EBURY PRESS

# FROM THE HEART OF NATURE

Running barefoot and climbing trees, Pamela Gale Malhotra spent every moment of her childhood in the woods. Rooted in the spiritual culture of her Native American heritage, her 'love affair' with Nature coincided with her lifelong journey with her beloved husband, Anil. A graduate of Colorado State University, Pamela worked with a major pharmaceutical company before training in natural healing methods.

Pamela's love of Nature has impacted everything she has done, the sanctity of Creation coupled with respect and devotion for the Creator being the key tenets she and Anil shared. Both enjoyed exploring wild places whenever they could, creating their first wildlife sanctuary on the Big Island of Hawaii. Eventually shifting to India, they established a model private wildlife sanctuary in Kodagu, Karnataka, with hundreds of acres of reclaimed, rewilded and preserved forests under their protection. The sanctuary was the fulfilment of Pamela's childhood dream, with Anil transforming that dream into reality. They also founded the non-profit charitable trust SAI (Save Animals Initiative) Sanctuary Trust to promote their cause. For more information, please visit www.saisanctuary.com.

Over the years, Pamela's environmental work and her efforts for women's empowerment have been recognized globally. She has received awards like India's Nari Shakti Puraskar (2017); Karnataka State's Environment and Conservation Award (2017–18); the International Institute for Peace through Tourism Women's Empowerment Award (2015); TOFTigers Wildlife Tourism Initiative (2014); lifetime achievement awards from Cauvery College and Kolkata's International Wildlife and Environment Film Festival (2016); Animal Activist in Defense of Animals award (2016); Indian Confederation of NGOs Karmaveer Noble Laureates (2008 and 2019); the Ramnath Goenka Social Service Award (2016); the Dharma Seva Trust Award (2016); and the Giraffe Heroes award (2021).

Pamela's goal is to inspire others to join the mission of protecting Mother Nature and rewilding the Earth for the benefit of the present and future generations.

# from the
# heart of
# nature

## The amazing story behind the creation of a private forest sanctuary in India

## PAMELA GALE MALHOTRA

EBURY
PRESS

An imprint of Penguin Random House

EBURY PRESS

USA | Canada | UK | Ireland | Australia
New Zealand | India | South Africa | China

Ebury Press is part of the Penguin Random House group of companies
whose addresses can be found at global.penguinrandomhouse.com

Published by Penguin Random House India Pvt. Ltd
4th Floor, Capital Tower 1, MG Road,
Gurugram 122 002, Haryana, India

First published in Ebury Press by Penguin Random House India 2022

ISBN 9780143442165

Typeset in Adobe Caslon Pro by Manipal Technologies Limited, Manipal

www.penguin.co.in

*To my beloved husband, Anil—my lifelong partner in this Journey of Love and Devotion—the one who turned my dream into reality.*

*May your life's work continue to be an inspiration for others to protect and preserve our dear Mother Nature.*

# Contents

## PART III: THE CANOPY SPREADS

# Preface: The Odd Couple

It's hard to believe that the original manuscript for this book was finished on 21 September 2019, International Peace Day, as designated by the United Nations. That's over two years ago!

So much has happened during those two years—so many challenges, personally as well as globally. I have had to deal with my own health issues, while the world has been in the grip of the COVID-19 pandemic, which has touched the lives of so many millions and spread to every corner of the globe.

Our sanctuary has remained beautiful throughout, filled with 'Life', including new species who have made it their permanent home. As I write this, I hear the call of one of our new 'residents' in the tree outside opposite me, asking me to come by to say hi. As I open the window, my new friend comes down on to the branches closest to me, just to 'chat' to let me know that all is well, and that very soon, there will be a new addition to the family!

Now the mother comes out into the open, followed by the father. The mom's tummy is indeed very, very big! It looks like she could give birth to my little friend's sibling any time now.

It's a unique family, made up of two different species—one dark and one light—living together in love and harmony. It is so perfectly representative of the sanctuary as a safe home for all seeking refuge from harassment and persecution—a secure haven for all those 'outcasts' and 'outsiders' in need—somehow reminding me so much of Anil and me—the odd couple!

Included in this book are many more stories like this, as well as a call to my own brothers and sisters of the human family to join us in lending a hand to those most in need at this time— Mother Nature's other 'children', both flora and fauna, and Mother Nature Herself. Together, let's explore the wonders of our Mother, understand the challenges that She faces and discover the ways we can help Her face those challenges, and, in the process, help ourselves.

# Introduction: My Childhood Dream

Since childhood, I had always dreamt about living in the heart of Nature. So powerful was this passion to live in Nature, surrounded by her forests and wildlife, that it shaped my life, and my goals in life. So powerful was its influence on my consciousness, that its fulfilment was shown to me in a prophetic dream many years before it became a reality.

In the dream, I saw a house on top of a small hill, overlooking a pond, with a river flowing past, within the heart of a wooded valley filled with wildlife, encircled by whitecapped mountains—the entire scene hauntingly beautiful and etheric in nature.

So vivid was this dream that I actually drew a picture of what I had seen—a picture that became a living reality many years later.

This is the story of the fulfilment of that dream, and the story of the life's journey it has taken to realize it—a journey that started on one side of the globe but was fulfilled on the other—from my childhood woods of America's Atlantic Coast to the snow-capped, rugged peaks of Colorado's Rocky Mountains, to the exquisite Pacific rainbow jewels that are the Hawaiian Islands, to the majestic and mystical Himalayas in India's north, to the biodiverse-rich, stunning, lush forests of the Western Ghats in India's southern peninsula.

It is the story of a childhood spent in those Atlantic woods, where the seeds of love for Nature were sown deeply in my heart; the story of my ancestors, and their own deep love and reverence for Nature as our Mother; of an extraordinary man who shared my love and transformed my dream into a living reality.

It is the story of a spiritual awakening into the truth of our being; of the opening of a secret door in Nature and of the revelation of the Presence of the Divine in Nature; of the realization of our Oneness with that Presence within and without as children of Mother Nature and the Divine Spirit.

This is also the story of Mother Nature and how being in Her heart heals our bodies, calms our minds and uplifts our souls; of how She cares for us in every way as we are Her children—part of Her Being.

But it is also the story of humanity; of how we have forgotten these truths, of how our ego has blinded us to these truths, has robbed us of our reason, our love and our soul, causing us to fight among ourselves while forgetting and forsaking our Mother, destroying Her forests, Her rivers and seas, Her wildlife and Her other 'children' in pursuit of satisfying our ego's greed, bringing upon the world the spectre of ecological apocalypse as a result—an apocalypse that threatens our own survival and the very existence of 'Life' on the planet, humanity acting like an all-consuming cancer, a parasitic plague killing its host, thereby ensuring its own demise as well.

It is the story of a world held hostage by a single species—us, humans—and how our activities are damaging the biosphere of the Earth to such an extent that ecosystems around the globe are on the verge of catastrophic collapse. Their collapse means the end of the services they provide—services that we are dependent on for our own survival, chief among these being water production and conservation, soil enrichment and crop pollination, climate regulation and mitigation of the disastrous effects of human-induced climate change.

Already, vital fresh water sources are drying up across the planet. The resultant desertification has turned a quarter of the Earth's soil to sand, severely impacting global crop production.

Already, half of Earth's tropical rainforests have been cut down with forests now covering only 31 per cent of the land area of the planet. Already, Nature's ability to rejuvenate herself is being crippled by the extinction of plant, insect, bird and mammal species. Our activities have caused these extinctions, wiping out Nature's 'Insurance Policy' of biodiversity which helps shield us from global pandemics too.

Already, higher temperatures are causing glaciers and ice caps to melt, raising the seas, inundating islands and coastal cities, with extreme weather events multiplying and intensifying across the planet—all this, a result of our actions. Already, thousands of human deaths globally have been caused just from rising temperatures alone.

So, this is also a story of hope—hope that humanity will awaken from its delusive nightmare quickly enough to change direction, to stop our mindless race to the precipice of extinction's abyss, to work together to revive and heal the Earth, to rise above our petty, ego-oriented differences to embrace a new Life-Affirming Ethic based on integrity, cooperation, compassion and love.

For, this is a story of faith, too—faith in the essential goodness of the human heart, of the purity of the soul that exists within us all and within every part of Creation, faith in the underlying Spirit that binds us all together as a family, our active conscience reminding us that humanity is here as the Steward of the Earth, the caretaker of the planet for the sake of all species today, and for those generations that are yet to come.

Finally, it is the story of my sanctuary, of our sanctuary, and of the struggles my husband, Anil, and I have had to endure, the obstacles we had to overcome to turn my dream into the living sanctuary of life that it is today; a story of the sorrows and joys, the wonders and awe-inspiring experiences I have been privileged to have living here in the heart of Nature. The sanctuary itself dedicated to the Universal Divine Mother, that is Mother Nature.

SAI Sanctuary is our living legacy and a model for replication across India and the Earth. It is a model for green sustainable living, and for preservation, restoration and rewilding of the natural ecosystems that once thrived here.

It has always been my hope, our hope, that our work, our sanctuary would inspire others to do whatever they can individually and collectively to help preserve, restore and protect Nature around the world.

I am heartened by the movements spearheaded by religious, indigenous and spiritual leaders in their efforts to instil a new perspective of the sanctity and sacredness of the Earth; to awaken the conscience of the present generation in terms of what we are doing to the planet and how our actions are compromising the future of our children.

The war on Nature must end. It is time to stop funding things that destroy Nature, and start funding things that help and protect Nature, so that we can help ourselves build a cleaner, healthier, brighter and more beautiful future.

It is critical that governments at every level—local, state and national, along with international governmental entities—act NOW to fund these programmes. In addition, it is vital that the business and corporate sectors get involved as well. After all, they use the ecosystem services that Nature provides to exist and carry on their businesses. By doing so, they protect their own ability to continue to exist now, and in the future.

In India, this concept of 'giving back' is already in place legally, through laws governing corporate social responsibility (CSR). But this needs to be expanded dramatically—voluntarily, if possible, or through taxation, if necessary—collecting monies for a 'Tax for Nature' to go into a special fund earmarked specifically for Nature-protection and enhancement, with strict transparency making the collection and dispersal of funds available for all to see.

As for funding of our own sanctuary, monies used for the purchasing of lands and management of the sanctuary have come from Anil's self-earned income. But for those who would like to help, a non-profit charitable trust called SAI (Save Animals Initiative) Sanctuary Trust was established here in India twenty years ago, the trust having government-approved 80G status, making donations to it tax-deductible. A similar non-profit NGO, with US IRS 501(c)(3) recognition, was established in the US several years ago, donations to it within the US also being tax-deductible.

With or without donations, the mission Anil and I started will carry on to realize my passion and my dream of creating a Living Legacy to give back to Mother Nature for all she has given me throughout my life.

I pray that his book will aid in the awakening of the conscience and the uplifting of the consciousness of all who read it, sowing the seeds of love for our Mother deep in each heart and soul. Come, walk with me on this journey, through the pages of my life.

# PART I

# The Seeds Are Sown

# 1

# Childhoods in Nature

*'When despair for the world grows in me*
*and I wake in the night at the least sound*
*in fear of what my life and my children's lives may be . . .*
*I come into the peace of wild things . . .*
*I rest in the grace of the world, and am free.'*

—'The Peace of Wild Things', Wendell Berry

Time stood still. In stunned silence I sat for what seemed an eternity. Finally, I whispered, 'No . . . no! It can't be!'

'I'm sorry, but I'm afraid it is,' the doctor replied. 'Come, see for yourself,' he said, pointing to the mass the ultrasound scan had revealed in my right breast—a tumour he suspected was malignant.

'You see that bright red colour in the centre? That is blood feeding the creation and expansion of the tumour. The edges of the mass are also irregular—another sign that this mass is cancerous. You need to do more tests and scans to confirm this diagnosis. I recommend you go to Mysore to start the process as soon as possible,' he urged.

3

I still could not believe that he was correct. After all, there was no history of breast cancer on either side of my family going back several generations. So how could it happen to me?

Seventeen days later, after a battery of uncomfortable and downright painful scans, biopsies and tests, I was lying on a hospital gurney in a Bangalore cancer hospital for the removal of the confirmed malignant cancerous tumour growing in my right breast. I was supposed to be in New Delhi for that week receiving another lifetime achievement award for our conservation work, meeting with the publishers for this book and giving another TEDx talk about the state of the environment.

Instead, I was waiting to be wheeled into an operating room, my husband, Anil, standing beside me, waiting with me. I looked up from the gurney into his face, into his eyes—the same eyes I had first seen forty-nine years ago in my hometown, half-a-world away; the same eyes that had inexplicably and instantaneously drawn me to him.

Would I ever be able to look into those eyes again? Would I survive the operation? I had never had an operation like this before, never had to undergo general anaesthesia before. Would I make it? Would I be able to fall into those eyes again as I did so many, many years ago?

This and countless other memories filled my mind of the life we had spent together—the decades that had started on one side of the Earth and could now be ending on the other . . .

Ours was an unlikely relationship from the very beginning, having been born on opposite sides of the globe and raised in very different economic, social and cultural circumstances.

Anil had grown up with the proverbial silver spoon in his mouth. His mother's family harked back to the nobility of the western district of Quetta of undivided India and was one of the wealthiest in the area. His great-grandfather was appointed governor by the British and 'diwan' or chief minister in the Muslim-run state of Baluchistan. His maternal grandmother was an extraordinary woman. Fluent in three languages, she composed poetry in Persian. Often the only woman in attendance at all-male conferences, she was a firm believer in the equality of men and women. Her choice of husband exemplified her independent spirit. Defying convention, she chose to marry a simple schoolteacher whom she fell in love with during a chance meeting on a train trip in 1919.

A love marriage in those days (July 1919) was certainly an unusual occurrence, especially for a family of her economic standing, not to mention that the man in question was a widower as well with a young son from his first marriage. But, supported by her own mother's approval, her father relented and agreed to the union. To secure his daughter's future, he even set up several business opportunities for his new son-in-law including an import–export business, construction-company contracts and land holdings which were later expanded to prime real estate in the beautiful Doon Valley and the Savoy Hotel—the crowning jewel of the hill station of Mussoorie. The couple's first child together was a daughter they named Janaki—Anil's mother.

Anil's father—Mulkraj Malhotra—was the eldest of seven siblings from a lower-middle class family. Even though Grandfather Malhotra was a doctor, there was never much money in their household. But Mulkraj had the drive to better himself economically and left India to study abroad in the USA, getting his engineering degree from Temple University in Pennsylvania. Always a hard worker, Mulkraj made a mark with his engineering expertise, working in both public and private construction projects and eventually went to Russia as the principal consulting engineer for the Trans-Siberian Railway. He returned to India from his travels abroad a successful and very wealthy man. His wealth brought him into the same social circles as Janaki's family, which eventually led to an arranged marriage between him and Janaki. Anil was their first-born child.

Though born in Mumbai, Anil's first childhood memories are from the natural surroundings of his home in pre-Partition Lahore, where his father had a factory. Anil was particularly fascinated by a bird species called *battera* that made frequent visits to the window ledges outside his house. He would go to the windows as often as possible in the hope of seeing them. The birds seemed to enjoy playing hide-and-seek to the delight of the young boy. They would often come to the sills and call to him, but then fly off as soon as he would reach the windows, only to fly back again to visit him a few seconds later.

A few years into Anil's childhood, the partition of British-controlled India took place. The horrors and sorrows of Partition left their scars on all who went through that tumultuous time, adversely affecting relations between the three countries India, Pakistan and Bangladesh even to this day. Dividing communities on the single basis of religion meant that people who grew up together as friends, who spoke the same language and shared the same customs for generations, were suddenly caught on different sides of a man-made border. The mass migration that followed, marred by tremendous violence, created many refugees and left many dead. But there were also acts of great compassion and heroism by people on both sides of the border in the defence and protection of those caught in the turmoil. Accounts of such deeds illustrate how people can rise above the labels and man-made barriers that can separate the human family.

This is what is so essential today—to transcend those things that divide us and seek the common ground, sometimes quite literally, that can and must unite us. Nature is the greatest teacher in this regard—she does not recognize any of these artificial impediments to the unity of humanity and instead, showers her blessings on all, regardless of caste, creed, origin, race, gender, etc. It is for this reason that the critical environmental issues that we face today underscore how vital it is for us to work together to resolve them. For example, climate change affects all of us. As former US secretary of defence Chuck Hagel has stated, 'Climate Change is a threat multiplier—it is a global problem. Its impacts do not respect national borders. No nation can deal with it alone.'[*]

The single greatest cause of climate change is deforestation. The droughts it causes with the subsequent lack of fresh water and food affect everyone because those who are denied these basic elements of survival have no choice but to seek them out wherever they can find them. The resultant forced migrations often lead to conflict. As Wangari Maathai—the first black woman and first environmentalist to win the Nobel Peace Prize—explains so simply and correctly, 'Gaining access and keeping control of natural resources is the root cause of all conflicts on the globe. All conflicts are the result of lack of resources or the greed to control them.'[†]

Global refugees numbered 83 million as of 2020, with over 50 million of these people being environmental refugees. As effects of deforestation and climate change intensify, that number could climb to 1 billion by the middle of this century. We must work together as a family to address these challenges for everyone's sake.

As a result of Partition, Anil's family lost all their businesses and landholdings in Pakistan, so his father became the manager for the Maharaja of Rajpipla in Gujarat. Their house there was surrounded by a jungle that was filled with all kinds of wildlife. Cheetal and other deer, birds and butterflies, and even the occasional leopard could be spotted in those woods. The family's next home was in the suburbs of the growing city of Jabalpur. By this time, Anil was old enough to start school and was therefore sent

---

[*]  US Department of Defense, https://www.defense.gov/Explore/News/Article/Article/603440/
[†]  Refer to the bibliography for source.

to the top boarding schools of Welham and then Doon, located in
the beautiful Doon Valley. These schools being in wooded areas
meant many excursions into the forest by the students with and
without teachers, including treks up to Mussoorie and further to
the foothills of the Himalayas.

Anil spent several wonderful years in these idyllic settings.
The sylvan surroundings helped to sow more seeds of love of
Nature and all her other 'children' in his heart during the most
impressionable years of his life when innocence, awe, wonder and
joy were foremost in his consciousness.

It was while attending Welham School that the events in
his mother's life would change Anil's forever. Janaki led a very
active social life that included both hosting and attending
glittering parties, on the one side, while supporting many service
organizations for the poor and disadvantaged on the other. Her
wardrobe was filled with the most beautiful saris and jewellery,
and she had an entire closet just for her shoes. At the same time,
she spent many hours helping hospitals, orphanages, schools and
other programmes for the destitute. Like her own mother and
grandmother, she was a great lover of the Arts, being both a fine
sitar player and classical dancer in her own right. Her love of music
eventually led to her first meeting with Sri Dilip Kumar Roy—a
famous writer and classical singer. Janaki was to preside over a
function where he was to be the chief guest, but she had fallen too
ill to attend. She sent him a letter inviting him to her home, so she
and her husband could still have the pleasure of meeting him. To
their delight, Sri D.K. Roy accepted.

A second visit followed a few months later, which led to
a series of letters from Janaki to Dadaji (as they called him,
meaning 'respected elder brother or grandfather') asking
him to guide her on the spiritual path. Each letter he sent in
response suggested she turn to his own guru for guidance—
Sri Aurobindo—and that she come to Aurobindo's Ashram in

Pondicherry to experience things herself. Eventually, Janaki did make the trip followed by another and yet another, until she finally took the plunge into spiritual life, completely forsaking the active worldly life she had so loved.

Her decision to move to Pondicherry forced Anil to make a choice as well—did he want to stay at Doon School which he had recently started attending, or did he want to join her instead and attend the ashram school in Pondicherry? He readily chose to be with his mother leaving behind the beautiful Doon Valley.

Thus began a different phase in Anil's life where the seeds of spirituality and internationalism were sown both at the ashram school and even more through his daily contact with Sri D.K. Roy (Dadaji)—a man who would bring with him not only his own rich personality, but also the essence of some of the greatest minds and spiritual masters of the twentieth century.

Under Dadaji's influence, Anil's vision of humanity expanded. Using his own personal experiences with great minds like Bertrand Russell and Romain Roland, Dadaji helped Anil to embrace the concept of the oneness of the humanity and equality of all regardless of place of birth or origin, race, culture, religious affiliation, or other man-made designations and to celebrate the beauty of the world as his friend Rabindranath Tagore so eloquently expressed in his writings. Recalling examples from the life of India's great patriot Subhash Chandra Bose (Netaji), who was his dear friend and college mate, Dadaji impressed on Anil the fundamental imperative of dedication to an ideal and of following one's conscience and heart no matter the obstacles or cost.

The highest ideals are those enshrined in mysticism and spirituality as exemplified by the lives of the great mystics, saints and spiritual masters of India, Dadaji explained. This encompasses the ethical ideals of integrity, honesty and justice, compassion and the willingness to sacrifice for others, coupled with the recognition of the Law of Karma—there is a reaction for our every action—so, whatever we do, be it good or bad, will eventually come back to us in one way or another.

But spirituality goes beyond these moral codes. It is the seeking of the highest truth and beauty, a search for the light of spiritual wisdom, infused with a recognition and all-embracing, expansive love for the Divine who is manifest as the inner core of all beings, of all creation.

This is the true purpose of our existence—the search for this highest state of being. This is the essence of what our life's journey should be, Dadaji would say, following the triune path of works (karma), worship (*bhakti*/devotion) and wisdom (*jnana*) as woven into a perfect harmonious integral system by his own spiritual preceptor and master, Sri Aurobindo.

There was one more, very important revelation of spiritual insight that Dadaji shared with Anil: Nature is the outer vesture and secret doorway into the heart of the Divine, and as such is guide and guru on the spiritual path. While most think of a spiritual preceptor or 'guru' as a human being, those attuned to Nature have a direct link to the Divine as spiritual teacher and guide. Sharing with Anil his discussions on this point with the great mystic, Sri Ramana Maharshi, Dadaji relayed Maharshi's words that Nature, in the form of the Holy Hill of Arunachala, was his guide and guru.

These revelations of spiritual insight helped to bring a new and higher dimension to Anil's love of Nature. She was the source of inspiration for many great spiritual seekers including Mahatma Gandhi. As Gandhiji told Dadaji during one of their many discussions over the decades that they were friends, 'I need no inspiration other than Nature's. She has never failed me yet. She mystifies me, bewilders me, sends me into ecstasies.'* Yet, not merely a source of inspiration, Nature was now revealed as guide

---

* 'The Bonhoeffer Legacy', *Australasian Journal of Bonhoeffer Studies*, volume 2.

and guru on the spiritual path, the hidden Godhead that we must recognize, as Sri Aurobindo wrote in his classic poem 'Savitri'.

A couple of years after Sri Aurobindo's passing, Dadaji and Anil's mother, who was now known as Indira Devi, moved to erstwhile Poona (now Pune), where they set up a small ashram. In keeping with his own beliefs in internationalism, all were welcomed at the ashram regardless of religion, cultural or ethnic origin, economic status, or nationality. Almost every evening, Dadaji would sing devotional songs and then give a discourse on some aspect of spirituality.

Anil had joined Shivaji Military Academy, which was also in Poona, and so spent all of his free time at the ashram with his mother and Dadaji. It was during these times together—often over a game of chess, which both the men loved to play—that Anil would pepper Dadaji with questions about life and spirituality.

As Anil got older, he saw the practicalities of life and living, of holding down a job and advancing economically, as major obstacles to living a spiritual life where one adheres strictly to truth and integrity, no matter what the cost. How does one please one's superiors or clients if truth and integrity stand in the way of executing the job they have given you to do? How does one square the concept of 'karma' in life when all around one sees many of the rich, famous and powerful getting away with all kinds of illegal activities or socially irresponsible actions?

When questioned about these ethical dilemmas and what seemed to be karmic contradictions, Dadaji would often answer, 'Anil, my boy, as you get older you will see the truth of the action of Karma in your life and in the lives of others. You will come to realize that short-term gain must never compromise ethics or the tenets of spirituality.'

Try as he would, it became more and more difficult for Anil to see the wisdom or feasibility in these words as time went by. After graduating from St Xavier's College and Government Law

College in Bombay (Mumbai), Anil entered the world of finance, graduating from London's Institute of Banking and becoming an officer at National Grindlays Bank in Kolkata.

As is the case with so many of us in our youth, Anil chose to rebel against all the strictures and restrictions he felt were constraining his life. Alcohol and cigarettes became his inseparable 'companions' as he partied often through the night with his friends and colleagues at work. It was during this period that he came in contact with the Indian film industry and fell in love with a beautiful and talented rising star. He quit his bank job and followed her to Bombay diving into the world of movie production and distribution. His family had already cut him off financially since he had refused an arranged marriage due to his love for his actress-girlfriend. So he lived off of what he made from his Bollywood connections and winnings from his bets at the horse races for over a year.

Next, the 'travel bug' bit him and Anil was off to Europe to see what adventures he could have there. He had always wanted to travel and see the world much the same way as Dadaji had done. This was another reason for his refusing to marry anyone—his desire to see new places and experience new cultures.

It was the latter part of the psychedelic '60s—a time of tumult and kaleidoscopic changes on so many fronts. The Vietnam War was raging with all the horror that came with it. Thousands of Vietnamese were killed and suffering while many US soldiers were being sent back home permanently scarred physically and psychologically with others sent back in coffins and body bags.

The vision of a modern-day Camelot based on peace, equality and justice had been shattered earlier by assassins' bullets first bringing down President John F. Kennedy (JFK) and later his brother, Robert (Bobby) F. Kennedy (RFK). Kennedy's plan to withdraw from Vietnam was never implemented by his vice president, Lyndon Johnson (LBJ). Instead, a ratchetting up of the war began, increasing the demand for both men and equipment.

The equipment was supplied by US corporations whose swollen profits increased their influence nationally and internationally. Vietnam became the testing ground for all kinds of new military hardware and devices. By the end of the war, the influence of the 'military-industrial complex' in the halls of government had grown exponentially from the first time former president Dwight D. Eisenhower coined the phrase and warned against this very thing during his final address to the US public in 1960. US foreign policy was increasingly aligned with the desires of US business interests around the world. The clout of this nexus of power continues to hold sway over policy decisions even more so today, this influence—evidenced by the massive expansion of the US defence budget—which is, today, the single largest expenditure of the US government.

To supply the requisite troops for the war, mandatory military conscription in the form of 'The Draft' was instituted. A lottery based on birthdates would determine which young men had to enter the military and fight. As a result of the Draft, opposition to the war, which had at first been restricted to a relatively small group, broadened to include far more of the American public.

Music was the key to the spread of the growing opposition against the Vietnam War and US policies both foreign and domestic which increasingly pushed the global agenda of big business. Some of the greatest poets, songwriters and musicians of the twentieth century were at the heart of this movement, raising inconvenient questions to 'the establishment' about the war and in fact, the lifestyle of people in the West. From a small core of mainly American folk artists like Joan Baez, Pete Seeger, Bob Dylan and Peter, Paul and Mary, the musical tidal wave of change grew as more artists from the US and abroad joined the flood, raising more questions about the conscience and consciousness of governance. Richie Havens, Jimi Hendrix, The Who, Roger Waters and Pink Floyd and of course, the Beatles, joined in. John Lennon's song 'Give Peace a Chance' even became the unofficial anthem for the anti-war movement with Europe soon becoming a leading global centre of opposition to the war. The powerful lyrics from these artists helped to break down the wall of apathy and illusion that had encircled so much of the US public, including the youth and including myself.

This, then, was also the time of Anil's political awakening, as he travelled through Scandinavia and Europe, often meeting young American men who had fled to Europe to avoid the war. Some were draft dodgers while others were war veterans who had gone AWOL (Absent Without Official Leave) after having witnessed the horrors of the war. All had harrowing stories to tell and willingly shared them when asked. West Germany became a centre for both war opposition and for concerts given by the musical groups spreading the anti-war movement. This is where Anil chose to pursue his PhD in politics at the University of Hamburg. The University of Hamburg was to West Germany what the University of California Berkeley was to the USA—a hotbed of opposition to the Vietnam War as well as a crucible of experimentation and change for an awakening youth. Marijuana and hashish were freely available, as were psychedelics. These helped to further drive the search for an alternate lifestyle from what was prevalent then—one not marked by warfare, violence, greed, hatred and discrimination coupled with the shallowness of conspicuous consumption and competition in every aspect of social life. There had to be better and more meaningful ways to live.

Anil enthusiastically dove headfirst into it all, going straight to the very heart of becoming a part of it. This inevitably led to brushes with the law, encounters that had major impacts on his life, further convincing him that there had to be more to life and living.

The seeds for an awakened and expanded consciousness had been sown within him years earlier. All that was needed now were the right circumstances and setting to help them sprout forth—conditions he found a few years later, in America, after meeting me . . .

# 2

# Deep Roots

I was born a little over twelve years after Anil, on the other side of the globe and hence, we were, quite literally, worlds apart. Just past midnight, with no doctor or nurse in attendance, my early arrival surprised everyone, including my mother, who told me years later that she experienced virtually no labour pains during the delivery.

Just another Jersey girl born in the USA, I spent most of my childhood and adolescence in houses built by my mom's maternal grandfather, Augustus Brandes. Born in 1853, Gus (as he was called) was an engineer who had emigrated from Germany to America when he was in his early twenties. His skills and expertise soon came to the notice of one of the wealthiest landowning families, the Throckmortons, in this area of Monmouth County in the US State of New Jersey. At one time, this family owned almost all the land between the two major rivers in the region, the Shrewsbury and Navesink. Mr Throckmorton made Gus the overseer of his various properties, putting him in charge of building numerous homes in what would become the small town of Red Bank (so named for the colour of the soil on the banks of the Navesink River). Gus also planted all of the trees like black

16

walnut, elm, sycamore and others, which initially lined the streets and were to be found in the yards of these houses.

Gus's hard work and dedication were rewarded when he married his German fiancée, Eva, upon her arrival in the United States. As a wedding gift, Mr Throckmorton gave the happy couple three of the houses that Gus had built. Five generations of my family would go on to live and grow up in those houses, including me. Gus and Eva were blessed with a baby girl in 1889, who was named Elizabeth, but was always called Bess. Bess would grow up to be my maternal grandmother, my beloved Nana, whom I was so close to as a small child.

My mom's father and paternal grandfather were very colourful characters. My great-grandfather, Emory 'Buck' McKee, was born in the Osage Mission at Caney, Kansas, on 2 April 1871. He grew up on his father's cattle ranch across the river from the Pawnee Indian Reservation located in the Oklahoma Territory. His mother was apparently a Native American, although no one is quite sure which tribe she belonged to. Over the years, he worked as a cattleman and horseman, published the first newspaper in the area and also served as sheriff of Pawnee County for several years before joining various Wild West shows. Eventually, he became the vaudeville partner of Will Rogers—entertainer, actor, newspaper columnist and one of the most beloved political radio commentators of America. Buck first met Will while he was still sheriff, ultimately taking the place of one of Will's previous partners, Jim Minnick, when he quit to return to Texas.

Buck was a horse whisperer—he had a tremendous gift for working with horses. As a result, he trained many of the horses used by Will over the years as well as his own, called 'Teddy'. Teddy was completely devoted to Buck, as newspaper accounts at that time have recorded, noting Teddy's intelligence and the mutual affection between him and his owner. He would follow Buck around town like a loyal pet dog, waiting outside of whatever building Buck would be in until he returned. If Buck took too long, Teddy would whinny his disapproval over the long wait until Buck returned. Teddy's intelligence and Buck's training were certainly on display at each show as they would burst through the curtains at full gallop stopping just short of the edge of the stage.

Will's skills with a rope would then be demonstrated as he lassoed Grandpa Buck and Teddy in several different ways. Their act was a hit on stages across America and Europe, with Buck and Will working together in vaudeville and Hollywood's silent movies for several years, including *The Roping Fool* (1922), until Buck left the act and moved to Roseville, California, in 1924, with his second wife, Maude, to open a horse farm.

By the year 1935, Will Rogers had already become Hollywood's top male box office attraction, but more importantly, America's most widely read newspaper journalist and radio commentator, reaching an audience of 60 million people. He was admired and respected for his humour as well as his incisive political commentaries which gave him open access to the Oval Office at the White House as well as to the Senate cloakroom in Washington. Although he claimed no desire to run for office himself, his sensible and intelligent views definitely influenced many in the highest seats of power in the country at that time.

Buck and Will remained friends and their last meeting took place at Grandpa Buck's horse farm in August of that year. During this final meeting, under the shade of one of the tall trees in the ranch, both of them sat enjoying and reminiscing—easy peace and calm in the air around the two of them. Buck asked Will to stay on and spend a few weeks with him at his ranch just relaxing and taking pleasure in each other's company, while watching the horses they both loved so much, roam free. Unfortunately, he declined and decided instead to join another friend, Wiley Post, a pilot, as he flew to Alaska . . . a fateful decision that ended up costing Will Rogers his life as the plane crashed a few days later on 15 August

1935. Who knows what additional contributions to America and the world this extraordinary man may have made had he stayed those weeks at Great-Grandpa Buck's ranch instead of boarding that ill-fated flight.

## The Osage Connection

Buck was just shy of twenty when he met and married his first wife, Margaret Dunlap. Margaret's parents were Robert Dunlap and his Native American wife, Mahotomoi (her name roughly meaning 'Moon-Sun'). Mahotomoi was the daughter of one of the chiefs of the Osage tribes. The young lovers first met sometime during the 1860s—a time of tremendous upheaval among Osage peoples.

The Osage had been one of the most powerful tribes in North America particularly in the Midwest. They had migrated from their eastern origins around the Chesapeake Piedmont region westward through what would become Kentucky and Tennessee, finally settling in the Mississippi and Ohio River valley areas around 700 BC.

When the Europeans first came to America, the Osage felt little impact, but as the European invasion of the eastern part of the continent grew dramatically, Native American tribes of the east were forced to move westward. This, in turn, pushed the Osage further west, with the tribes ultimately arriving and staying on in the Great Plains during the 1600s AD. They settled near the confluence of the Mississippi and Missouri Rivers—an area they called *Ni-U-Kon-Ska* meaning 'Middle Waters', since it was also the junction where all the other great rivers in that part of the continent met. Hence, the Osage called themselves 'People of the Middle Waters' or *Wazhazhe* meaning 'Mid-waters'. With an average height of at least six feet in men, with many reaching seven feet, they were among the tallest Indians in North America. They had strikingly handsome features, as captured in paintings by the artist George Catlin, the missionary Isaac McCoy calling them the finest-looking Indians he had ever seen.

The Osage were a profoundly spiritual people—a fact noted by Christian missionaries who described them as the most deeply spiritual Indians in North America. They considered all aspects of and changes in the universe, and all facets of life to be manifestations of a single, mysterious life-giving force, called *Wa-kon-tah*—the Great Spirit—and this sense of the spiritual being incarnate in Nature underscored every element of their way of life. They deemed humanity to be just one expression of the Great Spirit, alongside all other living beings and features of creation—every component of Nature and every living being was to be respected as a part of the Divine and conserved. Any abuse or misuse of creation would mean disrespecting the Great Spirit and disregarding the laws of life, which were enshrined in the orderly balance and flow of the universe by that all-powerful Force.

Careful observation of the weather cycles of the seasons and movement of the stars in the heavens, the behaviour of animals and changes in the land and bodies of water, the growth of plants and of human development and the interconnectedness of each of these patterns of Nature revealed to the Osage the orderly but delicate balance of creation. It was, therefore, the duty of each person to be a conscious and responsible participant of this balance, protecting and preserving it in order to ensure the continuation of the cycle of life for future generations.

The first Europeans to encounter the Osage were French and Spanish colonialists who found them to be most congenial and cooperative. The Europeans traded various goods, including horses, for information, food and other supplies from the Osage. With their villages spanning the Mississippi and Great Plains, the Osage were able to control the flow of commodities going east and west, building a strong trading empire and expanding their geographical influence as a result.

This mutually beneficial relationship ended abruptly in the early 1800s with the departure of first, the French, and then the Spanish from the region after they sold massive amounts of land to the US government; the sale is widely known as 'the Louisiana Purchase'. But, unlike the French and Spanish, the US government was not interested in trading with the Osage or any other Native American tribes as equals, but rather was interested in one thing only—their land to be lived on and used for more Euro-American settlers to push west across the continent.

Herein lies the critical historical difference between the goals and therefore, treatment of the indigenous peoples by the Europeans in India versus in the Americas. In India, the British and other European powers came purely for material wealth and economic gain. There was no real interest in or intent of settling in India *en masse*—only in controlling the land and its people to make money. In the Americas, the goal was not just to establish control over the people and the land, but also to live on and use the land for the growing population of the Euro-American invaders who were rapidly flooding in—to take over, even if achieving this goal came at the cost of genocide of the indigenous peoples.

Estimates of indigenous populations across the Americas before the arrival of the Europeans run as high as 112 million people, with a North American Native population of 18 million. The genocide waged against the North American tribes reduced their numbers to less than 250,000 by 1900—a reduction of 98–99 per cent of the original population across the continent.[*] The US government took over by performing the massacre in phases, principally using three methods—forced relocation, the introduction of deadly diseases and the destruction of the

---

[*]  https://www.democracyandme.org/learning-from-history-pandemics-are-nothing-new-in-native-communities/
Refer to the bibliography for more links.

most important food source for tribes across the Americas: the American buffalo.

The policy of forced relocation predictably triggered conflict and warfare between the tribes, as those relocated were forced on to the traditional lands of other tribes—something the US government used in its overall strategy to increase disharmony between the Indian peoples while spreading contempt and vilification of all Indians amongst Euro-American settlers. It was largely as a result of these wars that the Osage earned the reputation of being exceptionally courageous as well as fierce in battle—a reputation that made neighbouring tribes fear them. For over 125 years, their strength and tenacity had not only made them one of the strongest North American tribes but had actually shielded the tribes further west from the various hardships brought on through contact with the Euro-Americans. With the fall of the Osage, the massive tidal wave of suffering, cruelty and misery was unleashed in full force upon these westward tribes by the US government.

Both the wars and relocations helped set up conditions for the outbreaks and rapid spread of deadly diseases among Native Americans, the deadliest of these being smallpox. But the loss of the buffalo was perhaps the final tipping point, the biannual hunts being the cornerstone of tribal life for the Osage and other tribes. Recognizing just how important the buffalo was for tribal survival, the government encouraged their complete extermination through unbridled slaughter by including the US Army in its massive killing campaign. The government also ran trains on the newly laid, cross-country rail tracks with hunters ready in each compartment of the train. When a herd was sighted, the train would stop and the firing of guns would commence, wiping out every single buffalo in the herd, their carcasses left rotting on the ground for miles and miles along the tracks, the heaps of dead buffalo reaching 8 to 10 feet in height.

The campaign was so effective that it drastically reduced buffalo numbers from an estimated 30 to 60 million when the Europeans first arrived, to less than 400 individuals by 1893, thereby achieving the US government's goal of depriving the Indians of their main food source. With the loss of the buffalo, tribes had to rely on gathering local plants and nuts for food and medicine as well as planting certain crops. But these were far from capable of providing adequate means of sustenance. The government's handouts were supposed to fill the gap, but rarely did so even when the tribes were forced to resettle around US government Indian Agency outposts. Crowding people together in small settlements around these outposts strained both the sanitation and nutritional conditions leading to malnutrition, unhygienic surroundings and the outbreaks of epidemics, especially of smallpox, that spread like wildfire through the cramped villages.

Smallpox was unknown in the Americas before the arrival of the Europeans. Hence Native Americans had no immunity against it. Its introduction to the Americas was not by chance, simply being brought over by sick Europeans who infected Native Americans. While that was the case in some instances, it was also intentionally spread through the distribution of smallpox-infected blankets to the tribes.[*] This practice was first started by the British, historical documents show—their actions wiped out many tribes in the eastern part of the continent even before the independence of the American colonies in 1776. Other practices carried out first by the British and then continued by the US government include poisoning of tribal elders and paying bounties for Indian scalps. The lack of tribal leaders coupled with their weakened physical state left the Indians very vulnerable, with successive waves of smallpox killing thousands and literally decimating the Osage as

---

[*] Esther Wagner Stearn and Allen Edwin Stearn, *Effect of Smallpox on the Destiny of the Amerindian*, University of Minnesota, 1945, pp. 13–20, 73–94, 97.

well as other tribes from Canada to Mexico. The first epidemic of smallpox coincided with the first forced relocation of the Osage after they lost a major part of their territory to the US government. More treaties followed with more land loss and forced relocations unleashing more waves of epidemics and deaths.

It was at this point that my mother's great-grandfather, Robert Dunlap, became more closely involved with helping the Osage people, acting as an interpreter for them during the treaty negotiations with the US government. He had traded with the Osage for many years and was highly respected by them for his honesty and integrity as well as for his refusal to trade in alcohol—a substance whose consumption the Osage strongly discouraged. As per the existing treaties, Native Americans were to be provided adequate rations, medicines, clothing and other supplies as part of their annuities from the US government to make up for the shortfall that the tribes were experiencing as a result of having lost their land and with it, their ability to be self-reliant. All too often, the government failed in its duty to do so; it became a common practice for unscrupulous traders and middlemen to short-change the tribes and give them inferior-quality food in order to make quick profits. As a result, up to 50 per cent of the Osage population died within just one decade. Unless this desperate state of affairs changed immediately, there was the very real danger that the tribe would die out altogether.

In 1879, an Osage delegation helped by Robert Dunlap went to Washington, DC to address the situation, successfully negotiating an agreement with the US government to give the tribe all their annuities in cash rather than in goods, thereby becoming the first Native American people to be paid in cash. As a result, the Osage were one of the only Native American tribes to actually buy their reservation lands. Thus, they retained more rights and sovereignty over the lands including ownership over the minerals below the surface—something that would help them greatly, in monetary terms, in the near future. While the lands were poor for farming, they were excellent for grazing cattle as they were rich in bluestem grass. Consequently, income from grazing leases with Euro-American cattle ranchers became the best source of income for the tribe during the late 1800s.

Then, in 1894, oil was discovered below the Osage reservation. With the discovery of oil, the same regulations for grazing leases were used for oil-mining leases, bringing even more wealth to the tribe. It was at this time that the Osage elders approached Robert, offering to place the names of his entire family on the tribal rolls, the Osage calling him 'Pahapi' due to his love of popcorn—a common food made by the Osage. Robert's dedication to help the Osage during those previously terrible times had already earned him a place within the tribal family which culminated in his marriage to Mahotomoi and the birth of their daughter Margaret in 1869. The marriage of Buck McKee and Margaret Dunlap produced three children including their son Leo—my maternal grandfather who was born in 1891, the timing of his birth and that of his two siblings Frederick and Martha coinciding with the discovery of the oil.

With all their names now on the tribal rolls, the whole family would have benefitted from the land allotments, grazing, mineral and oil royalties that were to be divided equally among all members of the Osage tribe, with the Allotment Act stating that all persons listed on the rolls prior to 1 January 1906 or born before July 1907 would be entitled to a share.

Despite feeling highly honoured by the sheer magnanimity of their gesture, Robert refused, even though the entire family did indeed have a legal right to be on the tribal rolls. Robert felt it would be unethical for him and his family to profit monetarily at the expense of the other members of the Osage tribe. The more people on the rolls, the less each person would receive. He could not, in good conscience, do this after having personally witnessed the horrible suffering that the Osage people had endured over the decades—such was the integrity of this good man.

Ironically, this decision may have actually saved the lives of Robert and Mahotomoi's daughter, her husband and their grandchildren. By the early 1920s, the prosperity of the Osage, principally due to their oil royalties, attracted a large number of money-hungry outsiders. As royalties were passed on to the legal heirs of an individual Osage, even non-Osage could receive them. This led to many fake marriages, deaths and murders, and this period is often referred to as 'The Reign of Terror'. Between 1921 and 1925, at least sixty Osage are known to have been killed, the actual number probably being higher. The killings did not stop until the newly formed FBI (Federal Bureau of Investigation) was approached for help by the Osage, starting with the case of Molly Kyle—an Osage woman whose legal Indian heirs had all been murdered, leaving her Euro-American husband as the sole heir to her oil royalties. It was the first murder case for the FBI which they successfully investigated, with prosecutions leading to convictions of the key conspirators in the case including Molly's husband. The FBI also discovered that Molly herself was being poisoned, their discovery coming in just enough time to save her life. However, most of the other murders were never solved.

The tragic story of the cruel and outrageously unjust treatment meted out to the Osage was repeated with other tribes across North America with the US government continuing its attempts to not only rob the tribes of the reservation lands to which they were initially forced to migrate. Most of these forced migrations took place between 1830 to 1850—a period known as the 'Trail of Tears' when over one lakh (100,000) Native Americans from different tribes were forced off their ancestral lands and traditional hunting grounds, or confined to such a small percentage of them that it made it impossible to hunt enough bison or other animals to sustain them throughout the year.

At least 15,000 men, women and children perished due to the harsh conditions they had to endure during these illegally imposed exoduses, Chief Justice John Marshall of the US Supreme Court declaring the forced relocations unconstitutional. The then President Andrew Jackson—a renowned bigot and genocidal fanatic against Native Americans who had told his troops to systematically exterminate indigenous women and children after slaughtering Indian men—ignored the Court's ruling, stating, 'Marshall has made his decision; let him enforce it now if he can.'

Equally brutal but horrifically more heartless was the attempt to strip Native Americans of their cultural identity as Indians at all. These efforts became 'law' with the passage of a bill in the US Congress entitled the 'Civilization Fund Act' on 3 March 1819. A multipronged approach, this effort to force assimilation of Native Americans into white culture included 'outlawing' various Native American religious and cultural ceremonies.

Even more shocking and appalling was the forced separation and virtual kidnapping of Native American children from their parents at ages as young as three years old. Taken off the Indian reservation, they were then sent far from their homes to either government schools, or those set up by religious organizations with government funds. Forced to stay at these 'schools' for their entire youth and adolescence with no visits to or from their families or any member of the tribe, tens of thousands never saw their families again. Of those who did finally return, many found one or both of their parents had died during their coerced absence. One advocate for Native Americans labelled this despicable practice 'civilization by kidnapping' during a US Congressional hearing on the system held on 23 February 1927. In the US, there were at least 367 of these schools spread across the country including in Alaska, with 73 schools still operating today, attendance by Native American children made compulsory in 1891.

Opened in 1879, the Carlisle Indian Industrial School was the first of these boarding schools in the US and became the model for the more than 300 schools that followed. Its philosophy of teaching was 'kill the Indian, save the man' which meant, 'kill any semblance of Indian culture in the child in order to make him or her over in the image of the white man.' Hence, all Indian customs were banned including the practice of wearing long hair, with the hair of all children shorn up to their ears regardless of their gender. Speaking in any Indian languages was also forbidden.

The policy was carried out throughout the USA as well as across Canada, affecting hundreds of thousands of children and families. In Canada, more than 130 residential schools were set up by the Canadian Government, many operated by Christian churches until 1969, with the same horrific stories of indigenous children separated from their families and isolated from their communities. From 1863 to as recently as 1998 more than 150,000 (1,50,000) indigenous children were unwilling prisoners at these schools, having come from families of the First Nations (full-blooded Native American), Inuit (Eskimo) and Metis communities, Metis being the children of a Native American and a person of European ancestry; in other words, children like my great grandparents Mahotomoi and Buck McKee, my grandpa Leo, my mother and me along with my siblings since the classification of Metis included those whose great grandparents had Native American blood, the word 'Metis' being of French origin meaning 'mixed blood/mixed ancestry.'

Many children did not survive these forced 'internments,' being the victims of malnourishment, disease and abuse of every kind—physical, sexual, emotional and especially psychological. In 2021, mass grave sites were found on the grounds of these former 'schools' in both Canada and the US. Researchers estimate that over 40,000

Native American children are buried in these graves in the US and several thousand in often unmarked graves in Canada—revolting proof of the horrors these poor children were subjected to for over 150 years.

The overarching goal of all of these efforts to force the children and their parents to assimilate as individuals into the mainstream of English-speaking, Christian American and Canadian societies was to negate the concept that the different tribes were 'free nations' on their own. While Indians were given full American citizenship first in 1924 and reaffirmed in 1940, the concept of the tribes also being 'free nations' had been acknowledged in treaty after treaty between the different tribes and the US government through the centuries. But now, bill after bill was passed in Congress terminating US government treaty obligations to Indian Nations, ending all aid programs set up to help the Indians and rescinding US government 'recognition' of various tribes at all, ignoring the fact that the tribes had existed for thousands of years. All done in order to take over their resource-rich reservation lands.

Between 1945 and 1960, as a result of these 'termination' policies, more than 113 tribes were denied US government recognition as 'tribes', stripped of their rights to tribal councils, religious rights, access to any government aid programmes for Native Americans and lost over 1.4 million acres of their lands that the US government took over, selling it off to non-Indian businesses, groups and individuals.

Millions of acres of land had already been stolen by the American states and federal governments since the country's inception in the 1700s. An example of this was the case of Maine which illegally seized over 12 million acres of land from the Passamaquoddy and Penobscot Indian tribes in violation of the 1790 treaty they had signed, leaving a mere 5000 acres for the tribes.* The termination

---

* https://www.narf.org/nill/documents/nlr/nlr7-1.pdf

policy was in part an attempt to 'legalize' all of these previous
unethical and immoral land grabs by the various governments
while stealing even more millions of acres of Indian land across the
country; the non-recognition of tribes meaning that the Indians'
lands were no longer theirs and up for grabs to the highest bidder.

Fortunately, the 'termination' policy itself was terminated
in the early 1970s. Additional rights were returned to Native
Americans by three acts signed into law in 1978 by then president
Jimmy Carter: the Tribally Controlled Community College
Assistance Act which guarantees stable US government funding
for post-secondary education on Indian reservations; the Indian
Child Welfare Act which put an end to the shameful practice
of removing Indian children from traditional Indian homes and
placing them with non-Indian families; and perhaps the most
important, the American Indian Religious Freedom Act—this
act affirms the responsibility of the US government to protect
and preserve the inherent freedom of Native American Indians
to believe, express and exercise their traditional religious rights as
well as cultural and spiritual practices. It also guarantees Native
Americans' access to their 'sacred lands' and the freedom to
worship through traditional ceremonial rites which includes the
right to possess and use objects considered 'sacred' to them.

It was also President Carter who negotiated a settlement
between the US state of Maine and the Passamaquoddy and
Penobscot Indians who had lodged a case against the state for
violation of the aforementioned 1790 treaty and its subsequent
illegal seizure of millions of acres of Indian land guaranteed by
the treaty. Under Carter's settlement the tribes received federal
recognition once again and agreed to forfeit their land claims in
exchange for US $81.5 million, that money used to buy 3 lakh acres
(300,000 acres) of land for the tribes from nearby landowners—a
far cry from the 12 million stolen, but at least an adequate amount
for the tribes to try and become more self-sustaining.

With the opportunity for higher secondary education, Native Americans studied various trades and professions including law. Today many of them are lawyers arguing their own cases to secure Native American rights in US courts including holding the US government accountable to the treaties signed no matter how long ago, leading to landmark settlements of land and money given back to tribes that were deprived of their reservations.

One of the most recent examples of this was the historic landmark decision by the US Supreme Court handed down on 9 July 2020 which reconfirmed the binding legality of US treaties with Native American tribes no matter when those treaties were signed. The court decided in favour of the Native Americans, their decision on this case meaning that almost the entire eastern half of the state of Oklahoma is actually Indian land—land that the Muscogee (Creek) Nation along with the Cherokee, Choctaw, Chickasaw and Seminole tribes were forced to relocate to in the 1830s when President Andrew Jackson drove them out of their ancestral lands in what would become the states of Florida, Alabama and Georgia. Their tortuous travel to their reservation was 'The Trail of Tears' mentioned before. The court's decision is a watershed victory for Native Americans who have battled for centuries to uphold the sovereignty, tribal boundaries and treaty obligations of the US government. It also sets a precedent for other Native American claims across the continent whose rights and lands have been stolen, perhaps indicating a brighter future for Native Americans everywhere.

Some Native Americans have turned to politics in order to help their people regain the rights they have lost. Indeed, in 2018, two Native American women from two different states and tribes—Debra Anne Haaland of the Laguna Pueblo tribe of New Mexico and Sharice Lynnette Davids of the Ho-Chunk tribe of Wisconsin—made history by being the first Native American women to be elected to the US Congress. Perhaps with more dedicated Native Americans inside the Capitol Building, Indians will finally have a say in the future of this country which was theirs to begin with centuries ago.

Summarizing the struggles of all Indian peoples, one medicine/holy man—Amos McNac—who is also a justice for the supreme court of his own Muscogee (Creek) tribe states, 'We experienced genocide, assimilation, colonization, conversion policy by the government. We've survived. We still have our culture and our tradition.'*

Other Indians and tribes have worked to earn funds not just for their families but for their entire nation as well in order to buy back their sacred, ancestral lands. In some cases, the purchases have been hundreds to a few thousand acres specifically for their tribe; in other cases, the lands purchased have gone to a trust set up exclusively for this purpose. Indeed, 562 US-government-recognized tribes have purchased and put into a trust more than 55 million acres, reforesting the lands and protecting the wildlife returning to the renewed forests. In this way, Native Americans have become leaders in the environmental movement across the Americas, working to protect the future by protecting Mother Nature.†

The same story of oppression and genocide of Native Peoples has played out on various stages globally, where other indigenous communities have been victims of the cruelties of conquest and suppression, whether through arms or economics. Today economic subjugation is a key tactic used by governments to deprive indigenous peoples of their ancestral lands and heritage as greed for raw materials like aluminium, copper, iron ore and fossil fuels trump the legitimate claims of ancestral rights in the eyes of

---

*    https://www.nytimes.com/2020/07/11/us/muscogee-creek-nation-oklahoma.html?action=click&module=RelatedLinks&pgtype=Article

†    http://archive.boston.com/news/nation/articles/2009/12/27/indian_tribes_buy_back_thousands_of_acres_of_land/

governments that are dedicated to 'development at any cost'. As a result, in the current war being waged against Mother Earth, native peoples have taken on the roles of global leaders, battling with every means they have to save not only their own ancestral lands, but to also protect and safeguard the biosphere of the Earth upon which all life depends.

Hence, the history of the Native Americans and more specifically of the Osage gives me hope. For, in spite of all obstacles, all the suffering and deaths that brought the Osage population down to under 2000 people in the 1800s, the tribe endured and survived. Today, there are about 15,000 Osage, many highly qualified in Western education, yet careful to preserve the traditional wisdom, culture and beliefs of this extraordinary tribe of Native Americans to whom I am honoured to be related.

My grandfather, Leo, was very fortunate to have grown up with the love and influence of his own grandfather Robert Dunlap, whose integrity and character helped forge his own at a young age. He was also lucky to have Buck for a father, whose love for and special relationship with horses was something that he, too, had inherited—a gift that served him well as a young adult. When Buck joined the various Wild West shows, Leo went with him, touring across America. By the time Buck became partners with Will Rogers, Leo was already out on his own working at different jobs usually involving horses.

In 1916, while he was in Oklahoma, he met Jim Minnick— the very same person his father had replaced in Will Rogers' show. Jim was buying and training 'cow ponies' for polo to sell on the East Coast of the US. Leo decided to join him in the venture, being a competent polo player himself. When they reached the Armoury of Oceanport, New Jersey, where the ponies were to be stabled and sold, Leo's life changed forever. There, he met Bess, who was at the Armoury to ride her own horse. She was a very accomplished horsewoman, riding with ease not only in English and Western saddles, but side saddle as well. Leo quickly fell in love with Bess and they were married soon after. They then had to make a choice—did they want to go west and start their life together there or stay in New Jersey?

The young couple ultimately decided to remain in New Jersey, moving into one of the houses previously built by and gifted to Gus, at the insistence of Gus and Eva. Since working with cattle and horses was no longer possible, as he had done in his former life out West, Leo started doing construction work. Opting to follow in the footsteps of his father-in-law and become an engineer, Leo learned all he could on the job after he was hired by the county in 1918 as a 'rod man' in a survey party. By 1922 he had become a licensed, professional engineer and land surveyor getting his degrees in part from Princeton and Rutgers, doing additional studies on bridge engineering and highway traffic and safety. Many of the smaller bridges throughout the county were engineered and built under his supervision. Eventually he was promoted to the top position of county engineer for Monmouth County—a position he held for nine years until his retirement in 1959.

In 1918, less than two years after their marriage, my mom was born and named after a very dear college friend of Bess's—Helen. Four years later, a little boy was born. To honour the man he had so loved and respected in his life, the man who had done so much for his maternal grandmother and her people—the Osage—Leo chose to name their son after his own beloved grandfather—Robert Dunlap McKee.

My mom grew up during the Roaring Twenties and the Great Depression of the 1930s. Times were tough financially, but between Bess's teaching and Leo's engineering work, the family was far better off than many families in America including my father's. Early on, Mom came to share her mother and grandmother's love of gardening and teaching, while enjoying the passion both her parents had for horses and riding. She was a skilled rider and adored her horse 'Brownie' that her parents had given her.

When she got her degree in education, Mom got a job teaching the children of the military personnel posted at nearby Fort Monmouth in Eatontown. By this time, World War II had broken out and young military officers from all over the country were stationed at the fort. At a dance for servicemen and their friends at this fort, my mother met her future husband, my father, Clarence 'Dick' Stephens Gale.

## A Tale of Two Cufflinks

My father's family history follows the tale of two cufflinks that date back to at least the 1600s. The black onyx signet cufflinks set in gold with the old English 'G' etched in the centre were a gift given to John Gale when he left England to come to America in the early 1680s. John was my paternal grandfather's great-grandfather and a member of one of the most prestigious old English families of that time. He left England for America with two 'treasures' in his possession—the gold cufflinks and a land grant given to him by the British Crown for an estate in what became the state of Maryland.

John became a wealthy merchant and ship owner, trading commodities between England and America. He settled in what used to be Kent County (now known as Chestertown, Maryland) setting up Worton Manor Farm on Worton Creek as his home. He was the father of George Gale who, in turn, was the second husband of Mildred Washington—the paternal grandmother of George Washington, the first president of the United States of America.

Mildred had three children with her first husband, Lawrence Washington, before he died. George Gale was a loving and caring stepfather for the three children including the middle child Augustine who would grow up to be the father of George Washington. Augustine actually named his son 'George' in honour of his beloved stepfather. The connection between the Gale and Washington families continued through the birth of America as a nation with President Washington giving certain commissions and posts to the descendants of George Gale.

But let's go back to the cufflinks . . .

John Gale, Sr passed on his cufflinks to his son, also named John. John, Jr built Gales Wharf on the property which had a beautiful view of the Chesapeake Bay, where, coincidentally, the Osage tribes originated, who had long since moved west. Gales Wharf quickly became a principal shipping port, with the importance of the Gale family growing in the region. Gales Creek and Gales Town still bear the family name.

Years later, John, Jr. gave the cufflinks to his son William, who converted them to a ring and a lavaliere or pendant. In 1883, William's son, Clarence Stephens Gale, was born, with the ring and pendant passed on to him at the time of his marriage to Martha Griffith. In 1916, they had a son—my father—Clarence Stephens Gale, Jr. The ring and pendant were passed on to my dad at the time of his father's death and have since been passed on to members of the younger generation of the Gale family.

While my dad had been named after his own father, everyone called him 'Junior'. Grandfather Gale did not live to see his son grow up; he died when Junior was only eight years old. Martha remarried two years later, and the family moved from Easton, Maryland, to Raleigh, North Carolina. When Junior was in his teens, he was sent to Episcopal Prep School for his high school education. But tragedy struck again when his stepfather, Jim, who he dearly loved, committed suicide. It was the time of the Great Depression and Jim had apparently lost most of their family's money. Like so many others then, he could not live with the economic ruin and took his own life. My father was just sixteen years old at the time.

Twice, my most unfortunate father lost a father figure, and in Jim's case, it was he who found Jim's body. These traumatic experiences, especially at such young ages, must have left deep emotional scars. And yet, instead of giving in to depression, loneliness and melancholy, my father chose strength and the courage to fight on to achieve the goals he had set for himself, come what may. At this point in his life, Dad was virtually 'adopted' by a childless couple who truly loved him. Uncle Bert and his wife were extremely generous and protective of him, and he loved them dearly for all the kindness and compassion they showered on him.

Through their influence and financial help, coupled with his own hard work and determination, Dad finished his prep school years and went on to get his engineering degree at North Carolina State University. He also attended Reserved Officers Training Corps (ROTC) while at college to become an officer in the US army. The storm clouds of World War II had already gathered on the horizon and so, after graduating from college, he entered the army, enlisting full time. He was eventually posted at Fort Monmouth in New Jersey.

In spite of all that he had been through, Dad retained his wonderful sense of humour which so endeared him to everyone he met. While he was the editor of his college newspaper, he wrote a column called 'Reflections off the Cueball', which was a reference to his completely bald head. Later, at one of the dances, he and his partner won the dance contest. As he opened the box containing his 'prize', muffled chuckles rippled through the crowd—his prize was a hairbrush! The chuckles turned into a wave of uproarious laughter when he took the hairbrush out and used it as if he were buffing his bald pate to have it shine even more brightly under the dance-hall lights! Throughout his life, Dad would use this self-deprecating humour to connect with people or to lighten the tension in a situation. This was just one of the many endearing personality traits that caused my mom to love him so.

After their first meeting at one such dance at the Fort, my parents fell in love very quickly and got engaged on my mom's birthday, on 27 July 1942. On the heels of their engagement, they received the news that my dad was to be stationed almost immediately in the Pacific War Theatre. They decided, then and there, to get married before my dad left. So, with the blessings of my mom's parents, my parents were united in holy matrimony in a very rushed wedding on 3 August 1942. With no time to search for a wedding dress, my mother borrowed a friend's evening gown whose black ribbon border she and my Nana quickly replaced with white ribbons. My father shipped out just a few days later.

Throughout the war, Dad was stationed far from home, in the Pacific region. Holidays spent in such faraway places as Australia and the Philippines were extremely difficult, as he longed to be with his new wife and family. His loneliness was cushioned by the hospitality of the local people wherever he was stationed. The warmth and welcoming friendliness of the Filipinos, in particular, touched my father the most and so, he took a vow to return this same warmth and consideration to others he may meet in the future who had to spend their holidays far from home.

# 3

# Barefoot and Free

When World War II ended in 1945, my dad left active service but remained in the Army Reserves. Among other things, his duties included teaching foreign officers based at Fort Monmouth. His communication engineering experience from the war helped him land a job with AT&T as a construction engineer.

Dad and Mom quickly started a family with the birth of my two 'Presidential siblings'—so called because they were born on the same birthdates as two of America's greatest presidents. Their first child, named Peter, was born on 12 February, which was Abraham Lincoln's birthday, too. My elder sister Patty helped keep the 'link' between the Gale and Washington families going, being born on 22 February—the same date as George Washington's birthdate. I came along a few years later, on what has become International Women's Day—8 March, with the births of my younger siblings Pris and Paul following mine.

Five Ps in a pod—and I was the middle P. One can imagine my mother's consternation having to go through all five P's before getting the right name for the child she was scolding! We were a wild bunch of kids—over the years, we broke at least eleven doors in the house with our roughhousing! How my parents—especially my mother—coped with us, is beyond me.

The usual punishment for such destructive antics was 'hard labour' in the yards and gardens. Like her mother and grandmother before her, my mom loved gardens and gardening, and she had the veritable 'green thumb' to go with that love. Whether indoors or out, in pots or garden beds, anything and everything she touched seemed to blossom and grow. Lilies of the valley and irises, azalea bushes and pussy willow, tiger lilies and yellow forsythia, African violets, and Mom's favourite, dahlias, spread colour and cheer throughout our house and grounds. So, there was always plenty of work waiting to be done by us kids.

Composting was a way of life and the rich hummus obtained from it was added to a vegetable garden filled with yummy goodies to eat. Each year, the harvested fruits from the black grape arbour would be turned into the most delicious jams with everything grown with the greatest of love and patience. There is no doubt in the truth of the old adage that putting one's hands in the soil and helping 'life' to grow helps us grow too, and I feel ever grateful today for having had this wonderful training when I was young. But when we were kids, all we really wanted to do was just play!

Being the middle child in this wild bunch had both its advantages and disadvantages. The advantages were that I got to experience sibling relationships to the maximum—I got to be a 'big sister' to Pris and Paul and was able to tell them what to do, and also got to be the 'kid sister' of Peter and Patty, who I was able to blame for any trouble we got ourselves into. The main disadvantage was 'getting it from both ends'—I was either 'too old to act that way', being expected to set a proper example for the younger two, or 'too young' to be a part of my elder siblings' adventures.

This latter part led to my developing a favourite pastime: 'spying' on Peter, Patty and their friends. In order to not be seen or heard by them, I had to be very quiet and still. This actually turned out to be great training for observing wildlife, learning to sit in motionless silence, blending into the natural surroundings to avoid being seen or heard by the animals.

The Gale family was also in the middle of the McKee families: my mother's brother, Bob, lived on one side of our house while Nana and Grandpa McKee lived on the other. As my cousin Robert put it, 'It was one big extended family situation with the grandparents, aunts and uncles and cousins all living next to each other.' It was wonderful being encircled by family.

Patty and Peter would play outside with our cousins while Nana would visit us almost every day. I remember jumping down the stairs into her waiting arms whenever we would meet. I loved her dearly and grew very attached to her. When she passed away, my mom told me that Nana had gone to God's house. Feeling lonely and deprived of my beloved Nana, I was determined to go find God's house and ask Nana to come back home to us. I was just three or so at the time and had had no previous experiences with death, and so, fortunately for me and my mother, when a neighbour who lived a few blocks away from our house saw me riding my tricycle, she asked me where I was going. When I told her, this kind-hearted woman called my mom to tell her where I was so she could take me home.

Grandpa McKee was a huge, loving 'teddy bear' of a man with his broad smile and bright red hair. He would enthral us with stories of his own childhood and his experiences of growing up in what was then the 'Wild West'. He would howl like a wolf or coyote as he'd recount tales of the wildlife he had encountered, bringing his stories vividly alive in our imaginations.

Playing 'bear' with him was a favourite game. He would scoop us up into his arms and give us a big bear hug while pretending to chew off our ears, his prickly beard stubble scratching and tickling our necks and faces in the process as we giggled in delight. Even after he lost his eyesight to glaucoma and cataracts, he would still be able to find us using his walking cane.

He had grown up, worked and lived with some of the most iconic figures of the West, and so his personal accounts of these individuals were fascinating—people like Annie Oakley and Will Rogers, Pawnee and Buffalo Bill, as well as the famous couple, Roy Rogers and Dale Evans, (some of the biggest, most famous cowboys and cowgirls in America) to whom he introduced Peter and Patty, backstage after their show at Madison Square Garden in New York City.

After Nana passed away in 1955, Grandpa McKee remarried a few years later and moved to the home of his new wife in the then heavily wooded area of Lincroft. They had no close neighbours nearby—their house was situated on a small hill surrounded by forest, with a little brook flowing below. I loved visiting them there as it always gave me the chance to play in those magical woods.

With Nana gone and Grandpa having relocated, my parents decided to move into what had been our grandparents' house since it was much larger than the one in which we were living. My father drew up plans to remodel the house and did much of the work himself—from carpentry to electrical to wallpapering and painting.

Just prior to this, our cousins moved to the Rumson area, selling their house to the family of what would become my closest friend of my early youth. Her name was Joanie, and we did everything together. Some of my fondest childhood memories come from our times spent at the cabin her father had built deep in the woods. Amazingly, he had built the structure around a living tree—something that was utterly fascinating to me.

Fall was a favourite time at Joanie's cabin as the forest would be painted in the most beautiful autumn hues—orange and gold, yellow and deep red, scarlet and even purple—simply exquisite! The area had lots of wildlife including many different species of birds whose songs and sounds filled the air. Even as a young child, I could not help but be entranced by it all.

Our larger family home came with larger yards as well and included the old horse barn where my mom's and grandparents' horses were kept. Now it was home to the numerous bats that roamed the night sky after sundown, helping to clean the air of mosquitoes and other bugs. The areas beneath the barn served as a great home and nursery for small wildlife like wild rabbits and other small mammals and their young.

There were plenty of trees for us to climb, including those planted by great-grandfather Gus and others planted over the years to mark the birth of each child in the family—a custom passed down from my maternal grandparents' side. Anil and I went on to expand this custom, years later, by planting trees to mark all special events—births, deaths, Christmas, any and all occasions—calling the concept a 'Tree-volution'—a literal revolution and evolution of planting and nurturing trees to reverse the disastrous deforestation that has taken place around the globe.

Just imagine how quickly we could reforest the Earth if this concept of tree-volution became a tradition for peoples of all faiths and nations far and wide. Each special occurrence, each religious and national holiday would be marked by a fresh sign of life—a living tree. Each birth, wedding, graduation, new career and all other important events indicating a new chapter in life, symbolized through the planting of a tree. This would include honouring the memory of a loved one after their passing in this way—the continuation of their wonderful life in the form of a living tree.

Another family custom passed on by Nana and Grandpa to my mom was the making of 'seed balls' to help birds survive the cold winters. Cooking fat combined with various bird seeds would be rolled into balls and then placed on the branches of trees for birds and other small wildlife to eat during the cold often snowy winters when natural food would be scarce—a giving back to Nature for all Nature and her wonderful creatures give to us.

Anil and I have continued to do this throughout our lives, although the offerings may have changed from seeds to rice or other edibles, depending on the areas where we have lived. This practice would go on to help save our own lands and area in Colorado, years later . . .

Besides the many trees in our own yards, we were fortunate to be but a minute's run away from 'Eisner's Woods'—the wooded estate of one of the wealthiest families in the area. The patriarch of the family had emigrated from his native Austria to the USA in the mid-1800s making his fortune through a garment factory he set up that stitched almost all of the uniforms for the US Armed Forces during the World Wars.

He was very civic-minded and generous, eventually donating his home, which was overlooking the Navesink River, to the township of Red Bank for it to be made into a public library—a place where I spent much time as a child reading about exotic people, faraway places and the mysterious wildlife found there. Out of their fondness for children, the Eisners allowed the local kids to play in parts of their wooded estate, including sledding down Eisner Hill during the snowy winters.

When I wasn't in our own backyard, I was off exploring these marvellous woods, quietly watching the animals that had taken refuge there. The combination of Eisner's Woods coupled with our own numerous trees and flowering bushes meant our yards were filled with wildlife. Birds, bats, bunnies, squirrels, the occasional racoon and opossum—all these creatures were a part of our backyard menagerie. Being a part of this natural world gave me the greatest joy and happiness as a child and laid the foundation for my future path in life.

One of our most numerous of the wild residents was the grey squirrel. They were attracted to the tall walnut trees that not only provided them with lots to eat, but also plenty of places to nest and raise their young. One day, my younger sister, Pris, discovered a tiny baby squirrel on the ground below one of these walnut trees. The baby must have fallen out of its nest, but the mother was nowhere to be found.

So, my mom became the foster mother of little Mr Squirrel who became part of our family and stayed inside the house with the rest of us. He was very affectionate and loved to climb under our shirts to stay warm. Mom even allowed me to take him to school for 'Show and Tell' time in first grade so that my classmates got the chance to see and interact with him as well.

Mr Squirrel was indoors with us for several weeks until Mom decided he was old enough to be released back into the wild of our backyard. So, opening the kitchen's backdoor to the yard one day, Mom encouraged Mr Squirrel to go outside. As he scampered off and climbed a tree, we all thought we'd never see him again.

But when we sat down to eat our supper that evening, there was a scratching sound on the kitchen's backdoor. It was Mr Squirrel! He had come to join us for supper just as he had done for so many weeks as part of his nightly routine before going to sleep. So it was that Mr Squirrel continued to join us for supper every night thereafter.

Another special outdoor friend who became part of our indoor family was a special budgie parakeet we called 'Halo'. Budgie parakeets are not native to that part of the world, and this little one would certainly not have survived the approaching cold temperatures as it was already autumn when he arrived at our house. It was my elder sister, Patty, along with my mom, who rescued the little guy, bringing him inside so he could become a permanent and later favourite member of our family.

Halo was extremely friendly and loved interacting with us all. But he seemed to have a particular fondness for my father and his bald head, using it as both a launch site and landing platform causing my poor dad to wince each time Halo's sharp little claws 'danced on the cue-ball' to their own beat! In spite of the scratches his poor head endured, Dad was wonderfully tolerant of Halo's antics and actually seemed to enjoy the unique love and attention this very special flying friend of ours gave to him.

Our homes were always filled with animals. My earliest memories of some of the more traditional animal friends include two cats named Tom and Jerry followed by a beautiful collie called Lassie. Lassie was 'the lady of the neighbourhood', who went around meeting the various male dogs here and there. As a result of these many interactions, she gave birth to *fourteen* puppies—not a small number!

My parents sought to find good homes for all of the puppies when they were old enough to leave their mother. Friends would stop by and choose a puppy to take home with them, but each time someone would come, one particular puppy would be missing from the group. Eventually, my mom realized who the culprit was and why—I had fallen in love with that puppy and was hiding it so he wouldn't be taken away. She finally agreed to keep him with us, and I promptly named him Bobo.

A few years after Bo was born, my parents gave me a beautiful black and white rabbit I named Trixie. Trixie had his own special hutch to live in but was also free to roam our backyard and ended up with his own wild families over the years. He and Bo became best buddies. Whenever Bo would lie down, Trixie would join him, lying underneath Bo's chin in the space between his crossed front paws, often giving Bo a 'pedicure' by chewing on his nails.

Bo was unbelievably tolerant of this, but we'd frequently hear him let out a small yelp in pain when Trixie would come too close to his cuticles. Yet he never retaliated or harmed his little friend. And he made sure no one else harmed him either, being fiercely protective of Trixie.

Bobo lived a very full life of fourteen years. When he finally passed away, Trixie became terribly lonely for his life-long companion. Within barely eight days of Bo's passing, Trixie died, too. He just could not bear to live without his dearest and closest friend.

Those who question whether animals have the same feelings as humans have obviously never spent time with animals—either wild or domestic. It is virtually impossible to observe their interactions, their relationships, their family lives, their sharing and caring for one another, their love and joy, their pain and anguish, their extreme feelings of loss and grief when someone they have loved has passed on and not realize that they do indeed share the same feelings that we all share.

This is finally being acknowledged, accepted and understood in at least some sectors of the scientific world with studies about the way animals think and act with each other and with humans supporting this truth. They do indeed think, feel, care and love like us. And if we are lucky, sometimes, they share part of their immense reservoir of love and affection, of care and concern, with us as well.

According to the Native American Hopi tradition, the world has gone through several cycles. Reminiscent of the Vedic teachings of the four yugas/ages, it is said that during the very first cycle/age, humans and animals could communicate directly with each other because of the living realization that we are all 'One'—we are all connected to one another and to every aspect of creation in complete balance.

Then the human ego crept in and tried to find differences between the rest of creation and itself, between animals and humans, with humans starting to consider themselves somehow superior to animals and the rest of the species and aspects of creation. With this intrusion by the human ego, it is said humanity lost the privilege of communing and communicating with animals.

The human ego brought imbalance to the perfect balance of creation. Man's fall from perfection began . . .

## Nature Deficit Disorder

This then is a glimpse into the delightful years of my early youth spent outdoors so much of the time in our backyard and Eisner's magical woods.

One day, when I was running to those wonderful woods I was stopped in my tracks at the sight before me—devastation— complete and utter devastation. Bulldozers were pulling down trees and digging deep holes into the ground while men with saws were cutting the downed tree trunks into small pieces. Bricks and cement bags lay strewn all over. The ear-splitting noise of saws and bulldozers hurt my ears, while the thick dust and diesel exhaust being belched out by the heavy equipment filled the air making it difficult to breathe.

I was completely stunned. It was as if I had just walked into a horror movie. *Monsters*, I thought to myself. *My forest is being eaten by monsters!* I felt as if I had been punched in the stomach—I could not catch my breath. A huge knot in my throat gave me the sensation of being strangled. I was overwhelmed with feelings of grief, bewilderment and a terrible sense of loss at the destruction of 'my' forest and the disappearance of all my little forest friends.

It is difficult to overestimate the impact that this experience had on me as a child—the same experience that children across the world go through when their forest playgrounds are demolished for whatever reasons. It leaves deep, lifelong, emotional scars that can haunt one for decades to come and finally ties into the 'Nature Deficit Disorder', from which the vast majority of children suffer today.

'Nature Deficit Disorder' is a term used to describe a host of behavioural and physical problems that are very real and very dangerous for the future of our children and our planet at large. These problems manifest as a result of not spending time in Nature and a general lack of connection to Nature.

Its symptoms range from memory loss, attention-span disorders (ADD and ADHD) and lack of concentration to physical health problems like obesity, Vitamin D deficiency and myopia (from lack of exposure to natural sunlight), diminished use of our senses as well as emotional anxiety and turmoil including depression and even bullying.

Richard Louv first used the phrase in his 2005 book, *Last Child in the Woods*, to describe the high cost which humanity pays as a result of our disconnect from the natural world. Today, it is finally being recognized that adults suffer from the same syndrome. Studies from around the world have shown irrefutable proof that our alienation from Nature is the root cause of so many of our physical, psychological and emotional problems leading to negative impacts on our lives in all areas—personal, family and community life as well as professional.

One aspect that has extremely serious implications is that of increased bullying and aggression towards others. Studies show that children who grow up bullying others, who show a lack of empathy and concern for others, including other species, even resorting to physical violence at times toward others, including animals, often continue this pattern of violence and lack of caring and sensitivity as adults.

This certainly does not bode well for the future of peace on the planet. Indeed, the next generation seems to be hardwired for violence due to their estrangement from Nature and their often-obsessive exposure to violent video games.

It also has grave implications for our fitness as caring and responsible stewards of the Earth, entrusted with protecting and preserving the planet for the benefit of future generations. As children who have lost contact with Nature become adults, their interest in protecting and preserving the Earth is virtually non-existent, leading to an even greater uptick in exploitation and destruction of the natural world.

During the course of his research in the 1990s and early 2000s, Louv also interviewed children who suffered emotional and psychological turmoil similar to mine at the loss of their special forest areas. In his book, he relates his interview with a young poetess, who, unlike most of the children with whom he talked, spent almost every day in the forest in a place she thought of as her own—a beautiful part of the woods with a large waterfall and stream flowing past through the trees. It was her special place of freedom and peaceful solitude where she would come to be by herself, surrounded by the beauty of Nature.

Then, one fateful day, she lost her special place. Clearly, in deep distress and anguish upon reliving that day, her voice choked with emotion, she told Louv that when they cut down the woods, they cut down a part of herself.

She and I have shared the same deep sorrow and painful memories over the loss of our special forest places. Even today, I experience those same feelings whenever I come upon a scenes of annihilation of a forest or other aspects of Nature—the obliteration of life.

That is what Nature is all about—LIFE! And if we want to improve our own life, we need to re-establish our relationship with Nature in every way without further delay. Recent studies underscore just how critical our reconnection with Nature is in order to improve our lives physically, emotionally, psychologically and spiritually.

In today's world, we live virtually entirely removed from Nature in a lifestyle that is so sedentary, we barely move from our seat unless it becomes necessary, imitating the lifestyle of a brick rather than that of a living being!

So, just getting up and moving about is also an improvement. But while physical exercise of any kind can help one tone up and lose weight, a walk in Nature or just being in Nature gives benefits well beyond simply burning calories.

Called 'forest bathing' by the Japanese, some of these benefits documented by various studies include lower heart rate and blood pressure with an increase in the body's adiponectin levels. Adiponectin has anti-inflammatory effects on the cells of blood vessels which reduces the risk of heart attacks. Secreted by fat cells, it also regulates fat metabolism, weight gain and glucose levels while reducing insulin resistance, thereby helping to control diabetes.

Being in the forest also helps decrease the incidence of headaches and migraines while causing an increase in both production and activity of NK cells in the immune system—NK stands for 'natural killer' cells. These amazing cells selectively seek out and destroy cancer cells as well as bacterial infections, even targeting viral infections within a cell without destroying the entire cell. This enhances the overall ability of the body's immune system to fight infections as well as tumour formations.

Just breathing forest air is a bonus, not only because it is far less polluted, but because of the essential oils that trees emit into the air. These oils called 'phytoncide' help protect trees and plants from germs and pests, and they help us, too. Breathing them in, while in the woods, has been shown to improve our immune system and reduce inflammation throughout the body, both internally and externally.

This reduction of inflammation has major benefits for those suffering from a variety of health troubles including osteoporosis and other joint pain, skin diseases and conditions like psoriasis and eczema. Lung and breathing problems like asthma are also aided since phytoncides enhance oxygen production in the body.

Some compounds found in forest air, known as 'terpenes', are even helpful in decreasing inflammation in the liver, pancreas and brain thereby helping to reduce the onset of Alzheimer's and other degenerative brain diseases that stem from brain inflammation. These compounds also have anti-tumour properties effective against various cancers including those of the breast, liver, pancreas, intestine and colon.

The reduction of dopamine and the stress hormone, cortisol, are two more benefits of 'forest bathing', along with lower sympathetic nerve activity (which controls our 'fight or flight' responses) and greater parasympathetic nerve activity (which oversees our 'rest and digest' system). As a result, we feel far less stressed and far more relaxed and at ease in a forest environment compared to that of a city or urban centre. Simply put, we just *feel* good in every way whenever we are in the woods.

It is not just our body which gets a boost from being in Nature—our brain gets a needed rest and a boost as well. The 'command centre' of our brain—the prefrontal cortex, which is also the centre of sustained attention, conceptual and complex thinking as well as decision-making and social behaviour— is able to slow down and rest. The EEG readings of subjects taken before and after they spent time in Nature have verified this by registering a reduction in the energy coming from lower midline frontal theta waves, or the waves that measure conceptual thinking and sustained attention. There was also decreased activity in the subgenual prefrontal cortex, which is tied to depressive thinking.

It was Korean researchers who first documented the stark difference between how our brain reacts while in Nature versus in city settings using the MRI to see real-time brain reactions. When volunteers were shown urban scenes, the MRI revealed increased blood flow in their amygdala which is the brain's centre for fear and anxiety.

Conversely, when these same volunteers viewed scenes of Nature, the anterior cingulate and insula lit up. These are areas associated with empathy and altruism giving evidence for yet another plus from being in Nature—not only do we feel better about ourselves, we also feel more compassion and understanding for others including for other species.

Hence, these changes in our brain and social behaviour also help us in work environments. An increase of up to 50 per cent better creative problem-solving, cognitive functioning and improved executive attention skills like short-term memory, coupled with a rested, relaxed, rejuvenated workforce that is also socially congenial and mutually cooperative means far better performance on the job.

This is not lost on the government and business world of South Korea, where there used to be just three official healing forests. Today there are a total of thirty-seven state-run healing forests across the country located near almost every major town in the country.

While timber yields were the focus of the Korean Forest Service in the past, today the concentration is on human well-being as an official goal of South Korea's forest policy. Health rangers are posted across the country to help those seeking the various health benefits from these healing forests. This includes camping in the healing heart of Nature for children who have been victims of bullying.

This research has been further confirmed by real-life studies which demonstrate conclusively that isolation from the natural world causes stress and depression, while connecting to Nature helps stem depression while lowering stress and aggression in all its forms.

The patterns of physical, psychological and social breakdown seen with animals forced to live in unnatural surroundings are the same as those observed in human communities devoid of Nature.

These patterns include an increase in aggression and violent behaviour, disrupted and confused patterns in parenting, along with turmoil within societal structures and community hierarchies.

However, when surroundings are changed to include Nature, both animal and human communities benefit with a marked decrease in hostility and violence. In human communities, this reduction is seen across the board—from incidents of bullying in schools to violent acts committed by inmates in prison.

Officers at a correctional institution in Oregon reported that solitary-confinement prisoners who exercised in a room where Nature videos were playing, exhibited far calmer behaviour than those who exercised in a gym without the videos. In Chicago, researchers recorded far fewer acts of both violence and crime in areas with trees compared to neighbourhoods devoid of greenery. People in greener communities demonstrate more care for one another and for their communities.

This extends to schools, too—the more the trees, the less the bullying and violence among students. Just playing on a natural surface like grass compared to playing on asphalt helped to bring down incidents of bullying.

Walking barefoot in Nature centres us as we are literally grounded to the earth, helping to reset our own electromagnetic field (EMF) that is constantly under assault from the various technological EMF sources like wireless devices or cell phone towers that saturate our environments. There are few things as refreshing as walking on cool, green grass, or as stimulating as walking on sand, or as fun as squishing wet mud between one's toes while wading through water.

Add to this natural mix, contact with animals and there is an even greater change towards more peaceful and thoughtful behaviour. The emotional, physical and psychological uplift we gain from being with animals has been known for decades. The unconditional love they shower on us brings solace to the most confused minds and softens even the hardest hearts—from working with autistic children to helping the criminally insane, animals touch us in a way that nothing else does.

Interaction with animals also brings out our empathy leading to increased acts of gentleness and kindness towards the animal in our care while opening the doorway to better relationships with other humans as well. Through these contacts with animals and Nature, we learn to truly respect and love every form and aspect of Life.

Then comes the adventure of learning about all these different facets of Life and Nature—something which was an integral part of humanity's 'education' in eras past but is sorely lacking today. Indeed, in conjunction with 'Nature Deficit Disorder', there is 'Nature Knowledge Deficit', or the simple fact that we know far less about Nature and natural cycles today than our parents and ancestors knew even just a generation or two ago. This is a dangerous situation, especially in light of the environmental challenges presented by climate change today—challenges that will only multiply and intensify in the future.

Without an understanding of how Nature works, how can we try to reverse or at least cushion the effects on ourselves and future generations of higher temperatures and rising seas, extreme climate events whether of drought or flood/heat or cold, of missing links in the food chain due to the extinction of thousands of species and the consequential catastrophic collapses in the ecosystem that these extinctions will inevitably cause?

Hence, the results of these studies have great implications for our own future as a species and for the future of life on our planet. If we continue down the road we are travelling today, consumed by our obsession with technology and tech toys, denying ourselves the richness, tranquillity and rejuvenation that contact with Nature brings, mindlessly destroying what remains of the natural world around us, disrupting irreparably the delicate ecosystems upon which our own survival depends, then our future and the future of peace on Earth looks grim, indeed. For, in all probability, if we continue to assault Nature, we will continue to assault each other.

We desperately need to embrace the truth that we are a part of Nature. We evolved in Nature, are adapted to Nature and cannot live without her. Cut off from Nature, we become ill and unstable; reconnect with and respect her, helping to heal the wounds we have arrogantly and ignorantly inflicted upon her, we heal ourselves.

We who live in democracies have an even greater responsibility to bring to power genuine leaders who understand this connection between Nature and humanity and will work to protect and revive it. The actions of the South Korean government are examples of a good start, prompted as they are not only by the economic and health benefits for their population, but also by their cultural traditions of worshipping Nature-spirits. Forest bathing has been part of Japan's National Public Health Programme since 1982, with Japanese culture embracing appreciation of and for Nature for generations.

Indian culture has been similarly intertwined with Nature for millennia. Since Vedic times, the peoples of India have respected and revered Nature not only for her bounty, from which they were able to sustain their lives and flourish, but also for her connection to the Divine. Like my maternal ancestors, the Native American Osage, indigenous people across the Indian subcontinent have recognized this link of Nature with the Creator and hold it in high esteem as the outer vesture of the Divine.

Throughout ancient India, the native peoples showed their reverence for Nature by putting aside areas not to be touched by any humans, where all wildlife was free to roam unharmed, where no tree was to be cut down or even dead branches removed. These areas were the 'Lands of the Gods'—'Devarakadus' or 'Sacred Groves'—meant to be places of veneration and worship of the Divine as well as constant reminders of the fact that our existence here on this Earth is due to the unceasing benevolence and generosity of Nature, from whom all life has come.

Sacred groves spanned the entire length and breadth of ancient India, filling every corner of the landscape. Thousands of them brought green life to the peoples of the country; it was from these blessed domains that many of the holy rivers originated.

Today, these lands, once viewed as sacrosanct and untouchable, have been encroached upon, polluted and destroyed, and human greed has been the main culprit behind this devastation. At present, Indian culture, once vibrant with the life its contact with the natural world gave to it, is but a shadow of itself, cut off from the source of its strength and inspiration: Nature.

This must be reversed by the revival of our sacred groves across the country, and the little state of Sikkim in India's northeast is showing us the way. With Sikkim already one of the greenest states in the country, its state government is now encouraging people to forge personal, lifelong relationships with trees in an age-old practice known as *Mith*, meaning 'friend'.

Trees can also be adopted like a child or preserved in the remembrance of a departed loved one. The goal of the programme is to help foster friendship, reverence and love between people and Nature, in general. It is also identifying 'heritage trees'—trees whose large girth are testimony to their older age and must be protected as living legacies for future generations. Anyone who damages these trees or those trees registered under the 'Mith' programme will be charged with committing a forest offense and penalized accordingly by law.

This is a wonderful way to help rekindle humanity's relationship with the forest—enshrined as laws aimed not only at protection, but at rebuilding the admiration and adoration of Nature that we once shared, and to reawaken the child, that in truth, lies within each one of us, that we all may experience what it means to be 'barefoot and free' in the heart of Nature once again.

# 4

# Suds in the Water, Tar on the Beach

'Water! Water!! Please give me some water,' I whispered as loudly as I could to the nurse leaning over me trying to hear what I was saying. I had just awakened in the recovery room having survived the operation, but in a great deal of pain and discomfort. My mouth and throat were so dry, I could barely make any sound at all above a tiny squeak.

'You'll have to wait a little longer before you can have any water,' she replied. The pain in my dry throat was so excruciating I thought I would die right then and there if I did not drink some water, this experience being an agonizing reminder of just how important this element of Nature is. Simply put, none of us can live without water.

I have always loved water. Perhaps, it was written in the stars that I should have such an affinity for it—I was born a 'double fish' under the Zodiac water-sign Pisces, in a hospital called 'Riverview', overlooking the river which would become an important part of my early life and whose red banks gave my hometown its name. I have loved water and everything about water for as long as I can remember. There is something very special about this most precious element, and life on this planet as we know it would not have existed without it.

According to ancient Vedic teachings, creation is the result of the evolution of and interplay between the five basic elements. Each element has evolved from the previous, bringing with it a new attribute, quality and power for the creation and life. Our five senses have evolved and developed as a result of these attributes. With the senses, the ability to experience creation to its fullest becomes possible. It's a bit like a telescope—each new section emerges from but still remains connected to the previous. When all sections/elements with their unique attributes and powers are complete and in balance, with the five senses intact, the 'picture' of creation comes into sharp focus for us to enjoy.

Ether or space is the first and most subtle of the elements having just one attribute of sound, thus giving rise to the ear, so that we can hear. From ether, air or wind evolved, with its feature of feeling and powerful sense of touch. Fire came next with its quality of light and sense of sight. And then came this unique element of water. It has all the qualities and powers of the previous three elements—it can be heard, felt and seen—and then brings another one of its own—taste. The final element which evolved from water is earth which gave rise to the sense of smell. It is easy to experience the connection between water and earth whenever it rains. The rainfall brings out the full, rich aroma of the good, pure earth. Breathing in deeply, this extraordinary fragrance heals our body, lifts our heart and literally grounds our soul to Mother Earth.

One of the unique features of water, compared to the other four elements, is its unusual ability to take on different forms while still remaining structurally the same substance. Depending on the temperature of its surrounding environment, it can rise up into the sky as a gas, flow on the ground as a liquid, or become solid, hard as stone, when it freezes into ice. Whether as a gas, liquid or solid, water and its interactions with the other four elements creates remarkable habitats filled with life—some astonishingly beautiful, others strange and unexpected and some others, downright bizarre.

The different forms and sounds of water portray its different 'moods' while affecting our own as well, sometimes soothing and calming, at other times enthralling and exciting—the mist slowly rising from the hills covering everything in its white veil; the gentle 'pitter-patter' of the light rain shower or the torrential din of monsoon at its height; the exquisitely delicate snowflakes blanketing the earth in deep, hushed silence; the icicles hanging down from the bare tree limbs, sparkling in the winter sun, sending rainbow hues in all directions and tinkling like crystal chimes in the wind; the sound of frozen rivers 'singing' as the ice shifts above the liquid water below; the still pond mirroring the sky, the mountains and the forests around it, waves rippling across its surface as the breeze blows in unison with your own breath creating diamond reflections of sunlight shimmering everywhere; the changing rhythms of the ocean breakers crashing on the shore; the babbling brook laughing on its way; the white water rapids and raging waterfall cascades thundering over steep cliffs into the emerald green ponds below; the symphony of sounds as the river flows past, beckoning your soul to join it on its journey to mergence with the sea.

Water's perseverance to reach that goal of mergence gives great lessons for life. While being wonderfully gentle, flexible and adaptable, its persistence can wear down even the hardest rock, creating majestic canyons of stunning beauty as a result. It will overcome every obstacle in its path going over, around or beneath them to stay its course. With help from the other elements, it is constantly cleansing itself to keep its purity intact, sharing that purity with all. These amazing transformative properties that produce this rich array of sights, sounds and beauty, seem magical, mystical and even spiritual, since no matter what its form, water's essence stays the same. Maybe this ability, coupled with the intuitive recognition and practical reality of the fact that without water life is impossible, was what led humanity to venerate water from the time man first roamed the Earth.

Held sacred and holy by cultures and faiths throughout history, water has, in the forms of rivers and lakes, oceans and seas, been both humanized and deified. For many indigenous peoples, water is the origin of 'life' itself. For Native Americans, the credo 'water is life' is a living breathing fact. It was therefore the duty of every person to respect and protect water sources and their natural surroundings as well as the various animals that were specially connected to water in one way or another. These animals themselves were honoured and often considered sacred, too.

This sacred connection between water and various species of wildlife illustrates well how Native Americans and other indigenous peoples have understood the intricate workings of the web of life and the balance of Nature.

One example of this comes from the Blackfoot tribe of North America—one of the Great Plains tribes like my ancestors the Osage. For the Blackfoot, the beaver is a sacred animal and must never be hunted nor its habitat disturbed. This honour and respect for the beaver grows out of the recognition of the vital role beavers play in giving water to the dry Midwest of the continent. Beavers make dams that become green oases of life not just for the beaver, but for many other species as well, with the life-giving waters of the beaver ponds supplying water to the tribe while also attracting other species of wildlife like deer which the tribe could then hunt for food.

Another example is the North American salmon which is held in the highest esteem by many Native American tribes, especially those of the northwest. Salmon start their life in freshwater rivers and streams in the forests and then head out to the salty seas when they have matured, spending the rest of their life in saltwater oceans. Years later, individuals return to the very same freshwater river and stream where they were born to reproduce and die. This event of Nature is called the 'salmon run' since the fish 'run' or swim upstream to lay and fertilize the eggs of the next generation. Upon their return to spawn, salmon feed not only various Native American or First Nations tribes, but also many diverse species of wildlife, from birds to wolves to bears, making it the keystone species of the entire ecosystem. Without the salmon, the system would collapse, not just because of the loss of food for people and wildlife alike, but because of the special relationship that has evolved over the ages between the salmon and the bears in particular.

To help build up fat for their long, winter hibernation, both grizzly and black bears rely on catching huge numbers of salmon during this annual 'salmon run.' But since black bears are much smaller than grizzlies, they take the fish they've caught and go into the forest to eat in peace without danger from the larger grizzly interrupting or stealing their meal. The leftover remains from the salmon also 'feed' the trees in the forests by making available vital nutrients, including phosphorus and nitrogen. Scientific studies show that 70 to 80 per cent of the nitrogen these trees need comes directly from the decaying remains of the salmon left there by the bears after a good meal.

Indeed, trees on the banks of salmon-stocked rivers grow more than three times faster than those along rivers without salmon. An example is the Sitka spruce. These trees normally take 300 years to reach a width of 50 cm. But those growing where salmon are found, take just eighty-six years to become that thick. The trees aid the salmon as well by providing food, shelter and shade to the developing fish—a symbiotic relationship that benefits both species and by extension, the people who depend on them.

Hence, to summarize: without the salmon, the forests would not thrive; without the black bears, the salmon would not arrive in the forests; without the grizzlies, the black bears would have no reason to take their salmon catch into the forest; and without the salmon this unique ecosystem would not exist at all. How wonderfully intricate and mutually supportive the different parts of Nature are! The salmon's transformation from living in fresh water, then adapting to salt water only to readapt to fresh water is another marvel of Nature. For Native Americans, salmon represent determination, renewal and prosperity, and also serve as a reminder from the Creator to properly care for Nature in order to protect this vital food source, being careful to never take more than one needs to survive.

With water being so imperative for life and living, it is not surprising that my own tribe associated themselves deeply with water by identifying with the great rivers that abutted their traditional tribal lands, as mentioned in Chapter Two, subtitle 'The Osage Connection.' Many religious and cultural practices include the use of water for spiritual cleansing and as a symbol for rebirth—baptism by Christians, Hindu ritual bathing in the Ganga and a dip in the hot springs at the source of the Yamuna are just a few examples. Whether it is the calming reassurance felt while soaking in a hot spring or the shocking exhilaration following a full body immersion into an icy stream that makes the whole body tingle with 'life', water cleanses, heals and renews us in every way.

Hydrotherapy for various ailments has always been used by healers around the world, with water from certain rivers and pools considered especially potent in its power to heal and transform. Water from the Ganga is a case in point. Highly valued by British sailors for its ability to not become stale during the long journey from India to England, it also has certain properties that do not allow mosquitoes to breed in its water and inhibits mosquito-breeding in any water to which it is added: two amazing facts for which scientists are still trying to find a conclusive scientific explanation.

These anti-putrefaction qualities along with documented healings of various illnesses like cholera, dysentery, malaria, typhoid, tuberculosis, pneumonia and meningitis among others through ingestion of and/or immersion in the Ganges waters have puzzled scientists since 1896 when British bacteriologist Ernst Hankin scientifically demonstrated the antibacterial property of Ganges water against cholera for the first time. In addition, Ganga's self-purifying quality leads to oxygen levels twenty-five times higher than any other river in the world.

More recent studies have revealed the presence of over two dozen potent bacteriophages, which are viruses that eat up disease-causing bacteria. In addition to this, Ganga's medicinal waters also contain double-stranded DNA viruses never seen before which have the ability to heal several MDR (multi-drug resistant) infections—yet another complete puzzle that scientists are trying to unravel. Taking all of this into consideration, it is easy to see why Indians have revered 'Mother Ganga' for thousands of years.

Other indigenous peoples and cultures have also respected and revered water throughout human history. Today, among some secular court systems and governments in various parts of the world, including here in India, there is a change in attitude and practice at least with regard to some rivers. From gross exploitation and mindless manipulation of the entire riparian system, a shift is underway towards respect and preservation, including granting the status of 'personhood' to them in order to ensure that these ecosystems are granted the same rights and protections as human beings. This shift is based, in part, on cultural history in countries like Bolivia, India and even New Zealand. Certain rivers have been revered as 'holy' by the Maori people who came to the islands long before the white settlers ever arrived. But this change is also based on the scientific understanding of just how critical water is to life on the planet, including our own species. Without water, we cannot exist either.

Of all the elements, water is the key that scientists look for when seeking the possibility of life on other planets as well. As life evolved from water and specifically the oceans here on Earth, with oceans in particular still being critical for our weather patterns and the production of oxygen for our atmosphere, astronomers and other scientists theorize that a similar process elsewhere on another planet could mean a similar evolution and development to complex life there, too.

So, even apart from the spiritual aspect, it is very clear that protection of water and preservation of its natural surroundings, to ensure its purity and abundant supply, is the practical and intelligent thing to do to avert greater environmental damage.

But is that the way we are living today? Clearly not.

Our waterways have become polluted cesspools of sewage and other pollutants from manufacturing facilities which are directly flushed into them. These, along with chemicals from conventional agriculture in the form of pesticides and fertilizers, enter our vital waterways either directly or via rain runoff, poisoning them and often causing massive toxic blooms of certain algae, whose decomposition depletes the oxygen content in the water, suffocating aquatic creatures and aquatic plants, leading to massive fish kills numbering in the thousands, and 'dead zones' where no life exists at all.

The largest dead zone in the world is in the Gulf of Mexico where agricultural chemicals flowing into the Gulf from the Mississippi River are major culprits. This zone measures an astonishing 8,776 square miles—about the size of the state of my birth in the USA—New Jersey. But there are other dead zones in other areas around the world, with the one in the Arabian Sea being as large and the thickest dead zone in the world—something that should certainly concern all of us here in India!

Not just indigenous peoples, but environmentalists and scientists are ringing alarm bells about the perilous and deadly state of our global freshwater supplies today. All too often, these warnings are ignored by those in power, who disregard even scientific data and testimony in an insane rush, fuelled by a greed for oil, natural gas and other minerals and materials below the earth's surface. They continue to destroy and put at risk the ecosystems and habitats of the various creatures and systems of water that are vital to safeguard and preserve for all life.

Two examples of this come from the USA. The first is the mad fracking industry. Fracking entails pumping one of the most toxic chemical cocktails ever devised along with water into the earth at high pressure to force the rock below to crack and release pockets of natural gas for harvesting. These chemicals have been found in drinking water supplies where fracking is occurring and include such high amounts of methane gas that putting a lit match in the water causes it to explode and burn. The same thing happens with a lit match near water coming from a faucet—fire explosions from the extremely polluted water that is clearly unfit for any use—drinking, cooking, bathing, etc.

The second example is the struggle to stop the Keystone XL and Dakota oil pipeline. The project would not only bring pipelines to the border of the Native American reservation endangering their own water supplies but will also cross the most important underground aquifers in the USA—the Ogallala Aquifer. This aquifer, which spans eight states, is one of the largest reserves of fresh water in the world, providing drinking water to at least two million people while also supporting $20 billion in agriculture. The pipeline has to cross more than 1000 streams, rivers, aquifers and other water bodies on its journey from Canada to the oil refineries in the Gulf of Mexico, endangering key rivers like the Missouri, James, Illinois and even the Mississippi.

Because much of the pipeline will be underground, one leak will not only contaminate vital freshwater sources on the surface, but the leaked oil will also percolate down through the ground to poison this crucial aquifer for all time because, unlike surface water which is in a constant mode of cleansing through its movements, aquifers move but a few inches each year if at all.

Frighteningly, the track record from the original pipeline is horrific with at least thirty-five leaks in its first year of operation. This new pipeline addition has already leaked thirteen times including a major one in November 2017 where over 2,10,000 gallons (210,000 gallons) of crude oil extracted from oil sands in Canada spilled above and below ground in Nebraska. Native Americans have been joined by people from every walk of life in their fight against this insanity since this aquifer and the various surface water systems endangered represent the fresh water supply for millions of people throughout the Midwest from Canada to the Gulf of Mexico.

But when the ones with vested interests are also the ones in power, the struggle is difficult if not impossible without overwhelming numbers of the country's population standing together to stop these insanities and those perpetuating them. This is the very essence of a people's movement, especially in a democracy. The people can drive change if they care enough to act together to do so.

And change has finally come, at least in this case. Newly elected President Joe Biden has cancelled the Keystone Pipeline as one of his first acts after his inauguration in January 2021, revoking the permit for the pipeline. While Native Americans and environmentalists are elated by the move, they hope for even tougher, more permanent guarantees that the pipeline will never be allowed, regardless of who sits in the US White House. So, the battle to actually win the war against this and other fossil fuel polluting projects continues.

Then there is the mindless dumping of garbage into the oceans across the globe with our unnatural, non-biodegradable products like lighters, bottles and plastics of all kinds going round and round the ocean currents or gyres until they end up resting on shorelines often on the most remote uninhabited and otherwise pristine parts of the planet.

How much garbage? The garbage patch in the Pacific is more than three times the size of France containing at least 1.8 trillion pieces of plastic—enough to fill 500 jumbo jets, and that's just in one garbage patch! According to the UN, there is more plastic garbage in the world than there are stars in the galaxy with the weight of that plastic being equal to that of a billion elephants!

Worse still is that our garbage is mistaken for food by sea creatures and aquatic birds like the Albatross who then regurgitate it into the unsuspecting mouths of their innocent hungry chicks eventually killing them and other marine animals like turtles and whales. Recently, the autopsy of a seven-metre whale revealed it had swallowed at least thirty plastic bags and other plastic items, probably having mistaken the plastic for squid, its natural food. This doesn't begin to count the numbers of wildlife killed, crippled and injured by becoming entangled in our garbage—dolphins, seals, otters—with our trash even reaching the Arctic Circle tangling up polar bears swimming along the coast. Here, in India as well, wildlife is falling victim to our trash including some of our most iconic animals like tigers and elephants. Both species spend a good deal of time in water and are dying either from drinking polluted water or being entangled in or ingesting our garbage.

This plastic mess is a menace to human health as well and is literally killing us. Plastic does not biodegrade but breaks into smaller and smaller nano pieces. Globally, there are at least 5 trillion pieces of plastic floating in the planet's oceans with most of that being micro/nano plastics that are entering the food chain and poisoning life in the oceans and around the earth, including us.

In addition, international studies have found these nanoparticles of plastic in the tap water of every country in the world, with the highest concentration being found in the USA. India's water ranks third—a dangerously high ranking that must alarm us all and awaken us to act. This ranking means that rivers are dying as a result of the mass of garbage being dumped in them, choked to the point where they no longer flow, filled with such high levels of deadly chemicals that no living thing can survive in them.

Ingestion of these nano plastic particles can come either directly through tainted tap water, through consumption of fish and other aquatic foods, or through tainted produce which has used contaminated water for irrigation, with scientists even finding them in human placentas and mother's milk! The adverse effects on our health are many and varied. Some examples are weakness, headache and fatigue, nausea, diarrhoea, vomiting and liver damage, and neurological damage, endocrine disruption, birth defects and child development disorders, reproductive damage, DNA changes, damage to the immune system, asthma and other breathing problems, endometriosis, acute skin rashes and skin diseases as well as various types of cancer and multiple organ damage.

This is a grave situation and each and every one of us bears some level of responsibility for it. It is our manufactured goods, the packaging of the products we purchase, the 'throw-away' mentality of society today that is the cause of this. We must recognize our own hand in this tragedy and work to change it by being more conscious consumers, insisting on less packaging around the products we purchase while demanding that whatever packaging is used be biodegradable. We must become more inventive repairing, reusing and recycling everything, thereby helping to vastly decrease destruction of forest areas due to mining for raw materials as well as cutting down the requirement for both energy and water since recycled products require less energy and water than newly manufactured/one-use products.

The situation can be reversed only if we act both individually and collectively while also demanding that our elected officials act as well to ensure that laws be passed and implemented by the proper authorities in order to clean up this mess we have all created. It is after all our responsibility, our duty to revive and protect our sacred waterways upon which we all depend that they may once again be the source of life and joy for all species.

## Forests and the Elixir of Life

I have been fortunate to live near water in some form or the other for most of my life and have spent a good deal of my childhood playing in and around its various forms—from sledding down snow-covered hills to snowshoeing in the forests of the Rocky Mountains, from skating on Swanker's Pond near my home to sailing on the Navesink River and swimming in many water bodies including both the Atlantic and Pacific Oceans.

Red Bank is located just six miles from the Atlantic. My mother loved the ocean and spent every summer day that she could there on the shore. This is where she taught me how to swim and where I trained to receive my lifeguard certification. It is also where I used inflatable mats to ride the ocean waves into shore—a favourite pastime of my youth. If we were lucky, we would see a pod of dolphins or perhaps even a whale at sea while seabirds would search for crabs and other food at the ocean's edge.

These were happy, carefree times enjoying the wind, surf and sun, walking barefoot in the warm sand . . . that is until I unexpectedly walked on balls of tar in the sand, the thick sticky tar getting all over my feet and between my toes. The tar was very difficult to remove and was sometimes in the ocean water as well, getting on my bathing suit or even in my hair. What a mess!

These awful experiences with tar were my first awakening to the concept of 'pollution'. The tar was caused by oil leaks and spills from ships at sea. This and other garbage of various kinds and from different sources were also intentionally dumped in the ocean with no regard as to the consequences of such thoughtless and dangerous acts, polluting one of my favourite playgrounds.

Then there was the Navesink River which flowed through my hometown of Red Bank and was just a few blocks from my family home. Many happy hours were spent either on its shores, in its waters, or sailing its surface. Sailing was and still is a family affair. Both my mom and my dad enjoyed sailing when they were young. My mom raced sailboats on the Navesink itself with her brother, Bob, as her crew when they were kids. My dad sailed on the Chesapeake Bay in Maryland and continued to sail on the Navesink after the war.

Most of us kids 'crewed' for my dad at one time or another. But two of my siblings—Peter and Pris—became outstanding sailors in their own right. Peter raced different sailboats all over the country with his love of being on the water eventually leading him to join the Merchant Marine Academy at Kings Point in New York. Pris sailed on to win several National Championships as well as becoming the sailing instructor for young sailors at the local boat club. Today she is an international judge at various sailing regatta competitions.

I was never the sailor that either of them was but I still loved being on the water with the breeze blowing through my hair, the reflected sunlight sparkling off the water's surface as the waves lapped at the sides of the boat—just a wonderful convergence of the elements creating a peaceful and serene scene. My first sailing adventures were with a 'Sailfish'—a boat that looked like a surfboard with a sail. They were simple to sail on and could be easily righted making them great fun even when they tipped over dunking you in the river as a result. The only problem, however, was that very often, when I ended up in the river, I would break out in a terrible rash—not from jellyfish stings, but from the gasoline leaked into the water from power boats. This was yet another lesson in how our carelessness and activities can pollute vital water sources not to mention ruin an otherwise great way of spending the day sailing.

As mentioned earlier, the unique attribute of water is taste. There is nothing as thirst quenching as a drink of cool, pure water, and I drank lots of it as a child playing on a summer's day, drinking it directly from the kitchen tap. It tasted great. One time, on a visit to my aunt's house in Staten Island, New York, I asked for some water to drink. My aunt filled a glass from her kitchen faucet and gave it to me. With my first gulp of the water, I immediately stopped drinking and said to my aunt, 'This water tastes funny!'

Back at home in Red Bank I told my mom about the funny-tasting water at Staten Island. My mom said that the water there was polluted—that was why it tasted strange, adding that Red Bank's water supply was clean and safe because it came from an artesian well—not from polluted surface water like that on Staten Island. The artesian well was located below Eisner's Woods, and herein was my first lesson in the connection between forests and water.

While much of global rainfall is produced from evaporated sea water, forests are also critically important for rainfall production. Forests cause rainfall through the interaction of three processes. The first is photosynthesis, which is the absorption of $CO_2$ from the atmosphere by trees/plants and its conversion to sugars/food for the flora using sunlight and water, releasing oxygen back into the atmosphere during the process. The second process is transpiration. During photosynthesis, trees draw the water they need from deep underground through their root systems sending it up the trunk, out the branches and into the leaves. The leaves transpire or push out water vapour into the air from small pores on their underside. The released water vapour sets up conditions for raincloud formation. The third process is direct cloud seeding by the forest itself as trees, plants and especially forest mushrooms/fungi spew forth microscopic bits of potassium salts high into the sky. These salts become the nucleus around which the water vapour that the trees and other flora has released into the atmosphere coalesces/aggregates to make raindrops that form rainclouds.

The contribution of forest-generated rainfall is critical for the planet especially in the equatorial rainforest belt (between latitudes 30 degrees south and 30 degrees north) where over 50 per cent of all rainfall is created by the forests themselves. Researchers confirm that rainfall generated by forests has a chemically distinct potassium core from rainfall produced from evaporated sea water, adding that a high concentration of fungal spores are found in the study samples used, attesting to their forest origin.

The three-stage process of forest rainfall generation also cools the earth's surface not only because the moisture-laden air brings down temperatures, but also because these damp aerosols scatter/reflect sunlight back into space, thereby helping mitigate higher temperatures from climate change.

What is also quite amazing is that forests themselves activate the onset of the rainy season. Near the end of the dry season in equatorial areas, and as temperatures warm in temperate zones, new foliage starts to appear on trees. These new leaves boost the rate of photosynthesis and, as a result, boost transpiration as well. This increased transpiration puts enough moisture into the air to build low-level clouds intensifying air circulation (called 'shallow convection') that further moistens the air, destabilizing the atmosphere enough to start the transition from dry/cold to the wet, rainy season.

This 'shallow convection moisture pump' or SCMP initiated by enhanced transpiration first produces light 'pre-monsoon' rain showers which warm the atmosphere further causing air to rise, triggering a further intensification and strengthening of air circulation large enough to induce a shift in wind patterns that sends moisture-laden air from the ocean inland for the full onset of the rainy, monsoon season. Isotopic fingerprints of the atmospheric moisture unequivocally identify forest transpiration as the primary moisture source during this transition from dry to wet season.

In addition, air that passes over forest areas produces at least twice as much rain as air passing over little vegetation. In other words, the more the forests, the more the moisture the air carries and the more the rainfall produced, increasing rainfall even thousands of kilometres away especially in equatorial zones—a fact that is extremely important for India since most of India including the entire Western Ghats region lies within these zones.

This has important implications for government policies regarding the need to protect forest areas. If forests continue to be cut down, not only will there be higher temperatures and additional reductions in rainfall, but also a later onset of the rainy season inevitably leading to drought not only locally but on a continental/country-wide level.

In addition to rainfall generation, trees provide many other essential services on which we depend and from which we directly benefit. The forest canopy and fallen leaf litter on the forest floor help to capture rainfall, acting like sponges to soak up extra rainfall, thereby reducing water runoff and flooding. Each adult tree can absorb as much as 57,000 gallons (almost 216,000 litres).

This is in conjunction with their extensive root systems which act as a giant net to hold soil in place thereby reducing soil erosion. The roots not only hold the excess water until the dry season, slowly releasing it to ensure our waterways flow year-round, they also purify the water of toxins as they suck it up. This is a crucial service that is completely lacking in areas where deforestation has taken place. With no tree roots for purification, water sources both above and below ground become choked with debris, pollutants and toxins which end up poisoning us.

So, Eisner's Woods was not just my special forest hide-away and home for wildlife. It was an important part of the critical water cycle of life helping to increase rainfall, purifying it as well on its journey to the underground aquifer below—services from which I and everyone else in the area benefitted each time we drank a glass of water.

Unfortunately, virtually all of Eisner's Woods has been cut down over the years and replaced with apartment and condominium complexes. The same is true for other once heavily wooded estates in the area. Those wonderful forests of my youth along with all the amazing and essential ecosystem services they freely provided are for the most part no more . . .

Finally, I want to thank my then-representative to the US Congress—James J. Howard—for helping to drive home the truth that the most serious crisis humanity faces today is the destruction, pollution and disappearance of our fresh water sources. Representative Howard visited our high school one year while I was a student decades ago and gave a presentation that I remember clearly even to this day. Starting his presentation with a question to the students, he asked, 'What is the most serious crisis facing the USA today?'

This was in the late 1960s and the Vietnam War was in full swing. Quite naturally several students answered, 'The Vietnam War'.

'Wrong,' he stated emphatically. 'The most serious crisis facing America today is water pollution.'

A wave of sceptical laughter rippled through the student audience . . . until he started to show us photos and videos of New Jersey's waterways filled with garbage and choked with the most disgusting white foam as sewage and manufacturing pipelines belched out black liquids directly into rivers, ponds and lakes.

Stunned silence filled the room while Representative Howard explained what the results of this pollution meant for our own lives, the various deadly illnesses and birth defects these toxic effluents caused, the poisonous legacy being left to our generation and the next as well . . . if another were to be born at all.

I will never forget those photos, those videos, or the massive impact they had and still have on me. What is so unutterably sad and devastating to me today is that similar photos and footage of garbage-laden waterways with poisonous white foam floating on the top are now the 'norm' for so many of India's rivers, ponds and lakes.

While the local, state and national governments in the USA took bipartisan action in the 1970s to clean up its water, although in recent years, changes in administrations have sought to weaken those efforts. Here in India, the problems are so vast that governments on all levels have great difficulty enforcing laws already in the books to stop this poisoning of our waters.

In a democracy like that of the USA or India, it is as much the fault and responsibility of the people as it is of the politicians and bureaucrats. Nature neither recognizes nor respects political boundaries or agendas. She does not differentiate between the various man-made separations we humans so wrongly and erroneously impose on ourselves. She shares her abundance irrespectively with all. But all are also affected by the pollution and environmental fallout from deforestation and other destructive human activities that disfigure Nature and impair her ability to keep providing these ecosystem services upon which our very survival depends.

Unless the people join forces not just to insist on change, but to insist on change and enforcement of pollution laws, plus dive into action themselves personally and collectively helping to clean up waterways, plant trees, change our own wasteful polluting lifestyle and engage in purposeful actions—from purchasing only biodegradable goods to recycling/reusing/reducing waste of every kind, AND supporting and voting into power those individuals who will help bring about and enforce positive eco-sensitive and eco-sensible changes—the situation will only get worse.

In a democracy, we all have the ability and responsibility to ACT. This includes running for office as well in order to help pilot these necessary changes through the halls of government and make them the law of the land. We are all accountable for what kind of legacy we are leaving for our children and our children's children . . . that is, if more generations are to be born at all . . .

Will we clean up our act and leave them pure, abundant supplies of fresh water—the 'elixir of life'—or be cursed for having left behind a poisonous 'brew of death'?

The choice is ours . . .

# 5

## Dreams Beyond the Rainbow:
## A Collision of Worlds

When I was in the third grade, our class put on the play *The Wizard of Oz*. The script was written entirely by the students, of course with our teacher's help and guidance, and the class voted on who should play which roles. I was chosen to play the leading role of 'Dorothy' whose last name just happened to be 'Gale'!

The most beloved song of *The Wizard of Oz* is surely 'Somewhere over the Rainbow', the main song I sang for the play. For me, the song was and is so appropriate because I have always dreamt about going over and beyond the rainbow—travelling to other parts of the world, experiencing other cultures and peoples and spending time in Nature wherever I may go, to see the different wonders of the wildlife and scenic beauty of other lands. I was especially attracted to stories of the Middle East and Asia. There was something so familiar about these places—the customs, languages and even the clothing, especially that worn by the women, the veils and saris, were somehow all so familiar. Even as a child, I wondered if I would end up marrying someone who was born and raised in America like me or if my heart would be filled with love for someone from a land far, far away.

I mentioned how, years earlier, my father had made a vow to give the same kind of love and hospitality to foreign officers stationed in the USA as he had received overseas during World War II from the people of the countries where he was stationed. As a result, many holidays saw our home filled with guests from foreign lands, celebrating those special times with us. Coincidentally enough, most of these officers just happened to come from countries of the Middle East and Asia: Egypt, Israel and of course, the Philippines, where my dad spent so much time during the war.

My favourite foreign officers were Mar and Pedro, who were both Filipinos. They spent Christmas with us and joined in the family fun by helping to decorate the Christmas tree and singing Christmas carols, sharing their love with us as we shared ours with them, making it one of the most memorable Christmases of my life. My parents kept in touch with them right up to their passing, with my brother, Peter, visiting them during his own tours on naval duty, as required by the Merchant Marine Academy he attended. Peter's other travels included Europe and South and Central America. Listening to his stories of the places he went to and the people he met, fuelled my desire to go and live abroad.

Added to this were my interactions with the exchange students from South America who stayed with our family for some time. I distinctly remember two young women—one from Argentina and one from Brazil. While both girls shared the camaraderie of being from South America, there was friction between them over a natural wonder that both countries claimed as their own. This natural wonder is the spectacularly beautiful and majestic Iguazu Waterfall, whose headwaters start in Brazil and its waterfall cascades tumble into Argentina.

Here was yet another lesson for me to learn about the importance of fresh water and how access to it and control over it can lead to conflict between competing parties. Today we see how the possession and control of natural resources has affected the world and caused conflicts even within various countries where local and regional disputes over natural resources and especially freshwater supplies are increasing.

Case in point, the Cauvery River water dispute between the state of Karnataka and the neighbouring state of Tamil Nadu. Disputes between them over the dams on the Cauvery erected by Karnataka have led to cases being filed in the Indian Supreme Court and even to riots between the peoples of the two states, especially over the last few years as less rainfall in Cauvery's watershed areas in Karnataka have meant less water in the river. This is the ironic and tragic point here, since these conflicts, in most cases, are the direct result of humanity's actions of deforesting those very watershed areas which have helped to create these rivers, inland seas, lakes and other water bodies that we all depend on for survival. When forests are intact, rainfall is abundant enough to keep these vital sources full and flowing. But as soon as deforestation takes place, rainfall decreases, less water is available and conflicts begin.

How quickly can inland seas, large lakes and rivers disappear taking their precious water and wildlife with them? The answers vary, but the disastrous results are the same. For example, it has taken forty to fifty years for the Aral Sea in Central Asia and Africa's Lake Chad to virtually dry up. Whereas Iran's Urmia Lake and Bolivia's Lake Poopó have disappeared in less than thirty years.

Once Bolivia's second largest lake, spanning over 3000 square kilometres, all that is left of Lake Poopó today is the sandy bottom where water once stood. The loss of water has also meant the loss of fish and other food sources for the area's indigenous inhabitants, the Urus, their name ironically meaning 'people of the water'. Now forced to leave their ancestral homes or face possible starvation, they along with the lake and wildlife that depended on it are victims of the rising temperatures of humanity-induced climate change as well as the overuse and misuse of the tributaries that once flowed into Lake Poopó. Diversion canals and dams upstream plus poor agricultural irrigation practices mean less water to fill the lake.

We see similar consequences of these very same practices across the world, with lessons from the countries that have experienced the negative impacts of unwise schemes, being largely ignored. The result is always the same: drainage of vital water sources and disruption of the ecosystems, lives and livelihoods of people dependent on the original water bodies that have been disturbed and destroyed.

Rather than taking water from one area and transporting it to another, if intelligent reforestation programmes are implemented with follow-through to protect the saplings and young trees, ecosystems could be revived, wildlife would return to help keep these systems alive and thriving and humanity would again be the recipient of abundant rainfall and freshwater supplies along with all the other precious and irreplaceable ecosystem services which natural systems supply. Instead of competing to control vital resources, especially water, if communities, states and countries sought to cooperate in protection of these fragile and essential ecosystems, all would benefit from the enhanced ability of Nature to provide.

This idea of sharing cooperatively in both the protection of and benefits from Nature has been the very foundation behind the creation of Peace Parks, especially large parks that even transcend national borders. While the idea has been around since the early 1900s, the concept got a major boost in 1932, when the USA and Canada initiated the comprehensive cross-border plan to protect the Waterton Glacier area, thereby ensuring protection of the forests, wildlife and purity of the vital glaciers that are the source for many streams and rivers for both countries.

Here in India, Air Marshal K.C. (Nanda) Cariappa along with Kent Biringer (senior researcher for Sandia National Labs in New Mexico, USA) have promoted the establishment of a Peace Park in the Siachen Glacier region between Pakistan and India in order to demilitarize the area, lessen tensions between the two countries and help protect and preserve the Himalayan glacier field. This glacier field is a critical source for rivers that provide fresh water to at least 1.5 billion people living not only in India and Pakistan, but also in other countries such as China, Nepal, Bhutan, Thailand, Burma/Myanmar, Bangladesh, Laos and Vietnam. So, cooperative protection of these glaciers could go a long way in fostering positive relations between all countries in the region that are dependent on them. Another Trans-Boundary Wildlife Conservation Peace Park has also been proposed between India, Nepal and Bhutan, and a memorandum of understanding was drafted between the three neighbouring Himalayan countries in 2019.

Over the years, hundreds of Peace Parks have come up all over the globe, including many that span national borders. But it is on the African continent where this concept has had its highest degree of both implementation and success, with the establishment of the Peace Parks Foundation in 1997. Peace Parks have increased in size and developed into Trans Border Protected Areas (TBPAs), also known as Trans Frontier Conservation Areas (TFCAs).

These parks and especially their expansive expression as TBPAs represent the acknowledgement of the truth that Nature does not accept or respect artificial, man-made borders between countries. Weather patterns and the ecosystems that have evolved have done so according to Nature's laws, not man's. Waters flow and mass migration of wildlife over hundreds of kilometres occur due to millennia of natural evolution. TBPAs are a recognition of this fact and are an intelligent and desperately needed attempt to keep these natural systems alive and thriving for everyone's benefit, while promoting peaceful coexistence between peoples of different backgrounds and countries. For when Nature thrives, humanity survives with abundance, peace and joy.

In 1986, Canada decided to encourage even more support for the Peace Park concept through the use of global tourism as a conservation-friendly, development tool for local people, thus securing more monetary and local support for these parks and TBPAs in all countries while fostering peaceful interactions, cultural exchanges and goodwill between people across the world—a celebration of diversity on the one hand and honouring the oneness of the human family on the other.

The initiative is known as the International Institute for Peace through Tourism (IIPT) and is active in dozens of countries around the planet. IIPT drafted the first code of ethics and guidelines for responsible and sustainable tourism. It also worked in consultation with the UN to identify a state-of-the-art code of conduct for tourism and the environment. The code's aim is to help local communities while simultaneously protecting the environment. In 2015, India joined IIPT, embracing the view that every tourist can and should become an ambassador of peace wherever he or she may travel. In September 2015, IIPT-India held its first Awards for Empowered Women in India. I, along with four other women, were honoured to receive this award; my award was specifically related to my 'Services in Protecting Nature and Promoting Eco-Friendly Tourism'.

This idea that every tourist can and should be an ambassador of peace and goodwill is also one of the underlying principles of student exchange programmes, nationally and internationally. As young people travel the globe, experiencing different communities, cultures and lifestyles, a greater appreciation for the diverse peoples who make up the patchwork quilt that is humanity is engendered. At the same time, the realization that all humans share the same feelings, hopes, dreams and concerns dawns in the hearts and minds of both hosts and guests, helping to build bridges of empathy, compassion and love in spite of perceived surface differences that only appear to separate us from one another, both on a macro/national scale or micro/local community level. This is and must continue to be one of the key goals of education everywhere especially with regard to student exchange programmes—the celebration of each peoples' uniqueness along with the promotion of the sense of community and oneness of humanity in order to ensure peace and plenty for all.

For me, the exchange student who had the greatest impact on me personally was my childhood friend Joanie. Joanie was the first exchange student in our area to visit and live in India for a year. During her presentation to the high school after her return she wore a stunning sari, braiding her long dark hair into a single plait down her back as so many Indian women do with their own hair. I remember being struck by how beautiful she looked and how amazing her photos of India were—again that feeling of familiarity came over me as if distant memories had been unearthed and brought to the surface of my mind although I could not explain why. Little did I realize then that India was to become my own home for almost my entire adult life.

My participation in Girls' State was another opportunity that helped broaden my horizons. This educational programme held at Douglas College (sister college to Rutgers University) was designed to help students learn about democracy and the electoral system of both the state and national level. I along with other girls from different high school systems across New Jersey were chosen to take part in this week-long exercise which included mock campaigns and elections.

The African-American daughter of Christian missionaries who had spent many years living in Africa was chosen 'governor' of our Girls' State. Her family helped to set up educational and healthcare facilities in many different countries on the African continent. Listening to her stories of the adventures she had had there and the wonders she had seen helped convince me all the more that I must see the world with all its natural richness of peoples and Nature.

The closing ceremonies ended with the delegates' choir singing in beautiful harmonies the classic anthem, 'Let There Be Peace on Earth'—a song that eulogizes the one human family whose Creator is one and the same for all. With tears flowing freely down so many faces including my own, the words resonated deeply with each and every one of us as we sang, 'Let there be peace on Earth, and let it begin with me.'

As the thirst to travel and explore grew ever stronger, the question was how to quench that thirst. Should I join the Peace Corps and go to distant lands to help those in need as the family of our Girls' State governor had done?

My own parents were great examples of activism. They both served in various ways to give back to the community and help those most in need. Sometimes they were volunteering for church activities or working at the local soup kitchens, making food for the homeless and delivering it to shut-ins. At other times, they would be helping young people to get training and jobs through the Youth Employment Scheme, my father being a founding trustee of the programme.

But it was in the educational field that both parents were the most active. My mom was a teacher for forty-plus years in different school systems and was also very active in both the Teachers' Union and the PTA (Parents and Teachers Association) having been president of both. My dad was on the Red Bank Board of Education for over twenty-five years and helped steer the building of two new schools for the Red Bank Education system during the course of those years.

This parental activism in education did lead to some rather interesting and even humorous times, such as when my mom as president of the Teachers' Union ended up going to jail due to the teachers' strike against the Board of Education's lower-salary guidelines, my dad being the president of the board at that time! There was so much tension at the family dinner table you could have cut it with a knife! The irony of this particular situation was that the seniors of Red Bank High School led by my elder sister, Patty, became the mediators between the teachers and the board in order to resolve the situation and get the school year started again!

Thus, pondering my own future, I took a cross-country road trip with two of my friends to see America. I had already run a couple of businesses with friends including a small furniture store and an all-night coffee house below a discotheque. A frequent visitor to the coffee house was Bruce Springsteen along with his band then known as 'Steel Mill', Bruce being a childhood friend of my partners.

These business experiences convinced me that I had to return to college and get a degree that would help me realize my thirst for global travel. The cross-country trip was in part to search for the right college that would turn those dreams into reality. Of course, the college had to be in the right location as well with plenty of beautiful Nature close by.

While I saw many fine institutions and many magnificent places in Nature, my heart fell in love with the Rocky Mountains and Colorado State University (CSU) located in the foothills of these majestic hills filled with wildlife.

As my first year at CSU drew to an end, my future goals became clearer—I would enter the US Diplomatic Corps and see the world . . . or so I thought. It was during summer break from college that year that my life was changed forever.

## A Collision of Worlds

Summer breaks from college or school always meant summer jobs for me and my siblings to earn money for the coming year. I was working two jobs in different locations, so I needed the family car to drive to them. I had gone to get the car from my younger sister, Pris, who was working at an Indian restaurant in our hometown. I was walking into the restaurant when I first saw him—the man from over the rainbow, my future husband and partner-in-life—Anil. He was standing near the kitchen entrance dressed in a white turtleneck T-shirt and black pants.

It was his eyes that so transfixed me—so soft and yet so clear and penetrating at the same time. We didn't actually meet, as my sister came up to me rather quickly with the car keys since she knew why I was there and didn't want me to be late for my own job.

In any case, there was a woman dressed in a sari with two children around her, standing next to him. Leaving the restaurant, I thought to myself, 'Bad luck. He's obviously married.' Little did I know then that he had also noticed me and had asked my sister about me after I left.

Later that night, I was surprised to see him at the bar where I was working. Customers were few, so when he introduced himself, we were able to spend some time talking. Eventually, he asked me to go out with him the following night, which happened to be my day off. When I answered saying that I don't date married men, he said, a bit surprised, 'Who the heck is married?!' He then went on to explain that the woman in the sari was his partner's wife, adding, 'She's not even Indian. She's Jewish-American!'

I was still hesitant about accepting his date proposal as I didn't want to have it interfere with my sister's job in any way, so decided to ask my mom's opinion. She and my dad had met Anil a few times since Pris started working for him, including having meals at his restaurant. My mom encouraged me to go, saying that Anil seemed to be very respectful and family, oriented and had a great interest in politics—one of my favourite topics as well.

Little did she know that this first date would lead to my living half-way around the globe from her and the rest of the family for most of my life!

Our first date was one to remember as Anil told me about his rich family background, his mother's spiritual life and his own forays into the Bollywood movie scene. It all sounded quite unbelievable to a small-town, New Jersey girl—certainly out of my own realm of experience! I thought to myself, 'It's either all true, or the best line I've ever heard from a guy, especially on a first date!'

All that Anil had conveyed to me that night was confirmed on our second date. We had gone to New York City for dinner and to see the Broadway show, *Godspell*. During the earlier part of the evening, I met Anil's father and two young American followers of Dadaji (Shri D.K. Roy) and Anil's mother Indira Devi, affectionately called 'Ma' by their followers. Discussions just happened to cover the unbelievable points Anil had told me before, thereby confirming their validity.

Earlier, Anil had received a letter and photo about his mother's health. She had developed Parkinson's disease and was barely able to walk due to the trembling of her body. Anil had sent her medicines that were not available in India from the US. Unfortunately, she could not take the medicines due to her pre-existing heart condition.

As the Parkinson's quickly worsened, Dadaji decided that they should to Hardwar and that Ma should bathe in the Ganga seeking Mother Ganga's healing compassion. Literally crawling down the steps to the bathing ghats on the Ganges, Ma pulled herself into the water praying for the Mother's help.

The letter went on to relate that Ma had a vision of the Mother blessing her, after which she was miraculously 90 per cent healed of Parkinson's, now able to walk, talk and even use her hands to write again.

Coincidentally, two young Canadian tourists heard the commotion below their own room at Hardwar Tourist Bungalow and went down with their camera to investigate, taking a photo just at the moment of the astonishing healing. The photo of Ma's healing spoke a thousand words more than even the letter. I was dumbfounded by the entire thing.

But why would I doubt the validity of this event when I myself had experienced a similar one less than two years earlier? I had been hospitalized with symptoms of a nerve disease that doctors believed was the start of multiple sclerosis (MS). Examinations had revealed a loss of muscle tone, a diagnosis confirmed through an extremely painful operation done without anaesthesia since I needed to be able to respond to the doctor's commands to test the muscles.

As I was brought back to my hospital room, the minister of the church that my family attended saw me. His name was Father Best. He was there in the hospital to give solace and comfort to those ailing and in need. The compassionate look he gave me as he entered my room caused the floodgates of my emotions to burst. He held me like a small child giving me calm comfort and reassurance as I cried uncontrollably. By the time I was all cried out, his vestments were saturated with my tears. His gentle love gave me hope, and it so happened that from that moment onwards, my severe symptoms completely disappeared.

If this could happen to me, why not to someone else? Were my doubts about the manner of Ma's healing based on the fact that she lived on the other side of the globe and prayed to God in a different form than me?

This was the beginning of a pattern set in my early relationship with Anil. He would tell me something, I would doubt it and then confirmation of the truth of what he had relayed to me would end up coming from some independent, objective third source.

Like the fictional couple from the novel *The Notebook*, we argued about everything. Nowhere was this truer than in our fierce arguments about politics. We were on completely opposite ends of the political spectrum. He had been an anti-Vietnam War activist in Europe and a supporter of George McGovern when he ran for US President against Richard Nixon in 1972. I was from a Republican Party family whose parents supported the war and Richard Nixon, believing that the war was 'just' and essential for 'protection of democracy' and US interests at home and abroad.

It was my elder sister, Patty, who first raised questions to me about the justification and legitimacy of the war. Her views, coupled with my brother Peter's frightening accounts of the explosions, bombings and gunfire he heard while his ship was anchored at Tonkin Bay near Saigon did give me pause to wonder, but were not enough to change my views.

I grew up in an era of fantastic music and went to many concerts, including the Atlantic City Pop Festival in 1969. I was also supposed to attend Woodstock, with tickets purchased for the second day of the festival but couldn't get there as the massive crowds had forced the closure of the New York Freeway and all links to it from New Jersey. Even though I enjoyed listening to the music of some of the most outspoken anti-war musicians and groups, their questions, words and warnings somehow did not prick my conscience or penetrate my consciousness enough to help me realize the truth. It was Anil's thundering voice that finally shook me into action.

It was August 1973. We were having breakfast while on a trip to Puerto Rico and the US Virgin Islands while another heated political discussion raged on. Anil leaned across the table pointing his finger at me and said, 'You're a murderess! You supported Richard Nixon and the atrocities of the Vietnam War and all the other brutalities done by this government in your name. Haven't you ever heard of Bangladesh?! Don't you understand karma?!'

My mind was a whirl of questions—*What atrocities in Vietnam? Where is Bangladesh? What the heck is karma?!*

I knew he had to be wrong, wrong about it all. America could not be guilty of these things. So I made up my mind to prove that when I returned to CSU.

I had been fortunate enough to be exempted from lower-level courses due to my good grades and was taking graduate-level studies as an undergrad. This entailed researching a particular topic approved by a professor and then writing a thesis on it. I chose every foreign policy issue Anil and I had fought over, sure my research would prove him wrong.

But, as it turned out, my research showed Anil was right in virtually every case. Rather than standing as the beacon of freedom promoting genuine democracy around the globe, in most cases, US foreign policy primarily reflected the economic interests of US business. This often meant US support for brutal dictators who ruthlessly stifled any opposition to their rule with the bullet and the grave.

It also meant the destruction of forests, wildlife and ecosystems along with the indigenous peoples who depended on them with some of the most ancient, pristine, natural places falling to the bulldozer and the blade.

It was a global repeat of the mindless destruction wrought by colonizing forces in Africa, the Middle East and Asia, including in India, coupled with the same kind of genocidal brutality inflicted on my own Native American ancestors across the Americas— lands for cattle-grazing pastures replacing biodiverse grasslands and rainforests of life; rivers and lakes poisoned for mining and oil exploration; wildlife slaughtered in huge numbers—some for trophies, some just to empty the forests of any life for the sake of greed and 'development.'

But beyond the interests of business, since the end of World War II, global politics had become a competition between the USA and the former USSR (Russia today) to expand their spheres of influence though proxy wars and puppet regimes, the countries of the earth being mere pieces on the chessboard of the world stage, with the population of the planet held at ransom and at risk of nuclear annihilation if the Cold War suddenly turned 'hot', as it did for those twelve tense days between the 16 and 28 October 1962 during the Cuban Missile Crisis.

I was just a child of ten years at the time, but can still vividly remember the atomic war attack drills we had to do in school, huddling under our desks in classrooms for an imminent attack, or quickly filing downstairs to the school's basement, lining up facing the outer walls leaning into them with eyes buried in one arm and the hand of the other covering our heads.

But the most frightening drill was that done by the entire town with everything being shut down—businesses, stores, offices as well as schools. The drill started with us being at school. Some of the older students like myself were given the responsibility to walk younger children to their homes before going to our own.

After taking my last child to her home, I clearly remember standing in the middle of the road, about one block from my parents' house just listening. Silence—complete silence. Not a soul stirring, no sound of traffic anywhere, not even the sound of dogs barking or birds singing. It was as if the entire world was holding its breath. The experience was both frightening and extremely eerie. I can truly grasp the terror that children caught in war feel and the terrible lifelong psychological trauma this inflicts on the child's mind.

It was only years later that I realized the futility of these drills. Had an atomic bomb been dropped, none of us would have survived.

## So, What about Bangladesh?

It was one more example of the same global politics of competition between the US and USSR, but with a few twists. As mentioned earlier, Pakistan had been carved out of India on the eastern and western sides of India's original borders. Over the next two decades or so, the generals of the Pakistani army were the de facto rulers who controlled all policies in both the eastern and western regions of Pakistan—policies that always favoured West Pakistan over East Pakistan even though East Pakistan had a larger population.

After decades of military control, the first and only democratic general election was held in both parts of the country on the 7 December 1970, a democratic election meaning that the vote was based on population—one person, one vote. As a result, the Awami League of East Pakistan led by Sheikh Mujibur Rahman won the overwhelming majority of the seats in the national assembly.

Both the generals and politicians of the west refused to accept their loss of political power. Consequently, the military dictator General Yahya Khan postponed the opening of the national assembly indefinitely, disregarding the election results and instead, invoked martial law.

Then, during the early morning hours of 26 March 1971, the West Pakistani army launched a military campaign called 'Operation Searchlight' to crush the east and force the people into submission. What followed was mass murder on an unimaginably horrific scale, with tanks and machine guns turning the streets of the capital Dhaka red, the bodies of unarmed civilians lying everywhere. The bloodbath continued in Dhaka University with both students and professors shot as they slept in their beds or forced to line up in hallways where they were summarily executed *en masse*.

The West Pakistani soldiers then turned their attention to the women's dorm, setting it on fire, then mowing down the girls with machine guns as they ran from the burning building. The naked bodies of other women were found having been raped, killed and hung by their heels from ceiling fans—facts confirmed by the US consul general in Dhaka.

Widening the net of death further, the Pakistan Army sought out anyone they viewed as a potential opponent or who gave any help to those being rounded up for elimination. Intellectuals, officials, businessmen, industrialists and even other soldiers were slain and subsequently buried in mass graves.

The massacres continued with the Pakistan Army expanding their campaign of slaughter to every city and town in East Pakistan, eventually extending this tidal wave of terror, murder, rape and destruction throughout the countryside.

Harrowing stories of the carnage from refugees flooding into India in the millions, desperately trying to escape the butchery in East Pakistan, started being reported in the Indian and international press. The wide scope and utter brutality of the genocide being carried out, coupled with the nonchalant callousness of the Pakistani soldiers committing these coldblooded mass murders, shocked and appalled the world. Global opinion turned against West Pakistan with cries for an immediate end to the slaughter and for the granting of independence to East Pakistan—now called 'Bangladesh'.

Two of the people instrumental in raising awareness of the genocide and the suffering that was going on in Bangladesh and among the refugees, who continued to stream into India, were classical Indian sitar player Ravi Shankar and his close friend, the former Beatle George Harrison.

Being Bengali himself, Shankar had been following the events unfolding in Bangladesh for some time, informing Harrison of the situation in the early months of 1971. To awaken the world to the ongoing genocide and to raise funds to alleviate the suffering of the 10 million refugees in India, they organized 'The Concerts for Bangladesh'—two benefit concerts held in Madison Square Garden in NYC on 1 August 1971. The sell-out crowds of over 40,000 people heard music from the top music personalities of that time playing with George Harrison including Eric Clapton, Leon Russell, Billy Preston, Ringo Starr and Bob Dylan along with Bengali musician Ali Akbar Khan, who performed Indian classical music on stage with Ravi Shankar.

An act of conscience compelled a career diplomat and his staff to challenge the policy of their own president, sacrificing their careers as a result. The diplomat in question was the most senior at the American consulate in Dhaka, East Pakistan—its consul general.

Through a series of telegrams he sent to Washington, DC, the full brutality and savagery of the military operations against the people of East Pakistan/Bangladesh was revealed, along with the desperation of the US diplomatic staff stationed in Dhaka to have President Nixon intervene to stop the bloodshed, especially since the arms and ammunition being used in the massacres had been supplied to Pakistan by the US government.

The cables have become known as the 'Blood Telegrams' since the name of the US consul general was Archer Blood—an ironic and poignant appellation considering they were describing the horrific bloodbath being waged by the West Pakistanis on the East Pakistanis.

Blood urged immediate political pressure by Washington on West Pakistan for a political rather than military solution to stop the unbridled slaughter, his request backed up by US Ambassador Keating in New Delhi as well. His request was ignored.

Blood sent cable after cable detailing the ruthlessness of the country-wide campaign being waged by the Pakistani military against the people of the east so that no one in Washington could ever claim that they were ignorant of what was going on in the crisis. Each transmission was met with a deafening silence.

Finally, he, along with twenty of his colleagues, sent a telegram stating their condemnation of America's policy in the crisis, condemning the failure of the US to denounce the suppression of democracy, its failure to denounce Pakistani military atrocities, questioning its morality for supporting genocide and for doing everything it could to decrease any negative impacts from the international community on Pakistan.

The question is, why did President Nixon ignore his own diplomats? The answer lies with China. Nixon was virtually obsessed with opening diplomatic channels with China since he hoped China could help end the Vietnam War because North Vietnam relied on China for arms and supplies. To do this, Nixon relied on Pakistan's military dictator General Yahya Khan to act as his political liaison/go-between with China. Nixon believed that the twin diplomatic 'wins' of opening the door to China coupled with ending the Vietnam War would win him re-election in the upcoming US elections in 1972. Hence, Nixon was initially silent over the atrocities and later overtly supportive of Pakistan over India because China had been Pakistan's decades-long ally, secretly supplying arms to Pakistan.

The lengths to which Nixon and his national security adviser, Henry Kissinger, were willing to go to secure this connection with China via Pakistan is quite shocking—from illegally continuing to send Pakistan arms through third parties in contempt of a US Congressional ban, to even risking nuclear confrontation between the US, the Soviet Union and China.

On the night of 3 December 1971, Pakistan launched a pre-emptive air strike on India. Up to this point, India's armed forces had not been an active part of the Bangladeshi conflict, although it had given supplies to the Bangladeshi freedom fighters for months while also having to care for the 10 million refugees fleeing the genocide. But with these attacks well into its territory, India had no choice but to go to war with Pakistan.

This arrogant and self-destructive move by the Pakistanis was no doubt prompted by Yahya Khan's arrogant feeling of utter impunity in Nixon's backing no matter what he did. But what followed was a violent and very short, two-week war wherein the Indian armed forces thrashed the Pakistanis in every field of combat, the first week alone seeing the complete destruction of the Pakistani air force.

In desperation to save his valued collaborator, Nixon made one of his most reckless and dangerous moves yet. He ordered ships from the US Seventh Fleet to sail from the Gulf of Tonkin off Vietnam, where they were stationed, to the Bay of Bengal. The armada included cruisers and destroyers and a large amphibious assault ship, all being led by the largest warship in the world—the nuclear aircraft carrier, USS Enterprise, carrying seventy fighter and bomber aircraft.

The carrier arrived on 11 December 1971, Nixon's official justification for its presence being 'for evacuation purposes'—a thin cover for the actual reason of making the US presence in the region known to discourage the Soviets from intervening in the war.

However, Indian intelligence had intercepted the US transmission ordering the Seventh Fleet to the bay and quietly informed Moscow, requesting the activation of Article IX of their bilateral treaty of mutual protection signed on 9 August 1971— a treaty that Prime Minister Indira Gandhi had no option but to sign since all her attempts to get President Nixon to rein in Pakistan and stop the crisis were ignored as millions of refugees continued to stream into India from Bangladesh.

Moscow intelligence informed India that a British naval group led by a British aircraft carrier was also nearing Indian territorial waters. It was clear that the US and Britain had planned joint operations to intervene in the war on the side of Pakistan intending to simultaneously squeeze India from both the Arabian Sea and the Indian Ocean.

This is probably the most ironic and paradoxical event of the entire affair. The two leading Western democracies were ready to attack the world's biggest democracy to shield a ruthless military dictator and his murderous cohorts who were perpetrating one of the largest genocides of the twentieth century, communist Russia being the only country coming to the aid of democratic India.

The USSR kept its word to India, sending two groups of their own cruisers and destroyers armed with nuclear weapons and anti-ship missiles from their naval base in Vladivostok on 6 and 13 December along with six nuclear submarines to counter the presence of the USS Enterprise and Britain's own aircraft carrier.

The Soviet ships and nuclear submarines arrived before those of both the British destroyers and the US Seventh Fleet. Moscow ordered its six nuclear submarines to surface in full view of the American and British fleets to make their presence known, and then to encircle the two naval groups and train their missiles on the USS Enterprise, effectively blocking entry into the Bay of Bengal and the territorial waters of both India and Pakistan in the Arabian Sea.

At this point, the Soviets intercepted a message from Admiral Gordon of the British fleet to the commander of the US Seventh Fleet saying, 'Sir, we are too late. There are Russian atomic submarines here and a big collection of battleships.'

The British ships fled, heading towards Madagascar, while the encircled US fleet was forced to leave as well, the Russians blocking their ability to reach any Pakistani, Bangladeshi, or Indian port, trailing them until 7 January 1972—long after the war in Bangladesh ended on 16 December 1971 when the Pakistani army surrendered to Indian forces.

Thus ended a conflict that brought the world far closer to nuclear annihilation than most people are even aware. Richard Nixon did indeed win re-election as president in 1972, but at what cost? In a little less than nine months, up to three million civilians had been slaughtered, as many as 400,000 women suffered genocidal rape with countless more kept as sex slaves by the Pakistani military, over 30 million people were internally displaced within East Pakistan/Bangladesh and at least 10 million more fled into India as refugees, Nixon's arrogant, reckless and irresponsible behaviour brought the world to the brink of a nuclear conflagration.

As I researched the US congressional records at Colorado State University to discover the truth about the birth of Bangladesh, I came across an entry by Senator Ted Kennedy—youngest brother of slain President John F. Kennedy, and one of the main people behind the passage of the congressional embargo banning the shipment of any military goods including spare parts to Pakistan. He was reading a letter he had received from a Christian missionary based in East Pakistan, begging Senator Kennedy to have America intervene to stop the genocide taking place. He wrote:

There are so many dead bodies floating in the river that one can walk over them to reach the other side.

There is simply no justification that can be made for this human tragedy, this heartless apocalypse . . . none.

## And Then There Was Vietnam

By the time Richard Nixon became the US President in 1969, the Vietnam War was raging at its highest level. This was in spite of former president Kennedy's plans to withdraw all US troops from the country by 1963. Those plans were cut short by the assassin's bullet that killed him on 22 November 1963, his successor, Lyndon Johnson, instead ramping up the war exponentially.

Nixon was determined to win the war and announced that he was extending it into Cambodia. The news created a veritable tidal wave of protests that swept across America and around the globe, millions demanding an end to the war. More and more American young men were returning to the US from Vietnam in coffins and body bags. The war was hitting families across the country. By 1971, over two-thirds of the American population were clamouring for an immediate end to the war.

This helps to put into perspective why Nixon was so desperate for help from Pakistan's military dictator Yahya Khan. To win re-election, Nixon had to convince the communist Chinese to intervene with the North Vietnamese to end the war, and Khan was Nixon's only conduit to make that happen. But things in Bangladesh did not go the way Nixon had hoped. Fighting continued unabated with aerial bombardments of suspected North Vietnamese infiltrators in the south being carried out in earnest. By 1972, three times the total munitions used in all war zones of World War II had been dropped as bombs on Vietnam.

The bombs not only contained virtually every kind of explosive and incendiary known to man plus a gelling agent, but also dioxin-based defoliants called 'Agent Orange'. Used to help strip the countryside of any green cover and food for the North Vietnamese, the highly toxic defoliant was sprayed on millions of acres of land in Vietnam destroying up to half of the forests and mangroves of the country, the US basically committed ecocide. It was also sprayed directly on millions of Vietnamese people with the effects of its toxicity causing massive health problems even decades later with the environmental consequences still being felt to this day.

A temporary ceasefire was finally secured in October 1972, just a few weeks before the US elections. As mentioned earlier, Nixon did indeed get re-elected, but at what cost.

By the end of the Vietnam War, over 58,000 American soldiers had died with more than 150,000 wounded, up to 1,400,000 Vietnamese soldiers and at least 5,000,000 Vietnamese civilians killed, with more than 200,000 civilians in Cambodia and 30,000 more dead in Laos as well.

Between the slaughter of innocent people in Bangladesh and that of Vietnam, I could now certainly understand why Anil had called me a 'murderess' for having supported Richard Nixon. While it is true that I did not know what was going on in either country, that is no excuse for my blind, uninformed support of a person who was to occupy one of the most powerful and influential positions not just in America but in the world.

This is the point about living in a democracy—it is our duty to know, to stay informed, to look beneath the surface to find out the facts before we lend our support to anyone seeking a position of power as an elected official. For, those elected are carrying out their programmes in our name. Hence, we need to make sure that what they are doing portrays the compassion, intelligence and forward thinking that will ensure not just a peaceful planet, but one that will be fit for the next generations as well.

It is important to underscore the role that journalists played in bringing the truth of the atrocities and horrors of both the Bangladesh and Vietnam Wars to light. Without their courage, integrity and dedication, the general public would not have heard or seen what was really going on, and the global outcry against the genocides and ecocides being waged would have been impossible.

Two journalists stand out in the case of Bangladesh. The truth was being hidden from the world at large primarily because all foreign journalists had been forcibly incarcerated in Dacca's Hotel Intercontinental by the Pakistani military on 25 March just hours before the killing campaign began. They were then expelled from the country two days later with their notes, tapes and photos confiscated.

However, one escaped the military's dragnet—Simon Dring. Having viewed the death and destruction first-hand, Dring was able to leave East Pakistan with his notes and filed his report on the front page of the *Daily Telegraph* on 30 March 1971—an article that shook the world and brought a tidal wave of international condemnation crashing down on the West Pakistan military.

The second journalist of special note is Anthony Mascarenhas—then assistant editor of the West Pakistani newspaper *Morning News*. Risking his own life and that of his family, he flew to London on 18 May 1971 under the pretence of visiting an ill sister. Instead, he met with editor Harold Evans of the *London Times* telling him of the massive bloodbath he had eye-witnessed and offered to write an article about it.

Evans promised to run the story but had to wait until after Mascarenhas went back to Pakistan to get his family out of the country. While his family flew to London, Mascarenhas had to go on foot to Afghanistan to escape because, at that time, Pakistanis were only allowed one trip abroad, and he had already taken his. The story ran on 13 June 1971—the day after Mascarenhas was reunited with his family in London. Under the simple title 'Genocide', his article described in horrifying detail what he had witnessed, its deadly revelations bringing even greater condemnation from the international community.

It has been said that one photo is worth a thousand words, and in the case of Vietnam, this is undeniably true, but there were actually two. The first was the picture of Mahayana Buddhist monk Thick Quang Duc immolating himself at a busy intersection in Saigon, the monk sacrificing his life as the ultimate protest against the horrors of the Vietnam War. The extraordinary event was captured on film by *Associated Press* photojournalist Malcolm Browne on 11 June 1963, Browne being the only Western reporter there to witness it. 'The Burning Monk' became the photographic symbol of the cruelties and brutalities of the Vietnam War, pricking the conscience of the world as it was flashed on news screens and in print media.

The second photo was of a nine-year-old named Kim Phuc—a victim of a Napalm bomb whose back was hit with the burning substance, setting her clothes on fire, which she stripped off as she ran up the highway to a makeshift aid station. At the station were several journalists including *Associated Press* photojournalist Nick Ut who snapped the iconic photo, capturing on film the devastating consequences of this chemical warfare on the innocent victims of the war including the environment. The photo of 'Napalm Girl' shocked the world and added fuel to the growing global anti-Vietnam War protests, more and more of the general public appalled at the war's inhumanity and violence.

In order for the general public to stay informed, we must rely greatly on brave journalists like these four, and on what is known as 'The Fourth Estate'—the media. Today the media is under attack by authoritarian figures and regimes across the planet. Along with environmental conservation, journalism has become one of the most dangerous occupations in the world.

For the survival of democracy, for the survival of our planet, a strong independent media is critical—independent from government control, independent from the influence of 'big business' and from the military-industrial-surveillance complex as well.

Once again it was the dedication and integrity of two young reporters with the *Washington Post* that finally brought the downfall of Richard Nixon, exposing his role in covering up the truth behind the break-in at the national democratic headquarters in Watergate. As a result, Congress began impeachment proceedings against him, and a disgraced Nixon had to resign as president of the United States.

Karma eventually catches up with us all . . .

Years later in June of 1980, while flying 'over the rainbow' from our home in Hawaii to visit India beyond for the first time, I looked out the plane window to see the view below. The waves of a turquoise blue Pacific Ocean were gently breaking on to a long stretch of a white, sandy beach, the shore quickly giving way to thick tropical forests inland for as far as the eye could see.

'How incredibly beautiful,' I thought to myself. 'What an amazing place! I wonder where we are.' And then . . . it struck me. 'Oh my God! Is this Vietnam?!'

At that precise moment, a voice came over the plane's audio system: 'This is your Captain speaking. We are currently flying over Vietnam . . .'

Stunned by the realization and the exquisite beauty of the county below, all I could do was pray, 'Forgive me . . . God, please forgive me . . . forgive me . . .'

# PART II

# The Tree Takes Root

# 6

# Rocky Mountain Highs: Finding the Divine in Nature

While Anil and I certainly did have our battles on various things especially in the early years, we were still very much in love and definitely wanted to spend our life together. But that hope for the future was almost cut short not once but twice on a trip to the Caribbean.

The first incident was a near-fatal car crash. We were rounding a curve on the road while driving through the beautifully forested mountains of Puerto Rico when a vehicle coming from the opposite direction swerved into our lane, smashing into our vehicle with such tremendous force that our car was left teetering on the edge of a cliff, with one side completely crushed in. Had we been hit with a bit more force, we would have gone over the cliff—had the impact been just a couple of inches more towards the front of our car, I most likely would have been killed.

The second incident was when Anil and I were set to fly back from St Thomas in the Virgin Islands to San Juan, Puerto Rico. The plane was very small with just four seats—the one in front for the pilot and three behind him where we, the passengers, were to sit. St Thomas was a 'free port' which meant that liquor could be brought into Puerto Rico without any customs duty or sales tax. A man with several cases of alcohol wanted to join our flight but, at the last minute, he changed his mind and didn't join us.

About halfway through the flight over open water, the left engine of the plane started to sputter, eventually stopping altogether. A few minutes later, the right engine did the same. We were still at least fifteen minutes or more from the airport in San Juan, but too far from St Thomas to turn back as we would lose altitude too quickly. All we could do was hope that we were still high enough to be able to glide over the remaining sea to reach the airport. Otherwise we would crash into the ocean.

It was such a bizarre and paradoxical moment looking out the plane's window at the stunning beauty of the clear blue sky above and the turquoise sea below which was coming closer and closer with each passing minute. All I could do was pray, pleading in my prayers, 'Please God, not now! Don't take us now! Not when we have finally found each other!'

Fortunately, Mother Nature answered my prayers and helped us with her gentle trade winds from behind, lifting the plane as well as propelling us forward. Within a few minutes, land appeared on the horizon, with the plane just making it to the edge of the island, landing on the dirt ground before the landing strip began. When disembarking from the plane, my knees buckled and Anil caught me before I fell—both of us so very grateful to still be alive.

As it turned out, the pilot had neither properly checked the aircraft's oil nor its fuel before take-off, both of which were very low, hence the engines stopped. In addition, had the third passenger been on board with all his cases of liquor, the extra weight from those crates would surely have brought us down.

This was the third time in my life where Divine Grace had apparently played a significant role in the outcome of an event, my spontaneous healing in the hospital that I've talked about in chapter five, being the second. The first was relayed to Anil as he and I sat in Father Best's office for our pre-wedding conference in 1976.

Anil had commented on how beautiful the stained-glass windows were that lined the walls of our Episcopal Church, especially the large one of 'Christ, the Good Shepherd' over the altar. In response, Father Best quite unexpectedly said, 'Pam is responsible for saving these windows,' going on to recount the events that had taken place on Easter Sunday, a few years earlier.

A major fire had broken out engulfing the entire church in flames. The fire department was doing everything it could to try and save the beautiful stained-glass windows by spraying water on the exterior protective glass covering them. My family, along with many others, was watching in great distress, praying for God's help.

Suddenly the exterior protective glass over the Good Shepherd window shattered. Hearing the glass break, I ran as fast as I could around the corner to St James Catholic Church and went inside. Dropping to my knees, I prayed to God to please help—please save these irreplaceable windows.

When I returned to the burning church, my mom asked me where I had gone, so I told her, explaining what I had done. Shortly thereafter, the firemen finally got the blaze under control. When the smoke cleared, it was revealed that the church's roof had completely collapsed with some of the wall areas gone, too. But every single stained-glass window had survived, including the altar's 'Good Shepherd'.

The church was rebuilt in just one year with volunteer help from the whole congregation, making it possible for us all to celebrate Easter together in our rebuilt church just as everyone had hoped and prayed.

How Father Best knew where I had gone and what I had done, I do not know. Perhaps my mother had told him as she was the only person I ever told.

He then went on to tell us that he had read the Bhagavad Gita, pointing out the book to us in the bookshelf behind him. He said that he had found great beauty and truth, wisdom and inspiration within its pages, adding that the teachings of Krishna and those of Christ were very similar, indeed.

Father Best was the first person to draw a direct connection for me between God and Nature. Every year for twenty-six years, he told a new story about Christ's connection to Nature and animals at the children's Christmas service. Whether it was about the Christmas doves or the animals in the stable where Christ was born; the gift of the evergreen or the service the dogwood tree performed for Christ—each and every tale demonstrated the love and compassion of the animals and Christ, as well as the link between the Creator and His Creation. For me, his stories helped reinforce my own inner feelings of closeness to the Divine whenever I was in the heart of Mother Nature, communing in silence with the Spirit within and without.

During the first year of our relationship, while I was in Colorado and Anil was still in New Jersey, we wrote to each other as often as we could. One set of our letters was about that link I felt so strongly between God and Nature.

Earlier in his life and travels, Anil had seen a number of instances of hypocrisy with regard to what was being preached, on the one hand, by so-called 'religious' or 'spiritual' people, and what was actually being practised, on the other. This had led to a certain amount of cynicism with regard to organized religion which I had erroneously interpreted as a lack of belief in God.

I wrote to him, 'Whenever I go into the forests here in these magnificent mountains and see the incredible colours of the autumn leaves or the rippling streams flowing past, hear the sounds of birds singing as they fly in the sky or catch sight of a deer or fawn in a meadow, I can't help but believe in God. Who else has created all this beauty?'

Anil replied, 'I do not doubt the existence of God. What I abhor are the wrong acts done in God's name—the lies, the hypocrisy, the wars and brutalities through history that were done in the name of God. What upsets me is what humanity is doing to God's creation, how humans are destroying it and causing such pain and suffering to other species in the process. This is not the fault of God. It is our own.' Of course, he was right.

After my college graduation in the summer of 1974, Anil moved from New Jersey to Colorado to be with me, selling his successful Indian-food restaurant in the process. 'Love before money,' he said to friends and business associates in explanation for his actions.

Our first year living together was difficult as, in spite of our mutual love, our arguments on virtually everything continued. What saved us both as individuals and as a couple were our weekend trips into the forests of the Rocky Mountains. We owned no land of our own then but found one lovely, wooded place just off the highway, which became our regular weekend spot to stop, recoup and reconnect with Nature and with each other, letting the peace descend within us and allowing the love to flow once again. No matter the season or the weather, into the hills we would go, so vital was this weekly reconnection that would carry us through the long work week in the city of Denver.

It was here in these woods that we had our first encounters with the local wildlife, our first friend being a type of titmouse bird called the black-capped chickadee. On our very first time there, the chickadee came out to greet us. He would sit on a branch directly behind us, playing a game with us to see how far we could turn our heads to see him.

According to Native Americans, the chickadee is one of the most intelligent of all the forest folk. In comparison to other birds, their intellect matches that of crows and parrots. They are very friendly and highly observant of everything that happens around them. 'Being friends with all' means they are no one's enemies and so are never caught up in any fights. Always knowing what is going on around them helps them remain alert to any potential threats or dangers so that they can quickly adapt or leave to avoid any problems. Hence, they remind us to always be aware and cautious while keeping a positive outlook on life.

For the Osage and other Great Plains Indians, the chickadee is a symbol of good luck that brings success, prosperity and happiness. They are also associated with love, loyalty and lasting friendship, helping to emphasize the importance of staying together—a great reminder for Anil and me!

Identified with truth and knowledge, and as having a special connection to the higher worlds of Spirit, the chickadee is able to aid one in their thinking process and to reveal higher truths, as well as foretell the future. We could not have asked for a more wonderful friend than the chickadee on our first Rocky Mountain forest excursion together, nor a more prophetic one, as would soon be revealed.

As time rolled by, more animal friends joined us in our weekly visits. Each new friend would teach us more about the balance of Nature and their own special role in it. The squirrel, for example, was the distributor in the forest, collecting nuts and seeds and burying them for the winter, pausing now and then to eat one as well. He would also occasionally climb to the top of a tree and leave a seed or nut up there. Within a few minutes, a raven would land on that tree to take the squirrel's present with him. It was remarkable to see this behaviour which was truly suggestive of sharing among the two different species.

The squirrel was also helping to regenerate the forest with the seeds he buried, since, even during the cold winter months, he could never eat all the nuts and seeds he had hidden away deep in the earth. What he left behind would eventually sprout forth, growing into new trees to keep the cycle of life ever turning. This is why squirrels have been recognized and honoured as caretakers of the forest by Native Americans, who also admired their thriftiness and prudence in planning for the future, their trusting attitude towards us most endearing.

During the cold, winter days, we would put a blanket on the ground to sit on, while in the woods. Upon returning from a walk in the forest on one particularly cold day, we found our little squirrel friend relentlessly and repeatedly tugging on the corner of our blanket, which had become frozen to the ground. True to his role in Nature, he was trying to 'distribute' our blanket as well—a truly funny sight to behold! Perhaps he was planning to take part of the blanket home to his family and give the rest to Mr Raven!

Eventually, we were able to buy our own small, wooded parcel of land, measuring about three and a half acres and situated on the top of a hill. The location had spectacular views all around, giving us panoramic scenes of forested mountains and the peaceful valley below. Each season brought its own special beauty with it, whether of the autumn colours of the aspen tree leaves sparkling in the sun and quivering in the wind, or the clear views of deep blue skies and white puffy clouds on a warm summer's day, or the winter wonderland of deep snow cover all around us blanketing the mountain peaks in brilliant white.

Each weekend, we would make the drive up, bringing with us small food offerings, as I had been taught by my mom. The land was 9000 feet above sea level and received a great deal of snow in the winter, so, at that time of year, we would add suet-seed balls to our gifts to help the birds through this insect-free season, as well as a salt lick for deer. Summers meant putting up hummingbird-feeders filled with sugar-sweetened water for the many hummingbirds there, making sure to take the feeders down early enough in autumn so as to ensure our little friends would migrate south for the winter on time.

Our food offerings would only last a day or two, but they did encourage the wildlife to stay close by. The birds in particular stayed close, with the Steller's jays becoming the lookouts for the rest, noisily alerting the others on our arrival while flying alongside our car until we parked and then gathering around us as we walked up to the cliff to distribute food. This was especially true during the winter months when food for them was scarce.

Our small gesture of sharing paid rich dividends a few years later, when a warm winter coupled with drought led to a severe outbreak of pine beetle. These tree parasites can kill conifer evergreen trees in just three months, leaving whole stands of forest dead and tinder dry, with forest fires due to lightning often destroying what is left. Our neighbours lost many trees on their lands, but we didn't lose even one. When they asked us what chemical we were spraying on our trees to protect them from the infestation, we held up a few of our birdseed and suet feeders in response.

By encouraging these wonderful pest predators like woodpeckers and other birds to stay near for occasional treats, they did what they are meant to do—help keep the balance of Nature by protecting the forest's trees from parasites and pests like pine beetle. Soon, everyone started feeding the birds, especially during the cold winter. As a result, there was a major reduction in the numbers of trees killed by pine beetle in our area in comparison to other parts of the region.

Today, due to climbing temperatures of human-induced climate change, pine-beetle infestations have increased dramatically not only in the forests of the lower Rockies, but in the Canadian conifer forests as well, where problems with pine beetle were relatively rare in the past. Due to the severe cold temperatures during the previously normal Canadian winters, pine beetle would be killed off. But now, warmer temperatures in Canada have meant tremendous loss of forest areas due to pest infestations, which in turn have increased forest fires exponentially in occurrence and magnitude.

The warmer temperatures are also melting the permafrost that these same pine trees have relied on as their root base. As the permafrost melts, the trees' roots become dislodged eventually leading to the trees' deaths, adding yet more dry timber to fuel these fires caused by climate change—fires which, in the past, were very rare in this region. In addition, the melting permafrost also releases massive quantities of carbon dioxide and methane that had been trapped in the ice for millennia, thereby exacerbating global warming by raising the temperatures even higher.

It is true that certain areas of Nature are dependent on periodic wildfires for renewal and regeneration—examples include the grasslands and some forest sections of the Midwest and western USA. These natural fires would help clear dead brush on the ground and would rarely kill any trees in their path as they raced across the land quickly. Over the ages, some species of pine trees evolved in such a way that their cones do not open to drop their seeds for regeneration without the heat from fire. With the ground cleared by the brushfires, seeds would have a greater chance to sprout and grow, the fires also adding the nutrients from the ash to the soil, helping to enrich it.

As a result of the fires, wildlife would initially steer clear of the burned area and forage in other locations that the fires had not touched, which was helpful in avoiding overgrazing at any particular site. The regeneration of the prairie grasslands depended on rainfall, but also on the American buffalo that travelled across the plains. Native Americans became an integral part of this cycle of life. As mentioned earlier, for the Osage and other tribes of the Great Plains, the buffalo was the principal source of food, winter clothing and other essentials for life. Every part of the buffalo was used—nothing was wasted. Having understood this cycle of life, the peoples themselves would start controlled fires in one area in order to force the buffalo to move to another, thereby improving grazing for wildlife while aiding in this process of prairie regeneration.

We could see the process of balance and renewal playing out on our own small property, even though we only visited on weekends. It wasn't practical for us to live there then, due to our jobs in Denver, so we never built on it. For vacations in the mountains that included overnight stays, we needed to find a solution that would help us stay in the heart of Nature longer.

## Hummingbirds, Robins and Sacred Encounters

The solution came in the form of a wonderful place high in the mountains, near the ski resort of Winter Park, where we could rent a cabin overlooking a stream at a lodge called Millers Idlewild Inn. We would usually go during the off-season, starting from mid-spring until early autumn, before the snows would fall bringing skiers back to the slopes. Often, we were the only ones in the area, which meant very special times spent in silence and solitude deepening our connection with each other and with all aspects of Nature.

During our first visit in August 1975, we had many close encounters with a number of different animals, which led to friendships with them that lasted all the years we went there. Chief among these friends were yet another gift-distributing and forest-caretaker squirrel, an American robin couple and Mr Hummingbird.

Mr Hummingbird became a great friend and also taught me much. During our very first encounter, which was also my first-ever close encounter with hummingbirds, he flew directly toward my face at such a tremendous speed that I stepped backwards. This sent Anil into splits of laughter.

'What's so funny?' I asked him, rather annoyed.

'You!' he answered. 'I mean, really—look at your size and look at his, and *you're* afraid of him?! If you just stop being afraid and stand still, you may be in for a wonderful experience.'

Grudgingly, I heeded his advice and waited until Mr Hummingbird returned, which was in less than a minute. Again, he flew straight to my face with a 'Zoooop!' and stopped at eye-level, hovering just a few inches away. Then, with his extremely long tongue, he started playing with my hair, lifting it strand by strand, flying round and round my head, his wings going 'Trrrrrrrrrrrrrrrrr' just as my heart was pounding, 'Trrrrrrrrrrrrrrrrrrr!'

Hummingbirds beat their wings faster than any other bird— an unbelievable 80 to 120 beats per second. So, when in flight, their wings are always a blur. Their precision and control while flying is unparalleled and their ability to hover in place for long periods of time, unmatched.

My first encounter with Mr Hummingbird taught me three important lessons when interacting with wildlife, animals and Nature in general: The first is, **overcome your fear.** Fear can block us from having extraordinary experiences. Overcoming it helps open us up to a realm of possibilities and adventures when dealing with the various aspects of Nature.

The second lesson is, **show respect.** While we should not have fear, we should absolutely respect all species and Nature in general, understanding that each and every species has its role to play in Nature's exquisite balance. Nature has endowed all species with special gifts, attributes and talents in order to fulfil their roles. Whether it is the speed with which a snake can strike, or the intensity of the family bonds that keep an elephant herd together, we need to recognize and respect their talents, and respect all creatures.

Respecting an animal's space, making sure we do not crowd them in our excitement to be near them, is particularly important. Just as we would protect our children and family members from what we perceive to be an outside threat to them, so will animals—both wild and domestic. Hence, we must never get between a mother and her child or separate a family group in any way. Doing so causes great distress to the animals involved, possibly prompting an aggressive move on their part towards us in order to secure the safety of their beloved family member.

Respect also entails understanding of and appreciation for Nature's power and the process of constant change. We put ourselves in danger when we ignore the might of oceans during storms, the forces of erosion that can cause landslides in unstable grounds, how raging rivers and cloudbursts can cause catastrophes if we are foolish enough not to recognize and respect Nature's boundaries. When we build on the ocean shorelines, on the banks of rivers, underneath cliffs with areas of falling rock, on active earthquake faults or other geologically dangerous places such as on the slopes of active volcanoes, we are ignoring Nature's might—something our ancestors were never foolish enough to do. It is usually just a matter of time before Nature's law of constant change brings us hardship and often, heartache, for our foolishness and lack of respect.

Today, we see just how sad and dangerous that can be with the continuing eruption of Kilauea Volcano on the Big Island of Hawaii, its flowing lava having swallowed up over 700 homes during its 2018 eruption alone, leaving many people with nothing and nowhere to live. Our last home in America was also on the Big Island, but we lived on the slopes of the dormant volcano Mauna Kea which has not erupted in over 4600 years, choosing that site deliberately, keeping in mind the potential for eruptions in other areas.

The third and most important lesson is, **give love!** Animals may not understand our verbal language, but they definitely feel and respond to our vibrations. They are mirrors reflecting back to us our own feelings and thoughts. If we are fearful or have aggressive thoughts, they will have fear and either run away or react aggressively to defend themselves or their family. But if we feel love and have calm, peaceful feelings toward them, they will realize we are not a threat to them and will react accordingly by being calm and peaceful themselves.

These three lessons—**overcome your fear, show respect and give love**—are the tenets by which Anil and I have lived our lives, and have been abundantly rewarded by incredibly intimate and wondrous encounters with wildlife as a result.

Another fascinating aspect of our interactions with animals in general is their amazing psychic ability. An incident with Mr Hummingbird demonstrated this very well. While Anil and I would sit on the balcony of our cabin, I would start to think about him, wondering if he was still on the pine tree nearby. I would not even finish my thought before he would fly in front of us, perform his large loop-de-loops in the air, then stop in mid-air and look me in the eye as if to say, 'See—I'm still here!'

The robin couple had built their nest on the eave under the roof of our wooden cabin, with Mrs Robin incubating the eggs right outside our bedroom window. Mr Robin became fast friends with us, especially after the babies hatched, coming often for our little food offerings. When the babies grew big enough to leave the nest, he would bring them out of the brush into the open right below our balcony overlooking the stream so we could watch him feed them, demonstrating his tremendous trust in us.

Each year, when we would return to the cabin, the first 'friend' to greet us was always Mr Robin. He would fly to welcome us as soon as he saw us, even before we had checked-in. We observed that this was not his behaviour towards other guests. Hence, he was clearly recognizing us as his 'friends' from one year to the next.

Because of a story I was told in childhood, I have always associated the American robin with Christ. The story relayed that the robin was one of the birds present in the stable when Christ was born, the bird watching him grow into a man. At the time of crucifixion, it is said that the robin was so moved by Christ's pain that he flew to the cross and tried to remove the thorns from the crown of thorns piercing His head, a drop of Christ's blood falling on to the robin's grey breast in the process, turning it red. For this show of compassion, the robin's descendants would forever bear a red breast resembling the mark of Christ's blood, as a sign of gratitude from the Divine. Seeing one of these divine birds is therefore considered a blessing, coupled with the message that selflessness never goes unnoticed. This is one of the reasons why robins represent renewal and rebirth, their return to areas of North America after the cold, snowy winter coinciding with the return of spring as well.

Native Americans also revere the robin. For the Hopi, they are the directional guardian of the south, while for the Blackfoot, they are a symbol of peace and safety.

A story of the Iroquois conveys the robin's spirit of self-sacrifice for the benefit of others, always working selflessly to ease another's path. The tale tells how the robin helped a dying man. Alone and ill, the man could not even get up to tend the fire in his lodge to try and stay warm. As he was calling out for help, the robin answered, flying into the lodge to see what was wrong. When he saw the dying man shivering in the cold, he searched the ashes for an ember that was still glowing. Finding one, he then flew out of the lodge to bring small twigs and dry leaves putting these around and on top of the single glowing ember. After several trips, the robin began fanning the ember with his open wings trying to get it to spark back to life. Time and time again as he fanned the ember, he exposed his grey-white breast to the glowing ember.

Finally, the ember was hot enough that the dry twigs and leaves started to burn, the small fire growing with each new batch of twigs the robin now brought until it was burning properly, heating up the lodge and saving the man's life. The robin continued to stay with the man to keep the fire burning until he had recovered and was sound.

It was only after the man had recovered that the robin realized his own grey-white breast had been singed by the flames during his process of fanning them, his breast now itself glowing an orange-red colour. 'What does it matter?' he thought to himself. 'The man is alive and that is what is important.'

The grateful man asked the robin to stay at his lodge, and the robin answered, 'It is time now for me to fly south, but I promise you I will return in the spring—my presence will signal the time for the renewal of life.'

Good to his word, the red-breasted robin did indeed return in the spring. Making his nest in the eaves of the man's lodge, he raised his young there, his babies also having red breasts, as have all the rest of his descendants ever since. Hence, robins continue to make their nests near the dwellings of humans for they are always friends to them, and their red breasts are a testimony to their compassion and selflessness.

Native Americans also associate hummingbirds with the Divine or Great Spirit, even considering them to be 'celestial beings' that have come to help and heal those in need, as they open the heart and bring the 'medicine' of love and joy. Omens of good luck, they are esteemed as symbols of beauty, harmony and integrity.

Known for their intelligence and industriousness, they visit over a thousand flowers per day for nectar, remembering each and every flower in their area, as well as the best time to visit it for nectar. Their incredible memory stems from their large brain—hummingbirds have the largest ratio of brain to body among bird species. Considered the sacred pollinator, their mission is one of resurrection and regeneration, thereby bringing an abundance of new life to the earth.

Hummingbirds themselves 'resurrect' on an almost daily basis in some parts of the Americas, such as in the high Andean

Mountains, where night temperatures drop precipitously. In order to survive these freezing conditions, hummingbirds go into a hibernation-like state called 'torpor' during which their metabolism is lowered dramatically.

Their normal heart rate of up to 1260 beats per minute drops to just fifty, while normal body temperature of 40 degrees Celsius (104 degrees Fahrenheit) drops to a low of just 18 degrees Celsius (70 degrees Fahrenheit). This helps conserve up to 60 per cent of the energy they normally expend during daylight hours. People who see them in this state often think they are dead as they do not respond to sound or touch. Some are even found hanging upside down from hummingbird feeders! But though quite vulnerable in this condition, they are still very much alive, taking about twenty minutes to 'resurrect' from torpor to their normal constantly flying daylight state, visiting those 1000 flowers per day.

As a result of this ability to survive in colder climes, these flying jewels are critical pollinators for plants where insects are scarce or unable to live. Without them, some flora could not exist at all. Certain plants have evolved to be completely reliant on them for pollination, of which bromeliads and heliconias are just two examples. In fact, the *Heliconia Tortuosa* is even 'picky' about which hummingbird it will accept for pollination.

There are over 330 known species of hummingbirds, but this plant only releases nectar for two of them—the violet sabrewing and the green hermit—since only these two varieties have the long, curved beak necessary to reach deep inside its flower to lap up its sweet nectar, getting a proper dusting of pollen in the process. This particular heliconia is a keystone species upon which the entire food web of the Central and South American region depends, so without these two species of hummingbirds, the entire web would be in danger of collapsing.

There are various Native American stories that associate the hummingbird with water. Some narrate how he has intervened with the Great Mother (Mother Nature) on behalf of the people, pleading with her to bring rains to revitalize the earth so that the people may live.

Another recounts how he saved the earth and all living beings including the people when an angry demon spewed forth hot lava setting the land on fire. The courageous hummingbird flew to the four directions to gather the rainclouds, using their rain to extinguish the flames. It is when he flew through the rainbow in search of rain that the hummingbird got his brilliant, iridescent colours, especially those on its throat.

One legend describes the hummingbird's unwavering faith in the Great Mother and how this faith helped inspire the people to regain theirs. A long drought had come upon the people because they had lost their faith in the Great Mother and had stopped respecting her laws of balance. Only the hummingbird continued to thrive. Wondering how this could be, the holy sages and shamans followed him to discover the reason. They watched as the hummingbird went through a hidden passageway through a secret door that was open only to him, allowing him to go into the other realms to get nectar. Unlike the people, the hummingbird had never lost faith in the Great Mother and never stopped respecting her laws, confident that, as a result, she would always protect and provide for his needs.

The hummingbird's faith moved the people to trust and believe in the Great Mother again, and to respect and follow her laws, thereby ending the drought and she, once again, took care of them in every way. With this legend in mind, it is easy to see why hummingbirds are viewed as messengers between the worlds and the various dimensions of reality, acting as couriers to take gifts from the shaman to the Great Mother.

The hummingbird's inter-dimensional connection is illustrated even more directly in yet another tale, where humanity is living in an underground world of darkness. It is the hummingbird who flies above, seeking the light. Finding a spiral path upwards, he leads the people from this gloomy domain into the sunlit realm above.

Clearly, this last story is an allegory of the rise of human consciousness from the shadowy depths of mundane existence, up the spiral path and into the realm of light, love and spirit above. This rise in consciousness is what all mystics, saints and sages have sought to achieve in order to gain illumination, leading to the experience of 'Oneness' with all creation.

The hummingbird is the guide—the faithful, trusted friend and teacher, who urges us to seek that light above, to have faith in the Great Mother's love and care, to surrender all doubts and fears and let the light that is inside each and every one of us shine.

The spiritual power within us must wake up from its slumber at the base of our spine and ascend the spiral path, awakening and activating the seven 'chakras' or centres of spiritual energy with its ascension. Thus, an even more glorious and expansive joy is realized as our individual soul connects to the souls of all else in creation, finally merging with the All-Soul, the Divine Creator, from whom we have come and into whom we will merge again.

As a result of this mergence, we recognize ourselves in the eyes of our brothers and sisters and see that we all really are one and the same. We finally perceive that the Divine has been with us, within us and all around us all along, playing hide-and-seek with us until the veil of illusion and separation is finally dissolved in this blissful realization. Then, all is literally seen and known as part of the Divine and recognized as such—seeing the Divine in the eye of the squirrel looking back at us, clearly hearing the Voice from within. Time and space cease to have any relevance. All is sacred, all is perfection, all is GOD—G for Generating Principle, O for Organizing Principle, D for Destroying Principle.

This is 'gnosis'—spiritual enlightenment through realization of and union with the Divine through direct, personal, spiritual experience. It is what saints and mystics, sages and shamans from around the world have sought and attained. Through its attainment, an intuitive 'knowing' replaces intellectual 'thinking'. Things are instantly perceived for what they truly are, solutions to what seemed insolvable problems present themselves, a clear path of action for the future is shown.

Here in India, this same spiritual power is known as 'kundalini' and is likened to a coiled serpent 'sleeping' at the base of our spine. Once it has awakened and risen, we achieve enlightenment through a conscious union with God or God-realization. This imagery is also used by Native Americans, particularly in the central and southern areas of the Americas, the descriptions of the godman Quetzalcoatl* as 'the plumed serpent', reflecting this. For holy men, like the Native American shaman, this type of intuitive knowing as a result of inner divine guidance is exactly what is needed to fulfil their role of advising the members of their tribe about what course they should take.

It is also their duty to help keep Nature and Spirit in balance using the 'sacred smoke' provided by the hummingbird to purify the earth and to maintain that balance. The Great Mother in the personified form of the 'White Buffalo Cow Woman'† gave both the sacred pipe and the sacred plants to the tribes to use for this purpose and to keep that intimate spiritual connection between

---

* Quetzalcoatl was a God-realized being who lived/visited the Americas two thousand years or so ago. Some Native American tribes believe that he was the resurrected Jesus Christ who had visited them. There are many legends and even historical artifacts found regarding him and his stay in the Americas. On a symbolic level, he represents a God-realized being—a person who has raised the kundalini energy up his spine, opening his chakras to achieve God-realization, the kundalini often referred to here in India and among the native Americans as a coiled serpent at the base of the spine.

† The White Buffalo Cow Woman is considered the personification of the divine mother/feminine aspect of God. She is said to have come to the tribes with the gift of the 'peace pipe' to help them grow spiritually.

the people and Nature alive and strong. This is another reason that the hummingbird is known as the 'sacred pollinator' since it is critical for pollinating certain plants used for holy ceremonies as well as for individual spiritual quests.

The hummingbirds are key pollinators for several plants that are considered sacred, such as the trumpet flower species of *Datura* and *Brugmansia* which include plants like the angel's trumpet. Their long tubular blossoms make it impossible for other birds and most insects to reach their nectar. The sword-billed hummingbird whose beak is longer than its entire body is the only bird, in many cases, able to reach deep inside the flower for that nectar, getting dusted with pollen in the process. This pollen they then pass on to the next blossom they visit, thereby pollinating these sacred plants.

These plants have psychotropic and psychedelic properties and have been used by various indigenous peoples of the Americas to aid connection to spiritual realms and to the Great Mother as well. The use of plants for enhancing spiritual experiences has a very long history not only in the Americas, but in many places around the world, including here in India. According to researchers, Richard E. Schultes, former director of Harvard Botanical Museum and Albert Hofmann, former director of Sandoz Research Laboratories in Switzerland, who are also the co-authors of the book *Plants of the Gods*, virtually all indigenous peoples have done so, as they consider such plants to be 'gifts of the gods'.

For Native Americans, including the Osage, the use of these sacred plants and agents, including peyote, is taken very seriously and only done to gain illumination through inner guidance, especially when one has reached a crisis or turning point in one's life, and when one feels the need to commune with God.

The use of these psycho-active agents is done only with prior preparation and help from an experienced spiritual guide, and in conjunction with fasting and intense prayers in the proper environment, that usually being in the heart of Mother Nature. They are also used to facilitate vision-quests for young members of the tribe as they enter adulthood, helping the individual determine his or her role in the community.

This is the proper use of these sacred plants. Unfortunately, many today abuse and misuse them just to get 'high' or to 'space out'—something that is strongly condemned by native peoples as a gross misuse of the agent and the mind, both of which they consider sacred, warning that abuse can cause psychological problems for the abuser.

The true purpose of these psychedelic agents is to 'reveal the soul', bring about 'the vision of the soul' as per the literal translation derived from the ancient Greek '*psychē* (soul) *dēloun* (reveal, make visible)'. Another name given to them by researchers in 1979 is 'entheogens' derived from the Greek roots *entheos*, meaning 'God (*theos*) within' and *genesthe*, meaning 'to generate'. Hence, an entheogen is a substance or material that generates God or the Divine within someone, helping to cleanse the mind and heart so one can fully focus on the Divine to achieve mergence, union. As one spiritual master explained, then spiritual truths become reality, all the holy scriptures are understood and one fully comprehends the phrase 'God is love'.*

For me, comprehension and realization of that phrase is most easily attained within the heart of Nature. When in her heart, I feel the closest and most intimately linked to the Divine, as does Anil. So, while the forest with its wildlife is wonderful, magical and mystical, it is also without question spiritual and divine, being the 'outer vesture' of God.

We are not the only ones to experience this spiritual connection within Nature's heart and sacred encounters with her

---

* https://www.ncbi.nlm.nih.gov/pmc/articles/PMC4813425/
https://pubmed.ncbi.nlm.nih.gov/522165/

other creatures. Why else have mystics and saints from various faiths and cultures around the world spent so much time in Nature? But even scientific researchers have felt this connection while working in the forest and observing wildlife. One such researcher is Stephan Harding, resident ecologist at Schumacher College in the United Kingdom.

As Dr Harding explains, these sacred encounters in Nature and with wildlife are not the same as those when one is viewing things from a scientific or intellectual perspective.* Those can best be summarized as 'observations'. True 'encounters' go beyond the intellect, tapping into the intuitive level of perception and understanding, linking us with that upon which we are focusing. It could be any part of Nature—a mountain or a stream, the ocean or a woodland meadow. But it is most often triggered through encounters with wildlife, usually one-on-one.

There is a meeting of the mind, of the heart, of the being, of the soul, coupled with an immediate understanding of the essence of the animal involved, first as an individual and then as a representative of the entire species, their connection to Nature as a whole, to the Earth, with a corresponding expansion of one's own being as well, merging your being with theirs and expanding to merge with all of Nature and with the Earth as a whole.

My own amazing 'encounters' with wildlife continued to grow in both intensity and frequency with each trip into Nature being another chance to reconnect with the Divine Spirit as well. One involved a squirrel as it stopped on the limb of a tree and looked deep into my eyes. Time stood still as I could see myself reflected in his eye. My being merged with that of the squirrel, and then came the recognition that it was the Divine looking back at me through the eyes of the squirrel.

---

*   Refer to the bibliography for source.

One of my most memorable sacred encounters involved the robin. I had become overwhelmed with love for the Divine when, suddenly, everywhere we looked there were robins. The trees had become filled with them where we had not noticed them before, looking directly into our eyes—that same deep, penetrating gaze I had experienced with the squirrel. Overhead, robins were circling around in huge numbers where Anil and I were sitting on the forest cliff of our land. Two other friends were with us to witness this unbelievable and spectacular sight. Robins were everywhere!

As the feeling of love intensified, even more of them seemed to appear in every nook and corner of the forest; the sky filled with them as those on the trees flew up to join the others. It was an extraordinary experience as each new wave of robins coincided with a greater and more expansive feeling of love for them, all of Nature and the Divine Spirit that links us all together.

Whenever Anil and I go into the forest, we always follow the paths made by wildlife as they usually lead us to the most beautiful and isolated spots within the woods.

One time, when we were deep in the forests along with two close friends, it started snowing very heavily even though it was late May—not that uncommon for the Colorado Rockies. Snow had fallen the night before and was still falling in the morning. So we were already wearing our snowshoes and plenty of layers of warm clothes.

The snow stopped falling as we were making our ascent up the mountain. Reaching the summit, we beheld the most stunning view. The clouds had cleared revealing a spectacular 360-degree panorama of snow-capped peaks and thick pine forests, the incredible vistas taking our breath away. As I breathed in the cold, clear air, the wind responded with each inhale and exhale, the movement of the wind naturally synchronized with my breathing—in and out, coming and going—breathing with the wind as it swirled the powdery snowflakes all around us.

The snowflakes themselves were exquisite, each with its own unique pattern reflecting the sun's rays and transforming them into rainbows, every snowflake becoming a moving rainbow of colour. The fallen snow was radiant, shimmering in the sun's rays, with some areas appearing blue and others almost golden. A large bush seemed to stand out from the deep snow drifts around it. Absolutely glowing with such intensity, it almost appeared to be on fire.

Back in the forest, the evergreen trees had become covered with snow, the heavily laden branches bending under the weight. Snowshoeing through the woods, it truly looked like we were going through the literal heart of Nature as the snow outlined each and every curve and twig of each and every branch—astonishing in its intricacy and delicate, lace-like effects. At times we would hear, 'flump! flump!' as the snow occasionally slid off the branches and dropped in a heap on the ground below. Then all would be totally silent once again—the hushed pause between the breaths of the forest.

Finally, as we sat together on a fallen tree, we were greeted by various forest friends. The chickadees, different types of jays, woodpeckers and ravens all joined the forest mouse in saying, 'Hello!'

In this hushed silence, while deep in meditation, I had the most wonderful and extraordinary experience of 'Oneness' with all creation. My being, my very soul expanded far beyond the physical limitations of my body to encompass all 'life' surrounding us. I was connected to everyone and everything there—the birds and other animals, the trees and the wind, the falling snowflakes seeming to fall through me as they gently descended to the ground.

It was as if my body had become the base, the canvas upon which all of this incredible life had been 'painted' by the Divine. I was connected to everything—animate and inanimate—and could feel the even slightest movement around me as a part of myself. Each time there was a movement of a bird or the limb of a tree, I could feel and even anticipate the reaction that movement caused elsewhere—action, reaction—my body now One with the Earth and the Spirit that upholds it.

It was much later that I found a description in the Vedic classic *The Shrimad Bhagwat*, that paralleled my experience exactly. The holy scripture states that the human body is the 'sacrifice' upon which all of creation is based. As such, it is intimately connected to each and every part and aspect of it.

This was not the only time that I have had a spiritual experience first and then read a description of that same thing in a spiritual text later. Another incident took place a few years earlier at the same cabin in the heart of the woods. In this case, it was the ecstatic awakening of the kundalini—that spiritual power located at the base of the spine.

Music has always been a medium for spiritual upliftment no matter the culture or faith. It has the ability to move both our heart and soul to higher planes of being. Chants, hymns, ragas and beautiful instrumentals can move us in a way that nothing else can. So it was for me on that day. We were listening to the beautiful music of a Nature and spiritually-oriented group—The Moody Blues—their words of love filling my heart with intense devotion to the Divine.

At a point where the music built to a growing crescendo, that great spiritual power within me uncoiled and rose up my spine in symphonic synchronization with the music, bursting in my head like a thousand, diamond reflections accompanied by the most exquisite feeling of bliss—a spiritual ecstasy that I never even dreamt could exist, leaving me with the deepest sense of peace I have ever known. In Vedantic scriptures, this experience is called '*samadhi*', while the Christians have called it 'rapture' and 'agape'.

A few years later, on that beautiful snowy day, this intimate communion with the Divine in Nature lasted for many hours. The snow that had been falling ever so gently increased in volume, a thick, white veil now obscuring views as well as covering over the path that would lead us back to our cabin. During these treks into the woods, I would usually take the lead, just as I did this time. Although I knew the area somewhat, the now heavy blanket of snow made it difficult to make out the landmarks I usually used for guidance. So, I asked the Great Mother for help.

From that point onwards, depressions in the newly fallen snow became visible—depressions that had not been there before. Ever so grateful, I followed them with confidence. Sure enough, the trail made by them led us back to our cabin even though it was not the same trail we had used to climb up the mountain. Indeed, this one made by the Mother was easier and more direct.

It was only upon our return that we learned that we had been out in a full-blown blizzard that had stranded people and vehicles, and had closed highways and towns. For us, the day had been one of the most blissful we had ever had, filled with magnificent beauty and exceptional sacred encounters with wildlife, all spent in the comfort, security and protection of Mother Nature's divine heart.

I have shared these very special moments of personal history to help underscore the divinity inherent in Nature, to encourage others to understand her sanctity and to remind us of the secret door within her heart that is there for all who truly seek it—to enter therein to reconnect with the One who has created us all.

So many of us are lost in an artificial world of concrete and technology that is entirely cut off from Nature. We have forgotten the true purpose of life, which is to learn and experience all we can about the Divine. Science has become our new 'god'. Showing any kind of respect or devotion for the Creator of us all is somehow viewed as antithetical to scientific inquiry.

Nothing could be further from the truth. There is nothing contradictory about appreciating science while embracing spirituality. Both are valid because both seek truth. As Anil has said so many times, 'What is science but humanity's attempt to understand Nature?'

I love science. I love the scientific research into Nature, its seeking to comprehend the processes by which 'life' has evolved in the cosmos. As more scientific revelations come forth about the brilliance with which natural processes have developed, my admiration and esteem for the Creator is enhanced—not diminished—while my appreciation for science grows.

Ironically enough, it is scientific study that is leading us back to Nature, whether that be due to the positive physical, emotional, mental and psychological benefits we derive from reconnecting to Nature, or the recognition that humanity cannot survive without the ecosystem services Nature freely provides for us every day.

Science is also warning us that if we do not respect Nature—whether that be through overconsumption of her bounty or the polluting of her various elements—we will suffer, all life will suffer. Therefore, scientists across the globe are calling for a new approach to Nature, soundly based on respect, echoing what the sages and mystics have said since time immemorial. For truly, respect, coupled with love of Mother Nature, love of the Divine, is what will ensure on planet Earth the future of mankind.

# 7

# From Pills to Plants: A Life
# in Healthcare

When I was in high school, I was given a test to see what possible career choices I might want to consider based on my interests and aptitude. Afterwards, my school guidance counsellor said the tests indicated that I might want to contemplate working in the field of advertising.

When I relayed this to my mom later at home, she laughed and said, 'You will never be happy if you are not outside in Nature all the time.'

I knew in my heart that she was right.

Over my years in high school and college, I had worked at many different jobs in order to earn money for college expenses—from babysitter to waitress, store clerk to supermarket cashier, bank teller and coffeehouse partner, to selling Plexiglas furniture and waterbeds handmade by my business partner, wholesale and retail.

My favourite job by far was that of a camp counsellor for young children aged around eight to ten years or so, since we were always outside in Nature, walking through one of the state parks and exploring the marvels of Nature together. This work reinforced my desire to travel to see the wonders of the world, hence my initial choice to join the American diplomatic corps.

However, this career was no longer an option for me once I discovered the truth about US foreign policy, what the US was doing and the type of people in power it was backing in so many parts of the world. I could not be a part of that, especially after the revelations of Bangladesh, in particular, where the on-ground staff and the US high counsel in Bangladesh were completely ignored, forced to witness the genocidal horrors and being unable to stop them due to the powerful political figures in Washington.

In a way, my career actually found me as I was contacted by one of the largest pharmaceutical manufacturing companies in the country that was interested in hiring me. This was certainly not my speciality as I had mainly studied political science and history in college. However, the job involved a good deal of travelling, which attracted me. So, needing the work and looking forward to the travel, I accepted.

A whole new area of learning and knowledge opened up as a result which eventually led to my environmental awakening. My political awakening had come during college through research as a result of my heated political debates with Anil. My spiritual awakening had come in the heart of the forests of the Colorado Rockies with Anil. Now my intellectual awakening in the scientific world was to commence as I took courses in chemistry, biology, pharmacology and abnormal psychology, to mention a few.

Suddenly I was in the world of healthcare, meeting with doctors, going to hospitals and psychiatric centres, learning about the history of modern allopathic/western medicine and being confronted with both the benefits and dangers of this type of healing modality. While it was fascinating to learn about the human body and its amazing ability to heal itself, what was even more intriguing and illuminating was the fact that so many of today's modern medicines have their origin in plants and other natural substances used for centuries by Native Americans and other indigenous peoples, this precious knowledge of Nature's healing gifts passed down from generation to generation.

Ayurveda is one example of this wisdom here in India, along with other healing systems such as Unani. The use of these healing plants exemplifies the wisdom and understanding of these native cultures, their pharmacopoeia being the result of the cornucopia of plants that have evolved over the millennia on Mother Earth.

In addition, their keen observation of wildlife has often led to their use of a certain plant that they would see an animal seeking out to eat when it was ill. They also understood the importance of wildlife as propagators of these healing floras. An example of this can be found in a saying of the Osage, 'Healing plants grow where the buffalo rolls,'—an observation which is absolutely true. Buffalo love to roll or 'wallow' in the dirt in order to rid themselves of biting pests, as well as to shed their winter fur. In this process, seeds of various plants get lodged in their fur, dropping off when they roll in another location as they travel across the Great Plains.

One study conducted in Osage County, Oklahoma, found thousands of seeds from at least seventy-five different plants in the fur shed from just one buffalo, clearly proving how critical buffalos are to the dispersal of seeds in the prairies. Furthermore, the rolling of the buffalo compacts the soil beneath them, leaving depressions in the ground that fill up with water when it rains, creating small pools across the land that greatly benefit all species of wildlife there. When the water in the pools eventually evaporates, the various seeds from the buffalo's fur sprout forth, bringing the healing plants to life, bearing testimony to the truth of the Osage saying.

Some of these plants include sage, echinacea, mullein, spearmint and valerian, along with a host of fruits—from blackberries to raspberries. These in turn help treat ailments from coughs and colds, to flu and fever, from joint pain and inflammation to circulatory, respiratory and digestion problems, to boosting the immune system in general. Other plants are used for their antiseptic and anti-infection properties while some others are valued as anaesthetics and analgesics, or pain relievers, like the aspen or willow bark which contains salicin—the original 'aspirin'.

Allopathic/Western medicine has also benefitted from this knowledge, but with one very stark difference—instead of using the plant in its natural form, where all its components are in balance, allopathy isolates one or more active ingredients which are then synthesized for artificial, mass production. An excellent example of this is the use of salicin for aspirin. The problem with this approach is that it often causes side-effects when taking the medicines, which can sometimes be life threatening.

My work with this major pharmaceutical company gave me first-hand insight into this problem that often accompanies allopathic drugs. This motivated me to look for gentler, more natural methods of healing. The practices of Native Americans again helped guide my search, leading me to the use of flower essences and aromatherapy as well as hydrotherapy, including the use of saunas. Modern-day saunas mimic the Native American practice of sitting in sweat lodges to help the body rid itself of toxins through perspiration, the practice often accompanied by the burning of the leaves of specific plants whose fragrance when inhaled aids in the purification process.

While Native Americans relied on animals to show them healing plants, allopathy uses animals in a very different manner—as test subjects for new drugs and treatments—tests that are almost always horrendously brutal and painful for the animals that are used. Over 100 million animals are used by humans for these tests and studies ranging from dogs, cats and rabbits to rhesus monkeys and chimpanzees. The testing of cosmetics, cleaning agents and other non-medical products are also done on these same animals, not to mention exposing them to radiation and other substances to determine 'lethal dose' limits.

There are serious ethical questions that we must ask ourselves when condoning these cruelties inflicted on other species. What gives us the right to inflict pain, torture and suffering on another species, especially when the sole beneficiary of these tests and studies is the human species alone? These animals are abused in shockingly cruel ways, routinely being drugged, starved, and held in restraints for hours while being subjected to inhumane treatment.

Psychological testing is probably the most appalling and inhumane of all testing methods. Many behavioural study tests involve inflicting painful electric shocks on the animals to observe their reactions and to alter their natural behaviour, causing them to go mad and then killing them. Other heartless and atrocious tests include forcing animals to live in overcrowded conditions on the one extreme, or completely depriving them of social contact on the other. This latter procedure is inflicted on day-old primates that are separated from their mothers to gauge the reaction of the newborn babies.

Does it really take callous, sadistic, scientific, psychological studies like this to guess the extreme stress the infants experience as a result of the separation, or the terror they feel at being locked up alone in steel cages, to live out the rest of their days in a prison, to be treated as mercilessly as humans choose to treat them and murdered at a human's whim, all in the name of 'science'?

The ironic tragedy in this terribly sad and cruel waste of life is that the majority of animal experiments do not contribute to improving human health. Indeed, researchers have found that medical treatments effective for animals rarely translate to being effective for humans, including in cases of cancer and HIV/AIDS, according to the *Journal of American Medical Association* (*JAMA*).[*]

As for psychological testing, far more reliable results are obtained for human behaviour and reactions from closely observing humans, rather than extrapolating what human behaviour may be based on those observed in animals. We humans pride ourselves on being different from animals when it comes to justifying their use in these tests and studies, and yet, therein also lies the contradiction of that justification: if animals are so different from us, then how can tests on them be reliable for results in humans?

My views on these tests are the same as those held by Mahatma Gandhi. As the Mahatma said,

> Vivisection is the blackest of all crimes that mankind is committing against God and His fair creation . . . I abhor vivisection with my whole soul. All the scientific discoveries stained with innocent blood I count as of no consequence.[†]

Echoing the words of nineteenth-century German philosopher Arthur Schopenhauer, Gandhi states,

> The greatness of a nation and its moral progress can be judged by the way its animals are treated.[‡]

---

[*]   https://www.ncbi.nlm.nih.gov/pmc/articles/PMC2746847/
      Refer to the bibliography for more links.
[†]   https://www.petaindia.com/blog/mahatma-gandhi-quotes-on-animals/
      https://www.goodreads.com/quotes/340-the-greatness-of-a-nation-and-
its-moral-progress-can
[‡]   Ibid.

In his book, *On the Basis of Morality*, Schopenhauer underscores the need for compassion for all creatures and for the recognition of the presence of the Creator in all creation:

> Compassion for animals is intimately associated with goodness of character, and it may be confidently asserted that he who is cruel to animals cannot be a good man . . . The assumption that animals are without rights, and the illusion that our treatment of them has no moral significance, is a positively outrageous example of Western crudity and barbarity. Universal compassion is the only guarantee of morality.

> Because Christian morality leaves animals out of account, they are at once outlawed in philosophical morals; they are mere 'things', mere means to any ends whatsoever. They can therefore be used for vivisection, hunting, coursing, bullfights and horse racing, and can be whipped to death as they struggle along with heavy carts of stone. Shame on such a morality that is worthy of pariahs, and that fails to recognize the Eternal Essence that exists in every living thing, and shines forth with inscrutable significance from all eyes that see the sun!*

As Albert Einstein summed it up,

> The indifference, callousness, and contempt that so many people exhibit toward animals is evil first because it results in great suffering in animals, and second because it results in an incalculably great impoverishment of the human spirit.[†]

---

*   Howard Williams,, *Ethics of Diet, a Catena.*

[†]   https://www.azquotes.com/author/4399-Albert_Einstein/tag/animal-cruelty#:~:text=The%20indifference%2C%20callousness%20and%20contempt,impoverishment%20of%20the%20human%20spirit

In today's world there is no justification whatsoever for this continued cruelty, including in the medical field. Keen observation and computer simulations can yield far better results for studies—results that are not tainted with the blood of the innocent. We must seek gentler, more compassionate methods of healing—methods which are available for use right now and have excellent track records of success as well.

Each one of us individually and collectively must begin to take responsibility for our own health. So much of our illness is due to the unnatural, stressed-out lifestyle we lead. It seems easier to pop a pill than to change our way of living. But this drug dependence ultimately comes back to haunt us as the side effects kick in to numb our bodies and blur our minds.

Stress along with a sense that life is meaningless are afflicting many, leading ultimately to a state of depression. But the use of antidepressants is far beyond what is truly necessary with only a small minority of people actually suffering from severe clinical depression. This over-reliance on these drugs has led to a massive increase in their long-term use of five years or more all over the developed world, with addiction to them being a major problem. In the USA, the rate has tripled since the year 2000. The increase for two-year usage has soared 60 per cent since just 2010. One in four American women over the age of forty and 4 per cent of teenagers are taking antidepressants—shocking statistics.*

Stopping the use of these drugs is difficult as over half or more of those consuming them experience some form of withdrawal symptoms which include dizziness, nausea, headaches, irritability, fatigue, confusion, insomnia and paraesthesia—

---

https://www.inspiringquotes.us/author/3804-albert-einstein/about-animal-cruelty

*    https://www.nytimes.com/2018/04/07/health/antidepressants-withdrawal-prozac-cymbalta.html

described by patients as electric-shock sensations in the brain that many call 'brain zaps'. These symptoms can take many years to disappear even after ending the use of antidepressants completely.

The situation in India is not much better, with the use of antidepressants having skyrocketed over the last decade or so as well. Senior Indian psychiatrists are warning that the easy availability of these drugs make overuse and abuse a very serious concern as the sedative effect of these drugs appears to calm down patients when, in actuality, it is dulling the mind.[*] This is very dangerous as extended consumption of benzodiazepines and other antidepressants causes physical and psychological dependence.

Multiple studies have established an increase in mental illness with urban living.[†] Today, over 50 per cent of the world population already live in cities, and that number is rising every year, with projections of 68 per cent or more being crammed into metropolitan centres by 2050.[‡] Clearly, this swelling of population in urban areas will translate into higher rates of mental illnesses—from anxiety and mood disorders to a doubling of the risk of schizophrenia.

Indeed, in one recent study, researchers found a 50 per cent risk increase in the development of schizophrenia in people who grew up in areas devoid of green spaces, compared with those who

---

[*]    https://timesofindia.indiatimes.com/life-style/health-fitness/health-news/one-in-every-20-indians-suffers-from-depression/articleshow/56867750.cms
    Refer to the bibliography for more links.
[†]    https://www.thehindu.com/society/how-urban-design-impacts-mental-health/article31693107.
    More links in the bibliography.
[‡]    https://www.un.org/development/desa/en/news/population/2018-revision-of-world-urbanization-prospects.html

grew up surrounded by greenery.* This information is of particular interest to me due to my past work with the pharmaceutical company since one of the drugs they manufactured was a major tranquilizer, specifically used for the treatment of schizophrenia. While the drug was helpful to many patients, it also had several side-effects.

The drug's main action was to reduce the amount of dopamine in the brain. Once again, this is where reconnecting with Nature can be of such help and importance. As mentioned in earlier chapters, research has shown that just being in Nature does exactly that, not only decreasing dopamine levels, but also those of the stress-hormone cortisol, thereby lessening overall fearful feelings associated with urban living that can lead to schizophrenia.

Again, just being in Nature decreases activity in the brain's subgenual prefrontal cortex area, which is associated with depressive thinking. This coupled with lower activity in the prefrontal cortex—the 'command centre' of our brain responsible for complex thinking and social behaviour—translates into fewer chances of 'rumination' or excessive thinking associated with schizophrenia too—all benefits for our brain solely from reconnecting with Nature.

## Help from Nature: Sacred Plants and Ancient Wisdom

Medical and psychiatric researchers are continually looking to Nature for help in the ever-constant pursuit of good mental and physical health. The sacred plants used by certain indigenous

---

* https://www.sciencedirect.com/science/article/abs/pii/S0920996418301786
More links in the bibliography.

peoples are being investigated for possible utilization in various areas.* The use of cannabis as an aid for pain relief and for its anti-emetic/anti-nausea properties for cancer patients and those going through alcoholism withdrawal, as well as for its therapeutic uses in glaucoma and multiple sclerosis, among other illnesses, are just a few examples. Currently over forty countries have already legalized it for medicinal purposes, as have at least thirty-six states in the USA, with calls for the same legalization coming from certain quarters in India as well.†

The molecular structure of certain brain hormones closely resembles that of the compound that causes visionary experiences found in some of these sacred plants and their value and efficacy in treating psychiatric patients has been documented in studies as early as the 1950s. This includes their semi-synthetic versions, like LSD, which was first discovered by Albert Hofmann in the 1940s. Examples of conditions for which they have been helpful for include not only pain relief, but also depression.

Today, new research has underscored their worth in these areas as well as in others, as reported in the premier UK medical journal, *Lancet*, and confirmed in other highly respected publications.‡ With regard to depression, new studies have shown that psychedelic drugs have far higher rates of efficacy in combatting depression in comparison to common antidepressants. Their positive effects are immediate and long-

---

*    https://www.ncbi.nlm.nih.gov/pmc/articles/PMC4813425/
†    https://en.wikipedia.org/wiki/Legality_of_cannabis
     More links in the bibliography.
‡    Dr Robin L. Carhart-Harris, PhD, et. al., 'Psilocybin with Psychological Support for Treatment-Resistant Depression: An Open Label Feasibility Study', *Lancet*, volume 3, issue 7, 1 July 2016, pp. 619–27.
     More links in the bibliography.

lasting, without side-effects and with no requirement for daily medication over long periods of time.

These latter points may well explain why most of these new studies are being done by renowned scientists at prestigious universities like Johns Hopkins University and Imperial College of London, as well as non-profit pharmaceutical companies and organizations, and not by large traditional pharmaceutical companies. If only a couple of administrations of psychedelic drugs can have long-lasting, positive effects in patients suffering from depression and other ailments, that's not good for business because it means that they don't need to buy more pills.*

Due to the molecular structure of these sacred agents and their semi-synthetic versions, addiction to them is virtually impossible. This is because their activity relies on the brain's supply of serotonin, a neurotransmitter or a type of 'chemical messenger' that sends signals from one nerve cell receptor to another. Serotonin is the same neurotransmitter that antidepressants target. An increased supply of serotonin helps you feel happy, at ease, active and more sociable.

However, the brain can only produce so much and therefore releases a limited quantity of serotonin at a time. Once it's gone, it's gone, and it takes time for the brain to produce more. This time period is the key curb on the risk of physical addiction to psychedelic drugs which is why that risk is so low. Even with an increase in dose, the psychological 'high' isn't there for the user to enjoy if they are used too frequently.

Antidepressants work by raising levels of serotonin by increasing the activity of all the serotonin receptors in the brain. In addition, they block the brain's ability to reabsorb excess

---

* https://www.independent.co.uk/voices/antidepressants-drugs-pills-opioids-addiction-mental-health-a9131901.html

amounts of serotonin. This is one of the reasons that they can cause physical and psychological addiction.*

Psychedelics on the other hand target only certain subtypes of these receptors, specifically the 5-HT2A receptors, which are understood to increase cognitive flexibility, also playing a key role in regulating moods, anxiety, schizophrenia, sense of self and consciousness. This cognitive flexibility allows patients the 'mental agility' to overcome problems in order to achieve long-lasting results—something that is critically important when dealing with depression and other psychiatric disorders.

In addition, psychedelics shut down certain main 'connector hubs' in the brain. These hubs act in a similar way as hubs on the Internet do, which collate and then pass on information down the line. When major connector hubs are shut down, the brain's normal pathways for communication are disrupted, thereby causing an interruption of the brain's 'Default Mode Network' or DMN.

The DMN normally kicks-in when we are not concentrating on anything in particular—somewhat like a screen saver in computers—the brain on 'autopilot'. Associated with the sense of 'self' and consciousness, it is the area of the brain occupied with self-reflection, 'thinking about thinking', musing over past experiences, or wondering about the future—all essential activities for a mentally healthy individual.

However, an overactive DMN is associated with certain mental disorders such as depression, anxiety and OCD (Obsessive Compulsive Disorders)—all disorders associated with obsessive over-thinking, particularly negative thoughts about one's self.

When the well-worn, normal pathways for communication are disrupted and shut down, the brain starts to communicate in

---

* One of the main physical sensations is dullness of the mind, often called 'bluntness' of emotion and feelings, lack of motivation. Psychedelics do not target all serotonin receptors—only some, unlike antidepressants.

different ways—ways that often lead to new perspectives on life and one's problems. An analogy would be driving in a city or town.

Usually, we take one particular route to go from point A to point B—going from work to home, for example. We may normally travel on certain 'round-abouts' or circles to get from one street to the next and onwards to the main road before reaching home. But if these circles are blocked or the main road itself is closed, we have to find new ways of getting home. We are forced to make a detour using new routes. These new routes give us an entirely new view of the area in which we live. We are literally seeing things in a new way.

This is what happens when taking psychedelics—the disruption of the normal pathways for communication in the brain leads to the use of new pathways which provide a different perspective on reality, an altered state of consciousness. This causes the different regions of the brain to communicate with one another to facilitate communication. Their increased interaction is one possible explanation for the enhancement in creativity and problem-solving that is attributed to psychedelics.

Patients have relayed how their use helped them confront and deal with their fears, even aiding access to an 'inner voice' that guided them through intense self-reflection, which often involved a cathartic release of pent-up, negative emotions about themselves and others as well. This, in turn, led them to forgiveness—for themselves and others—followed by a new feeling of self-worth—not in an egotistical way, but in a recognition of their own goodness being still alive and well inside. All of these revelations prompted changes in both perceptions and lifestyles, ultimately leading to a deep, reassuring, profound and lasting sense of peace.

Around the world, thousands of emotionally and mentally troubled people commit suicide each year. In the USA alone, 120 Americans take their own lives every day, with twenty of them being war veterans. Many of these people, and most of the war vets have been suffering from Post-Traumatic Stress Disorder (PTSD)—a condition that often leads to severe depression, anxiety and addiction. One particular psychedelic drug that has shown dramatic success in the treatment of PTSD is MDMA (also known as Ecstasy). Once again, part of the reason for its success lies in the physical changes in the brain caused by psychedelics.

Like other psychedelics, MDMA decreases blood flow and brain activity in the amygdala—that same centre in the brain associated with fear and anxiety that are key factors in both depression, schizophrenia and PTSD. But they leave the prefrontal cortex online—that key area of the brain, coupled with the hippocampus, which deals with learning, rational thinking and decision making—critical for people suffering from PTSD since they have reduced activity in these same areas.

MDMA-assisted therapy has been more effective in treating PTSD patients than has any other therapy currently available. As a result, the US Food and Drug Administration (FDA) has given its approval to a roadmap for the legalization of MDMA for medical use by 2021.*

The controlled use of psychedelic drugs has also helped patients suffering from various addictions, including smoking and alcohol dependence, as well as anxiety disorders including end-of-life anxiety suffered by the terminally ill. When given doses of these sacred agents, terminally ill patients are not only freed

---

* https://www.nytimes.com/2021/05/03/health/mdma-approval.html
More links in the bibliography.
Please also note that MEDITATION has been shown to be very useful here as stopping the 'round and round' of the mind/DMN
https://medium.com/swlh/the-brains-default-mode-what-is-it-and-why-meditation-is-the-antidote-d0408ab989d6    https://www.cbsnews.com/news/psychedelic-therapy-tried-by-patients-for-mental-health-psychological-conditions/?intcid=CNM-00-10abd1h

of their pain, but have lost their fear of death, having finally understood the meaning of life.

I witnessed such an episode in the USA with a coal miner who was dying from black lung disease.* Throughout the experience of psychedelic-assisted therapy, he was guided by a trusted psychiatrist who had spent much time with him beforehand in preparation, helping him to understand what experiences he may undergo, the entire session of several hours being filmed. At the end of the session, the dying man said that for the first time in over a year, he had been completely free of pain. He added that he no longer feared dying since he now understood the meaning of life and death, going on to share some of his poignant spiritual experiences during the session.

When asked if he had any regrets, he stated that the one regret he had was that the members of his family could not experience what he had experienced, for then they too would understand and let go of their fears, pain and sorrow. The inability of his family members to experience what he had experienced is due to the illegality of these sacred agents in many, if not most, countries around the world—a prohibition that was imposed just fifty years ago in almost all instances, and even less in others. The Osage and others who belong to the Native American Church view these sacred agents as holy sacraments, and are the only ones exempt from this ban in the USA, with the additional exception of those engaged in psychedelic research.

This illegality makes no sense when looking at the history of these holy plants, or the immense help they have given to those

---

* This was an episode on the news documentary series *60 Minutes*. See this more recent episode https://www.cbsnews.com/news/michael-pollan-on-testing-psychedelics-as-a-treatment-for-depression/?intcid=CNM-00-10abd1h

https://www.cbsnews.com/news/magic-mushroom-psychedelic-may-ease-depression-anxiety/?intcid=CNM-00-10abd1h suffering from various emotional and mental disorders today. For over 10,000 years, indigenous peoples have used these agents for the correct purposes, which range from illness or crisis in one's life or within the tribal community, to connecting and communing with the Divine.

Their record outstrips virtually all present-day drugs for mental illness in efficacy and safety. The inability to obtain them legally forces those who either want or need to use them, to get them from underground sources—sources that are often unethical and mix various dangerous chemicals with the sacred agents. This is the real safety danger of psychedelics—that their purity when purchased on the street cannot be guaranteed, whereas legalization and government supervision could help ensure their purity by keeping a check on any adulteration.

But until that happens, we will have to continue relying on pioneers persevering in their research to carry on unlocking the secrets of these agents, adding to the highly impressive lists of successes and features that these very special gifts of Nature have and continue to offer to humankind.

It is important to emphasize once again that the use of these sacred agents is conducted under strict supervision by an experienced guide or therapist whose preparation of the individual involved and guidance through the experience is essential. While the use of sacred plants under this kind of strict supervision and guidance has been helpful to many, it is clear that just being in Nature has a wonderfully powerful and positive effect on us all.

Why? Simply put, because Nature is our Mother. The roots of our existence stem from her and are nourished by the time we spend in her heart. She renews us physically, emotionally, intellectually and spiritually. The awe, wonder and amazement we experience in Nature is what gives us real happiness, and that is the secret of a healthy, fulfilled life.

# From Carnivore to Herbivore

I was raised in a home where meat was usually eaten three times a day. My personal journey to vegetarianism/veganism was a process that began in high school when I first became aware of dolphins drowning after being caught in fishing nets meant to catch tuna. Schools of tuna often travel with dolphin pods, as dolphins are excellent in deterring ocean predators like sharks.

Unlike fish, dolphins and other cetaceans are air-breathing mammals like us, despite living in water. Being caught in these nets means they are unable to surface to breathe, and hence drown. They become the victims of an industry that often kills aquatic creatures other than those for which it is actually fishing. The fishing industry calls these innocent victims like the dolphins 'by-catch' having been caught 'by the way'.

I absolutely loved eating tuna-fish sandwiches, so it was not easy making the decision to give them up. But I was faced with an ethical question—could I really justify the death of these wonderful and highly intelligent dolphins just for the sake of my own taste buds?

I was faced with the same dilemma when I learned about the massive loss of aquatic life as 'by-catch' for another seafood favourite—shrimp. For each kilo of shrimp caught, there is approximately eleven kilos of other aquatic life caught as well, usually thrown back into the sea, dead. How could I justify eating something while so many other lives simply went to waste in the process.

The number of animals killed for the sake of scientific research may be in the millions, but they account for less than 1 per cent of those killed for food. Fifty-six billion farm animals are butchered every year for food. This figure does not even include fish and sea creatures whose death for humanity's meal tables are measured in the tonnes, and the figure is even higher when those killed as 'by-catch' are added to it.

Another push toward vegetarianism came from my work with the pharmaceutical company. As I learned more about the troubles with the side-effects of allopathic drugs, another disturbing problem surfaced with regard to antibiotics. The prophylactic use of antibiotics is a common practice in the raising of various animals for food, routinely given to cattle and other species destined for slaughter. One of the reasons is the overcrowding at feedlots where the animals are kept before being shipped for slaughter, this overcrowding causing dangers of spreading infections and illness among the packed group.

Having driven past cattle feedlots many times on the journey from Denver to Fort Collins to attend college, I could easily understand the concern as the feedlots reeked with the stench of faeces and urine from all the animals kept there.

This overcrowding of factory farm animals, coupled with the filthy and unhygienic state of the enclosures are horribly inhumane conditions to keep any animals. In addition, they are the principal causes of the outbreaks of various kinds of diseases that can also affect humans. Swine flu and bird flu epidemics are just two examples where the disease has jumped species to infect other animals, both domestic and wild, as well as humans.

However, this routine prophylactic use of antibiotics in these animals creates an even more serious dilemma that affects those eating the meat. As one consumes the meat, one consumes the residues of antibiotics left in the meat, thereby causing a build-up of resistance to the positive effects of the drugs when ingested as medicine. This has become a common problem around the globe, leading to the rise of the so-called 'super bugs' that the present spectrum of antibiotics available is unable to control.

Additionally, the use of antidepressants is now being linked to antibiotic resistance as well. Studies have shown that the key chemical ingredient found in some of the most popular antidepressants causes the body to build up a resistance to the positive effects of several types of antibiotics—a drastic development that makes those who consume certain antidepressants even more vulnerable to these 'superbugs'—a doubled danger from the dependence on and overuse of both of these types of allopathic drugs.*

My own mother died from such a 'superbug'. She had been hospitalized with ordinary pneumonia during the cold, snowy winter month of January, but had responded to treatment and was on the road to recovery when she became infected with a strain of 'hospital pneumonia'—a super antibiotic-resistant strain that could not be controlled. Though she had never taken any antidepressants, this super bug was just too strong. Instead of leaving the hospital for home in just a few days, as was the doctors' original prognosis, she died in the hospital in less than a week, a victim of the misuse and abuse of antibiotics not just in the medical profession, but in the factory farming of animals as well.

Considering these dangers, one would think that factory farms would clean up their act and abide by the laws already on the books in many countries dealing with the humane and hygienic conditions required to raise animals for slaughter so that the prophylactic use of antibiotics could be cut back drastically. But there is another reason for the use of these drugs in animals destined for slaughter—antibiotics cause water retention, thus increasing the weight of the animals at the time of sale for slaughter, meaning more money for those who sell them. The greed for money is the root cause for this medical and also environmental debacle that now affects us all—not just those who eat meat.

What's more, studies have now shown that the combined toxins of faeces, urine and drugs from the feedlots are polluting

---

* https://www.newsweek.com/fluoxetine-and-antibiotic-resistance-key-ingredient-antidepressants-linked-1113596
More links in the bibliography.

nearby water sources, the toxins being carried by rain runoff entering surface water sources like streams, lakes and rivers. This toxic brew also percolates down through the ground to poison whatever water bodies it reaches below, thereby threatening the purity of aquifers and other underground fresh water sources.

On top of that, factory farming of animals is also a major source of greenhouse gas emissions (GHGs) since cattle, in particular, release gas both through belching and through the biodegradation of their faeces and urine eliminations. Methane is the primary GHG released, which has 21½ times more potential for trapping heat around the planet than even carbon dioxide.

Another hidden environmental cost to the planet of factory farming is the loss of rainforests being cut down in Central and South America to make way for massive soybean farms, the soybeans used almost exclusively as a source of feed for factory farmed animals. The loss of tropical rainforests is particularly dangerous as they are both the lungs and water tanks of the earth. They absorb massive amounts of carbon while greatly cooling the atmosphere through the twin processes of photosynthesis and transpiration, also setting into motion weather-cycles that affect the entire globe, as mentioned in earlier chapters.

Changes in land use by humans which translates into deforestation in most cases is the single leading cause of climate change and our warming planet. The huge amount of land used for the raising of farm animals is one of the major factors in this with over 9 billion acres of land being used to graze livestock and another 3 billion acres or more used for feed production for these mostly factory farmed livestock.

In the USA as well as several other countries, the grazing of livestock is allowed on government land for a ridiculously nominal fee, thereby bringing ranchers into conflict with what little wildlife there is left, which is trying to survive on the few grasslands not already ploughed under to make way for mega-farms where feed for livestock is often grown. Today, almost 50 per cent of all agricultural output goes to feeding livestock, with over 67 per cent of all crops in the US Midwest going to feed livestock.

Governments routinely use these man-made conflicts as justification to kill off wild grazers like buffalo, elk, deer and antelope, but especially to exterminate predators like wolves, coyotes, bears and large cats like cougars who may occasionally kill a cow or two in their own desperate search for food and survival. Even the disgusting practice of 'denning' is allowed, where newborn pups and cubs of these predators are killed within their dens or homes.

How much life on this planet has been shifted away from natural systems and wildlife in general is illustrated by these astonishing figures: 96 to 98 per cent of all the vertebrate biomass on land today consists of humans, our pets and our livestock, with wild species accounting for only 2–4 per cent of terrestrial vertebrate life on the planet—a staggering fact to contemplate.*

It is true that in most cases, indigenous peoples around the world have been hunters and meat eaters, including my own Native American ancestors. But their harvesting of life was in balance with the ecosystem where they lived. The Osage, for example, only went on three annual hunts for buffalo, with each part of the animal used for some purpose and meat dried and stored for later use during the year. Their demand for food never outstripped Nature's ability to supply, be it from animal or plant sources.

That is not the situation today, where so much is wasted of the animals that are slaughtered. Additionally, human numbers

---

* https://www.ecowatch.com/biomass-humans-animals-2571413 930.html
More links in the bibliography.

have risen exponentially, increasing the demand for food accordingly, putting even more pressure on what little forest areas are left for wildlife to eke out an existence. As income rises, demand for meat products usually rises as well, multiplying the number of domestic animals raised and killed for food while intensifying the expansion of mega-farms and the destruction of forests as a result.

A switch to vegetarianism and veganism helps limit this destruction and also has major health benefits for those who refrain from eating animal products. It is also safer, which the final push towards complete vegetarianism for Anil and me illustrates well.

We had already given up eating meat on a regular basis, buying only certified organic, free-range roaming, humanely slaughtered meat from the health food store, if and when we did choose to purchase it. We had even stopped doing this, eating only freshly caught fish while living in Hawaii. But then, both Anil and I had severe bouts of food-poisoning from eating the freshly caught fish. The experience of severe food poisoning was horrible. I have never endured such pain in my life!

Afterwards, we found out that one of the nuclear submarines docked in Pearl Harbor port had leaked radioactive wastewater into the surrounding ocean, thereby poisoning fish and other aquatic life in the area—an event that neither we nor anyone else could have foreseen or controlled.

Clearly, with so many reasons to give up eating any form of animal life—ethical, environmental and health-related—we had no excuse not to do so. Our health has benefitted tremendously from the decision, as have our hearts and conscience. I would recommend vegetarianism and veganism to everyone who can make the transition. For those who cannot, at least choosing to eat less meat and seafood is a great start, making sure that the meat or fish eaten is organic and from humanely raised and slaughtered sources. We need to try as much as possible to live in a compassionate manner and frame of mind towards all species with whom we share Planet Earth.

# 8

## Colorado Rocky Lows: Missing Peaks for Uranium Tails

'Where am I? Why am I here? Who is talking near me? Why are these lights so bright?'

Question upon question was swirling around in my disoriented mind as I gradually awoke from the anaesthesia. I was thirstier than I had ever been in my life and the painful ache in my back was unbearable. I needed to move, to get out of the prone position I was in on the gurney. But the nurse stopped me, saying, 'Don't move yet. You have to stay here for a little longer.'

I was in the first recovery room after hours in surgery. The operation had started early that morning, and it was now already mid-afternoon. The cancerous tumour had been removed, but to verify that every bit of malignant tissue had been cut out, it had to be rushed to the lab for testing and confirmation that all the edges were 'clean' of cancer cells.

In addition, three of the 'sentinel lymph nodes' under my armpit had been removed for testing as well to make sure the cancer had not spread to them. Lymph nodes clear the breast of fluids, the 'sentinel' nodes being the first to receive anything from the breast. Hence, they would be the first areas outside the breast to receive cancer cells if the cancer had spread. Testing of the tumour and lymph nodes while I was still on the operating table under anaesthesia was one of the main reasons for the long duration of the surgical procedure. Only after confirmation that all was clear could the surgeon begin reconstructing my breast and then close the long incision.

When I was finally moved to the second recovery room, Anil was able to visit me. I could see the immense relief in his eyes as he looked down at me. My dear friend Tara was there as well and was an immense help in getting me into a more comfortable position.

For the next ninety minutes or so, more delivery of painkillers, antibiotics and antiemetic (anti-nausea) drugs through the intravenous (IV) cannula in my hand followed. Then I was discharged and began the almost two-hour drive back to our flat in Whitefield, Bangalore. Still terribly disoriented and now exceedingly nauseous, the journey was punctuated by bouts of vomiting and sharp pain whenever the taxi hit a bump or a pothole in the road. Finally reaching our building, Anil helped me up the four flights of stairs to my room where I collapsed on the bed.

Instructions from the doctor were to eat something bland and easy to digest as soon as possible to help settle my stomach, and then to bathe in warm water since the type of bandage used over the stitches in the breast was waterproof. A small meal of some rice and curd was followed by a warm shower. I cannot stress enough how incredibly grounding it was to have that stream of warm water flow down my body from head to toe. It was amazing! My nausea was gone and more importantly I was no longer disoriented at all! How healing, soothing and rejuvenating is this sacred element—water!

However, my ordeal dealing with cancer was not yet over. Four weeks later, I had to start targeted radiation therapy at the same hospital. Radiation therapy involves exposing areas that have, or have had, cancer to high doses of intense radiation to kill off cancer cells, thereby reducing the size of a tumour before surgery, or killing off any cancer cells that may have migrated elsewhere from the original tumour site. Hence, I ended up spending Christmas Eve to New Year's Eve in the hospital.

My radiologist—Dr 'L'—was a young but very experienced radiologist specializing particularly in targeted radiation therapy. This meant that instead of the whole body or large parts of it being exposed to radiation, only the area around where the cancer had been discovered would be exposed. This was a big relief for me as it meant less chance of damage to or killing off of healthy cells during the radiation process, making the chances of adverse side effects far less. However, since my breast mass was not enough to shield my lung from the intense radiation of CyberKnife therapy, Tomotherapy was used instead.

Spending the Christmas to New Year's holidays in a hospital was certainly not something I was looking forward to, especially because Anil and I usually spent these holidays together deep in the heart of Mother Nature at our sanctuary. But I was very pleasantly surprised and reassured about the whole process when I met Doctor L. He was an avid conservationist and wildlife lover who had already heard about me and followed our work. Meeting him was a great joy as we shared stories of wildlife encounters. His passion for Nature was displayed inside the large radiation therapy room as well, with beautiful large photos of Nature adorning the walls.

One photo of a forested mountain slope with the sun shining above was especially beautiful, and helpful. It was placed on the ceiling, so I would see it while lying down before therapy started. I then continued to imagine the sun as a focal point for meditation and prayers for healing after being moved into the rather claustrophobic tube for treatments. The picture and meditation were actually so appropriate since the sun exists and is powered though nuclear fusion, with its energy from its nuclear core reaching Earth in the form of radiation.

The whole concept of nuclear medicine as a healing modality may seem a bit contradictory and quite ironic. All forms of nuclear therapies use some quantity of radioactive materials, all of which emit radiation. In use with cancer treatment, controlled high bursts of concentrated radiation energy are used to kill off deadly cancer cells. And yet, nuclear radiation is itself extremely deadly. Any look at the historical use of nuclear weapons illustrates how lethal the radiation was from the bomb blasts, radiation poisoning continuing to kill people exposed to it even decades after exposure.

Herein also lies the core dilemma with the use of nuclear power as an energy source to produce electricity—with its radioactive legacy that lasts for tens of thousands of years.

## Glowing Carrots

My introduction to the nuclear power industry came in the mid-1970s while Anil and I were living in Denver. I was at a supermarket waiting in the checkout line to pay for my purchases when my attention was drawn to a magazine in a rack in front of the cashier. On its cover was a strange photo—a woman holding up a bunch of glowing carrots with a shocked look on her face.

'What the heck is this?' I wondered, picking it up. The entire magazine was filled with articles about nuclear power and the dangers it posed to the public—not just in general, but right there in Denver where we were living, as well as in Grand Junction, which was part of my work territory.

The articles covered every aspect of nuclear power—from its use of the rare element uranium-235 for its fuel, to how the uranium is split through nuclear fission releasing massive amounts of energy, to the highly toxic radioactive wastes produced as by-products of the process, creating deadly health risks each step along the way to humans and the environment from start to finish.

The first step is mining for uranium as fuel. U-235 is a natural ore found in the earth's crust, but it is also relatively rare. In 1943, Grand Junction became a major centre for mining and refining the ore when the US war department bought fifty-four acres of land there to build a uranium refinery for the 'Manhattan Project'— the code name for America's research and production of its first atomic bomb.

One of the by-products of the uranium refining process after the rock is crushed and uranium extracted is a grey sandy material known as 'tailings'. Piled outside the mills in mounds, the material was free to take. As a result, it was used extensively in place of sand for all types of construction—from roads, sewers and an airfield, to all kinds of commercial buildings; from homes, schools and a shopping mall, to street sidewalks and park walkways, including being used in sand traps on golf courses and for filling children's sandboxes in playgrounds. In Grand Junction alone, over 594 buildings including fifteen schools, and at least 5000 homes were known to have been built with these tailings.

There's only one problem with using these 'free' uranium tailings for construction—they are radioactive! And they remain radioactive for over 10,000 years!

Within a few years of the tailings being used, unusual health problems started being noticed, especially among children and the unborn who are the most vulnerable to the effects of radiation. Some examples include a three-fold increase in miscarriages, many more children born with birth defects and suffering from childhood cancers, as well as an increase in lung cancers across all age groups. Clearly, something was wrong.

Investigations into the health problems identified radiation poisoning as the culprit. It was also discovered that, before the uranium tailings were given away for free, the mills had simply discharged the tailings along with the radioactive waste liquids into the nearest waterways for over ten years, contaminating the waters and spreading that contamination downstream throughout the Gunnison River area of Colorado.

As mentioned earlier, Dr L did not use CyberKnife radiation therapy on me because he was concerned that radiation may pass through my small breast mass and damage my lung, possibly leading to lung cancer. In Grand Junction, the lungs of the occupants residing in those thousands of homes built with uranium tailings were exposed to the equivalent of more than 553 chest x-rays per year! Is there any wonder that there was a huge upsurge in rates of lung cancer?!

It took decades to deal with this radioactive tragedy. By 1998, over 15 million cubic yards (1,14,68,322.87 cubic metres) of radioactive material had been removed from building foundations, schoolyards, playgrounds, pathways and sidewalks in Colorado alone. This does not include figures from uranium clean-ups in other states.

Who paid the bill for this massive clean-up? Answer: the US taxpayer—not the companies that had profited from the mines and caused the massive environmental health problems to begin with. But then, isn't that the way it always seems to be?

The ones who bore the greatest costs were the innocent people who got cancer or whose loved ones fell ill, those who lost their babies and children to miscarriages and birth defects, those who had their lives cut short and filled with sadness and pain—their 'costs' can never be repaid.

## More Nuclear Nightmares: Rocky Flats

What about where we were living at the time—Denver? The answer to that is Rocky Flats.

Located just sixteen miles northwest from the city of Denver, Rocky Flats produced plutonium 'triggers' for nuclear weapons from 1952 to 1989. For thirty-seven years the plant operated under a shroud of secrecy carefully woven and kept in place by the US federal government along with its private sector business partner Dow Chemical, which jointly oversaw the running of the plant. The public was consistently kept in the dark and, of course, never warned of the dangers the plant posed to them or to their families.

Hence, people knew nothing about the countless fires, leaks and accidents at the plant over the decades, nothing about the plant's two main large fires in 1957 and 1969 which caused radioactive plumes to settle downwind of the plant directly over the Denver metro area. Nor did they know about the 5000 contaminated barrels at the plant that leaked plutonium into the ground, or the fact that toxic elements were being regularly carried by the wind and water into surrounding neighbourhoods.

But there were signs that something was definitely wrong—a spike in various cancers, miscarriages and birth defects were once again the warning signals.

One man who tried to warn the public was Dr Carl Johnson, the health director for the area from 1973 to 1981—the same time period when Anil and I lived in Denver. He carried out a number of studies on the levels of contamination and associated health risks that the plant posed to the general public, his results showing that Rocky Flats was saturated with radioactive material.

In return for his integrity and dedication, Dr Johnson was fired—a typical tragic pattern that is repeated time and again when those who actually care about the ordinary people collide with those who care far more about money and profits, those who care often being the immediate losers, but whose concerns come back later on to haunt those vested and financial interests in one way or another.

Some years later, studies conducted by the US department of energy confirmed Johnson's findings, verifying that various radioactive and toxic contaminants including plutonium had routinely escaped from the plant. The government studies came only after Rocky Flats was raided in a joint operation between the FBI (Federal Bureau of Investigation) and the EPA (Environmental Protection Agency) in 1989. The raid unearthed several deadly and serious environmental hazards that put everyone in Denver—including us—and the surrounding areas at risk. Those in charge of the plant received criminal environmental law convictions.

Some of the toxins that had leaked from the plant included strontium-90 and caesium-137 which have half-lives of thirty years or so, meaning that half their radioactivity will decay in thirty years. However, others stay radioactive for tens of thousands of years, the most dangerous of all being plutonium. Invisible to the human eye, inhaling or ingesting just one-millionth of a gram causes cancer and up to three tons of it had escaped into the environment, with another fourteen tons of plutonium stored unsafely at the plant.

How long is plutonium dangerously radioactive? Plutonium's half-life is 24,000 years! Repeating that once again—**24,000 years for just half of it to decay**! How does one safely dispose of a substance that takes longer to decay by half than the time-period that modern man and his civilization have been on earth, since archaeologists and scientists put that date at about 10,000 BC?!

To put that into perspective, perhaps a *New York Times* article written by Peter Metzger on 31 October 1971 can help.* Writing about the grave responsibility we have to future generations and how our decisions to use nuclear power could spell disaster not just for us, but also for them, Metzger points to the deadly legacy that still remains the most troubling and insolvable problem with using nuclear power at all—those lethal radioactive wastes that stay lethal for a very long time.

---

*   https://www.nytimes.com/1971/10/31/archives/-dear-sir-your-house-is-built-on-radioactive-uranium-waste.html

As he put it, if the Great Pyramid of Giza in Egypt had been used by our ancestors to store radioactive wastes, about 15 per cent of radioactive radium in uranium tailings like those in Grand Junction would be hazardous today. But if plutonium like that at Rocky Flats had been stored there, the natural decay even after 5000 years would still leave 90 per cent of the original radioactivity in that plutonium intact and lethal!

After reading the various articles on nuclear and 'glowing carrots', I was left with a flood of different emotions—fear and anxiety about the next nuclear accident which seemed all but inevitable, anger at government officials and elected representatives for not protecting us and for allowing this deadly industry to exist and disgust for the companies that continued to peddle their toxic wares with lies and distortions all for the sake of profits no matter what the cost to the environment, to humanity today, or for generations in the far distant future.

While numb from the revelations, I knew that I had to act, to do whatever I could to stop this injustice and dangerous threat to our very survival. Spreading awareness about the problems and dangers of the nuclear industry, whether nuclear power as an energy source or nuclear weapons, seemed to be the best avenue to take. After all, I had been unaware of any of this until I had read the articles in that magazine, so what about the rest of the ordinary people like me.

Relying on local, printed media to spread the word would mean reaching a limited audience. So, I turned to television instead—a much wider audience with national channels broadcasting across the country.

I wrote a letter with facts and references from the articles and studies on all aspects of the aspects of nuclear power and the industry in general, and then sent copies of that letter to various television news organizations including TV news documentary programs like *60 Minutes* produced by CBS News, hoping to get someone to do an in-depth investigation into the entire industry.

However, the response from the news organizations was anything but enthusiastic. Most didn't reply at all. Of those that did, it was nothing more than a form letter thanking me for my own letter and topic suggestion for investigation, along with a few words regarding 'choosing our topics for investigation based on interest from the general public'—a catch-22, no-win solution in this case. Here I was hoping to have the news media spread awareness to the public while they were telling me that they only pursue things the general public is already aware of and interested in!

But perhaps my letter wasn't completely ignored. About nine months later, *60 Minutes* did indeed air a programme about the industry on 8 February 1976. The title of the segment was 'How safe is safe?' While it did not focus on the problems at Rocky Flats or Grand Junction, it did delve into the question of overall safety of nuclear plants in general, which was the main point in my letter.

The programme created some controversy with backlash and condemnation on the segment coming from various corners. When asked how they got the idea for the story, the staff at *60 Minutes* stated that 'it just came to us' from people who oppose nuclear power plants.

Did my little letter have any impact on their decision? I'll never know, but it certainly was gratifying to see at least some examination of the safety issue being brought out for ordinary people to see and hear.

Three years after the programme on *60 Minutes* aired, the nuclear industry became THE number one topic of discussion for everyone across the country. Three words explain why—

## Three Mile Island

Three Mile Island was the site of America's worst-ever nuclear accident so far, although there have been plenty of other accidents across the United States. The accident here started early in the morning on the 28 March 1979 due to a valve that was stuck in the open position which allowed steam and water to escape from the reactor core. This caused the core to overheat to a point of meltdown, leading to radioactive steam vented into the air outside the plant with no warning given to the local population until four hours after the accident began.

The core had already reached 4300 degrees. If the temperature rose to 5000 degrees, there would be no way of stopping the nuclear chain reaction no matter how much water was dumped on the core to cool it. The core would melt through the pressure vessel, through the concrete floor and fracture the earth for a quarter mile in all directions with geysers of radioactive steam shooting up from the cracks—a truly catastrophic, apocalyptic event referred to as 'the China syndrome', the idea being that the hot nuclear core would melt its way through the earth all the way to China. The plant was only thirty minutes away from this cataclysmic event.

As the core continued to heat up, increasing radioactive gases inside the reactor dome created a growing bubble of hydrogen gas that looked as if it might burst, triggering a massive explosion that would spew radioactive materials for many miles around. This coupled with the meltdown of the nuclear core would render part of Pennsylvania a radioactive wasteland, uninhabitable for decades, even centuries, to come.

Fortunately, the nuclear core did start to cool down finally, having been fully submerged in water once again. As a result, the hydrogen-gas bubble started to dissipate as well, ending the threat of a catastrophic explosion. However, the core was completely destroyed, and the reactor could never be used again.

America was lucky. Ukraine and Japan were not.

In 1986, while Ukraine was still part of the former USSR, the reactor core in the nuclear power plant in Chernobyl suffered a complete meltdown, leading to a massive explosion. At least thirty-one people were directly killed by the blast, with millions more exposed to radiation. Tens of thousands of later deaths have been attributed to that exposure over the following decades. Birth defects in children as far away as Sweden have been documented, the fallout from the deadly radiation being carried on the wind around the planet. Decades after the disaster, the areas around the plant are still too highly contaminated for human habitation, although as many as five million people still live in the contaminated areas.

As illustrated by the nuclear accident at Three Mile Island, nuclear plants need large quantities of water to cool the nuclear reactor core. This is why these power plants are always located near the ocean or by other large bodies of water. But, when the water used for cooling is released back into the natural water system, its temperature is higher than that of the normal water, which causes sudden depletions in the water's oxygen levels as well. This, coupled with the sudden changes in temperature, traumatizes aquatic life, leading to 'thermal shock' and death.

Beyond the devastating effect on aquatic life, this necessity to have huge amounts of water puts nuclear plants themselves at risk of natural disasters, as was so dramatically illustrated by the major nuclear accident at the Daiichi Nuclear Plant in Fukushima, Japan, in March 2011. A major earthquake caused a giant tsunami/tidal wave to sweep across Japan's coastline, the wave smashing into the Fukushima nuclear power plant located on the ocean's shore. This in turn caused the plant's cooling systems to shut down and swamped the diesel-powered generator-run backup systems as well.

With no water circulating to keep the uranium cores covered and cool, the cores overheated to the point that they melted, leading to dramatic explosions of gases that built up in the reactor rooms. Massive quantities of radioactive materials were released into both the air and the sea, contaminating both. Hundreds of thousands of people living nearby had to be evacuated and at least

2000 people died as a result of the accident. Years later, the area is still too highly radioactive to allow any of the former residents to return—a fact all too graphically illustrated by the mutated plants and animals now found at both Fukushima and Chernobyl.

Catastrophic accidents like those at Chernobyl and Fukushima point out the dangers of nuclear power all too grimly, and there are far more accidents at nuclear power plants around the world than anyone may think. In the USA alone, there have been fifty-six nuclear accidents (as of May 2021), with twenty or more in Japan.[*]

Here in India, there were no less than six serious accidents between 1987 and 2002, and an overall total of at least seventeen. The most dangerous ones involved the plants' nuclear core—one at Kalpakkam in 1987 where the core was ruptured and one at the Narora plant in Bulandshahr, UP, in 1993, which almost led to a core meltdown like those in Fukushima and Chernobyl. All accidents involved a certain amount of radioactivity being released into the environment, with large amounts of radioactive materials leaked into the Rana Pratap Sagar River in 1995 from Rajasthan's Kota Nuclear Plant.[†] Half or more of these accidents have caused the nuclear power plants involved to be shut down for a minimum of one to two years for repairs—repairs that cost millions and in some cases, hundreds of millions or even billions of US dollars. Estimates for costs of the Fukushima clean-up are between $100 billion to $200 billion, with some long-term estimates at $1 trillion.

This does not include the costs of relocations of whole communities, or the medical costs of long-term illnesses suffered by those exposed to the radiation. Who really pays for these costs is still unclear—the company involved, or the country's taxpayers.

---

[*]   Refer to the bibliography for source.
[†]   Refer to the bibliography for source.

A more recent incident considered the second most dangerous nuclear accident in India took place on 11 March 2016—ironically exactly five years after the Fukushima disaster started. The Kakrapar Nuclear Plant in Gujarat developed heavy water leaks and had to have an emergency shutdown. The problem, however, was far more serious and worrisome than initially thought, as well as being totally unexpected. According to nuclear veteran Shiv Abhilash Bhardwaj, chairman of India's Atomic Energy Regulatory Board (AERB):

> . . . a leak of this nature in an actively running atomic station has never occurred in India. (There was) no inkling for such an incident . . .

The key question was how these leaks could happen since the pressure tubes of the reactors' coolant channels had been replaced with special zircaloy tubes just four years before the accident. This is a major concern for nuclear experts as the accident was unprecedented, the pipes being covered with corrosion resembling 'smallpox'.

Now these same top nuclear experts are calling for a complete review of the safety of all twenty-two nuclear reactors in operation in the seven nuclear plants in India, some even calling for all to be shut down until the review is conducted. They are particularly concerned about the seventeen other reactors that are of the same design as the one in Kakrapar. It is vital to ascertain whether this problem was an isolated incident, or if all reactors of this pressurized heavy water design (PHWR) could have the same weakness, Bhardwaj stressing that

> . . . all caution has to be exercised . . .
> until this is determined.

The seriousness of nuclear accidents may vary, but the point is that accidents do indeed happen, and they are far more frequent than we can afford. This is particularly true considering the deadly consequences of meltdowns and radioactive explosions, especially in view of the industry's alarming track record for major meltdowns—one per decade—certainly a figure to increase as older plants start having more maintenance problems and the frequency of natural disasters increases as well. This doesn't begin to deal with the question of security at nuclear plants possibly being targeted by terrorists, mentally unstable individuals, or during any armed conflicts or skirmishes between countries.

## Lethal Legacy

Beyond the question of accidents is the issue of the toxic waste that all nuclear plants create—waste that stays radioactive for thousands of years. After only five years in a reactor, nuclear fuel stops working efficiently and needs to be replaced. However, approximately 95 per cent of the spent fuel is still original uranium that is now extremely hot and hazardous having become mixed with fission products and deadly plutonium along with other materials.

The problem of what to do with this lethal mess has been one of the main drawbacks to using nuclear power since its inception and is still unresolved. Tens of thousands of metric tonnes of used solid fuel and millions of litres of radioactive liquid waste litter the earth, most kept in temporary storage containers that were never meant to hold these deadly substances for so long, some of the waste dating back to the 1940s.

Whether dumping it at sea, burying it in the ground in concrete silos, or even placing it in deep geological repositories, all methods have failed to stop the radiation from oozing out into the environment and contaminating air, soil and water. Virtually all dumping sites are leaking radiation, with plutonium levels in just one site measuring one thousand times above normal. Even sealing it in glass through vitrification and then storing it in stainless steel cannisters, as the UK, France, and some other countries do, will not work in the long term. Eventually the steel cannisters will corrode, allowing water to seep in between the steel and glass or ceramic, triggering a series of corrosive reactions in both glass and steel, leading once again to leakage of radioactive material into the environment.

At present, most nuclear waste is stored near the world's nuclear plants and processing facilities—a 'do nothing' non-solution to the problem, putting the burden of dealing with this lethal legacy on the next generation as the global and national stockpiles of these deadly materials grow higher and higher each day. A recent statement underscoring this dangerous situation stunned the world in April 2021 when Japan announced it will release more than one million tonnes of contaminated water from the destroyed Fukushima plant into the ocean despite the objections from its own fishing industry as well as from neighbouring nations like South Korea. The reason is that the storage capacity at the crippled plant for contaminated materials will run out in the fall of 2022.

Decommissioning of old nuclear plants that are no longer efficient or safe to run is another major cost and concern of going nuclear. The plants must be taken apart piece by piece with extreme care and disposed of in a manner that does not expose the surrounding environment to contamination—a process that takes up to sixty years. Considering the levels of radiation at these plants, this is very difficult to do.

In addition, while the safe operating life of a nuclear power plant is supposed to be between thirty to forty years, the actual life span is much shorter in almost every instance. Not a single nuclear plant anywhere in the world has been running for fifty years (as of May 2021) and several had to be closed down permanently, having run for no more than a dozen or so years. This includes

Three Mile Island which was only four months old at the time of
the accident!

Even when closed plants have been sealed in concrete, as
was done in Chernobyl, the radiation within the plant 'eats away'
at the concrete causing cracks that allow it to escape into the
environment, as has been documented in Chernobyl, the fractures
there appearing in less than thirty years.

Any way one looks at it, 'time' is not on the side of nuclear
power, and not just because of the problems with its long-lived
toxic radiation. Even building new nuclear power plants is not
a quick solution to energy needs at all since it usually takes a
minimum of a decade or longer to build a plant. Every new nuclear
plant around the world is behind schedule, and these delays are
increasing the costs of plants exponentially.

This is in part why virtually all of them are over budget,
costing far more than what was originally promised by those
building them—as much as a billion dollars more per plant,
the average cost of building a new plant running over $9 billion
(Rs 6,68,43,76,50,000) per unit.

Finally, climate change itself coupled with nuclear power's
need for water to cool the nuclear core may well be the final
death knell of the industry. As temperatures across the planet
continue to rise, they heat the very water sources nuclear plants
need to cool their cores. Today, water sources are becoming too
warm to use for cooling purposes even in plants operating in
Europe, so what about plants here in equatorial regions where
temperatures are even higher!

In addition, the increased droughts in various parts of the
world are making access to cooling water for nuclear plants more
difficult as water levels in lakes and rivers drop. Across the USA
nuclear plants have had to scale back production either because
of cooling water being too warm to use, or due to lack of water
because of diminished rainfall.

As climate change kicks in, more and more coastal areas will be flooded as a result of the continued melting of polar ice caps and glaciers. This will certainly cause even more problems for the nuclear industry as sea-level rise means flooded plants during storms and high tides.

Ironically, while nuclear power is being touted as an alternative to coal-fired plants to aid in stopping climate change, the truth is nuclear power cannot survive if climate change is not solved first!

In order to help combat climate change, we need viable, safe and economical replacement sources for energy now—not decades from now. As an industry that is already plagued with far too many problems and too few solutions, nuclear power clearly does not fit the bill with nuclear power currently accounting for only 1.8 per cent of India's national power production (as of the first quarter 2020).* But it is also true that reliance on fossil fuels like coal needs to be stopped immediately—something I came to understand decades ago while driving in the beautiful Rocky Mountains.

## Vanishing Tops

As mentioned earlier, one of the reasons I decided to take the job with the pharmaceutical company was because there was a good deal of travel involved. My work territory covered some of the most beautiful parts of the Western USA—Colorado, Wyoming, Nebraska and South Dakota, with occasional trips to New Mexico, Utah, Texas and Arkansas.

I was out on the road at least three weeks of every month thoroughly enjoying the unspoiled beauty of the areas I was driving through. Nature dressed in all her splendour, with

---

* Refer to the bibliography for source.

different colours and natural elements prevailing depending on the season.

Spring brought her flowers and vivid new leaves, with streams and rivers rushing past with the season's snowmelt. Summer's trees and plants wore deeper greens outlined by the brilliance of the sapphire-blue skies. Autumn's spectacular array of colours painted leaves and plants in brilliant hues of yellow, gold and orange, shades of pinks, crimson and deep reds, mixed with lavenders, violets and purples.

Winter's white cloak transformed everything into a wonderland of snow-covered mountains and forests, ice encasing branches and twigs while icicles hung down like crystal fingers off the ends of the boughs, buildings and even signboards.

My favourite area to drive through by far was the Rocky Mountains. There were special places throughout my journeys that I especially looked forward to seeing on each trip. A few of these included mountain streams and open meadows, often filled with herds of elk. The majestic antlers of the males would gleam in the sun as they would strut among the females, the rutting season bringing amazing displays of strength as the males would vie with one another for territory, females and the right to breed.

During winter, the boulders in the streams and along their banks would be topped with powdery snow, making them look like pure-white, giant, cotton balls. The streams' ice-encrusted waters flowing past would shimmer like silver ribbons in the middle of this pure-white landscape.

Some of the most breath-taking terrain was the mountain passes one travelled over to go from the eastern to the western slopes of the Rockies. It was fascinating to think that water from the rain and the snow that fell on the eastern part of the pass would eventually make its way to flow towards the Atlantic Ocean, while what fell on the western slopes would head toward the Pacific, often becoming a part of the Colorado River. This great river is the tool Mother Nature principally used to carve out one of the greatest wonders of the world—the Grand Canyon.

One fateful day, while enjoying the beauty of the mountains, I rounded a curve on one of the roads on the upper slopes, anticipating seeing one of the familiar peaks that had become one of my 'journey friends'. Looking up to see it, I was stunned—it wasn't there! It had vanished! But how could a mountain peak vanish? How could the whole mountain top be missing?!

Pulling off the road and stopping, I got out of the car to see if I could have already gone by it. But no—the mountain peak was gone. How?!

It was only after reaching Denver and asking around that I found out the awful truth—the mountain peak had literally fallen victim to one of the most environmentally destructive practices of coal mining called 'Mountain Top Removal' or MTR. In this process, the mountain top itself is blasted into a million pieces in order to reach veins, or seams, of coal beneath it.

Unlike traditional coal mining where a tunnel is dug into the side of a mountain or hill to access coal seams underground, this type of strip mining is used to access coal near the surface. It is far more destructive as the entire mountain from peak to base disappears, leaving behind nothing but mounds of rubble and dead trees littering the landscape.

Whatever streams or other water sources there may have been in the area become highly polluted, blackened by the sludge that results from washing the coal as it comes out. Amounts of over 3000 tons of various deadly heavy metals and other toxins such as arsenic, mercury, copper and lead are flushed into these waterways. All of these substances cause cancer and have other devastating effects on humans and on wildlife as well, especially affecting fish and other aquatic life living in water bodies located downstream from these noxious and disastrous mining operations.

Mounds of debris dumped into waterways slow or stop their natural flow, making the concentration of contaminants higher in the standing water. The toxins also percolate down to aquifers/underground water bodies below, poisoning them as well, rendering virtually all fresh water sources useless for supporting life including human life.

These valley fills do the most damage destroying headwater streams and surrounding forests—the very foundation and fabric of critical ecosystems. Over 2000 miles of vital headwaters have been poisoned and buried through debris mounds, along with 1.4 million acres of forest destroyed as MTR has already blown up 500 of America's most ancient and biologically rich mountains.

Coal mining and mining in general have had their serious effects on India's environment, too, as well as on the people living around the mining sites.

All of these mines are located in what were once pristine forest areas, developed in spite of objections from the local people. The valiant fight of the Dongria Kondh tribal community against the British mining giant Vedanta captured the attention of people not only in India, but around the world as the indigenous people struggled to keep their sacred Niyamgiri Mountain from being destroyed by Vedanta's plans for mountaintop removal. The entire ecosystem will be destroyed if MTR is allowed.

A true 'David versus Goliath' story with overtones from the movie 'Avatar', the Dongria Kondh used everything at their disposal to stop Vedanta—from roadblocks and human chains stopping bulldozers, to reaching out to the international community to bring pressure to bear on Vendanta.

It was India's supreme court that saved the day with a ruling in 2013 that mining could not be done in any area without the permission of the local village government—the Gram Sabha.

No matter where the mining is done, its destruction of vital, fresh-water sources is only the first of coal's impact on water. Coal-fired power plants consume literally tons of gallons (one gallon equals 3.79 litres) of the precious element, making it second only to agriculture in water consumption. When the plant's cooling water is released back into nearby water sources, its temperature is higher and contains less oxygen than that of normal stream water, causing thermal shock and death to aquatic life in the same way as the water used to cool the core of nuclear plants.

Coal's dangerous production of poisonous toxins does not end with mining either. In just one year, a typical 500MW coal-fired plant will produce 170 pounds (77.3 kilos) of mercury, 225 pounds (102.3 kilos) of arsenic, 114 pounds (51.9 kilos) of lead, 4 pounds (1.9 kilos) of cadmium, plus other toxic heavy metals.*

How dangerous is this? One-seventieth of a teaspoon of mercury put into a twenty-five-acre lake makes the fish in the lake unfit for consumption, with exposure to mercury causing brain damage, learning disabilities and neurological disorders. As small as fifty parts per billion of arsenic dissolved in water leads to cancer in those who drink that water, while heavy metals like lead, chromium and cadmium cause mental retardation, developmental disorders, heart problems and damage to the nervous system.

Besides polluting water sources, the mining, production and burning of coal causes massive air pollution which is disastrous for the environment, wildlife and humans. In an average year, the amount of just carbon dioxide generated by a 500MW coal-fired plant is 3.7 million tonnes—that's comparable to cutting down 161 million trees.

---

*   Refer to the bibliography for source.

Other toxic gases released into the air include sulphur dioxide, nitrogen oxide, heavy metals and particulate matter (PM) to name a few. Virtually all the pollutants are carcinogens (cause cancer) and have been linked with the entire spectrum of lung-related diseases such as inflammation of lung tissue, bronchitis, reduction in lung function, lung cancer including black lung disease, headaches, brain and heart disorders as well as birth defects.

MTR is especially polluting as the explosives used in this mining process cause massive amounts of dust particles to fill the air, coating everything and everyone around for many miles including water sources and farmlands. This dangerous layer of fine particles/PMs poisons the land and destroys topsoil, leading to desertification, all the while being inhaled into the lungs by anything that breathes, including people.

Even though laws in the US state that areas destroyed in this manner must be restored, they are never the same. How could they be since the entire topography has been changed from peak to flat barren land. The forests that once covered the mountain with wildlife and water sources they supported are all gone. The sparse non-native grasses and a few saplings planted in their place are a bad joke since many saplings will not survive to maturity in order to provide the ecosystem services that the mature forest had given free of cost. It will take many decades, perhaps generations before the lands really return to anything resembling the once pristine woodlands, meadows and waterways filled with wildlife that were once there.

Speaking of costs, coal is often promoted as a cheap source of fuel for power generation, but the opposite is true, as pointed out by a recent study by Harvard Medical School. To establish coal's actual cost to society, one must tally up all health, environmental and economic expenditures associated with the mining, production, transport and burning of coal for energy—an estimated $500 billion (Rs 3,71,35,42,50,00,000.01) annually—and then add those expenses to the price of coal. With the addition of these costs, the price of coal is tripled.

It is important to note that these annual expenses are not borne by the coal companies, but by the general public. Plus, this figure does not reflect the environmental costs of releasing heavy metals and carcinogens into waterways, the deaths and injuries of miners, or the social impacts of mining on mining communities. Clearly, the true cost of coal is far higher than what we all thought.

## Climbing Temperatures = Nature Out of Balance

Coal is one of the oldest fossil fuels used by humans. It is largely the widespread use of coal in the 1800s that fuelled the start of the industrial revolution that turned our basically agrarian societies around the world into industrial manufacturing systems—systems that have left many parts of the earth severely environmentally damaged, while taking a major toll on human health as well. From smog and acid rain, to dead water bodies and lost forests, coal costs us and the environment at every level in every way.

However, the most dangerous environmental impact of the use of coal is surely climate change, with rising temperatures threatening the very existence of life as we know it on the planet, including human life. Industrialization with the use of coal has been the principal driver behind the rise in global temperatures. The release into the atmosphere of greenhouse gases (GHGs) like carbon dioxide, methane and nitrous oxide along with a host of others through the burning of coal block the escape of solar radiation from the earth back into space. This is similar in effect to a blanket covering the planet.

The rising temperatures play havoc with the natural systems of the Earth upon which we depend for survival. From changing weather patterns and extreme weather events like devastating droughts to overwhelming floods that are quickly becoming the new 'norm', our climate is in a state of flux trying to cope with the higher temperatures to achieve equilibrium and balance once again. Meanwhile deaths from unprecedented hotter temperatures are global, with subsequent losses of food crops translating into malnutrition and starvation in many parts of the planet.

It's important to understand that virtually everything that happens in Nature does so on the basis of temperature. Blossoms bloom, leaf buds unfold, wildlife migrate and raise their young according to the temperatures of the seasons, with predators largely reproducing according to the life cycles of their prey species. This synchronicity of life cycles is what keeps Nature in balance.

As temperatures climb, these synchronistic life cycles are thrown off-kilter, often because prey species respond faster to environmental changes than do their predators. This is due to the shorter life span of many prey species. Each new generation shifts its reproductive and migration responses to changing temperatures that affect their food source.

Insects respond to the changes in temperatures that trigger the cycles of life, regeneration and death in plants since plants are the main source of food for so many of them. With warmer temperatures occurring earlier each year, trees and plants put forth their foliage sooner. Thus, the insects react with earlier arrivals in areas and earlier reproductive activities like the laying of eggs for the next generation as well.

Key predators of many insects are the various species of birds who also respond to these changes. But, due to their longer life cycle, the shift is slower, so it takes longer. This creates a disruption of this critical synchronicity of cycles. The birds end up missing the peak hatching season of insects, thereby having less food to feed their own young.

Human-driven climate change is upsetting the life cycles of plants and animals across the planet from pole to pole. With warmer temperatures thawing ice in the north polar region, polar bears are having great difficulty catching their normal prey of seals. The thawing ice means the bears cannot travel the great distances they need to in order to find adequate prey to eat to build up enough fat reserves to see them through the long winter.

In the south polar region, melting ice jeopardizes the birthing grounds of penguins, the now open waterways allowing ocean predators like leopard seals to penetrate further into the nursery grounds before the young are old enough to take to the ocean and swim away.

Warmer temperatures are creating apocalyptic scenes of destruction throughout the world's coral reefs. Coral is extremely sensitive to changes in temperatures. A rise of just one or two degrees causes coral polyps to expel the algae that live in them. Coral normally provide shelter for the algae, while the algae provide food for the coral in return through the process of photosynthesis, supplying 90 per cent of coral's nutritional needs. The algae are also responsible for giving coral their brilliant and beautiful colours. With the loss of their algae partners and therefore their source of food, coral literally starve to death—a tragic ending to this normally extraordinary symbiotic relationship that has gone on for millennia.

In the end, nothing is left but the brittle, bleached-white coral skeletons as testimony to the once thriving, life-filled ecosystem that existed there, these scenes of devastation also bearing testimony to the deadly impact human-induced rising temperatures are having on the world's oceans and the entire planet.

With the death of the coral reef which normally provides habitat for 25 per cent of all aquatic species, fish of all sizes disappear—from small species that used the reef for homes and hiding places, to all species that utilize it for egg-laying sites; from various fish species that ate the laid eggs and hatchlings, to sea mammals that would feed on this abundance of prey—all important players of this once-inhabited, biodiverse, essential ecosystem of life on planet Earth.

Humanity's use of coal and other fossil fuels is even changing the very chemical composition of the oceans due to the massive amount of carbon dioxide in their waters, further damaging coral reefs. Between 25 per cent to 50 per cent of all carbon is absorbed by the oceans, making them one of the Earth's main carbon sinks. Carbon combines with ocean water to make a weak form of carbonic acid. The more carbon there is, the stronger the carbonic acid.

The excess carbon dioxide humanity is pumping into the air is making ocean waters more acidic. This impacts the ability of many aquatic creatures to create the shells and exoskeletons they use as bodies since they make them from calcium carbonate—a substance that dissolves in carbonic acid—thereby threatening their very existence. Examples of affected species include not only coral, but also shellfish like oysters, mussels and clams, lobsters, crabs and shrimp and even some species of plankton, impacting the entire food chain from fish to whales.

Oceans of life are critical for the survival of life on the planet, including human life. If the oceans die, we die with them. They are one of the most essential parts of Nature's balance—a balance we are upsetting by our continued use of coal and other fossil fuels.

The question is, have we learned anything from our experiences using coal and nuclear power? Our ancestors valued the wisdom passed on to them from their elders and their own experiences, learning from them to avoid tragedy in the future. But unfortunately, present-day humans seem to suffer from a very short memory, and in spite of everything, profits still trump safety. This is even in the face of new reports showing carbon dioxide levels in the atmosphere hitting the highest concentrations in human history—419 parts per million in May 2021—the highest amount in millions of years.*

Still, scientific warnings are not being taken seriously. Russia, China and Australia, along with other countries, are still set on building new coal-fired plants. The huge additional quantities of greenhouse gases expelled from these plants will make it impossible to stop temperatures from rising above the goal of just 1.5 degrees Celsius increase. These higher temperatures will surpass environmental tipping points, triggering rapid, runaway, uncontrollable climate change, thereby endangering survival of all life on the planet including humanity.

All of these dangerous actions are being done just to heat water, to produce steam, to turn turbines, to produce electricity, the coal or uranium being the material used to heat that water. Is this really worth the risk?

Therefore, today we stand at a crossroads—which energy source should we use to supply the growing global demand for electricity. Clearly coal must be phased out if we are to prevent climate change from getting any worse. But nuclear power is obviously not safe enough to take its place.

Let's contemplate these facts for a moment—the coal and other fossil fuels we burn today started forming hundreds of millions of years ago. In just 200 years, we have burned up massive quantities, and there isn't much left, all the while endangering the future existence of life on the planet through global warming. The fuel source for nuclear power is also rare, and the process produces deadly wastes that remain lethally radioactive for tens of thousands of years, also endangering future generations of all life forms on the planet. Do we really have the right to do this?

---

* Refer to the bibliography for source.

We can answer that question using the wisdom of the great Native American prophet Deganawida who reminds us,

> In our every deliberation we must consider the impact of our decisions on the next seven generations.[*]

How many more generations will there be if we continue to seed the planet with radioactive 'timebombs'? How can life on the planet survive if we continue to stab Mother Earth in the heart, carving out deep caverns for the sake of black ore and other fossil fuels, turning her forests into wastelands and waterways into poisonous sewers? How can Mother Nature sustain her balance of life when the noxious smoke and gases from our continued burning of these fuels causes temperatures to rise so high that ecosystems collapse across the world, causing wars and conflicts over dwindling natural resources as a result?

Faithkeeper of the Turtle Clan, Chief Oren Lyons of the Onandago Nation of Native Americans answers these questions directly, stating,

> Leaders of the world, there can be no peace as long as we wage war on our Mother the Earth. Responsible, courageous actions must be taken to realign ourselves with the great laws of Nature. We must meet this crisis now, while we still have time.[†]

Perhaps some leaders actually *are* listening. For decades India has had to rely on its coal and nuclear power plants for energy production. But today, it is getting international recognition for its development and installation of solar power throughout the country. So, there *is* hope!

---

[*]    Refer to the bibliography for source.
[†]    Refer to the bibliography for source.

For thousands of years, indigenous peoples have lived in balance and harmony with Nature beneath the sun. Perhaps we should learn from them and embrace the sun as well . . .

# 9

# To the Land of Rainbows and Angels
# of the Sea

Emerald green jewels rising from a sapphire sea, girdled with a string of pearly white breakers lapping the shore; a double rainbow arcing in the sky—the beauty of the Hawaiian Islands took my breath away!

It was mid-October 1976. We were on our month-long honeymoon and couldn't wait to touch down in Honolulu to start our exploration of these stunning wonders of Mother Nature. Each island had been formed by the lava spewed forth from the earth's fiery depths, the molten rock first emerging through volcanic vents in the floor of the sea and then slowly rising up above the sea to become visible volcanoes.

We drove around the island of Oahu to enjoy the scenic beauty and later, went to an aquarium and sea park to see the various species of aquatic animals there. The main attraction for visitors was a 'show' featuring different animals, including dolphins and orcas, or killer whales.

The aerial acrobatics and synchronized jumps of the dolphins were amazing to see, as were the tricks performed by the orcas. We did not know then of the cruelty involved in much of the training of these magnificent creatures, or the high degree of intelligence that they possessed—higher than our own, according to some marine specialists. A comparison between the two reveals why these scientists say this.

When the brains of cetaceans like dolphins and whales are compared with those of primates like humans, cetaceans come out on top in a number of ways, starting with the fact that they can stay awake for two weeks and are semi-conscious at all times, turning off only half or one hemisphere of their brain at a time during sleep—a vital requirement since their breathing is under their voluntary control, unlike humans. Comparisons in the areas of communication and even emotion are even more revealing. The primary sense and means of communication for cetaceans, like dolphins, is auditory. Ours is a combination of visual, followed by verbal. We see something and then have to try to describe it in words, with something always being 'lost in translation'.

With the exception of baleen whales, most cetaceans use sonar to perceive something. They then directly project to others an exact auditory image that is identical to the sonar image that they have received. It is similar in concept to projecting a three-dimensional holographic image directly into the brain of someone else. This completely eliminates the step of 'translation' from one sense to another. They are even able to 'sonogram' fellow animals through their sonar, 'seeing' the condition of inner organs to determine the health and emotional state of one another. In this way, cetaceans are able to receive and convey twenty times the amount of information we humans can get with our sight or hearing!

Regarding emotions, it is the limbic system in the brains of both cetaceans and humans that deals with emotions and the formation of memories. But in comparison to the brain of humans, the cetacean limbic system is huge—so large that it actually 'erupts' into the cortex part of their brain as an extra paralimbic lobe.

Like humans, the brains of cetaceans also have spindle neurons—associated with emotions like love and grief, but also linked to the ability to perceive and communicate, recognize, remember and reason, understand and solve problems as well as adapt to change. This, combined with their exceptionally large limbic system, not only reveals the complexity of their brains, but also how much they think and feel. In addition, cetaceans exhibit a sense of self-awareness, as do humans, recognizing their own reflection and having individualized whistles that they use to identify themselves in the same way as humans use names. Clearly, this amazing mixture of abstract understanding and problem-solving, learning and cognitive thinking, a sense of individual self-awareness and deep emotional feelings gives great credibility to the argument that cetaceans are indeed smarter than we humans are.

However, both Anil and I were unaware of any of this. Nor were we aware that the cetaceans we were watching had been captured in the wild and cruelly separated from their family pods or groups. We had no idea that their family was first terrorized and then driven to shallow waters by boats, where those selected for capture, were separated from the rest. The remaining members of the family were usually killed in the process, in order to coerce those captured to become completely dependent on their human kidnappers for survival. Those kidnapped suffered not only the trauma of being kidnapped, but also of witnessing these bloody murders.

The chosen ones were almost always very young—adolescents and even babies—forcibly ripped away from their mothers and their other close relatives, all family members being deeply devoted to one another. Perhaps this deep devotion was due in part to the 'pack mentality' they may have had millions of years ago, when they were four-legged, dog-like animals roaming the earth eating both meat and vegetation.

Wild dogs and wolves that live in family packs are incredibly close, hunting as a group, eating, sleeping and caring for each other and for the pack's offspring together, for the good of the whole family. Similarly coordinated group hunting has been seen in both dolphin and whale pods—perhaps something carried forward over the millennia of their evolution, along with their devotion and love for each family member. Physical adaptations that took millions of years have transformed these previously land-based animals into creatures that not only live and survive in the seas but thrive in them.

However, clues to their previous form can still be found today in the skeletons of the flippers of dolphins that show the bone structure of their previous five-toed ancestors known as 'mesonyx'. Existing approximately 95 million years ago, these animals spent most of their time around marshy areas and other initially fresh water sources, to eat and hunt.

As they spent more and more time in the water, their bodies started to change drastically, adapting to a life spent in water. Examples of similar changes and possible evolutionary stages can be seen in other animals like otters, as well as in seals and sea lions. Front legs became pectoral fins or flippers with back legs disappearing, being replaced with horizontal flukes—the tail of a cetacean. Nostrils moved to the top of the head to become a blow hole as well as a key part of their echolocation system, external ears replaced with simple pin holes.

This evolutionary history of cetaceans that started about 50 million years ago apparently took place in the Indian subcontinent. Fossils documenting the various stages in their evolutionary physical changes and transition from a life spent on land to a life spent fully in the sea were first discovered in 1979 in north Pakistan, with subsequent findings in north-west India as well. They have had their present physical form for at least ten to fifteen million years, even though DNA evidence testifies to their previous ungulate/vegetation-eating past, their closest terrestrial relative today being the hippopotamus, with which they share a common ancestor. But again, Anil and I were completely ignorant of this incredible history of these creatures at the time.

We also never thought about the fact that they had to live out their lives in pools that, for them, were nothing but oversized bathtubs, or that being in these pools of captivity was literally torture for them since they navigate by using sonar signals and echolocation. Echolocation or bio-sonar is their ability to navigate and locate objects through sound. Cetaceans emit a sound wave that then hits an object and bounces back to them, enabling them to 'see' the location, size and shape of the object. They use this truly remarkable and highly advanced ability not only to travel, but also to protect themselves, and to locate and identify prey while hunting.

It is a complex process involving various organs and parts of the body. In the case of dolphins who have no vocal cords, sounds are generated through their use of nasal air sacs, the blowhole, larynx, lungs and an organ at the top of the head called 'the melon' which groups, amplifies and beams forward the sounds made. The sounds then bounce back from objects in the form of an echo which are received in the lower jaw, the teeth actually working like antennas to receive the signals. Perhaps, this is the main reason why baleen whales never developed echolocation, since they evolved small fibre-like baleen plates in the spaces between their teeth in their upper jaws to filter out food from water, these baleen plates eventually replacing their teeth altogether.

Through echolocation, dolphins can make and 'hear' sounds with a frequency as high as 120 kHz. In comparison, humans' hearing caps at 20 kHz, with dogs hearing up to 45 kHz and cats topping at 65 kHz. It is this acute sensitivity to sound waves that literally tortures cetaceans kept in the captivity of tanks since the reverberations from the sonar signals they send bounce off the walls of the tanks causing them terrible distress and suffering. As a result, dolphins have been documented banging their heads on the walls of these tanks while orcas have ended up wearing down their teeth from pulling at bars and biting the walls of their tanks.

Human-generated sonar from naval vessels is also causing terrible distress in cetaceans that use echolocation. Studies have now confirmed that the incidents of mass beaching or stranding of various species of cetaceans are tied directly to our use of sonar.* The sound pulses from the sonar act like a shot of adrenaline, literally scaring the poor animals to death. In this panicked state, their veins fill up with nitrogen gas bubbles, leading to severe brain haemorrhaging, damaging other vital organs as well. This decompression sickness is the whales' version of 'the bends', as a result of which the poor creatures suffer agonizing deaths. Researchers are now calling on sonar bans in all areas of the earth's oceans where whales are known to live and congregate to prevent these tragic and excruciating deaths of these wonderfully intelligent and gentle creatures.

In captivity, the suffering of these gentle beings is not only physical, but emotional as well. Cetaceans are social creatures that normally interact with members of their family groups or pods throughout their lives. Captive cetaceans kept in solitary confinement experience tremendous loneliness, leading to severe depression. Others are forced to perform tricks with fellow unfortunate captives, being solely dependent on their kidnappers for food, often only being fed when they perform their tricks to the satisfaction of their captors. The whole purpose of their imprisonment and performance of these tricks is to attract sufficient numbers of people who are willing to pay to see them.

As we gawked at them during their 'show', we had no appreciation of the boredom or suffering they had to endure, living

---

*   Refer to the bibliography for source.

out their lives in this dismal and depressing state. We had no idea that that can mean spending as long as sixty years for dolphins and up to eighty or ninety years for orcas—all this suffering for the sake of humans making money. These realizations came to us only later when we directly experienced the stark difference between captivity and freedom for these extraordinary, intelligent and loving creatures.

## In the Sea with Angels

We were spending Christmas and New Year's at a friend's place located in a thickly forested valley of Kauai, the oldest of the Hawaiian Islands. We stayed in their unique glass dome located by a mountain stream, surrounded by incredible rainforest beauty, enjoying the sights, sounds and scents of this pristine wilderness.

Our friends arranged for us to go on a rubber Zodiac boat to the North Shore of the island. That part of Kauai had no roads, so the only way to experience it was to trek and/or use the Zodiac boats to land on one of the deserted beaches there. We had already done day-treks, but the Zodiac allowed us to reach more isolated parts and trek further into this completely unspoiled part of the island. Mother Nature had created yet another perfect day for our outing, the brilliant sunlight sparkling like diamonds off the ripples of the sea. Going past these exquisite green mountains and valleys, with the occasional white-sand beach kissed by the gentle surf breaking on its shore, I was truly awe-struck.

And yet, deep inside, I was desperately hoping that we might be lucky enough to see a whale or better still, a family of dolphins. Saying some prayers to Mother Nature, I also sent out mental messages to whatever dolphins may be in the area, asking them to please, please come and visit us for a while.

The way out was uneventful, though we had a marvellous time in the jungle and on the white sand beach where we landed and spent a few hours. There is truly something special, almost overwhelming, stepping on to a beach that has no human footprints on it—it is the same feeling I get whenever I see a pure, untouched, snow-covered mountain or meadow. One is transported back in time when humans did not roam the earth—when all of Nature was unspoiled by man and still in perfect balance. One hesitates to make any imprint on this perfect, unmarked part of Nature, the only prints in the sand being those of various seabirds looking for food where the surf meets the shore.

The absolute lack of any human sounds was so calming, so purifying—listening to the rhythmic breaking of the waves, the rustling of the palm fronds on the shore and the seabirds occasionally calling overhead. Silence, solitude, peace—one dared not even open one's mouth to utter a sound, as it would shatter the depth of the stillness and communion of spirit with the mother and with each other.

As the hours melted away and it was time to leave, the spiritual elevation that both Anil and I felt was unmistakeable and so appreciated. And yet, as our Zodiac headed back, I couldn't help feeling a tinge of disappointment that my prayerful request to the dolphins had not been fulfilled . . . that is, until we were suddenly surrounded by a large family of them!

There were at least twenty of them, of all sizes, including small babies. Some adults were surfing off the wake of the boat on the sides and at the stern, with others surfing off its bow in front. They were thoroughly enjoying themselves as were we, watching them, with some leaping out of the water for the sheer joy of life!

We turned off the motor and let the boat drift. Then, slowly and carefully we slipped over its edge into the water. The dolphins swam all around us keeping just out of arm's reach. The babies were curious, but moms made sure they were between the babies and us. Putting our heads under water we could hear their clicks and squeals, chirps and whistles as they communicated with each other. It was without a doubt one of the most amazing experiences of my life!

The dolphins stayed with us for at least twenty to thirty minutes and then continued on their way, swimming, leaping and diving as they went. After experiencing their sheer exhilaration of life, of living free in the vast, blue sea, their loving bonds that kept their family group together, how could I ever enjoy seeing them in the prison of a sea park aquarium again?!

The same was true about the orcas or killer whales—such magnificent, highly intelligent beings with deep family bonds. Some orca pods stay in a certain area and/or return to it seasonally like clockwork, unlike other pods that just pass through. An example of this can be seen in the Salish Sea, off the coast of Washington State in the USA and British Columbia in Canada. In these waters, three family pods of southern resident orcas have lived for tens of thousands of years, long before humans inhabited the region.

Their society is matrilineal, tracing their ancestry through their mothers, grandmothers and great-grandmothers, with both male and female offspring staying with their family group their entire lives. They communicate with one another using their own unique calls and sounds that can travel ten miles or more under water. Just how close members of these family groups are with one another was recently illustrated in a heart-breaking way through the sad saga of Tahlequah and her little baby, who died shortly after birth.

It is a poignant story of how the mother Tahlequah refused to abandon her dead calf, continually supporting it to the surface of the sea, pushing it in front of her wherever she went for at least seventeen days, before finally letting it sink into the ocean's depths—a public display of sorrow that touched the hearts of everyone around the world who heard about it.[*] The mother was not alone in her grief. At sunset on the day her baby died, a group of five or six female orcas from Tahlequah's family pod gathered together to form a close, tight-knit circle at the mouth of the cove.

---

[*]   https://en.wikipedia.org/wiki/Tahlequah_(killer_whale)

Witnesses reported they stayed there at the surface for almost two hours in the moonlight, moving together in a circular motion as if participating in some ancient ceremony.

This incident brings to mind images of another matriarchal society whose members display similar acts of mourning over the death of one of their own—elephants. Elephants have often been seen examining the bones of their dead, apparently determining who the dead individual was, while perhaps bidding them farewell as well.

The unutterably pathetic and shocking truth is that Tahlequah's calf is not the exception, but rather what has happened to every baby born in this family group for the last three years. Indeed, over the past two decades, 75 per cent of newborn orcas have not survived. Why? The answer, once again, is human activities, namely overfishing of the orca's prey like salmon; the building of dams which has caused salmon numbers to drop precipitously as they are unable to reach traditional spawning waters to reproduce; and chemical pollution.

Studies by fisheries' ecologists and conservationists have found that wild salmon numbers today are a mere 1.5 per cent of what they were before the Europeans came to the western hemisphere.* Both the orcas and the Chinook salmon, upon which the orcas depend, have now become endangered species.

Massive water pollution, both from trash like discarded plastics and various chemicals from agriculture, manufacturing and other industries, is impacting all aquatic life, including the orcas. The heavy concentrations of mercury and especially PCBs (polychlorinated biphenyls) not only cause a host of various cancers and other illnesses, but also interfere with reproductive development, leaving both dolphins and whales unable to bear young.

---

\* Refer to the bibliography for source.

The dangers of PCBs and their by-products like dioxin affect humans as well—toxic effects known as far back as the early 1960s by the main company that produced PCBs—Monsanto. This is the same company that manufactured the notorious defoliant 'Agent Orange' used extensively during the Vietnam War, and whose disastrous environmental and health effects still plague Vietnam and its population today.*

PCBs are now banned across the globe. But its deadly legacy persists in soils and waters since it does not break down/ biodegrade easily or quickly in the natural environment, becoming concentrated in the fatty tissues of fish. Those fish are then caught by orca like Tahlequah and her family pod, as well as by humans who are poisoned with every bite they eat. This terrible situation for all cetaceans will not change unless we literally clean up our own act.

## Compassionate Hearts and the Dolphin's Tale

While the sad story of the plight of cetaceans certainly has its human villains, it also has its human heroes—compassionate hearts and dedicated individuals who devote their lives to protecting and defending our environment, while helping the wildlife that has suffered so much at the hands of man. Indeed, not all aquariums are 'prison parks' only interested in making money from their 'star attractions'. Some are wonderful 'marine hospitals' whose teams rescue and rehabilitate cetaceans like dolphins and orcas as well as other marine life, with the ultimate aim of releasing them back into the wild, whenever possible.

The extraordinary work of one such marine hospital was documented in the movie *A Dolphin's Tale*—the true story of a dolphin called 'Winter'. An Atlantic bottlenose dolphin,

---

* Refer to the bibliography for source.

Winter was found when she was only about two months old on 10 December 2005. She was caught in a crab trap—the ropes of the trap were in her mouth and tightly wound around her tail as well. She was cut free of the ropes and then transported to the Clearwater Marine Hospital and Aquarium in Florida. The ropes of the crab trap had cut off circulation to her tail, eventually leading to the need to amputate it. Without a tail, the prognosis for any dolphin is very grim. But that didn't stop the dedicated marine biologist at Clearwater from trying to help her.

Eventually, a brilliant prosthetics doctor was approached to see if he could fashion a tail for Winter. Through trial and error, success was finally achieved with Winter accepting the new tail and once again, being able to swim like a dolphin. The work done on Winter's prosthetic tail has helped revolutionize prosthetics for humans as well, in areas ranging from materials used, to the locking mechanisms holding the prosthetic limb in place. Her story has also become an inspiration for many around the world who have disabilities, lost limbs, or suffered from their own health problems, especially for young children who have gained confidence in their own abilities to overcome obstacles and keep striving on.

As the filming of Winter's story was drawing to a close, another two-month-old dolphin was found close to where she had been rescued. It was also a little girl who was desperately trying to nurse from her dead mother—a pitifully tragic sight to behold, indeed. The staff of Clearwater rescued her and named her 'Hope', hand-feeding her the same way they had done with Winter, exactly five years and one day earlier.

Dolphins, like all cetaceans, are not fish. They are mammals just like us. They bear their young live and nurse them on mother's milk, just like us. Throughout this nursing period, which can last at least 3 to 4 years or longer, the young are completely dependent on their mothers for food since, like us, they are born with no teeth to catch and eat fish. They are also totally dependent on their mothers for protection and for teaching them the skills they will need to survive in the wild, which is why dolphins and other young cetaceans stay near their mothers for several years. In the case of dolphins, that's up to six years.

In the case of orcas also, the calves nurse for at least two or more years and will stay close to their mothers their entire life if possible, thereby greatly increasing their own chances of survival. One study revealed that male orcas, in particular, are dependent on their moms, having an eight times better chance of survival if their moms are there, with females having at least a two to three times better survival rate. Clearly, moms are critically important for all cetaceans just like they are for us.

All of the individual members of a family pod that stays together live far, far longer, even into their nineties, in some cases. This is many years beyond their prime reproductive age, with females going through a menopause, just like humans, in their late forties. The dorsal fins of orcas are as individual as human fingerprints, which makes it easy for researchers to identify and track individuals, even over decades.

While Hope had not been injured like Winter, she had been orphaned too young in life to be released back into the wild. So, the Clearwater crew wished that little Hope would be accepted by Winter and vice versa so that both dolphins would have a lifelong companion. A second movie about little Hope and her journey of love and friendship with Winter has also been made—a truly heart-warming and inspirational tale of compassion, dedication and love that illustrates so beautifully the best qualities of human beings as well.

While Winter and Hope could not be released into the wild, the hospital crew have been able to help other rescued dolphins do just that. One such dolphin was called Mandy. Other rescued and released wildlife include pelicans and sea otters, with all species in need being helped by this wonderful group of compassionate hearts. Many of these animals had been injured due to the activities of man. Whether being entangled in the ropes of a crab trap or fishing lines or being caught in fishing nets or suffering from swallowing fishhooks, wildlife at sea suffers horrifically from both the activities and the garbage humans thoughtlessly dispose of in waterways as well.

The gentle manatee, as well as its cousin, the Indian dugong, are common victims of the propellers of our power boat motors which cut their bodies. Turtles end up with our discarded plastic straws stuck in their nostrils, which causes even more pain and problems for turtles as virtually all turtle species around the world are threatened with extinction due to human overexploitation and habitat loss. Whales and others die from ingesting the plastic refuse we so mindlessly toss away, with each death of a member of another wild species negatively impacting the marine ecosystems and Earth's biosphere as a whole. An example of this would be the critically important whales in our oceans.

## The Songs of Angels

'Look! Look! There they are—a family of humpbacks!' Anil and I watched in excitement as a group of humpbacks swam in the ocean in front of us. 'How incredible!' Anil exclaimed, as one of them breached, thrusting its huge body out of the water, coming down with a gigantic splash! Truly a spectacle that takes your breath away in its demonstration of power, magnitude and grace.

We were standing on the shore of the Kona Coast of the Big Island of Hawaii. The Pacific Ocean waters surrounding the Hawaiian Islands have been declared a National Marine Sanctuary by the USA. These waters are both the mating and birthing grounds for this iconic and wonderfully remarkable whale species—the humpback whale. We were privileged to see them many times over the years on both coasts of the Big Island.

Each year, up to 10,000 humpbacks migrate to Hawaii. The pregnant humpbacks that make this journey travel there to give birth due to the warmth of the Hawaiian waters. Unlike their moms, newborn calves lack that thick layer of blubber that insulates whales from the icy temperatures of the polar oceans. The waters of Hawaii give these babies a warm welcome to a life that will be lived in the sea.

It is in Hawaiian waters that these amazing giants sing their extraordinary, hauntingly beautiful songs, filled with astonishing intricacies of sound and variation. Each year brings new ornamentations and embellishments in rhythm, notes and key to the melodic theme of the previous year's song. While females do vocalize as well, is appears to be the males that engage in the more intricate song creations. All males in one area sing the same melody, with humpbacks in other areas singing their own distinct songs—songs that can last up to twenty minutes or more.

Scientists have yet to figure out exactly why the humpbacks sing. Initially, it was thought to be part of courtship—a way to advertise to females the presence of the males in the waters. While this may be partly true, male humpbacks have also been seen singing to other males, following the songs to meet each other. They have also been observed singing while accompanying a humpback mother and her calf as they travel together.

Whatever their reasons, singing humpbacks are both fascinating to watch and hear. Floating in an upright or perpendicular position with heads below the surface of the sea, they extend their exceptionally long pectoral fins away from their bodies, their pectoral fins being the longest of all whale species measuring up to fifteen feet in length. With their enormous fins resembling extended wings, these angels of the sea start to sing their heavenly songs—songs that seem to emanate from another dimension or heavenly realm of being.

Most unfortunately, human noise pollution has forced humpbacks to raise their singing tone an entire octave higher in order to be heard over the noisy motors of ships at sea, with motor and propeller noise as far away as 200 kilometres disturbing these sensitive, singing giants.

The humpbacks that come to Hawaii are making one of the longest migrations of any animal in the world—over 6000 miles/9700 kilometres usually arriving in Hawaiian waters in late October and staying until May. During their six-month stay around the islands, they do not eat at all, fasting the entire time. It is only when they return to the Arctic Ocean that they fill up on the rich aquatic food stocks found there.

This journey can be quite perilous for newborn calves accompanying their moms, as they run the oceanic gauntlet of predators they may meet on the way. In the past it was thought that the calf's only protection against these predators was their mother. But new video footage has now shown that this is not always the case.

Recent dramatic footage of a humpback mother with her new calf being pursued by sharks revealed something remarkable. At first, the mother tried to ward off the shark attacks alone. But her attempts to do so were failing. So, after some time, she dove underwater, apparently abandoning her calf to the hungry hunters.

About a minute later, the mother resurfaced by the calf's side, but this time, she was not alone. A large male humpback was with her. Though it was unlikely that this male was the father of the calf, he still took upon himself the task of protecting this baby with every weapon at his disposal.

First, he created a 'bubble wall' in the water to confound the sharks and hide the calf. He then slapped his pectoral fins close to the sharks to frighten them and break up the group. His fins, having barnacles on their edges, have the ability to inflict deep gashes on the body of anything they touch, not to mention the sheer impact they would have on anything they hit.

Finally, like an ascending avenging angel, he breached several times, propelling his massive body time and time again out of the water, then slamming it back as hard as possible on its surface. Any shark struck by those fins or his body would surely have been severely injured or killed. The tactics worked, and the sharks left to seek easier and less dangerous prey.

Now safe, the grateful mother and calf continued their northward journey with the powerful male travelling with them as their 'security escort'. This perhaps helps explain why humpback males have been seen singing and accompanying mothers and calves, the threesome travelling the seas in safety together.

Once they reach the Arctic waters, the time for gorging on the abundant food found there can begin. The whales often use loud vocalizations underwater and slap their pectoral fins and/or tail fluke on its surface to stun the fish and herd them close—the same action that the protective male did to frighten those sharks.

They also work together like pods of dolphins do, engaging in 'bubble net fishing'—an amazing cooperative fishing technique whereby they create air bubbles in the sea to form 'bubble nets' or 'bubble walls' that confound their prey, again as that protective male did to the sharks. But this time, the group of whales create the bubble walls in a circular pattern, which helps bring the schools of fish closer and closer together near the ocean's surface until they are swallowed in one gaping gigantic gulp.

That one gigantic gulp can contain hundreds of thousands of small fish, crustaceans, krill and plankton, with a single whale eating up to 5500 pounds (almost 2500 kilos) of food per day. While tons of water are taken through the mouth, the humpbacks filter food from the water through that fibrous 'baleen' material, keeping all fish and other prey inside their mouth while expelling the water before swallowing their catch.

## From Poop Plumes to Algae Blooms

While it may seem that whales eat so much in one day that it would be unsustainable, the opposite is true. First, the feeding season for these whales is only 120 days—just four months out of twelve in the year. In addition, studies over decades have shown that when there are fewer whales in the seas, there are less other fish and aquatic life as well. The reason is simple—what goes in through a whale's mouth must come out the other end, which it does in the form of 'poop plumes'.

These gigantic faecal plumes are incredibly rich in iron and nitrogen—nutrients that the whales have brought up from the depths of the ocean where they often feed. They always eliminate their poop near the ocean surface in what is called the 'photic or euphotic zones'—the uppermost 80 metres/260+ feet of the ocean where enough sunlight is able to penetrate for the process of photosynthesis to take place.

The upward and downward movements of the whales in the ocean while surfacing and diving helps mix their poop plumes with the surface water, keeping it from sinking. So effective is their mixing that it is roughly equivalent to the amount of mixing caused by all the world's winds, tides and waves combined!

Various forms of almost microscopic plankton live in this upper area of the sea. The plant plankton thrives on the nutrient-rich faecal matter the whales eliminate. Using the sun's powers while absorbing carbon through their pores, they produce the food sugars they need to survive through photosynthesis, releasing oxygen into the air as a by-product. Half the photosynthesis that takes place on the entire planet is done through this process in the oceans.

From the whales' poop plumes, phytoplankton algae blooms follow. The blooms are so huge they can be seen in space, the blooms producing 50 per cent of the oxygen in the earth's atmosphere while absorbing thousands of tonnes of carbon at the same time. Scientists estimate that in the southern oceans alone, the poop just from sperm whales that drives this process is responsible for sequestering 400,000 tonnes of carbon, with just a 1 per cent increase in phytoplankton activity equalling the carbon sequestration ability of 2 billion mature trees!

When phytoplankton die, they take all the carbon they have absorbed or sequestered with them to the bottom of the ocean. This makes phytoplankton one of the most effective carbon shields on the planet—all powered through the sun and whale poop.

Phytoplankton are the foundation of the marine life cycle as they are the food base of it all. Animal plankton feed on them and are in turn eaten by other small aquatic life, which are eaten by even larger creatures all the way up the food chain. In this way, the presence of whales actually helps to boost fish stocks due to their poop plumes that start the entire process from plankton to large fish and every aquatic creature in between.

So important is the monetary contribution of whales to the planet in terms of carbon sequestration, increasing fish stocks, and income from the huge Whale Watching industry that the International Monetary Fund (IMF) has estimated the value of a single great whale at US$2 million (Rs 14,86,90,000) which equals more than US$1 trillion (Rs 7,43,45,00,00,00,000) based on the present population of great whales in the world's oceans today!* Obviously protecting whales, as well as their food supply like Antarctic krill, protects us all!

In the Antarctic Ocean, krill is the keystone species for the entire food web. These tiny shrimp-like creatures feed on the

---

*   Refer to the bibliography for source.

algae growing under the sea ice, the algae absorbing carbon as they grow. The krill then goes to the ocean's bottom to drop their faecal sacs, leaving the carbon stored in the algae they've consumed permanently locked in the cold depths of the sea, cold water being capable of storing far more carbon than warm waters. This is one of the reasons it is so critically important to protect these waters as well as the continent of Antarctica.

Because krill have shells, they are susceptible to the acidification of ocean waters from excess carbon like other shellfish. Hence keeping these waters as pristine and undisturbed as possible helps protect the krill and the entire ecosystem of the region while ensuring yet one more carbon sink for capturing and storing carbon to mitigate climate change and stop rising temperatures.

Whales eat krill in vast amounts with the blue whale—the largest animal to live on the Earth—eating as much as four tons of krill per day. Yet these whales help the cycle continue through the fertilization of the ocean's surface through their poop plumes. Overfishing of krill by factory fishing vessels puts the whole ecosystem at risk, these ships fishing twenty-four hours a day, seven days a week, for the entire Antarctic summer, the krill caught being used in the production of Omega 3 among other things.

International NGOs have been working to try and limit this overexploitation and have fortunately obtained commitments from 85 per cent of the krill-fishing companies to support the creation of ocean sanctuaries where no fishing will take place. The ban went into initial effect in 2018 but has expanded to include more companies that agreed to stop krill fishing completely in certain areas of the Antarctic Ocean by 2020—an agreement that is being honoured by most of these companies today.[*]

---

[*] The voluntary ban has gone into effect.
https://wwf.panda.org/wwf_news/?1171341/Antarctic-Wildlife-to-Benefit-from-Fishing-Ban https://thefishsite.com/articles/in-for-the-krill

All of these efforts are done to help ensure a healthy and bountiful population of this critical keystone foundation species with whale poop being the 'fuel' that initiates the process. Hence it is clear that more whales mean more plant and animal plankton, which not only means more krill and fish, but also more carbon being sequestered.

Whales themselves are living carbon sinks individually and collectively. An average blue whale can weigh 90 tonnes. At least nine tons of that weight is sequestered carbon. Over its lifetime, a single whale can sequester 18,000 tons of carbon. Only very large trees can sequester more. When whales die a natural death, they sink to the bottom of the sea taking all that carbon with them. For an average humpback whale, that is approximately ninety feet long, that has lived its full lifespan of fifty to seventy years, its forty-ton carcass will take approximately two metric tonnes of carbon with it as it falls down to the ocean's bottom, effectively trapping that carbon there for all time. This makes whales one of the greatest natural $CO_2$ regulators on the planet.

It is estimated that before the advent of human hunting of whales, these extraordinary creatures removed tens of millions of tons of carbon from the air, actually regulating and even changing the earth's climate as a result.

But human hunting of whales has had an absolutely devastating effect on the populations of virtually all whale species. All have been mercilessly hunted by humans, wiping out some species while bringing many others to the very brink of the abyss of extinction.

Cetaceans fall into two main categories with the 'great whales' or baleen whales like the humpbacks who filter their food through the baleen plates in their mouths, being the first; the second category is 'toothed whales' which number over seventy different species—from dolphin and porpoise species to orcas, from the severely threatened, delicate vaquitas porpoise that is only four feet in length to great leviathans like the blue and sperm whales—the largest mammals and largest creatures to ever roam the ocean seas.

In three hundred years of human whaling, over one million sperm whales along with hundreds of thousands of baleen whales like humpbacks have been exterminated. This includes the various dolphin species that have also been brutally murdered over the years as well. Just how destructive whaling has been is reflected in the tiny fraction of whales left on the planet today. More than 90 per cent have been killed, leaving some species just barely surviving with only 7 per cent of their former population numbers alive.

Those most endangered include the 'great whales' like humpbacks and the critically endangered North Atlantic right whale, which may already be 'functionally extinct'. There are only 360 of these magnificent giants left, with only 100 or so being breeding females. Survey teams of the whales in 2021 saw hopeful signs as seventeen new babies or calves were counted—a huge difference from the preceding years where very few or no calves were seen at all. However, scientists are still very concerned as at least two dozen new calves need to be born each year if there is any hope of the species surviving.

Fewer whales puts any species at risk from a reproductive point of view. The fewer the individuals, the harder it is for them to find each other to breed and the greater the loss in genetic diversity, making the offspring from those that do reproduce far more vulnerable to genetic disorders and illnesses in general, biodiversity being Nature's insurance policy for stronger immunity in all species—the more diverse the genes, the more enhanced its overall health and wellbeing.

In truth, all species of whales are severely threatened with extinction. The great baleen whales like the humpbacks and bowheads almost disappeared due to human hunting. With their disappearance, medium-sized whales like the minke and sei are today slaughtered instead, their numbers dropping precipitously as a result. Even the seventy-plus species of toothed whales like the white belugas, narwhals and orcas are suffering from hunting as well as from chemical pollution like PCBs in the oceans' water, including the small vaquitas porpoises that are caught and die as 'by-catch' in fishing nets off the California coast, their numbers having plummeted to a mere few hundred.

All are endangered not only from hunting, but from chemical pollution, solid trash (especially plastics) in the oceans and ship propeller strikes, with the number of strikes climbing as international shipping increases each year. Warming oceans, with melting ice caps being the most graphic proof of rising ocean temperatures are also causing life-threatening problems not only for all cetaceans, but also for the prey upon which they depend for survival.

Another major danger not just to whales but also to their prey is the oil spills which poison the waters, the whales and their food, along with the search for new oil reserves for offshore oil drilling due to a new tool being used by the oil industry in their search— seismic sonic airguns.

As many as a dozen of these guns are tethered to the oil exploration ships at a time. Each one sends massive blasting sounds into the water to detect oil and gas deep underneath the ocean floor. The dynamite-like blasts go off every ten seconds for weeks and months at a time.

Sound waves in water travel much faster and are far louder than sound waves in air. So this deafening noise not only disturbs whales and other aquatic life where the ship is located, but causes problems as far as 1200 miles/2000 kilometres away, killing off plankton and krill through its sonic shock waves.

Researchers have found a 64 per cent reduction of animal or zooplankton within one hour of the blast, with a two to three

times increase in deaths of both adult and larval-stage plankton.*
Adult krill was found stunned and damaged by the sonic blasting
with 100 per cent of all larval krill killed by the deafening and
deadly sound waves—catastrophic figures that have apocalyptic
consequences since plankton and krill are the very foundation of
the entire marine ecosystem, being the very base of the food web.

The massive loss of whales from all threats and hunting in
particular in just 300 years has grave implications for today's
warming planet considering the amount of carbon sequestration
whales themselves store and help to sequester through their
essential role in the 'food to poop to food' cycle of life in the
oceans. It is estimated that the loss of whales in just one century
of whaling is equal to the carbon released from the burning of
seventy million acres of forest!

When trees are burned, the carbon they have sequestered
over their lifetime is released all at once. However, when they die
naturally, that same stored carbon takes many years to be released,
as they slowly decay to become part of the soil again. The same
is true of whales. When whales are killed by humans through
hunting or other means, the carbon in their dead bodies is released
quickly as they are cut into pieces or lie rotting on the ocean shore.
But when a whale dies a natural death, their body sinks to the
bottom of the sea, taking that lifetime of sequestered carbon with
it, to be stored in the ocean's depths for all time.

## Whales: Marine Ecosystem Engineers

From the largest to the smallest, from whales to microscopic
plankton, each creature in creation plays its vital role to help the
web of life continue to thrive, with each thread woven into this

---

* https://www.researchgate.net/publication/317821328_Widely_used_
marine_seismic_survey_air_gun_operations_negatively_impact_zooplankton
More links in the bibliography.

great tapestry of life, interconnected and dependent on the others as well. As we continue to pull out the living threads woven so carefully and intelligently by Mother Nature over millennia, we put our own species at risk as well, the whole tapestry weakened with the removal of each strand.

As the obvious disappearance of whales in our oceans has grown, governments and international organizations finally acted to put an end to whaling. In 1986, a complete ban on commercial whaling was put into effect by the International Whaling Commission (IWC), but even today, three countries continue to flout that ban, those countries being Japan, Norway and Iceland. Certain indigenous peoples have been exempted from the ban as well, specifically certain groups of Eskimos and peoples living in the Arctic who do subsistence hunting as they have done for thousands of years.

But even this type of hunting is having an impact and is threatening species of whales whose numbers have been decimated by commercial whaling. Evidence also shows this exemption is being abused and commercialized as whale meat is being sold to tourists and served in restaurants in violation of the law.

As a result of this, coupled with increased scientific understanding of the criticality of having healthy whale populations in the world's oceans, the IWC passed the 'Resolution on Cetaceans and Ecosystem Service' in 2016.

This proposal put forward by Chile states that all cetaceans must be considered for the ecosystem services they perform from which the entire planet, including humans, benefit. From carbon sequestration and helping combat climate change, to providing the nutrients for phytoplankton to flourish, thereby helping to rebuild fishing stocks as well, the whales of the seas are essential for both marine and terrestrial life on the planet.

This cycle of life that depends on whales has come to be called 'the whale pump'. It is an example of a 'trophic cascade' whereby ecological processes start from the top of the food chain and impact other species all the way down to the most basic and simple life forms. In this case, the whole marine ecosystem is primed and run off of whales and their poop. A similar situation can be seen in Yellowstone National Park in the USA where the return of wolves reintroduced after decades of extinction in the area has helped lead to the recovery of the entire ecosystem there.

Both in Africa and here in India one can see how the presence of elephants can trigger trophic cascades due to the massive amounts of seeds they spread through their dung as they migrate many kilometres per day literally spreading the green forest cover with each ball of dung they drop behind them.

As more understanding has dawned in the scientific community about the essential role cetaceans play for the wellbeing of the entire biosphere of Earth, they have warned governments around the world of the dangers of emptying our oceans of cetaceans and life in general. All the ecosystem services cetaceans provide, their high level of intelligence and cognition, their self-awareness and dedication to family has been recognized by scientists and ethicists around the globe. As a result, the 'Declaration of Rights of Cetaceans' was announced on the 22 May 2010 in Helsinki, Finland, by eminent global figures. It states:

> We affirm that all cetaceans as persons have the right to life, liberty, and wellbeing.[*]

The declaration goes on to emphasize that cetaceans are indeed endowed with the sense of individual awareness just like humans;

---

[*]  https://www.reuters.com/article/us-whales/human-rights-urged-for-whales-and-dolphins-idUSTRE64M0UC20100523

that no cetacean should be held in captivity or removed from its natural environment or be viewed as the property of anyone; that cetaceans have the right to protection of their natural environment; and that international laws should be enacted to protect and guarantee these rights of cetaceans.

One of those eminent individuals involved with forming this declaration was Dr Sudhir Chopra—a former professor of law at Calcutta University, National Law School of India in Bengaluru (Bangalore) and lecturer at Delhi University, who is also associated with several top universities around the globe. He was also India's first environment law officer in the Department of Environment, Government of India. In May 1984, his farsightedness was evidenced at Canberra's ANZAS Congress when he raised the issues of the ozone hole in the atmosphere, climate change and the melting of the Antarctic ice.

Dr Chopra, along with co-author Professor Anthony D'Amato, wrote one of the key inspirational documents used in the formation of the Declaration for Cetaceans. Entitled 'Whales—Their Emerging Right to Life' and published in the *American Journal of International Law* in January 1991, the article lays out the legal, moral and ethical reasons that became the basis for this declaration.

In a wonderfully cogent manner, Chopra and D'Amato explain the six stages and incremental changes in perspective involved in the shift from viewing something merely as a 'thing' or 'resource' to be used in whatever way one wants, to a recognition of the innate right it has to live and to exist freely on its own, without the threat of human interference or destruction. That pathway of thought develops from 'free resource', to conservation, to protection, to preservation and finally to legal and moral 'entitlement to life'.

As they explain, this last stage of 'entitlement to life' represents a higher evolutionary stage for human consciousness—a stage that is absolutely essential today if humanity is to change the dangerous path of annihilation and extinction of species across the globe that we currently tread. This transformation of consciousness brings with it a recognition and affirmation of not only the right of all species and aspects of creation to exist, but also our own dependence on and interconnectedness with them—an indispensable realization, without which, the future of humanity and life on the planet itself is in peril.

I was fortunate to correspond with Dr Chopra and talk with him over the phone several times to discuss his ground-breaking work and to get his own assessment on the future of cetaceans and humanity's own consciousness.

Just three years later, in May 2013, the Indian Ministry of Environment, Forest and Climate Change (MoEFCC) recognized cetaceans as 'non-human persons' whose right to life and liberty must be respected and protected, adding that they should have their own specific rights. The MoEFCC stated that it was morally unacceptable to keep cetaceans in captivity for entertainment purposes, acknowledging cetaceans as individual beings with consciousness and self-awareness that were not to be treated as property.

Through this governmental action, India became the fourth country in the world to ban the capture and importation of cetaceans for commercial purposes or entertainment, joining Costa Rica, Hungary and Chile. The governmental action was the result of a major campaign by various wildlife protection and animal rights groups including our own SAI Sanctuary Trust, spearheaded by FIAPO (Federation of Indian Animal Protection Organizations).

Considering the evolutionary history that cetaceans have with the Indian subcontinent, i.e., that confirmation of their ancestral evolution from a land animal to a fully aquatic one was first discovered here, India's actions to protect these 'Angels of the Seas' is so fitting. India has also designated the highly endangered Ganges river dolphin as the nation's marine animal, this dolphin being only one of five species globally that still spends its life in fresh waters like its ancestors millions of years ago. This dolphin is also viewed as the 'vehicle' for the personification of Mother Ganga.

Due to the number of iconic terrestrial animal species India has, we often forget that the Indian Ocean, Bay of Bengal and Arabian Sea that embrace the country's vast peninsular extension are filled with wondrous marine species that are equally extraordinary and awe- inspiring. Beyond various species of fish and turtles like the olive ridley and others who actually breed on Indian beaches and the massive whale shark that makes these waters their home, 120 marine mammals grace the seas that kiss our shores. This includes whale species large and small—from the giant blue whales to its pygmy cousin, from humpbacks and fin whales to minke, Bryde's and sei, along with the massive sperm whale and its dwarf cousin. Dolphins and porpoises also frolic in our seas with the melon-headed whale often accompanying them. The very special dugong, a cousin of the western hemisphere's manatee, also calls Indian waters home.

We, in India, have a duty to protect these marvellous and even angelic beings as part of our heritage. We also must remember that protecting them and their environment is protecting our own future as a species as well, due to the ecosystem services they perform for the entire biosphere of the planet. Hence, our actions of protection are also prompted by our own self-interest and self-preservation and therefore not totally selfless. The innumerable examples of protection and compassion demonstrated by cetaceans, on the other hand, with regard to helping humans in peril are, indeed, completely selfless, examples of which have been observed and even recorded for hundreds and even thousands of years in ancient manuscripts.

Recent examples of cetaceans aiding humans in danger come from all over the globe. They report either individuals or whole pods of cetaceans protecting swimmers and/or divers from sharks. Other examples include cetaceans helping stranded people stay afloat, like the beluga whale that saved a lone diver by lifting him to the surface when he was injured, or the dolphins who rescued an unconscious scuba diver in the waters between England and France in 2006.[*]

There are also reports where dolphins, in particular, have led rescuers to missing divers or struggling swimmers at sea. One well-publicized case happened in 2004, where rescuers were unsuccessful in locating five British divers lost in the Red Sea for over thirteen hours. Rescuers describe how individual dolphins from a family pod literally started jumping over the bow of their rescue vessel to get their attention and then led them to where the exhausted divers were located, thereby saving the divers' lives.

Another example is that recounted by *National Geographic* researcher, Maddeleana Bearzi. She and her research group were studying dolphins near the shore when one dolphin broke off from the pod and headed out to the sea. The rest of the pod quickly followed, causing Maddeleana and her group to follow them. About five kilometres (three miles) from the shore, they found the pod of dolphins encircling an eighteen-year-old girl struggling in the water and suffering from hypothermia. Had the dolphins not notified the researchers and led them to the girl to rescue her, she would have surely died.[†]

One extraordinary rescue by a humpback was for whale researcher and biologist Nan Hauser, who has dedicated her life to protecting whales for over twenty-eight years, the incident

---

[*]    https://www.dolphins-for-kids.com/do-dolphins-really-save-humans
        More links in the bibliography.
[†]    Refer to the bibliography for source.

actually caught on video in May 2018. In this case, the male humpback protected her from a very large eighteen-foot-long tiger shark—a shark she had not even seen heading straight for her. While a female humpback kept slapping the surface of the ocean to ward off the shark, the male humpback kept pushing Nan forward, lifting her out of the water away from the shark to get her back to her boat, not leaving her side until she got into her boat safe and sound.

Incredibly, four days later, on Nan's birthday, while out in the ocean doing research, the second whale (the female) came up to her boat, encouraging her to get into the water with her, which Nan did. The whale proceeded to give her a 'whale hug' with her pectoral fins—a wonderful birthday gift for sure!

Even more incredibly, one year and fifteen days later, while Nan was again doing research in her boat, a male whale came straight to the side of the boat and stared at her intently with his enormous eye. Finally, Nan recognized him—it was the whale who saved her life from the huge tiger shark! Slipping into the water to be near him again, he nuzzled her with his massive head, again lifting her onto his pectoral fin, giving her a very warm and loving whale hug.

Finally, eyewitness reports from various parts of the globe demonstrate that this compassion and selfless behaviour of cetaceans towards other beings is not limited to just humans, these accounts mainly involving the altruistic actions of dolphins and humpback whales—something confirmed by whale biologist Nan Hauser.

Humpbacks have been documented intervening in attacks by predators like orcas and sharks on smaller sea creatures like seals, sea lions, porpoises and grey whales. Nine out of ten of these encounters were 'rescue missions' by the humpbacks on behalf of the other smaller animals, with only one out of ten being to protect humpback calves like the one described earlier. The rescues usually involve two humpbacks against the hunting predators, but many times even a single whale will act to protect the weaker animal, with their defensive efforts against the predators going on for several hours, if necessary.

Beyond acts of protection, there are also accounts of remarkable empathy demonstrated for other creatures that are lost and confused. One eyewitness account from New Zealand in 2008, relates how a dolphin led a stranded pygmy sperm whale mother and her calf back out to sea, after several attempts by humans to do so had failed. All of these remarkable stories clearly illustrate why cetaceans are indeed the 'Guardian Angels of the Sea'.

# 10

# Awakening Compassion and Conscience

The sound of rushing water filled the air as we inched our way around the steep slope. Then we caught our first glimpse of the waterfall cascading over the cliff—stunning in its beauty, thundering in its powerful descent. This was it! This was the land we had come to see and possibly purchase—an exquisite piece of tropical paradise bordering the government forest preserve—thirty-seven and a half acres of pristine perfection, heavily forested with not one but two perennial streams—one on the border with the forest reserve and the other with this magical waterfall flowing through the very centre of the property. The streams themselves were the headwaters for the two most spectacular waterfalls on the Big Island of Hawaii: Akaka Falls and Kahuna Falls.

We could scarcely believe our eyes as we drank in the magnificent natural wonders all around us. It was October 1976, and we were near the end of our honeymoon, the Big Island being the last of the Hawaiian Islands we visited. The land was shown to us by a friend who lived there and knew the island and its forests well. From that very first sight of the waterfall, we decided then and there to buy the property. This land would become our first sanctuary—a place where we would learn so much about living off of and in harmony with the land and the rest of Nature.

It took us about three years to pay for the land, so we had to remain in Colorado, working to earn the money. Most of it came from the commissions Anil received for securing refinancing for various existing buildings or other structures. These commissions also afforded us the ability to invest in existing Hawaiian real estate as well, purchasing existing homes or condos, renovating them and then selling them.

By April of 1979, we had enough funds to move from Colorado to the Big Island of Hawaii. We decided to drive cross-country to see the beauty of that part of the USA, taking our two Siamese cats, Sathi and Bandhu, with us. Utah, Nevada and California had some spectacular wildlife and places to see. It was interesting seeing many of the same as well as 'cousin' species that we had gotten to know and love so much in Colorado.

However, one stop in California near Lake Tahoe was very disturbing. The scenery was beautiful—heavily forested with a small lake in the middle. But there was no wildlife around at all, not even the sounds of birds. Why would what appeared to be such a pristine place be devoid of wildlife?

Then the answer presented itself in the form of a sign on a post by the lake's shore. It said that the lake had been poisoned, and it warned not to touch, drink or swim in its waters. Looking more closely, we saw signposts with the same warning all around the lake.

Looking at its water, one would never suspect anything was wrong, as it looked clean and pure. But there was something missing—any sign of life within the water—no sign of fish of any size, no frogs, no ripples of movement of any kind in the water, not even air bubbles rising to the surface from the depths below. It was so eerie . . . the beauty of Nature's trees everywhere, but no sign of life at all—an unnatural silence pervaded the area.

The scene reminded me of Rachel Carson's book *Silent Spring*. In this case, the silent spring had become a 'silent lake' poisoned with man-made chemicals that killed everything. The whole experience was unnerving and seemed so unreal, like some scene out of a horror movie.

When we reached California, we flew from Los Angeles to Honolulu Airport with our two cats and proceeded to Hawaii's quarantine area for pets being imported into the state. Hawaii was free of rabies, so animals arriving from the mainland had to go through a four-month quarantine period to ensure they were free of rabies or any other disease. It was difficult seeing our babies in one large kennel together, but there was no choice. Since we would be living on the Big Island, we hired a Honolulu-based compassionate and loving woman to visit six days a week to groom Sathi and Bandhu and just give them the love they needed. We flew back to Honolulu from the Big Island on the seventh day to visit them until their quarantine period was over.

This mandatory quarantine led to our learning about the environmental impacts that introduced, non-native species of both flora and fauna has had on the Hawaiian Islands—impacts that have been felt on many other islands small and large throughout the world in the different hemispheres of the planet including Madagascar, New Zealand, the Galapagos Islands and even Australia.

Being one of the most isolated places in the world, Hawaii has had a tremendously high level of biodiversity of both plant and animal species but has now gained the unwelcome title of 'Extinction Capital of the World'.[*] Accounting for only 0.25 per cent of the territorial area of the USA, 25 per cent of America's endangered species are located in the Hawaiian Island chain.

Much of Hawaii's biodiversity has been lost and/or is critically endangered, due to the introduction of various species by humans.

---

[*]   Refer to the bibliography for source.

Before humans came to Hawaii, there were no mosquitoes, flies, rats, dogs, cats, pigs or goats here. All of these insects and animals were brought over by humans intentionally—as in the cases of dogs, cats, pigs and goats—and unintentionally, in the cases of mosquitoes, flies and rats. Their impact on the islands has been catastrophic, not only bringing various diseases through mosquitoes, flies and rats, but also causing the extinction of dozens of native Hawaiian species, including at least half of the original 140 known Hawaiian bird species—seventy species of birds are already extinct.

Lost and severely endangered species also include the sperm and humpback whales, as well as other unique endemic/native species found only on the islands, such as the Hawaiian monk seal, Hawaiian hoary bat, various species of snails and flora found nowhere else on the planet. Once lost, these species are lost forever.

One of the most damaging species introduced by humans has been the rat. While Captain Cook and his British crew have been blamed for bringing rats to the islands as stowaways on their ships which first landed in Hawaii January 1778, more recent evidence suggests that rats hitched a ride with the original Polynesian immigrants who came to the islands centuries earlier. Once on land, the rats caused havoc that led to the extinction of a number of bird species in particular. Because of the lack of predatory animals, many species of Hawaiian birds nested on the ground, rather than in trees. For rats, it was an easy 'free lunch' eating both eggs and chicks of these ground-nesting birds. For the birds, the cost was extinction.

Observing this situation, the British decided to step in to 'right the wrong' of whoever unintentionally brought rats to the islands. They turned to the Indian mongoose as the answer, releasing it into the forests of the islands. There was only one problem with this strategy—mongooses come out during daylight hours, while rats generally come out at night—the two species rarely, if ever, meet!

Additionally, one of the most important prey species that mongoose eat are snakes. But there are no snakes in the Hawaiian Islands. With no choice but to change its own diet, the mongoose also selected the easiest thing for it to catch and eat—the eggs and chicks of ground-nesting birds, thereby causing even more unique bird species to disappear.

This is an example of what happens when we humans think we know more than Mother Nature and start playing 'god' by introducing species where they do not belong.

## Shredding the Tapestry of Life

Introduction of non-native species is one of the five main causes of the present sixth wave of species extinctions sweeping across the planet. There have been at least five previous extinction events in Earth's geological past, but all of the previous ones were due to natural causes. Only this present event is caused solely by the activities of man.

In addition to introduction of non-native species in an area, the other four extinction causes are hunting/over-exploitation, deforestation/loss of habitat, islandization—which is an offshoot of deforestation—and pollution, which includes the pollution of our atmosphere with greenhouse gas emissions (GHGs) like carbon dioxide and methane that are leading to climate change.

The introduction of non-native species is not restricted to animals, but also includes plants and trees like the eucalyptus tree. The eucalyptus is native to Australia, where the adorable-looking koalas are famous for eating its leaves. Due to its fast growth, it has been used here in India and Africa as a 'quick fix' reforestation solution. But this short-term 'solution' is actually a major long-term headache for genuine reforestation efforts to restore the ecosystem services lost when forests were cut down.

The problems with the eucalyptus are five-fold:

They require large quantities of water to grow, thereby draining water sources rather than replenishing them

They disseminate a chemical in the soil around them that acts as a toxin that kills off and/or inhibits the growth of other trees or plants.

Eucalyptus oil within the tree is highly flammable and literally explodes during forest fires, sending hot sparks all over, thereby spreading the fires.

Eucalyptus leaves are of no use to cattle or endemic species in either India or Africa, since there are no koalas in either location and are therefore useless even as a food source.

Eucalyptus leaves are very tough and do not break down or biodegrade easily. Hence, they are of little help in replenishing nutrients in soils to further enhance reforestation efforts while soaking up whatever nutrients were already there.

The effects of planting the eucalyptus trees have been so negative that some countries in Africa have actually banned their import and planting. We need to do the same thing here in India and plant our own native trees on a large scale for each and every reforestation project throughout the country. This will not only save us from the negative impacts of eucalyptus, acacia and other non-native trees, but will help preserve the incredibly rich biodiversity we have in the country; biodiversity that has evolved over millennia for each different ecosystem of the nation; biodiversity that is rapidly being lost.

There are many countries that are trying to rid themselves of non-native species, which is certainly understandable, considering the damage many of these species have had on native ecosystems and wildlife. But programmes working toward this goal need to be carried out in a compassionate manner when dealing with non-native animals. After all, these poor creatures had no say in their introduction to these new areas. In most cases, they were brought there by man intentionally, usually as sources of food for humans, either being raised and slaughtered or released to be hunted.

Whatever their impacts on their new environments, these animals are not at fault—humanity is. These animals are just trying to survive as best they can in the new area they have been forced to inhabit. It is because of man's typical short-sightedness in making such introductions that these ecosystems have been destroyed and native species suffer. Hence, it is man who has to deal with the situation using intelligent and compassionate measures to try and right this wrong and solve the problems he has created.

We must not forget that every species has an inalienable right to life. This requires us to seek every alternative to euthanasia first before resorting to taking the lives of these innocent animals. Non-lethal measures can include restoring damaged habitats and nesting areas that will aid in the recovery of native species. Repopulation programmes for endangered native species to actively aid in raising their numbers to be released in restored wilderness areas is another method that has been successfully used for critically endangered species from condors to pandas.

However, as Jane Goodall has expressed, wherever a lethal option must be used, it must be carried out in as humane, compassionate and empathetic a manner as possible to minimize the stress and suffering caused for both the species and for each individual animal involved. To act otherwise is to display a lack of conscience and hard-heartedness that has gravely ominous implications for those involved in these acts and for society as a whole.

There is a dangerous trend in some countries that is engendering hatred and malice for non-native species.* One of these countries is New Zealand, where even children as young as four or five years

---

* http://www.janegoodall.org.nz/jgi-nz-campaigns/compassion-in-conservation/

More links in the bibliography.

of age are engaged in killing contests, glorifying the deaths of these unfortunate animals. Some schools hold annual hunts and competitions, encouraging children to participate directly in the slaughter of these animals, even having young children take babies or 'joeys' from the pouches of their mothers and then drowning them in a bucket of water. This is so wrong on so many levels in so many areas.*

There is no question that children need to be educated about the problems that non-native species, both flora and fauna, can cause in an ecosystem. But to actively engage children in the killing of these animals, to vilify these poor creatures and encourage malice and mistreatment of them, can cause lifelong damage to the psyche of children.

The development of empathy, compassion and healthy attitudes toward other forms of 'life' happens when we are young. Psychological studies have shown that once these values are instilled at young ages, they usually continue with us for our entire life. Children that engage in these kinds of brutal activities and/ or are fed a steady mental diet of contempt for any living creature become de-sensitized to violence, lack empathy and extend that type of negative discriminatory behaviour towards other people as well.

These attitudes impact their conduct right into adulthood. Several studies have shown a definitive link between abuse of animals as a child and aggressive/abusive behaviour as an adult, not just towards animals, but toward humans, too. Hence, it is imperative to engender not cruelty and meanness, but compassion and respect for all species, for all of life, for all of Nature.

With respect to what to do about non-native species in ecosystems, conservation must strike a proper balance between

---

* Refer to the bibliography for source.

protection and compassion. That approach will help foster respect for all life while helping to inspire creative, efficient and empathetic strategies to deal with this important issue.

## Cruelty Can Never Bring Beauty

In some cases, certain non-native species were introduced for the sake of the fur industry—one of the most cruel and barbaric industries on the planet with a record of cold-hearted abuse of animals that is utterly disgusting, deplorable and inexcusable. 'Fur for Fashion' is an example of the extent of cruelty that humans will engage in, just to stroke their own ego. Those who show off their fur apparel do so as if it is some kind of a status symbol. In reality, what it shows is the terrible status of the wearer's heart, conscience and consciousness. Wrapping one's self up in the dead skins and furs of creatures whose own beauty has become their cause of death is most certainly a demonstration of the wearer's ignorance, or worse yet, their insensitivity to the pain and torture that they have supported through their purchase of such blood-soaked products.

Every year, more than one billion rabbits and at least 50 million other animals are hunted or raised in appalling conditions to pander to humanity's vanity. 'Cruelty for Vanity' is the deadly and ugly truth behind the touted beauty of the fur industry. To make just one full-length fur coat costs the lives of at least one hundred chinchillas (a small squirrel-like rodent native to South America), sixty minks, forty rabbits, or twenty-four foxes, depending on the species used.

These figures do not even touch on the amount of inhumane suffering these animals have undergone before being killed, their death coming through various means, including being gassed, bludgeoned to death and even skinned alive. How can such cruelty ever lead to true beauty?!

The outcry against this cruelty inflicted by an industry that is totally unnecessary, fur being nothing more than 'frivolous fashion', has moved many countries to ban fur farming altogether, within the boundaries of their nations. The United Kingdom, Austria, Croatia, Slovenia, Norway, the Czech Republic, Luxembourg, the Republic of Macedonia, Serbia, the Netherlands, Denmark and Japan have all banned fur farming.

Others, like Germany and Sweden, have passed laws to ensure the humane treatment and living conditions of fur-farmed animals. These laws usually mean the eventual end of fur farming over a short period of time since they make the trade economically unviable.

Bans on fur farming, however, do not necessarily mean there is no import of fur products from animals killed in other countries, whether through fur farming, trapping or hunting. The UK is an example of this contradiction in compassion: it was the first country to ban fur farming back in the year 2000. Yet, it allows some fur imports from other countries that have added up to 650 million pounds and at least 2 million animals slaughtered annually, just to meet the demands for UK imports.*

This was partly due to being a member of the European Union (EU), where single EU trade laws overrule laws and restrictions of the individual countries, making it impossible to ban the import of fur from other EU countries. With Brexit meaning the UK's exit from the EU, the UK now has the opportunity to completely ban the import of all fur products into the country, making it a compassionate, totally fur-free nation.

This is exactly what UN ambassador of peace and world-renowned conservationist Jane Goodall is asking the UK government to do.† Many other conservationists have joined

---

*   Refer to the bibliography for source.
†   Refer to the bibliography for source.

her plea, including veterinarian doctors, experts and over thirty celebrities, including Dame Judi Dench. They point out that there is no justifiable reason not to ban imports of fur and skin products because there are plenty of cruelty-free substitutes that are also extremely beautiful and fashionable, which are available. 'Faux fur' and 'mock croc' are just two examples of cruelty-free products already currently available and widely sold in global markets.

At present, some countries have stringent restrictions in place on the importation of fur and skin-related products from abroad. The question is, why not restrict the sale of furs and skins completely to bring an end to this unnecessary cruelty that other species suffer for the sake of human vanity. This is especially true in countries like the UK where polls have shown that 93 per cent reject wearing animal fur with at least 72 per cent or more of the general public in favour of a total fur ban with only 3 per cent actually wearing fur.[*]

Where national governments have failed to completely ban the sale of fur, many cities across the globe have passed their own total prohibition on fur trade including London, São Paulo in Brazil and San Francisco in USA, with West Hollywood, California, being the first city in the world to do this back in 2013, willingly forfeiting the economic boost from the annual 2-million-dollar fur trade within its city limits, choosing compassion over blood-soaked cash.

Here in India, there have been some very positive changes as well. In January 2017, as the result of a long but determined effort by various animal rights groups, environmentalists, wildlife conservationists and others, India's union government prohibited the importation of the skins of reptiles, mink, fox and chinchilla. Maneka Gandhi (member of Parliament (LS), Sultanpur,

---

[*] Refer to the bibliography for source.

environmentalist, animal rights activist, founder and chairperson of People for Animals) was instrumental in the implementation of this ban, with the Ministry of Environment, Forests and Climate Change (MoEFCC) and Animal Welfare Board of India lending their support for the prohibition, stressing the need for India to join in the movement for ending this barbaric and unnecessary cruelty being inflicted on innocent animals.

Then, in April of 2018, India joined thirty-six other countries in barring the importation and commercial sale of products made from seal fur and skins. Thousands of seals—especially baby seals—are brutally shot or clubbed to death each year, mainly in Canada. The notorious Canadian commercial seal hunt is the largest slaughter of marine mammals in the world.

However, like fur farming, this industry has been dying for decades due to the global public outcry against it. This has meant huge economic losses for the barbaric trade as the conscience of humanity has translated into fewer and fewer markets for their blood-soaked products.

## The Disconnect from Conscience

We—the consumers—actually wield the power in determining which products are sold in the world. If we use this purchasing power to buy goods that are environmentally sensitive and ethically obtained, products that demonstrate compassionate thinking and a long-term view of their impact on the Earth's biosphere, its forests, wildlife and animals in general, on climate and sustainability, we can help usher in a new era of conscience and of consciousness in production reflective of our own raised consciousness. For it is what we purchase that dictates which industries survive and which do not.

Unfortunately, there is often a 'disconnect' between what we claim to be our set of values and the demonstration of those values at the marketplace. Most people say they like animals and many keep pets, also claiming to have a love for wildlife and Nature in general. And yet, they will buy a 'fashionable' fur-trimmed coat or hat, or a full-length leather jacket and trouser set, thereby illustrating the contradiction between what they say and what they actually do.

I was one such individual. I always claimed to love animals and wildlife. When I was in high school, I almost bought a knee-length, rabbit-fur coat for myself. Trying it on, all I could see was the beautiful fur. I could not look beyond the fur's beauty to the cruelty that had gone into the production of that coat. I didn't think of the forty or more rabbits who had suffered torment, torture and death in order to make that one coat; I could not hear their high-pitched squeals of pain as they were violently grabbed by humans and then killed in any number of horrific ways. All I saw was the beauty of the fur I was wrapped in, forgetting that that fur had come from dozens of rabbits just like my own beloved Trixie.

Fortunately, I never bought that coat, but looking back on this incident today, it graphically portrays the contradiction I was living—the same contradiction so many people are still living now.

This is one of the consequences of the manufacturing society that dominates the present world. Most of us live at least one step or more removed from the brutality and even grotesque realities of this manufacturing process since we do not engage directly in the killing of animals for food or fashion, or the actual cutting down of ancient forests for 'designer furniture' or for the tar sands underneath their forest roots. Hence, we are disconnected from the consequences that our own choices have had on the world, on the environment and on the rest of the species that also inhabit this planet. If we had to actually be a part of that process, I believe many of us would make different choices.

There are some individuals in the world who appear to be completely cold-hearted, without compassion, empathy or sympathy and devoid of conscience, and hence kill without compunction or hesitation, much less remorse. But I believe their numbers are tiny in comparison to the whole of humanity.

I believe that most people in the world are truly good at heart. They can, and do, feel empathy for others, including other species or aspects of Nature. Faced with the reality of inflicting pain on another living thing, or with dismembering a magnificent part of Nature, I believe most people would stop, think and refrain from doing so.

One of our closest friends in Hawaii helped to drive home this point to me, decades ago. He relayed how he had been quite in need of work and so took up a job at a slaughter factory near where he grew up on the mainland USA. He was a meat-eater then, so had no initial qualms about killing animals for food . . . until he actually had to do it himself.

He described the terror he saw in the eyes of the animal being killed, its cries of fear and then the pain as it was being killed, the panic and terror in the eyes of those waiting in line for their own death, the stench of dead flesh and fresh blood everywhere, blood splattered on walls, ceilings, floors and on himself. He told me about the horrible nightmares he had that robbed him of sleep, of waking in terror himself as the cries of slaughtered animals filled his ears, seeing himself in line for slaughter as well. Not only did he quit his job, he also immediately stopped eating meat.

Please understand, people who eat meat and/or wear fur are *not* bad people. Just like me they lack awareness and have not connected the dots between their choices and the consequences those choices cause. Even someone as compassionate and spiritually evolved as the Dalai Lama can be unaware of what is happening at times, as the following incident illustrates.

Since the 1990s, when certain groups of Tibetans became more prosperous, it had become popular to show off their newly acquired wealth and status by wearing the skins of various animals, reviving an ancient tradition that had formerly been abandoned. The demand for skins of tigers, leopards and otters in particular skyrocketed with the illegal trade in skins of these critically endangered animals as well as those of the fox, lynx and other animals also escalating as a result.

Wildlife conservationists and animal rights advocates approached the Dalai Lama about this distressing situation, explaining to him the terrible cruelty that was being inflicted on these creatures by trapping and killing them, as well as imperilling the very existence of many of the species whose pelts and skins were being worn.

When the Dalai Lama was shown pictures of Tibetans wearing various pelts, he was extremely upset. He relayed his concerns to a huge crowd that had gathered to hear him speak in January 2005 on the occasion of the annual Kalachakra ceremony (the initiation ceremony for Buddhists). The crowd included at least 10,000 Tibetan pilgrims who had travelled from Tibet to take part in the function.

During the course of his sermon, the Dalai Lama said he was ashamed to see images of Tibetans decorating themselves with skins and furs. In an emotional appeal to his people, speaking particularly to the Tibetan pilgrims there, he said:

> When you go back to your respective places, remember what
> I had said earlier and never use, sell, or buy wild animals, their
> products, or derivatives.[*]

The response from the Tibetan people was immediate, with bonfires of burning pelts lighting up the sky in accordance with

---

[*]    Refer to the bibliography for source.

the wishes of this great, compassionate and enlightened spiritual leader. One Tibetan activist compared the bonfires of burning furs to those that lit up the skies of India decades earlier, during India's struggle for freedom from British rule, when another compassionate and enlightened leader—Mahatma Gandhi—called upon the Indian people to burn the British clothes they had as a symbolic gesture of liberation from British domination, choosing instead to wear simple, Indian, cotton homespun, with dignity and pride of being Indian.

Similarly, as a result of the Dalai Lama's moving plea, Tibetans across the country spontaneously started burning their animal skins, enthusiastically throwing into the fires any fur garments they had—hats, gloves, coats and shirts, including their traditional Chubas costumes. As Belinda Wright of Wildlife Protection Society of India (WPSI) noted:

> The reaction of the Tibetan people (i.e., the burning of wildlife pelts), now that they have been made aware of the results of their actions, gives a little bit of light at the end of the tunnel for the Indian tiger.[*]

This is an example of true leadership, of an individual who recognized the truth and immediately acted in accordance with his conscience born from his new level of awareness, urging others to do the same. It is this type of genuine leadership we need much more of across the planet.

This is also a graphic illustration of the second major reason for the extinction of species around the planet—hunting and over-exploitation. Our purchase choices once again are critically important when addressing this major cause of species extinction. Fashion has been one driving force of extinction as

---

[*] Refer to the bibliography for source.

we have seen with the example from Tibet. Even species that seem to be so abundant that the question of their extinction could never be expected, can indeed be completely wiped out due to commercial demands.

One example of this from the USA is the passenger pigeon—a bird at one time considered to be the most numerous in the world, their flocks numbering in the millions of individuals, blackening the sky for hours when they flew past. Nevertheless, they fell victim to overhunting for food and to the 'fashion curse' when it became fashionable to wear the dead birds as decoration on women's hats in the US and in Europe. From an estimated 50 billion birds before the Europeans came to the Americas, their population plummeted to zero, being totally wiped out in just 100 years!*

This relentless slaughter of birds for their feathers continued, bringing many other bird species to the brink of extinction, until two women stepped forward to stop it—Harriet Lawrence Hemenway and Minna Hall. These two women are best known for setting up the Massachusetts Audubon Society. But, at a time when women did not have the right to vote or hold office, Harriet and Minna used their formidable persuasive powers with members of the United States Congress to enact the first environmental law in America—the Lacey Act of 1900—the law which outlawed both the national and international commercial plumage trade, and which became the foundation of conservation law enforcement and subsequent conservation protection laws for the country.

John F. Lacey of Iowa—author of this landmark legislation—was also an avid lover of birds and Nature as well as the moving force behind the creation of America's first National Park—Yellowstone. Commenting on the sorry state of America's bird populations at that time along with the lack

---

*    Refer to the bibliography for source.

of conservation and protection of Nature and her wildlife in general, Lacey stated:

> We have given an awful exhibition of slaughter and destruction, which may serve as a warning to all mankind . . . The immensity of man's power to destroy imposes a responsibility to preserve . . . Mankind must conserve the resources of Nature, or the world will, at no distant day, become as barren as a sucked orange!*

Words of wisdom we need so desperately to take to heart today, as calls for 'development at any cost' echo across the world, costing us the very existence of thousands upon thousands of species globally. Indeed, one species goes extinct every twenty minutes, putting the very fabric of life that sustains us all at risk.

True leadership like that demonstrated by Harriet and Minna as well as John Lacey will lead people on to the right path even when 'cultural traditions' are used as an excuse for continuing the slaughter of wildlife—especially endangered species—as demonstrated by the actions of the Dalai Lama and others globally who have encouraged indigenous people to adapt to the new realities of scarcity in the natural world today. Whether it is feathers in the hats of the rich or the use of the skulls and beaks of various species of endangered hornbills, or the skins of threatened species of squirrels and other mammals, the bottom line is the 'death' for the animal involved.

Spreading awareness and education of ground realities is always the first necessary step towards change. This, coupled with creative alternatives, such as headpieces moulded in the image of a hornbill that still honours 'traditions' without involving the death of the animal, help in engaging local communities in becoming

---

* Refer to the bibliography for source.

part of the solution, instead of being part of, and worsening, the threat of extinction.

## Our Choices, Our Future

Once again it all comes down to the choices each of us makes—choices in the way we choose to live as well as choices in what we purchase. The way we choose to live has a major effect on our own life and on the burden we place on the planet each and every day.

We can either:

- conserve energy and move to truly green alternative energy sources; or waste energy and continue to rely on fossil fuels while ignoring the horrific consequences of both their extraction and of their use, as global rising temperatures lead to ever more dangerous and frequent extreme weather events and climactic changes across the Earth;
- practise reuse and recycling; or throw away one-time use products into the ever-expanding mountains of trash and non-biodegradable plastic;
- use sparingly precious resources like water and food; or discard huge amounts of food while others starve and forests continue to be razed to the ground with the excuse of needing to grow more food for the global human population;
- decide not to purchase frivolous items that waste resources; or continue to mindlessly consume with literally no thought about the impacts our consumption has on us and on the future of the planet;
- decide to be aware, responsible custodians of the planet, seeking to preserve and protect it for the future generations of all species; or destroy what was given to us by our ancestors, which took millennia for Nature to create.

The choice is ours, and how we choose to live and what we choose to buy dictates to businesses how they should themselves act and what goods they should sell.

Like the passenger pigeon and other birds, tigers and other big cats in India have suffered a similar decimation in their populations in part due to fashion, but also due to the demand for their body parts that are used in traditional Chinese medicine.

For twenty-five years, China had a ban on the sale of tiger bones and rhino horns in the country. While the ban was openly flouted, it did still help curtail their use to some degree. But, in October 2018, China inexplicably reversed itself, allowing the sale of tiger bones and rhino horns yet again throughout the nation. While it is claimed that only body parts from government-approved sources will be allowed, it is highly doubtful that the enforcement of this 'check' will be employed at all.*

Global outcry at China's move has forced its government to reconsider the lifting of the ban. But this demonstrates just how easily such 'bans' can be reversed whenever the government of any country chooses to do so or chooses to ignore established international laws and global public opinion to satisfy vested interests its own nation.

And why did China suddenly lift the ban? The answer is what it always is, in this day and age—money. China has longed to have its traditional therapies recognized on a global scale so it could have yet another global market for its goods. This is one way they may hope to achieve that goal, purposely turning a blind eye to the catastrophic declines in the populations of both species, with the number of rhinos having dropped over 90 per cent globally because of the demand.

Tigers and rhinos are not the only victims of the insatiable appetite principally coming from China for animal body parts;

---

*    Refer to the bibliography for source.

bears are similarly hunted and even imprisoned on 'farms' where they suffer terrible torture as their bile is harvested for use in these so-called 'remedies'. Other endangered species in demand include seahorses, sharks, manta rays, leopards and lions. Over 150 million seahorses have died for use in traditional Chinese medicine. Pangolins—Asia's cousin species of the western hemisphere's armadillo anteaters—are hunted down and killed for their body scales, mainly for use in Southeast Asian countries. Over the last ten years alone, over one million of these wonderful and timid creatures have been brutally murdered.

The tragedy of this whole sordid and disgusting animal body parts trade is that it is completely unnecessary:

- First, the efficacy of these 'remedies' still remains completely unproven;
- Second, if there actually are any health benefits from the animal body parts used, the active ingredient can be easily synthesized in laboratories instead of killing the animal in question;
- Third and more importantly, there are plant sources that can be used to replace animal parts in the formulas for every single 'remedy'—traditional Chinese herbal medicine has plant alternatives for all ailments that are supposedly 'treated' with 'remedies' that use animal body parts.

So even the choices we make in the healthcare field can have hidden impacts on individual species, the ecosystems which they are a part of and even on the biosphere of the planet as a whole. Take the example of which vitamins to purchase.

As mentioned earlier, part of the unsustainable harvesting by humans of the Antarctic Ocean's keystone species 'krill' is driven by the demand for vitamins that contain Omega-3. While Omega-3 is principally found in fish and other aquatic species like krill, there are vegetarian alternatives such as seaweed and kelp, Spirulina being one of the most readily available sources of it.

The unsustainable and unnecessary use of krill for Omega-3 puts in jeopardy the entire Antarctic Ocean's ecosystem. Hence, it is essential we think about the consequences of our choices, awakening both our conscience and compassion to guide us to the right path that will ensure the health and viability of precious ecosystems that sustain life on the planet, including our own.

# 11

# Keystone Species: Cornerstones of Life

The unsustainable harvesting of any species endangers the balance of Nature since every species in an ecosystem is linked to every other, directly or indirectly. But this is especially true of keystone species. As mentioned in Chapter Four, salmon is the keystone species for the entire forest ecosystem of the Pacific Northwest of the North American continent, the salmon being food for various wildlife and the key source of essential nutrients for the forest trees. Anil and I have walked through these forests on trips we took to Canada and Alaska in the mid-1980s—trips where we enjoyed great beauty, peace and 'life', as well as some extremely frightening and downright terrifying experiences!

One of these trips was to the forests around the Salish Sea and its tributaries—the same area where Tahlequah's family pod of orcas lives today, her ancestors having lived there for many thousands of years. A small ferry took us and our rental car far upstream into one of the main tributaries. Even though it was a grey day with a light drizzle falling, it was still a lovely journey that lasted almost three hours. Thick forests—mainly of very tall Sitka spruce—came all the way down to the water's edge, with each bend in the river bringing new views of natural splendour.

When the ferry finally docked at a wharf, we disembarked with our car and drove off into the woods, heading for the cabin we had rented for our trip. After meeting our hosts and eating a quick meal, we went to sleep listening to the crackle of the small logs ablaze in the wood-burning stove heating the cabin. It was November and temperatures were very cold, well below freezing, so the warmth from the fire was greatly appreciated!

That night it snowed heavily, and we awoke to a fairytale winter wonderland. The ground was blanketed with several inches of powdery white snow, its weight causing tree limbs to bend low. Hanging down off the eaves of the cabin, long icicles glistening in the early morning sun beamed rainbow colours in all directions. The cold, brisk air filled with the strong scent of pine was delightful and so refreshing. Inhaling deeply, we felt completely invigorated and exhilarated!

We had come prepared for the wintry weather, having packed plenty of warm clothing, including knee-high, comfy, cosy hiking boots. Ready to set off into the woods, we waited for our 'guide' to show us the way. The 'guide' was the hosts' beautiful golden retriever dog who seemed to know exactly where we wanted to go—the river. Leading us through the snow-covered forest for some time, he took us straight to the edge of the woods where we could see the river a short distance away. He waited until we 'thanked' him, telling him what a wonderful friend he was, and then turned to go back home—quite a remarkable and friendly companion, not once did he bark or cause any problems for the local wildlife.

Looking out on the snow-covered clearing leading to the river's edge, where no human footprint could be seen, I was again transported to that same feeling of awe and wonder I experienced on the white-sand beach in Kauai—stepping back in Earth's past when humanity did not exist, when Nature was its original harmonious perfection and all life was free and at peace. A hushed silence enveloped us both, lifting our souls to a higher realm of seeing and being, the river flowing in the distance and the call of a bald eagle overhead the only sounds one could hear.

Walking in silence to the river's edge, we marvelled at the incredibly beautiful, pristine scene—huge, stately spruce trees covered the hills on both sides of the river, their limbs heavy with the night's snow, their crowns reaching into the cloudless blue sky; boulders topped with white, puff-pillows of snow dotted the river and its bank, the boulders being of various colours from yellow to rust to black and brown; cold, crystal-clear waters flowed swiftly past us in the river's rush downstream to join the sea. Sitting on some logs on the river's shore, wrapped in an aura of tangible peace, we drank in the stunning views while watching several bald eagles circle overhead, the azure firmament above so vibrant, it almost seemed to pulsate with 'life' around the great birds.

The presence of the bald eagles was especially significant for me. Native Americans view the bald eagle as sacred and as the leader of the birds because he is the most powerful and flies closest to the Creator. Therefore, he carries our words, our prayers on his wings, high up in the heavens—carrying them as the messenger who reaches closest to the Creator. Seeing not one, but several bald eagles circling above us filled me with a sense of immense gratitude that so many high 'messengers' were there to take our thoughts and prayers to the divine Creator. As we continued to sit in silent stillness, in deep meditation and prayer, I felt profound appreciation and great veneration for the Creator who had showered so many blessings upon us.

Later, while following a small tributary to the river uphill into the forest, we were stopped in our tracks when we came upon a spectacular waterfall. Part of the falls was frozen while the rest tumbled down behind sheets of transparent ice. The frigid temperatures had coated everything touched by the spray from the cascade with ice—the walls of the cliff, rocks, plants and ferns, branches of trees, wherever the spray reached—all appeared as if they were encased in glass. Everywhere one looked were the exquisite creations of Mother Nature—sculptures of ice more delicate and breath-taking than the greatest, blown-glass pieces ever wrought by human hands. Awe-struck, all we could do was silently gaze in wonder of Nature's stunning display of beauty and power.

Wanting to experience the spectacle more closely, I climbed down to the bottom of the waterfall. Sunlight streaming through the trees, sparkling off the icy cascade and spray, created bands of rainbow colours everywhere. Ferns and plants, coated with frost from the falls' mist, appeared covered with tiny diamonds glittering in the light as they trembled and quivered in the breeze. It was as if I was in the centre of a giant prism, reflecting and refracting divine light all around me—an astonishing and overwhelming experience!

After spending some time in these majestic and magical woods, we descended the mountain and reached a very large pond. Walking in the forest along its banks, we noticed a number of stumps of white birch and other small trees. Then we realized it was the work of beavers! This large pond had been created by beavers using nothing more than their four powerful front teeth to cut down the trees to make their dam!

## Beavers: Nature's Eco-Engineers

As noted in Chapter Four, the beaver is considered a sacred animal by certain Native American tribes, including the Blackfoot, who actually credit the beaver with helping to create the world—an honour that is nowhere near as farfetched as it may initially sound.

On the contrary, it is in recognition of the vital ecological contributions of this amazing creature, and an accurate description of the eco-engineering that this extraordinary being carries out for its environment. Indeed, beavers are Nature's principal construction engineers as well as the architects of biodiversity, making them a critical keystone species across the entire North American continent and Europe. Beavers are particularly important in the western part of the American continent, which has traditionally been dry. Only 2 per cent of the total land area in this region is wetland, but these wetlands support 80 per cent of its biodiversity—a fact recognized by Native Americans who not only valued the ponds of fresh water the beavers created, but also the abundance of wildlife attracted to beaver ponds—wildlife that they were able to hunt for food.

While writing this book, I was privileged to stay in a wooded area that contained five contiguous beaver dams, all created by a family of beavers that had been there for decades. My cabin was next to the pond of old grandfather beaver, the other four ponds being looked after by his children, their children and their children's children! It was fascinating watching these industrious creatures at work. Grandfather beaver's daily routine included circular rounds in his pond, inspecting every inch of his dam and repairing it wherever he found a breach. Using mud which he carried in his front paws and arms, he would walk upright with a waddle to any broken area and fit the mud in place, adding a branch or two for extra support if needed. Then he would pat it all down to ensure it was tightly joined to the rest of the muddy bank, being careful that water levels never got so high that his home-lodge in the middle of the pond would get swamped.

In the process of making their dams, the beavers had opened up the forest canopy, creating new habitats and ecosystems as a result, their freshwater ponds becoming oases for all kinds of life. It was a sheer joy to watch the butterflies and bees flitting past while sipping on the innumerable wildflowers blooming everywhere. Numerous species of birds kept flying by and singing overhead, including beautiful, red-winged blackbirds with their distinctive calls. Dazzling hummingbirds were also there, flying at top speed, then hovering above the abundant flowers to lap up the sweet nectar delight. Ducks, geese, swans and other waterfowl that had nested in safety within the pond's grasses would bring their tiny ducklings, goslings and cygnets out to swim in the morning sun, the bodies of fish gleaming in the sunlight. Often at sunset, bear and deer would amble by, munching on the lush greenery growing on the pond shores, while the croaking of different species of frogs filled the evening air, glorious reds, golds and yellows streaking across the sky as the sun disappeared behind the forest-covered hills. The incredible amount of beauty and biodiversity of plants and wildlife there was astonishing.

It doesn't surprise me, then, that one study documented an unbelievable cumulative increase of 148 per cent of species enrichment in areas where beavers had returned and built their dams—an example of the 'biodiversity multiplier effect' of the beaver, and a lesson for humanity on how helping or hurting even a single species has ripple effects on dozens and even hundreds of other species as well. Each species adds its own unique thread that is woven in harmony and balance with all others, helping to create and repair the delicate and intricate tapestry of life of which we, too, are a part.

The wonders of beavers and their ponds do not stop there. These life-giving freshwater pools filter out pollution from the water flowing through them, reducing agricultural pollutants downstream from the ponds as much as 40 to 50 per cent while helping restore degraded stream areas and storing water for use not only by other wildlife, but by humans as well. Water from the ponds percolates slowly into the ground, recharging underground aquifers and keeping soils moist through the dry season, with some of that water often percolating back up above ground to keep small streams flowing for the benefit of nearby flora and fauna.

This water-banking aspect of beaver ponds is critical today as sources of fresh water are disappearing due to overuse and climate change. With mountains receiving less snowpack and their glaciers melting due to climbing temperatures, beaver ponds help offset the reduction from these fresh water sources. The thousands of acres of water created by beaver dams also cool temperatures enough to actually stimulate precipitation. This helps break periods of prolonged drought with the ponds even acting as firebreaks. Hence, these industrious little creatures are an essential part of climate change adaptation in the areas that were once their natural habitat across North America and Europe.

Previously, beavers were only valued for their pelts. Hunted relentlessly across Europe and particularly in the UK, they were completely wiped out in Britain as early as the 1700s. At the time of the arrival of Europeans to North America, an estimated 400 million beavers existed across the continent, helping to keep rivers flowing and biodiversity growing, wherever they were found. Uncontrolled and incessant hunting by the European immigrants brought them to the very brink of extinction, being wiped out completely particularly in much of the dry West, where their ponds had helped to keep the area green and filled with life in the past.

Their prolonged absence not only translated into a loss of biodiversity, but also contributed to the spread of desertification and drying out of whatever forests were left. The bone-dry legacy of humanity's avarice and stupidity can be seen today in the form of over two million acres of forest and thousands of homes burned, with hundreds of people killed in massive forest fires in a single year (2018) in just one state—California—the state that has lost more wetlands than any other in America, and where beavers were almost completely extirpated by hunters in just sixty years, almost two centuries ago.

Fires have gotten even worse in the last three years, with the fire season in the west for 2021 outpacing all historic records, millions of acres going up in flames, with smoke from the fires in the west darkening the skies across the country right to New York City on the east coast. One of the greatest tragedies of forest fires is that as many as 90 per cent of them are caused by humans—a horrific percentage illustrating most graphically human thoughtlessness, lack of care, conscience and conscientiousness—a searing legacy of humanity's slaughter of beavers, mindless destruction of Nature in general, and human-induced climate change.

Greed has so often blinded man to the effects his actions have on the future. Today, more than ever, we need to look at the future through eyes of compassion, understanding and a view of the survival not just of a single species, but of all species, including humanity. In doing so and acting to save, rather than squander the natural riches of Mother Earth, we will ultimately end up reaping economic benefits as well—a fact demonstrated in the results of many studies, including a recent one on beavers—i.e., the restoration of beavers in just one river basin has translated into tens of millions, and even hundreds of millions of dollars in economic benefits each year. This is due to the ecosystem services their activities create such as water purification, moderation of extreme events like flooding and drought, creating habitat for other species which translates into increased biodiversity, nutrient cycling, greenhouse gas sequestration and increased water supplies to name a few.

Restoration programs for the former habitats of these eco-engineers are indeed taking place across Europe, parts of the USA and Canada. In America, at least two attempts were made to reintroduce beavers into Yellowstone National Park because of their importance in slowing the currents of rivers through their dam building. However, these attempts failed. It became very clear that another major link in the chain of life in Yellowstone was missing. For beavers to return, another keystone species had to return first—the apex predator who would help keep elk and deer populations under control—the wolf.

## Wolves to the Rescue

Wolves were exterminated in the continental USA in the 1930s. Hunted as 'vermin' because of their occasional kills of livestock raised by the Euro-American ranchers, their absence from the ecosystem in Yellowstone led to disastrous effects causing catastrophic cascading ecosystem collapse—a collapse that actually boomeranged on the ranchers themselves.

Without wolves preying on grass-eating animals like deer and elk, the populations of the unguents exploded, leading to uncontrolled browsing. Young trees and saplings of birch, aspen and willow weren't given a chance to grow and eventually died, leaving only much older trees alive—trees whose normal lifespan is about seventy years. By the 1990s, these older trees started dying off as well simply from old age, leaving the 'forest' bereft of trees.

The heavy browsing by elk and deer of the shrubs and bushes in meadows and along the rivers meant less food for other wildlife like birds, squirrels and especially grizzlies and black bears, who relied on various berries from these plants to bulk up for the months of winter hibernation. No berries meant less fat reserves, leaving the bears facing starvation and death during their cold winter months' fast.

The shrubs and grasslands had also held the banks of rivers together with their firm root systems. With these now completely gone, having been totally eaten too, there was nothing left to hold the soil in place. As rain fell and snowmelt swelled the rivers in spring, the banks of the rivers and streams collapsed, leading to severe soil erosion and actually altering the flow of rivers from their natural, slower, meandering pathways to straight torrents, which, in turn, led to massive flooding of the cattle ranches and farms downstream from the Yellowstone National Park. This was the main reason for those failed attempts to reintroduce beavers into the park. In addition, beaver dams can hold up to 30 per cent of the water released during heavy rainstorms or massive snowmelts, again helping to stop flooding downstream.

But the loss of birch, willow and aspen had meant no food for beavers either, especially to carry them through the winter as they would normally store the leaf-filled branches of these trees inside their lodge to eat during those frigid months. Without the trees, beavers disappeared altogether. As long as the number of unguents/ grazers remained too high, the unchecked browsing continued. Hence, there were no new aspen, birch, or willow saplings for the beavers to eat or use as building material for their dams.

In 1994, with the ecosystem in Yellowstone in catastrophic collapse, conservationists were finally allowed to reintroduce wolves back into Yellowstone National Park on an experimental basis, to see if their presence could help restore the balance of the ecosystem. The changes in the park in both flora and fauna were nothing less than astonishing in both their extent and speed— changes visibly seen and documented within just two to three years of their return.

With the wolves back, elk and other unguents could no longer denude an area of its vegetation. Wolves on the hunt would force them to run for their lives quite literally, chasing whole herds as far as five miles a day in a single hunt. This gave grasses and shrubs on the sides of rivers the chance to re-establish themselves, and tree saplings the chance to grow to heights where the browsers were no longer a threat to their survival.

As riverbanks stabilized and stands of birch, willow, aspen and other tree species were naturally restored, this very special keystone species—the American beaver—finally returned to the park. Its return marked another milestone in the recovery of this intricate and fragile ecosystem, delicately woven together with the 'threads' of different species creating this magnificent tapestry of life.

This rapid and astounding recovery of Yellowstone's ecosystem after the reintroduction of the wolf is an example of a positive 'trophic cascade'—where the return of a species at the top of the food chain can bring phenomenal beneficial effects all the way down to the smallest species of both plants and animals in the ecosystem.

From wolf to beaver to salmon—no matter the size of a keystone species or its placement in the food chain, the huge impact its presence or loss has on its ecosystem is overwhelming and incontrovertible. We could see this clearly from the beaver's pond. It was teeming with aquatic life, including salmon. Indeed, recent studies have documented just how critically important beavers are to healthy salmon populations, and also how those salmon become food for countless other species including insects.

As with Yellowstone, a beaver's dam slows down the waterway where it is located. Slower, calmer waters are precisely what is needed for baby salmon to live, grow and find food. By creating habitats for salmon, beavers not only help one species, but all the species dependent on the salmon for food—from bears and other mammals, to birds and countless insects—all benefit from the beaver's pond that give salmon a home—a wonderful example of the biodiversity multiplier effect of beavers in action. Looking above us to the number of bald eagles circling in the sky, as well as those perched on the tall trees on the edge of the beaver pond and river downstream, it was clear this was true.

It was also clear to see how the salmon that were living in the river and beaver's pond were critical for the forests of this area as well, since their remains left in the woods supplied up to 80 per cent of the nitrogen needed by the forest trees. Douglas fir, Sitka spruce, western hemlock and red cedar were all thriving due to the nitrogen obtained from leftovers of the bears' salmon meals. In our travels across Alaska and Canada, Anil and I could definitely see the easily measurable difference in height, girth and health of forest trees near salmon-stocked waterways and those without— the salmon forests far better in every way.

In addition, these forests are not just important to the local wildlife and people that live in the region. They are critical for the entire world. Scientists state that this area of forest known as 'Taiga or Boreal Belt' which encircles the northern hemisphere stores more carbon than all of the world's tropical and temperate forests combined, storing about twice as much carbon dioxide per acre when compared with tropical forests— obviously a critical carbon sink needed to mitigate global effects of climate change.

Without salmon, many of these forest areas would be at risk, lacking the nutrients they need to be healthy. An unhealthy forest means a reduction of the ecosystem services it supplies to the Earth's biosphere and therefore to humanity as well. With the loss of a keystone species like the salmon, catastrophic cascading ecosystem collapse is the consequence as we saw in Yellowstone.

This vital link between certain animals and the health of the people and forests that depend on an ecosystem was obviously understood by the indigenous peoples of the northern hemisphere. Hence, they are considered sacred and often recognized as guardians of the people. They are also honoured in various ways, including their depiction on totem poles, often representing an animal's relationship to the family group who has made and erected the pole.

Anil and I saw a number of beautiful, very colourful totem poles while traveling through western Canada and Alaska, especially in the Sitka area of Alaska, where the magnificent forests there were again the result of the salmon-nutrient cycle. Salmon, bear, wolf, beaver, orca and eagles (depicting the Thunderbird—creator of thunder and lightning with the beating of his wings) were animals we saw most often on these poles, along with one other keystone species of critical importance to life in the Pacific Ocean—the sea otter.

## The Otter Side of Life

The Pacific Ocean, off the western coast of America and Canada, is filled with giant kelp forests. Kelp is a type of algae that can reach heights of thirty to forty-five metres in a single growing season. Indeed, reaching for the sunlight near the surface of the sea, giant kelp can grow between ten to twenty-four inches in just one day! These forests are every bit as rich in species diversity as are tropical rainforests and coral reefs. Like coral reefs, they provide excellent areas for fish and other small aquatic life to reproduce, the kelp forests affording them areas to lay their eggs as well as plenty of hiding places for their various young to stay in until they grow large enough to strike out on their own in the great blue sea.

The top predator in these giant kelp forests is the sea otter. There are two different species that live almost their entire lives at sea, amidst these great forests of giant kelp—the northern sea otters and the southern, or California, sea otters. Otters like living in rocky areas where large populations of mussels are found, mussels being one of their staple foods. When they pry the mussels off the rocks, gaps are left for other species to inhabit, thus increasing the biodiversity of the area. Besides mussels, their main sources of food include different species of shellfish like crabs, sea urchin and abalone—a sea creature that is also a favourite food of humans. Hence, otters were viewed as unwanted competitors for the abalone by fishermen and massacred as a result.

Furthermore, sea otters were hunted for their pelts as early as the 1700s by the Russians since otter fur is extremely thick, warm and virtually waterproof. When Euro-Americans and Canadians started hunting otters along the continent's Pacific coast as well, populations crashed dramatically in just a few decades. By 1911, sea otters were virtually extinct, with fewer than 1000 individuals left in the wild.[*]

---

[*]   Refer to the bibliography for source.

The lack of sea otters in kelp forests caused a massive ecological disaster. With no sea otters to eat them, the sea urchin population exploded and completely destroyed the kelp along the entire western coastline. Without these kelp forests, the nursery grounds for all kinds of fish and other aquatic creatures disappeared, with populations of these species plummeting. This included the abalone, whose numbers had a similar drop, their loss and that of fish and other aquatic species bringing economic ruin and near total collapse of the US fishing industry there.

At this point, an international treaty banning the commercial hunting of sea otters brought an end to the slaughter. With strong laws to protect them finally put in place, sea otters started to make a comeback, albeit a slow one that took many years. With their return, the explosion of sea urchins was brought under control, which allowed the vital kelp forests a chance to grow. With kelp nurseries now available, fish and other aquatic creatures returned to reproduce, helping to recreate the vast abundance that had once been the norm in these extraordinarily rich, biodiverse underwater forests of life.

Over the years, numerous studies have shown that otters were never to blame for declines in the number of abalone in the Pacific at all. On the contrary, otters are now being credited with the abnormally large size of abalone in areas where abalone and otters co-exist, in comparison to parts of the world where otters are absent, such as the tropical Indo-Pacific region. In the Indo–Pacific waters, abalones are tiny creatures, no more than two inches wide. But in coastal waters shared by abalone and otters, abalones grow to the size of dinner plates, being as large as seven inches across.

Researchers believe that the explanation for this huge size difference comes from the protection of giant kelp forests by the resident otters, the otters keeping the population of destructive sea urchins under control. This gives abalone and other species an abundance of rich, nutritious kelp to eat, while the abalone uses the rock crevices cleared of mussels by otters, as hiding places. Simply put, wherever otters are present, kelp forests flourish, along with all the diverse fish and aquatic species that make the kelp forest their home. Where otters are not present, kelp forests have disappeared completely, as has all the biodiversity, and the area's barren ocean floor is littered with oversized sea urchin corpses which add to the empty, eerie death scene all around.

This five-million-year-old relationship has benefitted otters, abalone and innumerable other aquatic creatures, and proves that any drop in abalone or other fish stocks is clearly not the fault of otters, but the fault of the 'newcomer' on the block, humanity, with its overfishing, pollution and destruction of habitat. Indeed, otters are finally being recognized for what they are—a critical keystone species whose presence is essential for the ecological health of the oceans where they live, whose impact touches all other species in their coastal regions and whose contribution actually extends to the entire biosphere of the Earth.

Kelp forests absorb wave energy and slow water currents by more than two-thirds compared to currents outside the forests, thereby protecting coastlines from erosion, especially from extreme storms that are becoming the norm in this era of climate change. As mentioned earlier, much of the carbon that humanity continues to release into the atmosphere ends up in the oceans, turning them more acidic. Being enormous plants, these giant seaweed forests help to de-acidify the waters around them by absorbing carbon from the water during photosynthesis, thereby protecting shellfish and marine life in general.

The carbon-capturing abilities of healthy kelp forests are amazing—they can absorb billions of kilos! In one study comparing a world with otters protecting kelp forests with a world without otters, the difference in the annual carbon absorption of kelp photosynthesis is between 13 and 43 billion kilos. Clearly, the sea otter is a species whose protective presence is essential for the entire planet.

Anil and I were fortunate to observe these wonderful creatures in their natural habitat when we visited Alaska in the mid-1980s. Floating on their backs in the icy waters against a backdrop of unimaginable beauty—pure white glaciers and stunningly exquisite, sapphire-blue icebergs—they presented the perfect picture of contentment, resembling adorable balls of fur, bobbing up and down among the small waves rippling past. Several of them had large stones on their chest which they used as an anvil, hitting the hard shells of various prey they had caught to crack them open. Some mothers carried little babies on their body, hugging them close to their hearts and occasionally blowing air into the baby's fur to puff it up even more so that the little one would float if he or she fell off mom. This is crucial to do since the fur of the young babies is not waterproof, and if saturated by the sea water, the little one would sink and drown since babies don't yet know how to swim. Their friendly, endearing nature touched our hearts, instantly making them one of my all-time favourite animals. My love for otters endures to this day, which includes the wonderful otters that have made our sanctuary here in India their home, too.

Little did we or the otters know on that day, decades ago, that in just a few years, thousands of otters would be killed by the massive Exxon Valdez oil spill in Alaska's Prince Edward Sound in March 1989—a devastating catastrophe whose effects continue to plague the otter population there to this day, thanks to spilt oil still lingering in their environment more than thirty years later.* Nor were any of us aware that a new threat to their recently recovering numbers was looming on the horizon—a new predator that would be forced to seek them out as prey for its own survival—orcas or killer whales.

Prior to 1991, no attacks by orcas on sea otters had ever been confirmed. But when sea otter populations started to drop

---

* Refer to the bibliography for source.

precipitously during the 1990s, researchers were reminded of similarly plummeting populations, first with harbour and fur seals, and then with sea lions, in the 1970s and the 1980s. It was discovered that the population losses were due to orcas.

However, the real culprit here was humanity. Prior to commercialized whaling, orcas fed primarily on great whales in the North Pacific Ocean and Alaska's Bering Sea. One whale would feed the whole family pod with ease for several days, depending on the size of the whale and the number of orcas.

Unfortunately, with human greed bringing the great whale populations to the point of extinction, orcas had no choice but to seek out food substitutes to eat. Those substitutes were initially harbour and fur seals. Many more seals had to be killed by the orcas to sustain themselves compared to the killing of just one great whale; but the only other choice for the orca was to starve. Sadly, human covetousness for the pelts of these seals for fashion severely impacted their numbers. Since the early 2000s up to 2021, the 'allowable catch' of seals during Canada's annual hunt has been set at 400,000. That means up to two million seals have been killed over the last five years in Canada's seal hunt alone, with 97 per cent of those slaughtered being young seal pups, less than three months old.

With this unsustainable butchery lowering seal populations dramatically, the orca had to shift to sea lions instead. But sea lions were also targeted by humans for hunting, bringing about a steep decline in the numbers of yet another species due to human avarice. Tragically, by the 1990s, the orcas were forced to shift once again—this time to sea otters—a much smaller food source that had to be eaten in even greater numbers by the orcas just to stay alive, resulting in a massive drop of sea otter populations.

This terrible turn of events was not just a tragedy for otters—it was a disaster for the oceans and biosphere of the planet as well, considering the critical role sea otters play in mitigating the effects of climate change. With otter numbers declining, sea urchin numbers climbed once again, and great kelp forests died as a result, being eaten away to nothing—all of this the result of humanity's insatiable desires and unsustainable exploitation of various species to the point of their extinction, which will ultimately lead to our own extinction as well!

It is critical for us all to understand that each and every part of Nature is connected to each and every other part, directly or indirectly. When the numbers of one species unnaturally and abnormally climb or plummet, ripple effects of the change are felt throughout the fabric of the tapestry of life. When just one species is removed, all the threads of life are weakened. Each catastrophic ecosystem collapse that follows results in gaping holes in this great tapestry, which spells environmental ruin for us all.

In India, the main animal credited with eco-engineering like the American beaver, is the Asian elephant, whose presence in our forests is critical for their health, rejuvenation and expansion. This includes the creation of small ponds and channels for freshwater capture during rainfall—by the deep depressions they make in the earth while scraping the ground with their feet—and through their migration routes, the soil becoming compacted and pressed down by their weight and their repeated use of the same paths.

India also has its own otter species that are essential parts of each ecosystem where they are found. Smooth-coated otters frolic in larger rivers, while here in our sanctuary, the families of the diminutive, small-clawed river otter are the ones playing hide-and-seek with us along with a third species that has just made a comeback in our area—the Eurasian!

Otters are particularly important, as they are 'indicator species', which means that they indicate the purity and health of the waterways where they live. If there is too much pollution, the otters will not remain in the area, since the amount of fish, crabs, mussels and other prey they need to survive will shrink having been poisoned by human pollution.

Most regrettably and appallingly, all three species of otters in India are threatened with extinction principally from unlawful hunting for their pelts. Their slaughter is closely linked to the criminal poaching of tigers and leopards, making up about 25 per cent of the wild animal skins seized and confiscated from illegal poachers in North India alone, in 2017. Between 1980 and 2015, 2,949 otter pelts were seized by authorities trying to control this disgusting trade in South and Southeast Asia, with 53 per cent of the overall otter pelts seized involving India.*

In 2019, the Convention on International Trade in Endangered Species (CITES) put smooth-coated and small-clawed river otters into Appendix I of their listing for endangered animals in the hopes that this would give them greater protection from unscrupulous traders. This is the highest listing and is the same as the listing for Bengal tigers. But to really control and eventually crush the illegal wildlife trade requires help from the general public to stop the demand for animal parts to begin with.

Once again, this raises the issue of the purchase choices that we make on a daily basis—what clothes we choose to wear, what trinkets we buy, which foods and medicines we purchase—they are all tied into one of two systems, either 'sustainability' or 'exploitation leading to extinction'.

What we choose to eat is just as critical, if not more so, than the garments we choose to cover our bodies. The mindless, irresponsible and even unethical consumption of certain foods can spell extinction for a species. Two examples of such foods are shark fin soup and sushi.

Between one and two million sharks are killed every year, mainly for use in shark fin soup. This unbelievably cruel, senseless and unsustainable slaughter is pushing sharks to the abyss of extinction, not to mention the inhumanity of the way the sharks are treated. Most sharks are caught, have their fins cut off and

---

* Refer to the bibliography for source.

then tossed back into the ocean to die an agonizing, slow and torturous death. Eating this meat endangers the human diner as well, since sharks are at the top of the food chain, which means that dangerously high levels of mercury, cadmium, arsenic and other heavy metals in the smaller fish that the sharks have eaten also become concentrated in the meat of the shark, poisoning the eater of the shark's flesh, too, by extension.

Shark populations are down by 95 per cent, with the populations of other large predatory fish like marlin, large cod, tuna and swordfish dropping by 90 per cent, over the last few decades.* The loss of these top ocean predators is already having damaging effects on the health of our oceans and overall marine food chain, effects that impact the health and liveability of the planet, as a whole.

And then there is humanity's insane obsession with eating raw fish in the form of sushi—a potentially highly dangerous food to consume as the raw fish can and has been found to contain bacteria, parasites and viruses as well as high levels of mercury that can have devastating effects on human health.

A brief history of sushi shows that its original purpose was to preserve fish over longer periods of time when there was no refrigeration, having its origin not in Japan, but in China in the second century BC. The traditional Chinese dish *narezushi* was made with fermented rice and heavily salted raw fish, the fermented rice and salt used to preserve the fish longer and to help control the growth of bacteria and microorganisms in an era lacking refrigeration. In fact, the fermented rice was not eaten with the fish, but discarded instead. The dish spread to Japan and became 'sushi' only in the eighth century AD, the Japanese using vinegar to ferment the rice faster, again for preservation of the fish due to no refrigeration.

Over the centuries, the dish changed in many ways, especially once it was introduced to the west, with the fish no longer being

---

*   Refer to the bibliography for source.

raw but cooked. This meant that the dangers of getting ill from bacteria or parasites was greatly reduced. Today, sushi has gone through many changes, including being deep fried as fast food, to becoming vegetarian and even vegan. In vegetarian sushi, the fish (raw or cooked) in the centre is replaced with mushrooms like the flavourful Shitake, eggplant, avocado, cucumber, cooked and/ or fermented soybeans, or other ingredients like bamboo shoots, all rolled up in seaweed and rice. There is even 'egg and/or cheese sushis' for those who like eggs and cheese. All of these vegetarian/ vegan choices mean no dangers of poisoning from any toxins in or on the raw or cooked fish including mercury.

They also mean no killing of the traditional species of tuna that have been used in sushi. This is critically important as these species are highly threatened with extinction. It is the consumption of traditional raw fish sushi that is literally wiping out both the blue fin tuna and yellow fin tuna. Only 2.6 per cent of the original population of blue fins survive today,* with growing concerns that this iconic fish will disappear completely from the Indian Ocean in a matter of a few years according to new studies released in 2021, with complete extinction in less than a decade being a real danger, as demand for traditional raw-fish sushi continues to grow. Considering the fact that these tuna can live to be forty years old, grow to lengths of nine feet and weigh 1000 pounds, it is absolutely criminal to catch them for the sake of 'fast food' on the one hand, or a 'status symbol' on the other when delicious and far healthier alternatives are already available.

Be it shark fin soup or raw fish sushi, our demand for 'delicacies' and animal foods is negatively impacting wild species and the entire planet in multiple ways, including fuelling the illegal bush meat and fishing industries to feed that demand. But the most abhorrent form of hunting has to be trophy hunting.

---

* Refer to the bibliography for source.

# 12

# From Europe to Alaska: Signs of Grace during Terrifying Encounters

'You're not a real man if you don't hunt.' This is what Anil was told when we were in Austria on our trip across Europe in the mid-1980s. Wanting to experience some of the most beautiful natural areas in Europe, we had already been to Switzerland and Germany, staying in B&Bs in the homes of local people throughout our trip.

Now in Austria, we were anxious to see the mountains and forests celebrated by that iconic movie *The Sound of Music*. While in Salzburg, we visited the actual wedding site of the real people— Sister Maria Augusta Kutschera and Captain Georg Von Trapp. They were married on 26 November 1927 at the Benedictine Abbey of Nonnberg in Salzburg where Maria had indeed spent two years of her life in the convent as a novice. The grand cathedral made famous in the wedding scene of Sister Maria to Captain Von Trapp is actually the basilica in Mondsee—a town about one and a half hours away from Salzburg. It was so fitting for us to be there then as we were celebrating our tenth wedding anniversary, the wedding scene from the movie making me remember our own beautiful wedding ceremony a decade earlier. Upon entering the church, I felt a definite hushed, spiritual uplift, a divine atmosphere filling and permeating the building, and me—a very elevating experience.

Then, it was off to those spectacular mountains—part of the Salzburg State Alps—to fill our hearts with the songs that Nature has sung there for thousands of years . . . except when we got there, we scarcely heard any 'songs' at all, except for the babbling brook behind the place we stayed. It was called *The House of Maria*, and the woman who ran this B&B was really named 'Maria'. Her son was a champion ice-motorcycle racer, having won a number of races across Europe, earning him a very good income as a result— an income he shared with his widowed mother.

The location was lovely—in the valley floor with woods all around and that 'singing' stream in the back right beneath our bedroom window, the stream fed by meltwater from the glacier further up the mountain. We were quite excited about exploring the woods and hiking up to that glacier. We had seen magnificent glaciers before while visiting Alaska, but that was from a boat in the ocean. We had never actually walked on one before.

It was mid-October, so the weather was cool, crisp and bracing, the air made even colder as we neared the glacier. It truly was an amazing feeling standing in front of this huge frozen river of ice. Walking on top of it was even more extraordinary knowing that it was moving imperceptibly under our feet. The surface of the glacier itself appeared a bit dark in areas from both dirt and what looked like soot. But on one side of it, crystal clear meltwater raced downhill to join that laughing stream where we stayed.

Meeting some local people there, they commented that the meltwater was much more this year than it had been in the past, adding that the glacier itself had shrunk in size, not extending down the mountain as far as it had only a few years ago. Signs of climate change and a warming planet were there to see, along with clear evidence of the effects of acid rain caused by the burning of fossil fuels for energy and other manufacturing industries—signs we recognized, having done research on these issues for our first book in the early 1980s. But few others realized it back then. Signs in the forest included a number of pine trees turning orange and dying due to acid rain as well as an increase in pine beetle populations, several winters being warmer than what had been normal in the 1970s.

Hiking through the forest was a sad 'repeat' of what we had experienced in the forests of Germany and Switzerland—no sounds or signs of 'life' anywhere, no animal scats, no deer droppings of any kind, not even birds singing. The girth and height of the trees in these forests were somewhat better than what we had seen before. This meant that at least these woods still had some older trees left in them. But on the trees, scattered in different locations in the woods, elevated wooden hunting platforms had been constructed, as they had been in Germany and Switzerland. Hunters would climb up on to them, wait in silence for any wildlife to come by and then shoot them from above. It was clear that hunting was a major activity in these forests, now bereft of wildlife as a result.

As we walked through the woods, we came upon a number of small wooden shrines dedicated to Lord Jesus. All of them portrayed His crucifixion on the cross, with Mother Mary and usually two other women praying at the base of the cross. Clearly the people of the area were deeply religious. This made it all the more contradictory and paradoxical to us when the son of our hostess made this statement to Anil: 'You're not a real man if you don't hunt.'

Anil asked him, 'Was Christ a "real" man?'

'Of course! He was the best of men. He was the Son of God,' replied the young man.

'Was Christ compassionate?' Anil asked.

'Yes, of course! It was because of His compassion for us that He died on the cross for our sins,' he answered.

'But Christ never hunted anything. On the contrary,' Anil said, 'Christ freed the animals meant for slaughter as "sacrifices" to God. Remember what He said? "God does not want the sacrifice of innocent blood of animals! What He wants is the sacrifice of your ego, your pride, your hate. Sacrifice those for God and be redeemed as a result!"'

The young man was stunned into silence. You could see from the expression on his face that he was reflecting on Anil's words and comparing them to his own actions of hunting. It was a very moving moment, seeing this man reflect on his actions, with hope that his reflection would lead to change.

It is important to note that in the decades since our visit, a tremendous amount of positive conservation work has been done across eastern and western European countries, the countries of the UK as well as throughout Scandinavia. Old-growth forests have been protected from logging and are still standing tall. Reforestation efforts have made tremendous strides with forests recovering throughout these regions. Critically endangered wildlife species have been brought back from the edge of the extinction abyss, with new life breathed into them through the heroic efforts of so many dedicated individuals, organizations and even various governments in different countries, with cooperation on a number of rewilding programmes crossing borders from one nation to the next.

This is wonderful news and a huge step in the right direction. These positive actions should inspire us all, no matter where we live, to get involved in similar efforts within our own communities and countries and to encourage our elected officials to create and implement similar conservation policies. In doing so, these policies will not only help wildlife and forests, waterways and seas, but the general public as well since healthy ecosystems will once again be able to provide us with the ecosystem services we all need to survive.

## 'I Believe in Miracles!'

The next country we were going to visit was Yugoslavia. We wanted to see the beautiful mountains and forests around Sarajevo—the site of the 1984 Winter Olympics—and to visit Medugorje—the site of apparitions of the Holy Mother that had been going on daily since 24 June 1981.

Prior to boarding the plane in Vienna, we had to identify our luggage on the tarmac of the airport before it could be loaded on to the aircraft—something we both had done many times before in other airports. However, when we landed in Belgrade, my suitcase was missing. Only Anil's had arrived, with no sign of where mine had gone, leaving me with just my small carry-on bag that only contained some cosmetics and jewellery. We made out a report at the baggage desk and were told to contact the customs officials in Sarajevo as well when we landed there. I was quite upset about the lost bag as now I had nothing to wear other than the clothes on my back. But I was soon to get downright terrified.

After getting our carry-on bags scanned, a very large policeman came over to me and gestured for me to follow him. He was well over six feet tall and very muscularly built. I cannot adequately express how absolutely scared I was! Being an American who had grown up during the height of the Cold War, seeing this giant of a man with the communist red star emblem on his cap positively petrified me, Yugoslavia being a communist-socialist country then. Looking at Anil with panic in my eyes, we both followed him into a small room where he closed the door behind us. Pointing to my bag, he made me empty its contents on to the table. Gesturing with his hands at the various jewellery boxes, he asked me in German why I was carrying so much jewellery with me and where I had gotten it.

Anil came to the rescue, answering for me in German, Anil's fluency in German having helped us throughout the entire trip in every country we visited, especially because people would look at me with my blond hair and blue eyes and expect me to know German. They were always surprised when he—not I—would answer, saying that I didn't understand German at all!

Anil explained to the policeman that I was his wife and that I had met my Indian mother-in-law for the very first time on this trip. He went on to clarify that it was the Indian custom for the groom's family to gift the new bride jewellery that the mother-in-law had been saving since the birth of her son for his bride. This was the reason for so much jewellery.

Then Anil talked with the policeman about the very special relationship India had with Yugoslavia since India's Nehru and Yugoslavia's Tito had been the driving force behind setting up the Non-Aligned Movement or NAM—a group of nations whose common goal was to stay out of the Cold War between the US and USSR to avoid being pawns or puppets in the hands of either super-power and instead, steer their own countries on the course that was best for their individual populations. This instantly struck a chord with the policeman, who immediately dropped his chilly demeanour, speaking warmly to Anil about their 'special relationship' as if they were old friends.

Watching the entire exchange, I had no idea at all what was going on. It wasn't the first time on this trip that I wished I understood German! From that point onwards, the policeman was as helpful as he could be, telling me to put all the jewellery back into my bag and to come with him right away. He radioed ahead to the gate where we were to embark on a plane to Sarajevo, telling them to hold the plane as he had two passengers that needed to get on. Running to get to the gate, we were the last two passengers in the last two seats on a completely full flight. I quietly cried during the entire flight to Sarajevo, a combination of relief and fright pouring out all at the same time.

When we landed in Sarajevo, we met the head of customs to lodge our complaint once again about my missing bag. The person in charge was a woman who spoke excellent English to my delight! She asked us why we were there in Sarajevo and what our plans were for our stay. We told her about our love of Nature, and that we were also going to drive to Mostar—a famous large town with an iconic bridge that attracted tourists from all over the world. She asked us if we were going anywhere else in Yugoslavia. Anil answered, 'Medjugorje.'

She stopped writing and looked at us individually in the eyes. Then, lowering her eyes, she said very quietly, 'I believe in miracles.'

To understand the importance of these words one has to remember once again that at that time, Yugoslavia was officially an atheistic socialist-communist country where religion was considered 'the opium of the people' (to quote Karl Marx) and 'miracles' did not exist. For this government official to admit that she believed in miracles, and to trust us by telling us this, certainly put her and her job in jeopardy.

She quickly finished filing the paperwork to track down my luggage, and then gave us her personal telephone number, telling us to check with her every other day to see if my suitcase had yet arrived. Wishing us a very warm and loving 'goodbye', she gave us directions to the hotel where we were booked in Sarajevo.

After a few days of shopping for clothes for me and trekking through the beautiful pine forests outside the city, we drove to Mostar where we did indeed walk on that beautiful, old, iconic bridge. We then drove onwards to Medjugorje where we had made arrangements to stay with a family within the small village. Arriving late morning, we went to our host's house, unloaded our luggage and quickly went to the village church. The apparitions normally took place in the evening at 6 p.m. in a room off of the main church area. But, during the day, small groups of pilgrims were being allowed to visit that room.

When it was our turn, we entered the relatively small room which had a little altar to the left side with chairs in front for sitting. There was also a window on the wall opposite the door which was fully open. It was the third week of October and already quite cool during the day and downright cold at night—a problem for me as all of my warm nightwear was in my lost suitcase! And yet, after sitting in the apparition room and praying for a few minutes, I was engulfed in an inexplicable warmth, experiencing the same warm feeling within as well. After Anil and I left the church, I mentioned the strange occurrence to him, but didn't share it with anyone else.

A few hours later we were back at the church again for the evening apparition. Of the six children who normally saw the daily apparitions, only four were there that night. The two not in attendance were Marijana since she already received all ten of the prophetic 'secrets' the Holy Mother was passing on to them, and Vicka, who was doing a month-long sacrifice of abstaining from the visions as requested of her by the Madonna or 'Gospa', as they called her.

After the apparitions, messages for the general public were translated into various languages and posted on the church walls for all to read. The messages usually underscored the Madonna's main focal points of peace, prayer, penance, fasting and conversion entailing a return to and love for God coupled with living a spiritual, morally righteous life. The Gospa also stressed that all are Her children no matter their religion, culture, or place of origin—all humanity is one family—children of the same Divine Creator no matter what name one uses to identify this supreme being and should, therefore, live in peace and harmony, mutual respect and tolerance, always demonstrating love towards one another.

Back at our host's home, we bathed and then had dinner with the rest of the guests staying there—a priest from Ireland and an older woman travelling with an American couple who were her friends. Discussions around the table focused on the events of the evening as well as sharing experiences they had had or others had had while in Medjugorje, one of which immediately resonated with me. The Irish priest mentioned how some of the pilgrims he had met over the years had felt a strange warmth surround their bodies while in the apparition room even though the room itself was quite cold! I looked quickly at Anil, but we both kept silent.

The following morning, we trekked to the summit of Mount Podbrdo where the people of Medjugorje had erected a huge cement cross many years before the apparitions began. It was a long climb upwards, on a zig-zagging dirt path that was certainly not an easy thing to do for the infirm or elderly. Yet, we saw many people of all ages and conditions making the uphill hike. This included one older paraplegic woman who had been in a wheelchair for years. While we were ascending the mountain, we met her and her nurse as they were descending. Anil asked the nurse with the woman, 'How did you go up the mountain with the wheelchair?'

The nurse, mentioning that her patient is German, replied in English, 'I didn't take the wheelchair all the way up. My patient got out of the wheelchair and ran to the top on her own!'

Anil then asked the patient in German, *'Was hast du gemacht* (what have you done)?'

The woman patient replied, *'Ich weiß nicht. Es ist die Mutter* (I don't know. It is the Mother)!'

An inexplicable occurrence—one of many others we witnessed and heard about while there, including seeing the word 'MIR' ('Peace' in the local language of Croatian) written in letters of light across the sky—an event witnessed by dozens of people in the Medjugorje valley below, the Holy Mother identifying Herself as the 'Queen of Peace' to the visionaries.

When we reached the cross at the summit of Mount Podbrdo, we looked out on to the beautiful valley floor below, the steeples of Medjugorje's church rising high in the centre of the valley, with woodlands, orchards and farmlands all around. The peace of the lovely, panoramic, pastoral landscape was suddenly shattered by the loud whirring of a government helicopter overhead. We had been taking pictures of the scenery along with the giant cross, so Anil snapped a couple of photos of the helicopter, too!

Two men there, 'suited and booted' (as Anil would say), who did not look like pilgrims at all, but rather like undercover government intelligence agents saw Anil taking the photos and asked Anil in German what he was doing. Anil countered, asking, 'What are you both doing here? Are you here for the Mother and the cross?' Flustered, they mumbled something and left.

Only later, at dinner with the other guests, did we learn how dangerous that action could have been. The priest relayed how a number of pilgrims who had brought what the government considered 'seditious' or 'religious propaganda', and/or had taken photos of the government's routine helicopter buzzing of pilgrims on Mount Podbrdo and Apparition Hill had been taken into custody, their literature, photos and cameras confiscated, the pilgrims then forced to leave Yugoslavia at once. We were lucky!

The next morning, we decided to climb Apparition Hill—the site of the first apparition of the Holy Mother on 24 June 1981. The hill was much lower than the mountain, but still afforded us some beautiful views, the atmosphere being very peaceful, and much quieter compared to Mount Podbrdo, with far less pilgrims, too. We spent some time there praying and meditating, absorbing the peace and spiritual aura all around us.

As we were walking back to our host's house through the village, we happened to come upon the home of Vicka—the

(*Right to left*): Anil, his mother, Indira Devi, and her guru, Sri Dilip Kumar Roy, called Dadaji.

My mom and dad with Anil and me, on our wedding day, 9 October 1976.

The Gale Family: Peter, Mom, Dad, Patty; (*left to right, back*) Pam, Paul and Pris.

The Five Ps, grown up. Pam, standing with Peter. (*Seated*) Paul, Patty (*in the centre*) and Pris (*on the left*).

Anil, his mom and me, on our first day together at the ashram in 1986.

Old photo by the river below the house. Notice how open it is. Today, the place has far more trees.

Anil and me in front of one of our favourite waterfalls in Uttarkashi.

Anil and me, on the roof of the house looking out at the sanctuary.

Anil and me, in what is now known as the Uttarakhand region, when we owned land and lived there.

Me on the river.

Anil and me, sitting at the river.

Credit: Naseer N.A.

Me at Corbett, above the river where we met 'northern cousin' otters.

Me with the Nari Shakti Award at the Rashtrapati Bhavan, 8 March 2017.

Anil and me below the face of the Bhagirathi mountain peak above Gaumukh, where the Gangotri glacier ends and the Ganga starts flowing.

Trekking through the Himalayas.

Anil, my beloved rainbow man.

A reverse autumn. A fresh flush of red growth adorns the sanctuary's trees post monsoon.

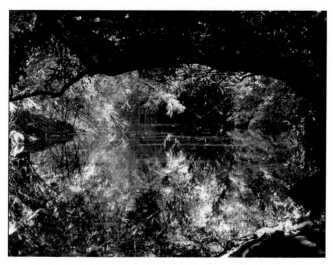

Reflections in the pond under a tree arch.

Natural grasses, incredible colours, in our natural meadow areas that grazers love.

The heart of the sanctuary.

Years later, our lush green sanctuary. The bird
seen here is the graceful white egret.

View of the sanctuary and the Brahmagiri hills
from our rooftop.

My friend Crabbie the crab.

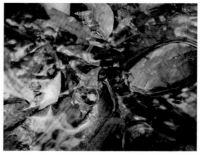

Terri the terrapin.

The Malabar hornbill drying its feathers
in the sun after a dip in the river.

A kingfisher dad feeding fish to
his baby.

Clover, finally free. One of our rescue
parrots released into the wild.

Tigers, being creatures of habit, often retrace the well-worn paths they take. This one came back in April 2020 and again in January 2021.

A gaur eating leaves at the edge of one of our largest natural wetland meadows.

A different meadow area called View Field, with a sambar fawn walking across at dawn.

Lav, Sita's baby.

Cheetal (spotted deer) does with a fawn.

Three members of the elephant family, at home
in SAI Sanctuary.

Palm civet.

Open-billed stork.

A Malabar giant squirrel enjoying
a jackfruit.

Mr Otter in our big pond, popping up to say hello!

SAI Sanctuary: A butterfly haven.

Some more butterflies.

A group of blue tiger butterflies.

Different species of butterflies grouping together in wet sand to drink up the minerals.

A male Malabar trogon.

The Neelakurinji flowers that bloom only once every twelve years.

The Nilgiri langur, very rare and only found in the Western Ghats. Their tail is as long as their body.

The Asian leopard cat. They are the size of a house cat, and have been roaming freely and reproducing at SAI Sanctuary.

Sambar alpha buck's 'peek-a-boo' to the camera.

Still from a video taken on 6 March 2021. He soaked in our 'sanctuary spa' for fifteen minutes!

The SAI Sanctuary logo.

visionary who was doing the month-long sacrifice of not seeing the daily apparitions of the Holy Mother. She was in her courtyard chasing a chicken to put it back into its enclosure—a funny sight indeed! Seeing us smiling at her, her face lit up with a most radiant smile. Giggling, she motioned for us to come in, and then extended her hand to shake ours, holding on to my hand for some time and posing with us for photos.

It was only later that we learned Vicka had been diagnosed with a malignant brain tumour—a diagnosis confirmed through a brain scan, the location of the tumour being in an area that was surgically inaccessible. But the tumour was discovered only after the Gospa had asked Vicka to do this one-month sacrifice. This explained why her hands were ice cold! Vicka had already told her priest that the Gospa would cure her of this tumour, the Holy Mother telling her the exact date when the tumour would disappear. Vicka wrote down that date on a piece of paper, then put the paper into an envelope and sealed it. She then put the sealed envelope into a second envelope and sealed that, giving that envelope to her priest.

Two weeks after we left, the tumour miraculously disappeared on the exact date Vicka had written down, her priest only opening the envelope when Vicka asked him to do so. The disappearance of the tumour was confirmed by brain scans—it had vanished, leaving no trace of it anywhere. Vicka recovered fully and completely with no brain damage whatsoever. Absolutely miraculous!

Right after meeting Vicka, we got news from the customs lady that my suitcase had been found and was due to arrive at the airport that Saturday night. We left early the following morning, drove straight through to Sarajevo, calling her upon our arrival, only to find that the airport was closed as it was a Sunday. This put us in a real bind because we had tickets to fly from Belgrade to Canada on Monday morning, so had to get to Belgrade that Sunday itself.

This wonderful woman proceeded to open up the airport just for us to clear my suitcase through customs so we could leave. But before leaving, she insisted that we accompany her to her apartment where she, her mother and her sister lived. She had just celebrated her birthday and wanted to share some chocolate cake and Turkish coffee with us before we left. We stayed with her and her mother for at least three hours, eating cake and talking about God, miracles and spirituality. She was so open and interested in all we shared with her, drinking in every word. We left one of the spiritual books I had been reading with her and asked her if we could send her more through the mail. She thanked us for the kind offer but said that could be very dangerous for her—a reflection of the reality of the country where she was living at that time.

Bidding her and her mother 'Farewell', we took off for the long drive to Belgrade, arriving late at night. I finally got to open my suitcase in order to get nightwear out and a change of clothes for the next day. It was only then that I realized why my suitcase had been 'lost'—at the bottom of the bag was a copy of our first book *The Phoenix Returns*—a book of comparative philosophy and prophecies that included references to the apparitions of the Madonna there in Medjugorje and the very negative attitude of the atheistic government towards them. Had the government officials found this book in my suitcase in Belgrade, I could well have been arrested!

Instead, I had been the recipient of tremendous grace and protection, with my suitcase having journeyed to *'Manchester, England, England—across the Atlantic Sea!'* as the lyrics say in the hit Broadway musical *Hair!*—a play written to protest both the forced conscription of American young men into the US army, commonly called 'the draft' (as mentioned in Chapter One) and the Vietnam War in general, many of its songs becoming anthems for the anti-war peace movement. Anil and I saw the premier of the movie version in 1979 while living in Denver—just a few years before our visit to Yugoslavia.

Unfortunately, we were never able to reconnect with this spiritual, loving woman or her family again due to the outbreak of yet another war—the brutal genocidal war that broke out in 1990 consuming the entire country of Yugoslavia, breaking it apart into seven separate nations with the most shocking and gruesome violence and scenes of mass ethnic-cleansing horrifying the world. Sarajevo was bombed relentlessly by Serbian forces, each new airstrike causing us to think of her and her loved ones, hoping and praying that somehow, some way they had escaped the carnage safely and were out of danger.

Since the messages began, one of the main points the Holy Mother kept emphasizing was an admonishment for not practicing and believing in the power of fasting and prayer. As She put it:

> You have forgotten that with prayer and fasting you can stop a
> war from happening.
> You can suspend natural laws.

Since the end of the war, a few of the ten secrets the Madonna gave to the children about future events on the planet have been made known—some of them referred to the coming of this war and the turmoil it would bring. But Her message above is still relevant today as 'Peace on Earth' has yet to be realized. Her call for peace, prayer and reconciliation with God truly are the divine formula to transform the ever-hopeful dream of world peace into a living, breathing reality for us all.

## More Divine Protection

On our summer trip to Alaska, Anil and I had another terrifying and yet extraordinary experience while flying from Juneau to

Anchorage. The plane we were on was a small commuter aircraft that was filled to capacity. The weather was not good at all—heavy dark cloud cover with rain and gusts of wind buffeted the plane up and down, and from side to side—without question, the worst turbulence I have ever had to endure while flying. Everyone in the plane was very concerned if not thoroughly scared like me! I held on to Anil's hand and just kept praying for God's help to get us all through this turmoil and land safely in Anchorage. I could hear other people nearby praying as well.

Suddenly, a woman behind us shouted, 'Look!' pointing out the window towards the clouds near the plane. Looking out, we could clearly see the image of a woman dressed in a long gown with a shawl over her head, standing in the midst of the clouds! You could hear people gasp with disbelief at the sight, while others tried to take photos. As soon as the image in the clouds appeared, the turbulence subsided. Then the rain stopped, the dense cloud cover parted in one area and the sun's rays came shining through just as the plane reached Anchorage; the aircraft finally landing safely to everyone's relief!

The following morning our hostess showed us the local newspaper. We had told her about the scary flight and incredible sight we had seen, but of course scepticism is often difficult to avoid in such events. Now, however, she was more convinced—on the front page of the paper was a photo that one of the other passengers on the same flight had taken. The image of the woman in the clouds was very clear, many saying it was the Holy Mother that had come and helped us all.

This led to a discussion about miracles and prophecies. We shared several of them from our first book, mentioning that increased earth changes and changes in the climate for our times had not only been foretold by seers and prophets, but were now being verified by scientists around the world. Just as Anil finished saying this, an earthquake shook the house! It was not a large quake, but certainly enough to make us all stop talking. It was as if Mother Nature was adding an exclamation point to what Anil had said!

Alaska is spectacularly beautiful! At that time, it still had many dense old-growth forests filled with wildlife. One of the highlights of our trip was our visit to Denali National Park. Among its many awe-inspiring sights was the undeveloped, unspoiled, pristine, snow-covered mountain peaks of the Alaska Mountain Range glistening in the sunlight, the mountains rising majestically above the Arctic Tundra terrain dressed in early autumn colours of golds and orange.

The open landscape made viewing of wildlife easier—moose, a mother grizzly bear with two cubs, a lone wolf, an Arctic fox still in his summer coat of brown fur and many bald eagles were just some of the animals we were fortunate enough to see. Visiting at the end of summer, we experienced close to twenty-four-hours of daylight, the sun rising by around 5.30 a.m. and just starting to dip below the horizon after 10.30 at night. But it did get dark enough an hour or so after sunset that we were able to witness the astonishingly exquisite aurora borealis—shimmering vibrant waves of green, yellow and pink, violet, red and blue dancing across the darkened night sky—a spectacle I will never forget and will always cherish.

However, sometimes travelling through Alaska was also like stepping back in time from the point of view of consciousness. It was as if we had suddenly entered the Wild Wild West once again, where guns and drinking saloons went hand in hand! For most of our drive from Anchorage to Denali National Park, the only establishments we saw on the highway were liquor bars and gun shops, that too, usually next to each other—what a combination!—one of the gun shops actually having an effigy of a man hanging from a noose outside its front door!

What was far worse were some of our experiences walking in the forests there. Usually, we would follow whatever waterway was in the area, trekking upstream since it would often lead to an area where wildlife would congregate for drinking. As I normally took the lead, I would always check for signs of recent wildlife activity on the trail—any tracks, hoofprints or pugmarks of any kind, recent deer droppings or other animal eliminations, broken twigs, branches, or nibbled leaves of plants and, of course, any sounds like the rustle of leaves or footfalls as well as calls or animal 'chattering'.

While hiking through Tongass National Park near Juneau, we followed a deer trail next to a small stream in the hopes of catching sight of a deer or two since there were quite a few fresh deer droppings on the trail. The woods were lovely and it was a bright sunny day making it easy to see through the trees. All was peaceful and calm, with the sound of the stream and singing of birds all around delightful to hear. Suddenly, the peace was shattered by gunshots behind us. A couple of bullets went whizzing by, hitting the trunk of a tree to our right. Someone was shooting at us!

Anil was furious and wanted to confront the hunters.

I said to him, 'Are you crazy?! They may shoot you before you even reach them! Let's run and get out of here!'

We ran down the trail as fast as we could, following it as it took a bend to the right around the base of a small hill, hoping the hill would give us cover from any more shots. Finally, we found our way out of the woods a few hundred metres up the highway from where we had parked our car. Jumping in, we drove as quickly as we could back to the B&B where we were staying, passing another parked vehicle—probably the hunters'—not far from where we had parked ours.

Going over the terrifying event in our minds, it was clear that the hunters had to know that there were other people inside the forest since our car was clearly visible on the road. In addition, the woods were not that dense—you could see plenty of metres ahead of you since logging had been done in this forest years earlier.

On top of that, it was not yet hunting season, so why were they in the forest with their rifles at all?!

There is no question that I was definitely traumatized by the incident, all these unanswered questions swirling around in my head, while also profusely thanking God for protecting us and keeping us safe. I just couldn't wait for us to get on the plane the following day and head for Anchorage! Of course, little did I know then about the panic I would experience on that flight, thankfully followed by a tremendous outpouring of more divine grace as mentioned before!

Yet another frightening and disturbing confrontation took place while we were hiking through the forest of the Kenai Peninsula. Emerging from the forest at the top of a high open hill, we started making our way down to the road below. About halfway down, I was suddenly filled with an uneasy feeling that intensified to a terrible sense of foreboding.

I said to Anil, 'I feel like we are in the rifle sights of a hunter! We have to get down as fast as we can!'

The hillside was quite open with little tree cover due to the clearcutting of the original forest that had been there years earlier, leaving us completely exposed to anyone looking up the hill. Literally running the rest of the way down, we finally reached the road where, sure enough, there was not one, but two hunters waiting below with rifles in their hands.

Walking directly over to them, Anil asked them what they were doing. They seemed flustered by his very direct approach, mumbling 'Nothing . . . nothing . . .' in response. They quickly got into their pickup truck and drove away. Clearly my fearful premonition was accurate!

As we made our way back to the house of our B&B hostess, we crossed a small wooden bridge. Coming from the opposite direction was another man who turned out to be a local Native American. Meeting in the middle of the bridge, Anil introduced himself as an east Indian to the American Indian who had never met any east Indians before. As East met West, there was a feeling of instant kinship towards each other, the two 'brothers' embracing one another.

When Anil relayed what we had just experienced with the two white hunters, the Native American replied that white hunters often trespass on their reservation lands to kill wildlife—not for food, but for 'sport'—even cutting down trees and hauling them away—all illegal activities since the reservation is 'off limits' to non-members of the Indian tribe. But there was little they could do to stop it since the local authorities did nothing to curb these criminal actions even after repeated complaints lodged by the tribe.

Anil then stated, 'My people in India have prophecies about these times which warn that uncontrolled deforestation and hunting, along with pollution and complete disregard for Mother Nature, will bring horrible consequences for humanity, even bringing us to the brink of extinction.'

'We too have similar prophecies,' the Native American replied.

'It's important to warn people of the dangers coming if people don't change their ways and continue on this path to destruction,' Anil said.

'We have tried, but they do not listen to us or our warnings,' he replied.

'If they don't change, then they will bring destruction upon themselves.'

'They will never change,' the Native American said sadly. Sharing one last warm embrace, we parted.

## Demented Minds, Empty Hearts, Dead Souls

The house of our B&B hostess in Kenai Peninsula overlooked a cove where various fishing vessels were docked. Upon our arrival at the house, we told her all that had happened, including the encounter with the Native American and the discussion about prophecies. Echoing what the Native American said, she added, 'The mentality among some of the men here is very cruel. They often kill sea gulls and then cut them in half, stuffing them into their crab traps as bait! It's very sickening to watch, but being a woman alone here, it's dangerous for me to raise my voice.'

Her remarks reminded us of what another B&B hostess had relayed to us in Fairbanks. A lovely, lively woman, she was a cancer survivor—breast cancer—having fought the deadly disease not only with allopathic methods but with alternative therapies too. She credited a book by another cancer survivor with giving her the courage and strength to face the illness, as well as the step-by-step alternative-therapy methods outlined in the book she believed helped her conquer and win her battle. She then gave me a copy of the book *Cancer Winner* by Jaquie Davison—the story of a woman with fourth-stage, malignant melanoma who triumphed over cancer in the most amazing way. Little did she or I know that decades later, I would be facing the same battle that she had fought and won!

About the mentality of hunting, our hostess shared her own exasperation with many of the white hunters she knew—their cruelty and lack of any restraint in hunting wildlife at all, calling them heartless so-called 'he-men', all members of the 'macho men's club'. The hunters that disgusted her the most were the same ones that disgust us—trophy hunters—engaging in a so-called 'sport' that is anything but sporting—killing animals for the sheer pleasure of killing. One has to wonder what kind of pleasure anyone can get from killing an innocent, unarmed and defenceless animal!

This 'thrill to kill' has to indicate some kind of psychological and/or emotional instability in the people who indulge in it—an instability that could have consequences on society as a whole, with the 'target' changing from wildlife to human—something that has happened a number of times already over the last few decades.

Studies have shown a definitive link between hunting and violent behaviour. Research done by Dr Murray Strause (director of family research at the University of New Hampshire) found that the states in America which had the highest number of hunters were also the ones that were most prone to violence, having the highest rates of homicides by teenagers who had been introduced to hunting at a young age. Researchers also found undeniable links between the incidences of hunting and child molestation, child abuse and human massacres; the obsession with guns has been found to have caused a rise in aggression, violence and crime.

The act of hunting itself desensitizes the hunter to cruelty, abuse, bloodshed and pain, turning killing into a thoughtless, casual act, deadening any thoughts or feelings of empathy, compassion, or remorse. This is especially true of the young. With most hunters usually being initiated into this mindless act of murder at an age just past puberty, it is important to note that the area of the brain that is active during hunting is also active during sex. The Genetic Economic Analytics Group has documented this neuro-physical link between sex and man's compulsion to hunt and kill animals, with brain scans confirming this fact.

Dr Karl Menninger earlier explored the correlation between hunting and sex, stating that hunting was a substitute for sexual gratification. Founder of the world-renowned Menninger School of Psychiatry and awarded the Presidential Medal of Freedom by then-president Jimmy Carter for his lifelong, groundbreaking work in psychiatry, Dr Menninger's research found that inflicting pain on another person or being gives rise to sexual excitement for the deranged abuser, his findings published in his paper titled 'Erotic Sadistic Motivational Theory of Sports Hunting'.

Dr Menninger noted that sadism may take a more socially acceptable form such as hunting and other aggressive and brutal 'sports', with all these actually representing the destructive and cruel energies of man directed toward more helpless creatures.

Building on Dr Menninger's work, the conclusions of researcher Dr Joel R. Saper of the University of Michigan and clinical psychologist Margaret Brooke-Williams, underscore this link. Basically, according to their findings, hunters are seeking reassurance of their own sexuality and the feeling of power from killing an animal brings them some temporary relief from their own sense of inadequacy and sexual unease.

Hunting is an overwhelmingly male-dominated activity, with 98 per cent of hunters in the USA and elsewhere being men. For young, mainly male teenagers with sexual hormones having begun to pump in excess, the act of hunting easily slips into a hunt for sexual conquest. So, as the teenagers seek their first kill, their brains treat it the same way as seeking their first sexual conquest. Their tendency to kill anything and everything in sight—which quickly changes to a craze for killing as many as they possibly can—mirrors their teenage tendencies in the context of sex, where they go after as many sexual conquests as they can in order to brag about it to others. It is clear to see the characteristic, albeit childish, immaturity at play in the younger hunting enthusiasts trying to prove their 'manliness' through acts of crudeness and cruelty.

It is no coincidence that the name for deer meat—'venison'— comes from the name for the goddess of love, Venus, or that the term 'venery' not only means the 'art of hunting', but also the 'pursuit of sexual pleasures'.

It is important to point out that the act of hunting *does not* bring the hunter any kind of sexual climax any more than the harassing persecution of another person by a bully. In both cases, the ones doing the killing and the ones doing the bullying are trying to cover up their own fear of failure, incompetence and ineptitude, their actions being an unhinged and unstable attempt to 'prove' themselves to others.

The search for higher social status 'with the boys' continues as they start to go for the best kill, killing the deer, elk, sheep, etc., with the largest set of antlers or horns. This is a particularly disruptive and destructive action from an evolutionary point of view for the species being killed, as human hunters removing 'the best' of the species means their removal of the alpha males, the biggest bucks and the matriarchs of a family group, which leads to a depletion in the gene pool of the species killed, the genes of smaller, weaker members being passed on to the next generation, instead of those of the strongest, which is the exact opposite of natural selection.

This is a critical problem with human hunting when compared to natural predators. Natural predators seek out the old, sick, weaker members of a species to kill as they are easier to catch. This helps support the evolution of the prey species, leaving the best, strongest, most intelligent, adaptable and resilient individuals to pass on their better genes through propagation. Human hunting does the opposite, which is counterproductive in passing on the improvements and adaptations needed for any positive evolution of the species in the future. It actually leads to the propagation of genetic weaknesses across the full spectrum of physical and intellectual development of the group, literally causing the 'devolution' of the animal species being hunted.

Studies have shown that species typically targeted by hunters have had an overall decrease in size by as much as 30 per cent over the last few decades, specifically for this reason, putting the entire species at risk since those left to procreate are not as fit or resilient as the larger individuals killed by human hunters. The act of killing the alpha male or female in a pack or herd animal causes stress, disruption and chaos for the entire family unit, and also puts them at risk from rival packs due to a lack of survival skills among the less-experienced family members.

Killing the matriarch of an elephant herd is a good example to illustrate this point. She is responsible for the welfare of her entire family and has knowledge of areas where water and food can be found, whereas the younger, less-experienced members do not. Killing the alpha male in a lion pride also has similar chaotic effects and puts the entire pride at risk. All cubs previously fathered by the slain male are usually quickly killed off by any new male that comes around trying to stake his claim to the now-vacant territory and the females in the family pride. The mother lionesses will try their best to defend their children, risking their own lives in the process.

This chaos was graphically documented when one beloved alpha male at a National Park in Zimbabwe, named Cecil, was killed by a hunter. His untimely death threw not one but two lion prides into disarray.*

## The Murder of Cecil

Cecil was a beautiful, majestic lion, dearly loved by the people in Zimbabwe where he lived, as well as by tourists from around the world. His calm demeanour, lack of fear of humans and exceptionally handsome features made him a prime favourite with photographers and researchers alike. The territory of the two prides which he 'ruled', along with his subordinate 'brother' Jericho, was located in Zimbabwe's protected Hwange National Park.

Cecil, along with other lions, had been part of a study being carried out by researchers from Oxford University for several years. As a result, he had been fitted with a GPS tracking collar so his movements could be easily monitored. The collar was still on Cecil when he was murdered. The tragedy of Cecil's death was compounded by the way he was killed, which is the next rung on the 'ego-status ladder' sought by hunters—the method by which creatures are killed, using lures and bait and/or killing with bows and arrows rather than using a high-powered rifle, which is usually a quicker death.

---

* Refer to the bibliography for source.

On that fateful day in July 2015, Cecil was lured out of the safety of the national park through the use of an elephant carcass, the scent lure extending from the park's border to the carcass almost one kilometre away. The poor elephant itself had fallen victim to a trophy hunter a few days earlier. Cecil's murderers lay in wait for him on an elevated hunting platform above the elephant carcass. As soon as Cecil stepped outside the border, following the scent lure of the elephant carcass, the hunter—an American dentist—shot him with an arrow, causing agonizing pain but not immediate death. The killer's skills as a hunter were so poor that he failed to hit any of Cecil's vital organs or arteries, because of which poor Cecil had to suffer in agony for over fourteen hours before he finally died.

This hunter and others from his murderous group could hear Cecil's pitiful groans and cries of pain. They heard his struggle to breathe, his excruciating and heart-breaking torture for fourteen full hours and yet were not moved by a shred of compassion to at least end Cecil's suffering quickly through the use of the guns the murderers had with them.

How disgusting can humans be! The entire episode revulsed people around the world and the ghastly photo of the smiling killers holding up poor Cecil's lifeless head nauseated those who saw it. What kind of perverse people kill for the fun of it? What type of demented individual can take joy in causing such torment and suffering and be proud of it?

The pain and agony suffered by this lion is suffered by millions of animals annually, who are wounded but not immediately killed in a hunt. In the USA alone, 4000 tons of toxic lead in the form of bullets is introduced into the environment by US hunters, leading to death by poisoning of 20 million animals each year. Over 100 million animals die each year at the hands of hunters. Even those that are part of scientific studies are not spared, as evidenced by Cecil's murder as well as over sixty other GPS-collared, male lions killed by trophy hunters, just in the fifteen years between 2003 and 2018.* So, imagine what of those who are not collared!

The number of lions in Africa has dropped from 200,000 to just 20,000 over the last century, with a 42 per cent drop occurring in just the last twenty years (from 2000 to 2020).† This includes one of Cecil's own sons, Xandu, a six-year-old, just starting the prime years of his life, who was murdered by yet another trophy hunter in 2017, just two years after Cecil's death, further crippling the gene pool for the species and compromising its entire survival.

Elephants are faring no better, with ninety-six elephants being killed every day, mainly for their ivory, but also by bloodthirsty, cold-hearted and insecure trophy hunters in search of status and reassurance, regardless of their gender. No one who kills an innocent animal is courageous or brave. They are cowards of the worst kind whose own life was never endangered by the poor animal they've murdered, but who are in desperate need of being stabbed in the heart with an injection of empathy and compassion, an awakening within their own soul of the horribly cruel and barbaric acts they are performing.

The few women who do hunt are clearly more preoccupied with 'manliness' over the empathetic nurturing often associated with femininity that is so desperately needed today. Their cruel actions are exactly the opposite of the loving, compassionate, understanding and protective role models that children all over the world need and should have, to help bridge the gap separating the peoples of the Earth.

It is important to remember that the strongest, fiercest creature in Nature is not the male, but the mother protecting her young from whatever threats come its way. This is true courage; this is real bravery, and this is what we human mothers must do as well,

---

*   Refer to the bibliography for source.
†   Refer to the bibliography for source.

by saying 'no!' to those who label cruelty as 'sport'; who mindlessly murder other beings with no remorse, who think so little of their own children that they endanger their future by shredding the tapestry of life through acts of toxic masculinity for nothing more than the gratification of the ego.

The individuals engaging in this disgusting behaviour are examples of the grotesqueness and disgrace to which some members of humankind can sink. They are that small group of humans who actually enjoy inflicting pain on other beings without a thought of regret or shame.

Those who claim that hunting can be a positive tool for conservation are guilty of outright distortion of facts. To date, no species has been 'saved' through being the target of hunters. No habitat or ecosystem has been 'saved' through the mindless act of exploitative hunting. This is but an attempt to justify the continuation of the murders along with the excuses like the need to feed their families or 'subsistence hunting' for survival.

The truth is that when the costs of hunting-licence fees, equipment, ammunition and time are all added up, those using these excuses could live on a diet of the costliest beef sold—filet mignon—for far less than it costs to hunt!

The truth is that Nature and wildlife ecotourism produces forty times more revenue than trophy hunting to the communities and countries involved. The truth is that the funds from trophy hunting overwhelmingly go to lining the pockets of a few individuals and are a major source of corruption in the officials of the countries involved.

There are hunters who evolve enough to no longer need to kill to prove their masculinity anymore. They finally discover what is truly important—their connection to Nature, the peace and joy they feel while being in the woods away from the din of humanity and the stress, tumult and turmoil of the artificial life we humans are leading today.

Within the heart of Nature lies salvation for us all. It is our duty and our privilege to protect that heart in any and every way we can, first and foremost through the choices we make in life. We must make conscious choices in what we eat, what we wear and how we live. We must endeavour to live in harmony and balance with Nature—preserving, not destroying; protecting, not poisoning—and live with the realization that, unless we do so, the future of our own species is not ensured at all. For that is the next cause of species extinction—poisoning of the Earth through human-generated pollution. That pollution poisons every element that makes up creation, inevitably leading to the poisoning of species across the planet, including our own.

# 13

# Embracing the Sun
## amidst a Poisoned Paradise

Peace, beauty, pure water, rich soil and abundant wildlife—these were the gifts given to us by Mother Nature when we bought the lands that were destined to be our first small sanctuary. In return for protection of this pristine place, Mother Nature provided us with all we would ever need to live comfortably as well as in balance within her heart.

Choosing a spot deep in the forest near the cliff overlooking one of the waterfalls, we set out to build a small wooden house where we could stay and soak up the purity and living spirit surrounding us, overjoyed to be beginning this adventurous part of our life together.

The names of the two carpenters who built the house were so very appropriate: Noah and Path. The sanctuary would certainly become an 'ark of life' protected from hunting, development and the other negative impacts that humanity has had on so much of the Earth's forests and wildlife. And we had indeed chosen to walk the path less travelled—a path that would require a great deal of learning and adjustment on our part as well as sheer physical strength and endurance since there was no road into our land. We had to walk through heavy rainforest to get to it and our building site. That meant packing everything on our backs and trekking through the thick mud to get there.

Our dear friends helped, as did some young men we hired for the work, one of whom had just finished his US army basic training. While walking in front of him carrying tools and other things, I could hear him muttering to himself, 'What kind of people live in a place like this! Only crazy people would live in a place like this! This is worse than basic training!'

We would be living off the grid, not connected to any utility company. So, if we wanted electricity, we would have to rely on Nature to provide it for us in a green, sustainable manner. The answer and logical choice was to 'embrace the sun' quite literally, using solar panels for electricity and solar heating for hot water.

We had been introduced to solar a few years earlier, while living in a condominium complex in Kona on the sunnier and drier western side of the Big Island of Hawaii. At that time, Anil was on the board for the homeowners' association, when President Jimmy Carter passed a tax credit on US income taxes for those investing in solar technology—an intelligent and hugely popular strategy to wean people away from fossil fuels and on to truly green alternative energy sources.

The installation of solar hot water heaters in the complex saved homeowners tens of thousands of dollars in electricity bills annually since water for the complex was previously heated through electricity. So, we had already experienced first-hand the value and efficiency of solar power for heating water.

Its use for electricity was something new for us but was again equally profitable and dependable even though our house was located on the eastern, wetter side of the island, and that too high up on the mountain slope where the rainforests there meant cloudier skies and far more rainy days than in sunny Kona. Still, the upfront investment in purchasing solar equipment was more than recovered through savings in electricity bills over the years.

We did, however, have to take far more care in hot water and electricity usage to ensure we had sufficient amounts of both when needed. These were great lessons in learning to use less, in conserving precious resources and in not overburdening, but living within, the ecosystem's ability to renew itself while still providing our essential needs.

For our water supply, we relied on rainwater harvesting, even though we had the only two perennial streams on the island within our land. We used a catchment system that directed rain falling on the roof of our car shed into an above ground tank for storage and use. This was yet more practice for us in conserving precious resources, especially the most essential and precious of all—water.

Then there was the question of living off the land, harvesting local plants and fruits to eat and growing our own food in the good, rich earth all around us. We had invested in a cast iron heating stove that used small wood pieces to burn for warmth on chilly, rainy nights, but also for heating up food. It had a steel plate on the top directly above the fire where cast iron cooking vessels and tea pots could be placed. Some years later, we got a gas stove and a small refrigerator that ran on either electricity or natural gas too.

As for food, the parents of one of our closest friends were absolutely incredible, both in harvesting and cooking local plants as well as in growing every kind of fruit and vegetable imaginable. D's parents had moved from the Philippines to Hawaii decades earlier. Economically speaking, they were initially quite poor. But their treasure trove of knowledge about Nature was precious and invaluable, living off what Nature gave to them and their young children in abundance.

D's mother showed me how to harvest the new unfurled leaves of certain ferns, cooking them into a very tasty meal. Everything they touched burst into life, growing beautifully and profusely without the use of chemical fertilizers or pesticides. They passed on their encyclopaedic wisdom to our dear friend D who shared it with us and helped us set up our own organic farming area within the sanctuary.

Embracing organic foods was something we had already started years earlier, buying organic whenever and wherever we could. Growing organic was a continuation of my gardening days with my own mom years earlier, along with composting and employing the concept of companion planting—planting two different types of plants next to one another or interspersed to help each grow and also to ward off any pests, an example being growing holy basil (tulsi) with tomatoes. But this was on a larger scale.

To discourage birds from eating some of our crops, we planted sunflowers around the entire border of our vegetable garden. This gave the birds a treat while encouraging them to fulfil their predatory role by eating garden pests like grasshoppers and other insects.

The feral pigs first introduced to the island by the original Polynesian settlers were another potential problem. The solution came in a silent agreement between us and the feral pigs—they could stay in our sanctuary safe from hunters eating all the roots and fallen fruit in the jungle they wanted, but in return, they were not to raid our vegetable garden. Amazingly, this silent agreement worked beautifully for us and them!

With D's help, our veggie and fruit gardens blossomed profusely, giving us a cornucopia of fresh and pure organic food to eat. The bounty was so great that we shared it not only with friends, but with the island's women's and children's crisis centre as well; the centre gave refuge to abused women and children, protecting them and helping them start a new life beyond their painful pasts. The regular deliveries of our organic produce, coupled with clothes and toys we sent for the children, helped to somewhat ease the torment they had endured for years, in some cases—the blank look on many of their faces changing to surprise and a bit of hope that perhaps there really were people out there who actually cared about their plight, who had the compassion and empathy to reach out and extend a helping hand to them to lift them up once again.

Love and compassion are surely the greatest 'medicines' one can give to another—'remedies' that can touch the mind, heart and soul as well as the body. The spirit of 'Aloha' felt in Hawaii is precisely that—the spirit of love, the word 'aloha' actually meaning 'love' in the Hawaiian language as well as peace, compassion and mercy. 'Aloha' also has an even deeper spiritual meaning. 'Alo' means 'being in the presence of' while 'ha' means 'the divine breath of life.' Hence, 'Aloha' literally means 'being in the presence of Divinity—the Divine Breath of life.'

Living in the islands and even just visiting them, one can't help but tap into that spirit and breathe with that divine breath of life even unconsciously. One dear friend of mine who tries to visit the Big Island annually has told me that he always feels 'grounded' whenever he is there, reconnected once again to that Divine Spirit through the peace and beauty of Nature that surrounds him. It literally enfolds you in its soft arms of love.

But if the body needs some direct care to heal itself, then turning to a trained healer or doctor sometimes becomes necessary. We were extremely fortunate and blessed to have access to some wonderful healers, and one particular doctor who was a UK-trained osteopath and naturopath, and who became a good friend—Dr T.

While my experiences in Colorado with allopathic/western medicine had demonstrated how this healing modality had its uses particularly in certain areas, it also instilled in me the deep conviction that there had to be gentler, kinder ways of healing the body, mind and soul too. Having Dr T as our doctor opened up a whole new range of healing methods that worked both gently and wonderfully in manifold illnesses and areas of healthcare—

hydrotherapy, aromatherapy, homeopathy, the use of flower essence tinctures, vitamin and mineral supplements, dietary restrictions and additions making food the 'medicine' for the body that it is meant to be, along with complete fasting from food in some cases to give the body a rest from continuously having to digest food, thereby allowing it the time and energy it needed to work on healing itself.

The focus was always on purification through avoidance of processed foods, excess sweets, or overindulgence in anything that brings an imbalance to the physical frame and its various systems. He also taught simple techniques for relieving mental stress and tension while encouraging flexibility and bodily strength through yoga and other physical activities like swimming, fast walking and hiking in Nature.

With the unnatural, sedentary lifestyle that so many of us lead today, it is no wonder that our spine and skeletal system gets out of alignment, thereby causing pain. Dr T's spinal adjustments were literally lifesaving at times, bringing instant relief from the pain and restrictions of normal movements caused by this lack of proper alignment. In the early 1980s, Dr T put his vast repertoire of healing knowledge into a book which has been published, reprinted and sold around the world. For us, it became our 'health bible' that we still use today, not just for ourselves, but to help others too.

In addition to the healing wisdom we imbibed from Dr T, we also took courses in massage therapy and reflexology—a technique similar to Japanese shiatsu and Chinese acupressure and acupuncture, but without the needles. Applying pressure to certain points on the body helps bring relief from pain and aids in overall healing. The soles of our feet along with the palms and fingers of our hands are miniature maps of the body and its corresponding reflex points. Pressing on these points causes a reflexive action in the organ or area of the body needing the healing—something especially helpful in cases of accidents or where direct contact with the afflicted area is not possible or recommended.

In addition to these wonderful healing methods, I took courses in basic first aid as well as CPR (cardiopulmonary resuscitation)— emergency aid treatments and techniques that can literally mean the difference between life and death sometimes. Since we had made the decision to live our lives in remote areas, it was important to know what measures we should take in case of an injury or any other health emergency. This training has certainly come in use over the years both in the USA as well as here in India.

While living in America, I had also delved deeply into martial arts, studying a number of different styles and forms. My passion for these arts started when we lived in Colorado and was triggered by a television series called *Kung Fu*. The story followed a Buddhist monk of mixed Chinese and American heritage who trained in a Buddhist monastery from childhood to adulthood, before being forced to leave China to live in the old west of the USA. The contrast of the spiritual teachings and wisdom that he had received in China against the backdrop of the often violent 'Wild West' was fascinating. It was my first exposure to Buddhist philosophy. Little did I know then that both the philosophy and even the martial arts had their roots in India's spiritual wisdom and ancient martial disciplines, along with the teachings of yoga.

The goal of all these disciplines is to align body, mind and soul. Through this alignment and unification, one's thoughts, words and deeds become based on the intuitive guidance of the individual soul which is always connected with the All-Soul or Creator. With this conscious unification with Spirit, one's life is lived in harmony and balance attuned with the will of the Divine, with the Divine Spirit flowing unhindered through the mind and heart to guide each action taken that it may perfectly reflect the essential goodness of God.

As with yoga, the physical movements are meant to aid with that attunement, many, if not most of the stances and actions mimicking the movements and actions of different animals who are virtually always naturally balanced and alert, Nature once again being the principal teacher and guide for achieving this balanced, unified harmony of body, mind and spirit.

Being in our Hawaiian sanctuary was so conducive to this balance, helping us to connect to the Spirit that connects us all. It was so easy to feel rooted to the good earth within the Mother's heart, the exquisite beauty of the emerald-green cliffs surrounding us, blocking out all human noise from the outside world.

The pristine stream flowing past would take whatever cares and worries we had with it. The sweet songs of birds filled the air as the breeze played with my hair while showering us with the fine mist from the waterfall in front of us. Sunlight sparkled like diamonds off the stream rippling by as rainbows danced across the waterfall cascade tumbling down, its thunder vibrating through the ground and through my soul, the primordial 'OM' reverberating everywhere without and within.

How easy it was to slip into a deep reverie, my being filled with light, bliss, joy and a profound peace . . . that is, until that peace was abruptly shattered by the horrible roar of the engine of a low-flying plane overhead. My entire being was violently yanked away from the peace and joy within by the ear-splitting racket of this 'monster' flying at treetop level above.

## Poisoning Paradise: A Volcanic Response

It was the crop-dusting plane of the sugarcane company spraying its deadly toxic defoliant on the sugarcane fields below our sanctuary—a defoliant whose main ingredients were used so widely by the US during the Vietnam War—the same defoliant whose toxicity in the environment still plagues Vietnam even today over twenty-five years after the war ended.

The crop-duster was spraying its deadly payload over the fields to cause the leaves of the sugarcane to die and dry up. As soon as the leaves had dried, the sugarcane was set on fire, the billowing black smoke from the raging crop fires spreading its toxic ash residue everywhere the wind went—on to any homes nearby, on vegetable farms and soil, on the forest lands and into the streams and rivers that were used as water sources for the island's communities, those waterways eventually emptying into the sea taking the poisonous defoliant ash with them.

The chemical fertilizers and pesticides used on the sugarcane fields, as well as fields of other conventionally grown crops, added to the toxic cocktail entering the streams, rivers and finally, the sea, along with highly chemically laden soil. We would see this happening every time it rained, as we would drive down the mountain from our sanctuary towards the coast below.

Besides the soil from the cane fields, the clay soil from ginger fields would turn the ocean a sickening rusty red as it entered the sea. The fields had no trees or shrubs planted on their borders which would have helped slow down the rain runoff and stop the loss of the topsoil at the same time. The fine soil particles covered and smothered the coral reefs offshore, causing many to die off. These coral reefs are not only vital for the aquatic life that uses them as homes and nurseries, but also as a barrier to tidal waves. The coral reefs act as walls, helping to break up the waves and diminish both their speed and force before reaching the shore, thereby protecting humans and their communities located near the shore as well.

The devastation of the earth was continued by the sugarcane company as they brought more 'monsters' into the burnt fields to harvest the sugarcane crop. Huge cranes with giant steel claws were used to lift the dead, burned cane stalks from the ground, dropping the stalks into oversized transport trucks that would take it to the sugar manufacturing plant. The cranes and trucks belched out black diesel exhaust, polluting the air, this destructive and deafening process continuing throughout the day and on through the night, huge searchlights used to illuminate the area being harvested so the work could continue uninterrupted.

Between the roar of the engines and the exceptionally bright searchlights used there was no way one could even sleep. *Monsters!* I thought to myself. *Monsters are destroying the Earth and the peace of the Earth as well!*

It was illegal for the company's crop-dusting plane to fly over forest areas like our sanctuary, and especially over the island's forest reserve, those forests being the watershed catchment area for the entire island. But that didn't stop the planes from doing so, the toxic defoliants wafting down on the forest, poisoning and burning plants, trees and wildlife wherever it landed.

We witnessed the result of this contact on a bird covered with the disgusting stuff—a beautiful, red, male cardinal. We saw him as we were leaving our sanctuary. He was sitting dazed on the side of the road. Picking him up very carefully, we bathed him as best we could with cool, fresh water to wash the burning chemical off of his feathers, face and body. His poor face had clearly been scorched from coming into contact with the toxic spray. After administering what aid we could, he appeared to revive a bit. We then released him next to our house in the sanctuary, leaving plenty of water and bird seed to help him recover more, along with prayers for his complete recovery. He stayed close by for some time and then flew away, hopefully having recovered enough to survive on his own.

This was just one bird who had suffered being doused by these lethal sprays, the whole episode reminding me of the photo of 'Napalm Girl' from the Vietnam War. How many more birds, butterflies, insects and other wildlife had suffered a similar, agonizing fate as this poor cardinal!

A few years later, the sugarcane company finally closed down, its failing economic fortunes bringing about its end. While the aerial spraying of these toxic chemicals was finally over, that did not mean poisons, principally from large agricultural companies, were not still being used across the islands. One example was the use of the highly toxic chemical heptachlor as a pesticide on pineapple fields for decades.

When the pineapple plants were harvested, the green leaves on top of the plant were pulled out and then used as fodder for dairy cattle. This 'green chop', as it was called, was fed to the dairy cows principally on the islands where pineapples were grown as it was a cheap form of vegetation for dairy farmers to use, versus having to graze their cattle in open fields for enough hours a day to keep the cows healthy.

However, this 'cheap meal' for the dairy industry ended up coming at an exceedingly high cost when traces of that deadly chemical were discovered in the milk they were selling in 1982. Hundreds of thousands of gallons of milk were pulled off the shelves of grocery stores and thrown away, gallon after gallon literally poured down the drains that eventually led back to the sea, the heptachlor thereby poisoning the ocean in its toxic journey from plant to cow to milk to sea.

In addition, multi-million-dollar lawsuits were brought by dairy farmers against the pineapple industry with the Hawaii state government also being drawn into the legal mess, damages in dollars not coming anywhere close to the health damages this lethal contamination caused many of the residents specifically on the main island of Oahu. Heptachlor is a known carcinogen, with studies linking it to liver, kidney and breast cancer along with Parkinson's disease in humans exposed to the now-banned pesticide.

Commercial pineapple was not grown on the Big Island where we lived, so our milk supplies were not affected. But the shock of the news certainly underscored once again this horrific 'paradox in paradise'.

This once pristine Eden that was blessed with an incredible array of unique species of both flora and fauna, with the purest water one could hope to drink, with the freshest clean air one could breathe, scented with the matchless perfume of extraordinary flowers, with breathtaking beauty from its untouched sandy beaches, white surf and sapphire sea, to its forests filled with life, to its snow-capped volcanic peaks, all held in the tangible embrace of the Spirit of Aloha—all living in the presence of the Divine Breath of Life—was now poisoned, corrupted and devastated, tainted by the commercial blindness and greed of one species—humans.

As if in response to the mindless destruction caused by humans on the island that is her own 'home', the Hawaiian volcano goddess Madam Pele, burst into action on 3 January 1983, her spectacular fiery eruption coming from Kilauea Volcano's crater which is said to be the body of Madam Pele herself. Fountains of lava shot up into the sky with molten lava flows streaming down the volcano's slopes towards the sea, the lava producing massive clouds of noxious 'laze'—a deadly combination of steam, acid fumes and glass-like particles—wherever it entered the ocean.

A volcanic haze settled over much of the island, obscuring vision and tainting the air with the smell and taste of sulphur, the volcano smog or 'vog', as it is called, causing breathing problems for many—not just on the Big Island, but on other islands as well—the airborne sulphur also tainting water sources, particularly for those relying on rainwater catchment systems like our own.

Was the volcano goddess showing her condemnation of humanity's foolish and dangerous actions, man's stupid and senseless destruction of the forests, water, wildlife and environment in general of her home, destruction that would come back to haunt him in the end? It was indeed as if Madam Pele was censuring humanity, rebuking and warning all that if humans did not mend their ways and lifestyles, a terrible chastisement would follow.

We had become aware of the prophecies of indigenous peoples from around the world regarding the karmic repercussions of humanity's disrespect, abuse and destruction of Nature—prophecies echoed in the scriptures of virtually all religions that were now being repeated by global scientists regarding climate change, species extinction and the deadly dangers our chemical pollution was having on Nature and humans. We ended up putting the findings from our research into our first book—*The Phoenix Returns*—in an attempt to help spread awareness in the hope that at least part of humanity would heed the warnings and change.

And so it came to pass that Pele awakened the great 'Long Mountain'. While Hawaiians revere all five volcanoes that make up the Big Island as sacred, many have considered this Long Mountain—Mauna Loa—as the original home of the volcano goddess. Enormous in size, Long Mountain is the largest subaerial volcano on earth.

Covering an area of 5271 square kilometres (2035 square miles), Mauna Loa makes up more than half the land area of the Big Island of Hawaii. From its eruptive base under the sea to its summit towering in the sky, its total height is 17,170 metres (56,000 feet), literally dwarfing even Mount Everest whose total elevation is just 8848 metres (29,029 feet).[*]

For thirty-four years, Mauna Loa had remained quiet. Indeed, it was not common for both Kilauea and Mauna Loa to erupt at the same time. The last time this had happened was back in 1868. But on 24 March 1984, Mauna Loa once again rumbled to life, sending a long lava flow in the direction of Hilo—the capital of the island, where we had another home outside the sanctuary, from which we ourselves worked.

---

[*]    Refer to the bibliography for source.

Now both volcanoes were erupting, but the lava flow from Mauna Loa was the greatest threat as its lava continued moving directly towards Hilo. The mayor of the island finally made an announcement about the eruption, calling on the people of Hilo and all living on the island to pray. For, as he put it, only God can stop a volcano from erupting.

Christian churches and Buddhist temples on the island were filled to capacity in response to the mayor's plea, adding their own prayerful pleas to the Creator and volcano goddess to stop the approaching lava and save their homes. With the night sky being illumined by the lava flow close by, even we started packing our things to move to our house in the sanctuary as that was located on the slopes of the dormant/inactive volcano Mauna Kea, which has not erupted for thousands of years and was hence not in danger.

In addition, the air and catchment water at our sanctuary continued to be totally pure, unaffected by either the vog or the sulphur contamination causing great distress and problems for others on the island. Truly, the Great Mother was enfolding the sanctuary and us in her protective arms of 'aloha' on the slopes of the most sacred of all peaks in Hawaii—Mauna Kea—'the White Mountain'—named thus due to its snow-covered peak, measuring 10,000 metres (33,000 feet) from its peak to its oceanic base below the sea, making it taller than Mount Everest as well.

Considered the region of the benevolent gods by the ancient Hawaiians, Mauna Kea's Hawaiian name of 'Mauna a Wakea' shows its connection to Father Sky, literally meaning 'the mountain of Wakea—the Sky Father' who, along with Mother Earth, were the Creators of heaven and earth and the first parents of human beings, according to ancient Hawaiian beliefs. How blessed were we to have been given refuge on this sacred mountain!

Meanwhile, within just a day or two of the mayor's plea, followed by the prayers made by the whole community, the great wave of lava flowing toward Hilo stalled just six kilometres (four miles) from the first houses of town, piling up on top of itself as if a giant hand was holding it back, the photos and videos of the event astonishing us all.

Shortly thereafter, two natural levees higher up its path broke off from this main flow, thereby diverting the lava away from Hilo. The eruption of Mauna Loa ended shortly thereafter, the volcano having erupted continuously for twenty-two days. The Great Mother had responded to the earnest prayers of the community and showered her grace in this case. But the eruption of Kilauea goes on unabated, now being the longest continuous eruption of any volcano anywhere in the world. Its rivers of lava have swallowed up over one thousand houses since it began erupting, including two whole towns in its 1990 eruption—Kalapana and Kaimu—along with the famous black sand beach that Anil and I had visited several times while living on the Big Island. In its May 2018 eruption, two more subdivisions were destroyed, with a 600-foot-deep lava lake created during its latest eruption that started on 20 December 2020, only ending on 23 May 2021.

And this must give us pause and question why? Why did the Great Mother shower her grace decades earlier, but seem to have withdrawn it now? Perhaps the answer is that we humans have still not learned to respect Nature and her laws of life and balance.

Since Mauna Loa's joint eruption with Kilauea back in 1984, the population of Hilo has grown by over 35 per cent, according to US Census figures. This is putting a far greater strain on the area's ecosystem, deforestation of the island's forests being one of the consequences. Further, most of the food and other supplies used on the islands in general have to be flown in from the continental USA, making the cost of living in Hawaii 30 to 40 per cent higher across the board compared with living on the mainland.

Much of the expansion of homes on the island has ended up being on the former lava flows of both volcanoes—a dangerous move that illustrates a complete lack of respect and disregard for Nature and her forces.

Living on an island taught me that I had to live within Nature's balance; I had to put a limit on my demands upon her and her ecosystems. To not recognize these limitations on Nature's ability to replenish herself ultimately spells disaster as shortages of both food and water are its natural consequence.

Similarly, Planet Earth is an island in space. She has limited resources that must be used sparingly and shared judiciously with all life forms on the planet. To not recognize this truth is to put the very survival of life on the planet at risk.

And what about chemical pollution on the islands? Has that changed? Unfortunately, no.

Citing just one example, US Navy records have verified the existence of a huge subsurface oil plume beneath the navy's tank storage facilities in Pearl Harbor Naval Base on the island of Oahu, the toxic plume being at least five million gallons (16,000 metric tons) spread across at least twenty acres—that's about half the amount of oil spilled during Alaska's Exxon Valdez catastrophe mentioned earlier.[*]

But this is only one of more than 700 areas of contamination in the 12,600-acre Pearl Harbor Naval Complex, the entire complex being put on the US Environmental Protection Agency's Priority List of Hazardous Waste Sites in 1992, with the EPA warning people not to eat any type of fish/aquatic life from the area.

The food-poisoning bouts that both Anil and I had from eating freshly caught fish (mentioned earlier in Chapter Seven), which was attributed to the leak of radioactive wastewater from a nuclear submarine, may also have been related to contamination from these very sites, since records show that these spills have been going on for several decades. Not so coincidentally, the US Navy

---

[*] Refer to the bibliography for source.

has been working with the EPA and Hawaii State Government since 1983, trying to tackle the problem—the same time period as our own incidents of food poisoning—and yet little has been done to address the mess as the leaks and poisonings continue.

As I sit here writing about all this horrific pollution, I can't help but wonder whether my breast cancer actually had its origins in Hawaii. Such a pristine place, and yet such dangerous chemicals spewed across its land, in the air and dumped in the sea. Chemicals can stay in the environment—and in the human body—for years, even decades before they break down *if* they break down at all into harmless materials that biodegrade or are naturally eliminated. But some never lose their fatal properties.

It can also take a long time for cancer to rear its ugly head, the poisonous chemical 'seeds' unknowingly 'planted' in the body sometimes taking years to erupt within, perhaps triggered by some kind of stress or emotional event temporarily weakening the immune system just enough for them to spread their lethal influence in the body—like the toxic tentacles of a deadly monster.

This is why it is so vital today for humanity, for all of us to literally clean up our act! Our pollution in its innumerable forms is killing us and the ones we love, while killing our Mother Earth as well. And without a healthy, vibrant Mother Earth, resilient and in balance, none of us will survive.

Finally, another aspect of Mauna Loa Volcano has drawn worldwide attention to the Long Mountain—the existence of an atmospheric observatory near its summit. The main function of the observatory has been to measure carbon dioxide readings in the atmosphere. Records of these readings started being logged in 1958 under the direction of Dr Charles Keeling, the readings today known as the Keeling Curve. This was the first scientific documentation that human-generated greenhouse gases (GHGs) were changing the atmosphere around the planet, causing changes in our climate as a result.

In the 1960s, one of the first persons Keeling shared his graph with was his own mentor—Harvard's Dr Roger Revelle—who, in turn, shared it for the first time publicly with some of his students, including the future vice president of the United States—Al Gore. In his groundbreaking book *An Inconvenient Truth*, Gore relays how seeing the graph set off alarm bells in his mind, bringing him to the inevitable question, 'What does this mean for the future of life on the planet?!'—a question we all need to ask, but more importantly, understand the implications of its answer.

Today, we stand on the precipice of runaway climate change due to our continuous belching of GHGs into the atmosphere. Extreme climate events from floods to droughts, melting ice caps and rising seas, catastrophic fires and seasons out of sync are already in evidence. Indeed, calamitous consequences of our polluting activities are taking place across the planet – consequences that are "just guaranteed to get worse," according to Linda Mearns, one of the 234 authors of the latest report by the International Panel on Climate Change (IPCC) approved by 195 governments and released in August 2021.

Called a '*Code Red for Humanity*' by the United Nations, the report foresees even greater and more numerous deadly effects of the ever-increasing buildup of GHGs in the atmosphere by humans. With every part of the globe affected, there will be, "No place to run, nowhere to hide," as one scientist put it. Asia is set to see some of the most devastating fallout. In fact, many parts of Asia will become unlivable due to high temperatures, lack of freshwater and rising sea levels that are already happening faster than the global average, with coastal cities facing watery graves if strong, meaningful action is not taken immediately.

We all need to step up, speak up and act *now* to stop these deadly emissions, changing our way of living, eating, growing, building, doing business, being educated—basically changing virtually everything we do in order to transform our currently bleak future to one of hope and 'life'. This is our duty for the sake of our children and the children of all the species living on Mother Earth.

As Buddhist monk Thich Nhat Hanh has put it:

We need a Revolution: It starts with falling in Love with the Earth.

During these past two years (2020 and 2021), we have all had to change our lifestyle in every aspect due to the Covid-19 pandemic. This proves that we *can* change *if* we believe that the risks of *not* changing are far more dangerous and deadly than the temporary discomforts we must endure for some time during these changes. Climate change is an existential threat to humanity's survival and the survival of millions of other species on the planet. So how can we *not* change when we recognize this truth based on scientific facts?

In addition, by cutting emissions of carbon and other GHGs now, embracing truly 'green' alternative energy systems, turning to organic agriculture and protecting our wildlife as well as expanding our forests and other ecosystems and natural habitats on land and sea, we ensure a healthier, happier, more beautiful and much saner future for ourselves and for every living being that calls Mother Earth 'Home'.

One of the best ways to start this change is to stop deforestation immediately since it is one of the greatest causes of the deadly carbon dioxide build-up in the atmosphere. Indeed, today scientists recognize it as *the* single greatest cause of climate change when amounts of carbon released through cutting down and burning forests, *plus* the loss of its carbon-capturing services provided by its trees and wildlife are added together.

It is also the fourth and greatest cause of species extinction, deforestation having killed off more species than we can count, bearing in mind that over 70 per cent of the Earth's total species (flora and fauna) live in forests, as we shall see in the next chapter.

# PART III

# The Canopy Spreads

# 14

# The Holy Himalayas

It was the arrival of a telegram that changed our lives forever. 'Dad unwell. Come quickly.'

The telegram had been sent by Anil's mother. Although an American citizen, Anil's dad had returned to India in 1981 to retire, after having spent some time with us in Hawaii. He was living in Pune at the ashram established by Dadaji and Anil's mom some decades ago.

Dadaji (D.K. Roy) had passed away a year earlier on 6 January 1980—the same year as my first-ever trip to India seven months later in July. I had visited India alone then as Anil was unable to join me, the trip itself being both an incredible adventure and a daunting experience, not having lived for any time in another country or culture.

Travelling across the Pacific Ocean, I stopped in Bangkok to spend a couple of days there before flying on to India. The culture of Thailand (formally known as 'Siam') had fascinated me from the very first time I saw the movie *The King and I*, the film somewhat loosely based on the real-life story of the British teacher Anna and her experiences in the country as the tutor of the children of the then king of Siam.

The architecture of the ancient buildings and temples of Thailand was amazing. Thailand is predominantly a Buddhist country. Buddhist pagodas and temples are everywhere. And yet, there are some temples that have extraordinary wall and ceiling murals dedicated to India's Lord Rama and his consort, Sita. In one temple, the entire Ramayana—the story of Rama's and Sita's lives—is painted in exquisite detail, a written script being unnecessary for anyone familiar with the ancient tale.

It was beautiful seeing how wonderfully interwoven the influences of both the Buddhist and Hindu religions were in Thailand, the peaceful coexistence between the followers of both faiths based on a sense of mutual sharing, with a deep respect and even reverence for India evident as well, India being the birthplace of both creeds since both Lord Rama and Lord Buddha were both born in India.

When I finally landed in India, a few days later, at the then Bombay International Airport (now Chhatrapati Shivaji Maharaj International Airport), I was relieved to see Anil's cousin Arun, with his wife, Sheila, in the massive crowd outside the airport terminal. Arun and Sheila visited us twice in Hawaii over the years, so seeing their smiling faces was certainly reassuring as I was definitely taken aback by the sea of humanity that seemed to stretch endlessly in all directions.

For an inexperienced traveller like me, India can easily overwhelm you. One's senses are at once assaulted and uplifted by the kaleidoscopic sights, sounds, smells, tastes and the rush of different feelings which can be quite overpowering!

Arun and Sheila quickly whisked me away in their car to their apartment overlooking the sea. Here I was able to recoup for a day or so before leaving for another rather daunting experience— meeting my mother-in-law for the first time. I had never visited an ashram before, let alone stayed in one, so, the prospect of doing so, coupled with meeting my mother-in-law, was both exciting and a bit scary.

Riding the train from Bombay was yet another adventure. It was monsoon season and the entire countryside was decked in various shades of green. As the train climbed up the mountains or Ghats, stunning views were revealed with each twist and turn of the track—spectacular waterfalls cascading down steep cliffs everywhere, the sun creating crystal rainbows in the spray from the falls in all directions.

As the train reached the top of the Ghats, it slowed and then stopped briefly in an area known as 'Monkey Hill', so-named for all the macaque monkeys that made this area their home. The monkeys gratefully accepted the food handouts that the passengers shared with them from the train's windows. No one was bothered by the train's delay. Instead, they enjoyed the company of the monkeys and the antics of the young ones on the trees nearby.

This was one of my first experiences contrasting the different perspectives of 'Time' of East and West. In the West, 'Time' virtually ruled everyone's life—the clock was a dictator indicating the start and finish of every human event—work, school, even playtime and family time were, most often, dictated by the clock. But here in India, Time was relative—it was more important to slow down and *live* each moment people were given rather than 'chase the clock' and pass up enriching one's life with encounters and events like this—the joy one received simply from sharing one's food with another living being.

Anil's mother greeted me with great love and affection when we finally reached the ashram, as did the rest of his family members as well as the various devotees and followers of Dadaji and Ma gathered there. I was instantly put at ease with the laughter and smiles that were in abundance.

Like Dadaji, Anil's mother had a great sense of humour which she shared with everyone all the time. One of the first examples of this was illustrated with regard to the Indian custom of touching the feet of one's elders and respected individuals. Since most of the people gathered there were older than me at that time, I would have to go around the room touching one pair of feet after another—a process that could take quite a while.

After a couple of days of doing this, Ma said to me, 'Look here—I am now going to show you a quick way to do this.' She then proceeded to go to the middle of the room, bend her knees with her hand extended forward and twirled around quickly in a circle, symbolically 'touching' everyone's feet in the process! Her antics sent all of us there, including me, into splits of laughter.

## From Jeans to Saris: Chaos and Common Sense

Living at the ashram meant wearing Indian clothing at all times. During the day, I was usually clothed in various styles of the Punjabi salwar kameez—tunic tops with matching pants, the ensemble always including a dupatta or scarf usually worn over the chest and shoulder areas. While the outfits were fairly loose and quite comfortable, keeping the dupatta in place could be difficult as it would tend to slip down and fall off, or get in my way while eating or doing any chores.

Evenings meant wearing saris since going to the mandir/temple every night for prayers and singing was a must. Putting on a sari was a real challenge for me because, back in the USA, I was normally clad in jeans and T-shirts or in the long Hawaiian dresses called 'muumuus'. It took a lot of practice learning how to drape the sari, make the pleats and deal with its decorative end piece called the 'pallu'. Yet, I came to love saris after I finally learned how to wear them. Practical hints of tucks and safety pins here and there from those teaching me helped tremendously. In a short period of time, I truly fell in love with the beauty and elegance of this most versatile and feminine style of clothing. Even after all these years of travel to different countries around the world, I still consider the sari the most beautiful garment a woman can wear, with the Bhutanese 'kira' placing second.

When I arrived in Pune, Anil's mother gave me a large collection of saris. But petticoats and blouses of matching colours still had to be made. So, Anil's '*masi*' (mother's sister) and her husband, Noti uncle, took me to the bazaar to purchase them. Before leaving the mandir compound, Noti uncle stopped the car and '*pranaam*-ed' the various statues of the temple gardens Ma had made near the ashram gate, reverentially bowing to each one.

As we drove into the street heading for the bazaar, I burst out laughing as I began to suspect his pranaams were not mere gestures of devotion, but also prayers for protection! The only words fit to be used to describe the traffic would be 'insanely chaotic!'

Cars, lorries/trucks and buses plied the roads, along with three-wheelers or 'rickshaws', bicycles and motorbikes, each driver seemingly oblivious to everyone else and anything else on the road, the latter including horse-drawn carriages and human-driven cycle rickshaws along with cows, goats, chickens, dogs and people everywhere, the cows in particular, appearing not the least concerned with the swirling maelstrom all around them, calmly lying in the middle of the road, chewing their cud! It was absolutely unbelievable to behold for a person like me, who had grown up and learned to drive in the West where driving in proper lanes is a strictly enforced law.

Here in India, no one stayed in their lane, each driver ignoring the others, being solely focused on reaching his or her destination as quickly as possible. Reckless driving was truly the norm, rather than the exception, with the approaching vehicles from opposite directions driving in the wrong lane until the very last second, before swerving sharply to avoid a head-on collision!

While driving in India has improved over the decades, it can still be a hair-raising experience for the uninitiated. Today, I drive myself everywhere, but this is only after years of being subjected to more 'near-misses' than I care to recall! As the consummate 'backseat driver' I left deep impressions of my fingers on many a front seat, until I finally decided that enough was enough and I had to start driving myself around instead! While being a driver in India certainly has its own challenges, I still feel safer with me at the wheel rather than someone else!

During my first visit to India, I wrote to Anil every day. One day when my pen ran out of ink, I tossed it into the trash can, pulling out another one to use, when the woman cleaning my room at the ashram handed my pen back to me with the words, 'We can get an ink refill for this pen. There's no need to throw it out.'

Having been raised in the 'throw-away society' of the USA, that simple statement had a profound impact on me. I was suddenly confronted with my own unconscious behaviour of needlessly wasting reusable items.

Then there was the question of using paper goods. Single-use tissues, paper towels, paper napkins and other paper products come from trees. By switching to cloth handkerchiefs, cotton cleaning cloths and napkins like those being used at the ashram, all of which could be washed and reused, I would actually be helping to save the forests that I loved dearly.

As I opened my eyes and my consciousness more, I could see examples of practical recycling of goods going on all around me. What a revelation! 'Reduce, reuse, recycle' was no longer just a slogan but the living reality being played out before my eyes right here in India—a reality that so desperately needs to be revived here in India once again, as the mountains of garbage mindlessly discarded today in this country and around the world are literally burying the Earth, while poisoning us and the rest of life on the planet at the same time.

Returning to the USA from this first trip to India with this new perspective, changed the way I live to date. Simple, easy changes in our lifestyle can truly have profound cumulative effects on ourselves and the Earth at large.

Just a few years later, I would return to the ashram in Pune, this time with Anil. After receiving the telegram about Anil's father, we made our plans to visit India. As fate would have it, we actually ended up in southern India first before making our way to Pune. It was on our first visit to Nagarhole National Park that we met some of the top conservationists of the area and the country who were just in the process of setting up 'Project Tiger'.

After spending time with them and explaining what we had done in Hawaii, the then-wildlife warden of Nagarhole, who was a Coorgi or a Kodava, strongly encouraged us to remain in the district, to purchase lands there to establish another wildlife sanctuary like we had in Hawaii.

But that was not to be. At least, not initially.

## To the Holy Dhams: Sacred Abodes of God

After our arrival in Pune, Anil's father's health continued to deteriorate. He finally passed away early in the morning on 1 July 1986. For four days, prayers and ceremonies were done at the ashram in remembrance of Anil's dad and for his soul. Then Anil was entrusted with the task of taking his father's '*asti*' or ashes to Haridwar for immersion into the waters of the holy Ganga. I accompanied Anil. It was on this trip that Anil and I fell in love with the holy Himalayas and the sacred Ganga for the first time.

We stayed in the same hotel on the bathing ghats that Anil and Dadaji had visited so many times in years past—the site that had witnessed Ma's miraculous healing of Parkinson's disease, thirteen years earlier. The atmosphere was serene, with temple bells and holy chants filling the air at sundown, mystics and holy people clad in saffron-coloured robes passing by, doing their ablutions on the banks of this most holy of rivers.

Anil and I had no intention of staying permanently at the ashram in Pune. Our hearts were with Mother Nature. Having fallen in love with the holy Himalayas, we decided to go higher into the mountains to search for an area where we could live on a full-time basis. Anil's mother suggested we look for land to purchase around another holy town called Uttarkashi. Uttarkashi was a six-hour drive from Haridwar.

The trip up the mountains was very dangerous as the roads, cut into the mountains, were narrow and without any kind of barriers on the side. The drop from these sheer cliffs to the valley below was frightening. Many had, indeed, lost their lives going over the edge of these cliffs in buses and cars. Each time we would go around a bend, I would hold my breath hoping there wouldn't be another car or even worse, a truck or bus, coming from the opposite direction. Passing each other on these narrow roads at these heights was truly terrifying!

Our first few nights in Uttarkashi were spent in an ashram on the banks of the Bhagirathi River—the same river that eventually becomes the Ganga downstream. In the evening, there were prayers and various ceremonies including walking around the central statue of the mandir/temple. However, only men were allowed to join in the procession, something to which Anil immediately objected, asking why women should be excluded from this practice if they wanted to participate.

The monk in charge of the ashram explained that it was not the fault of the women that they were excluded, but the weakness of the men; proximity to women in this practice could distract men from their prayers and concentration on the Divine. To this, Anil suggested that the men then should be excluded rather than the women, since they couldn't keep their minds on God while the women could!

Over the years, I have seen this kind of exclusion of women from religious ceremonies relatively often. There were no such exclusionary practices at Dadaji and Ma's ashram, nor at the ashrams that I have come to honour and respect the most for their clarity of teaching and recognition of the one Spirit that pervades, animates and binds us all together as equals in Oneness.

## Grace and Wisdom from Mother Ganga

A similar event took place when Anil and I went to the holy city of Gangotri. We needed a room for the night and Anil went to see if we could stay at one of the ashrams there. But when the monk in charge saw that I was a foreigner, he refused us a room.

Thus began a discussion between Anil and the monk, Anil pointing out that spirituality and spiritual growth of individuals is determined by their dedication and devotion, progress and singlemindedness and not by their caste, gender, the colour of their skin, or the country where they had taken birth. Each soul was on its own journey back to union with the Absolute, the Godhead, and was thus not to be prejudged based on external factors by anyone, least of all those who claim to be devoted to this journey themselves.

To his credit, this monk was humble enough to recognize the truth of what Anil said, saying that both of us were welcome to stay at his ashram any time we wanted. He then went on to concur with Anil, adding that many 'city Indians', as he called them, think that the surrounding mountains are only rocks, pointing to the rocky peaks around us.

'No,' he said, 'these are the souls of great sadhus and mystics doing tapas/spiritual disciplines and meditation to the Holy Mother, to God.'

The visual validity of the monk's words came the following day, when we trekked towards Gaumukh—the origin of the holy

Ganga which flows forth from the Gangotri glacier. As we rounded a bend in the path, the great Bhagirathi Mountain appeared before us in all its snow-capped glory. The sight literally stopped me in my tracks, as I saw that the entire peak of the mountain was a human face. There was no question about it! One cannot look at that mountain and not see a face!

I stammered to our guide, 'There's a face on the mountain peak.'

The guide nonchalantly said, 'Oh, yes. People say it is the face of King Bhagirath who did great tapas/penance on the mountain praying to Mother Ganga that she would descend from the heavens to the earth and flow forth to the valleys below to bring water and life to the earth.' He went on, 'Others say it is the face of Lord Shiva in deep meditation. As Ma Ganga's descent to the earth would be an extraordinarily powerful event, Lord Shiva consented to allow Ma Ganga to fall on the matted locks of hair on his head as only he would be able to withstand the force of her descent.'

The symbolic meaning of this is said to represent the descent of liberating divine consciousness (personified as Mother Ganga) that flows from the head of a spiritual teacher (like Shiva) to purify everyone with whom it comes into contact. Hence, Ganga, as the pure Supreme Consciousness, represents the shakti, or the feminine spiritual force, which descends to purify our mind as well as our bodies of all sins or errors of the past, thereby granting enlightenment and liberation to seekers of the Divine. On the physical plane of existence, her descent is synonymous with the falling rain that gathers into sacred streams and rivers which nourish and sustain all life on the earth.

The face in Bhagirathi Mountain wasn't the only face or figure we saw on the trek to Gaumukh. There were others as well, including an extraordinary one of the Aum or Om symbol (ॐ) with a line connecting it to a triangular face above that had two eyes, a nose and a circular mouth that looked exactly like someone saying, 'Om!' It was all amazing to me, and so uplifting as well.

That night we stayed at the government rest house in Bhojbasa. It was late October and very cold. The following morning, we continued our trek to Gaumukh. When we finally reached it, we were overwhelmed by the beauty and significance of where we were. We sat at the mouth of the glacier with the holy Ganga flowing out from the opening beneath and meditated for some time.

There was only one structure there, which was the tent-like *kutia* or home of a mystic known as 'Nanga Baba' along with his single disciple. Upon meeting us, he invited us into his small hut and had his disciple make us a delicious vegetarian meal with excellent chai.

Nanga Baba asked Anil why he had married a foreigner instead of an Indian. Anil replied that, though my physical form may be foreign, my soul—like his—was on the same path to union with the Divine.

The sadhu then asked if Anil liked the forests there in America, to which Anil answered, 'Yes.'

Nanga Baba then said, 'But there is one difference between the forests here in India and there in the USA. Only the forests here have saints living in them.'

To this Anil pointed out the Native Americans also mentioning my own Native American ancestry. The sadhu responded, 'Yes, they were the true saints of the Western World. But they have been killed off by the white man,' he added sadly.

When we had finished eating our meal, we went to the Ganga to wash our hands. The water was absolutely frigid with ice crystals and pieces floating in it. I could barely feel my fingers afterwards. But it wasn't just the water that was cold—the air temperature was near freezing as well. Hence, we were wearing knitted ski hats with down parkas over sweaters, long-sleeved turtlenecks and thermal underwear, with thermal gloves on our hands as well.

The sadhu laughed at our discomfort and our reaction to the freezing temperatures. His humour was certainly understandable, considering he and his disciple were completely naked (*nanga*, meaning 'naked')! All that covered them was a layer of ash and long locks of hair! And yet they didn't feel the cold at all!

The sadhu and his disciple were living proof that those who are one with the Supreme Absolute are unaffected by the physical discomforts that temperature and pain usually cause to the human body and mind, literally being insulated by their single-pointed love and concentration on the Divine.

What an extraordinary encounter! What almost unbelievable proof that God truly takes care of those who surrender to the Divine wholeheartedly body, mind and soul.

One more incident illustrates the depth of compassion the Divine can shower even on an ordinary person like myself. Anil and I were more than halfway on our twelve-kilometre trek from Gangotri to Bhojbasa when a man leading a mule came from the opposite direction blocking the path completely. In order to let them pass, I went uphill a bit above the path to give them room. In doing so, I dislodged some rocks on the slope which proceeded to crash down on both of my feet.

This could have turned into a disaster as there was no way to get help from Gangotri or Bhojbasa this far away from both points. Fortunately, I was able to stand and continue walking with no hint of pain whatsoever. Indeed, I felt no pain at all for the next three days which included our trek to and from Bhojbasa to Gaumukh (an additional twelve kilometres—six kilometres in each direction), nor for most of the fourth day on the return from Bhojbasa to Gangotri (again twelve kilometres) until we had crossed the bridge spanning the Bhagirathi River at the entrance of Gangotri town.

By the end of the crossing, both my feet were throbbing with pain. Taking off my hiking boots and socks to have a look, I was stunned to see that my big toes were now swollen and deep red with black and blue setting in. I eventually lost those toenails (they grew back later), and yet, throughout our journey spanning four days, I had experienced no pain or swelling whatsoever.

What grace the Mother had shown me; what amazing compassion she has for us all! Her grace and compassion to us included being able to meet Nanga Baba since he is rarely seen by others who make the trek to Gaumukh, hardly ever speaking to those who do see him, much less inviting them to eat with him in his kutia! Our trip to this holy *dham*, this very sacred abode of our Mother, filled our cup of joy to overflowing!

Anil and I also took a trip to Yamunotri—the birthplace of the Yamuna River, the Yamuna being the main tributary of the Ganga as well. The Yamuna issues forth from a glacier and lake of ice high in the mountain above, Yamunotri, the sacred waters flowing down the mountain to the valley below. According to the ancient stories, Yamuna is said to be the twin sister of Yama—the god of death—and the daughter of Surya—the sun god. Bathing in her waters is said to free one of sins as well as the fear of death.

The Yamuna River is also associated with Lord Krishna since much of his younger life was spent near its banks, making her the 'river of romance'.

The sacred hot springs that are close to Yamunotri are said to be gifts that Yamuna asked of her father Surya for the benefit of those pilgrims who would come to pay their obeisance to her. The journey to Yamunotri is long and difficult, and the soothing sulphur pools nearby help relieve the aches and pains the pilgrims suffer as a result of the arduous trek, something both Anil and I can confirm since we soaked in the healing hot springs after making the difficult ascent.

## Healings with Help from Mother Nature

Our search for land in the Uttarkashi region first focused on an area known as Fold. It was a beautiful area of hills and forest some kilometres away from the main town of Uttarkashi. There were some fabulous views of the snow-capped Himalayas in the distance and a stream flowed below the low hills close to one of the parcels we considered buying.

There were three villages in the area—two that mainly had people of the Kshatriya (or warrior) caste like Anil, and one which was mainly peopled by Brahmins (priestly caste). While travelling through the villages, we came upon a woman whose child was very ill with colic, fever and diarrhoea. She asked us if we had any medicine as her young baby was not responding to the allopathic medicines the doctor in Uttarkashi town had given her.

At that time, I knew no Hindi at all. So Anil had to translate everything from Hindi to English and back again. I instructed her on how to use the simple UNESCO formula to try to help stop the baby's diarrhoea—one teaspoonful of sugar with a pinch of salt dissolved in a glass of water. She was to give the baby small teaspoonfuls of the formula throughout the day and night to keep the child from getting more dehydrated.

For the child's fever, she was instructed to finely chop fresh garlic to be put on the soles of the child's feet after smearing a layer of ghee (clarified butter) on them, covering the mixture with a loose cloth and socks to keep it in place. The ghee would protect the child's tender skin from being burnt by the raw garlic while allowing the garlic's antibiotic properties to be absorbed into the child's body.

For the colic, I advised the mother to stop eating food like cabbage, hot spices and oily fried foods as their greasy properties were being passed on to the child through her own milk that the baby was drinking, giving the baby a gassy painful stomach as a result. The following day, we got word that the baby was fully recovered—something we were so happy to hear.

The news of the child's healing spread throughout the villages prompting others with health problems to seek us out for help.

One case in particular was quite dramatic in the speed of the patient's recovery. The brother of an elderly woman in her late seventies came to ask for help as his sister had been running a high fever for several days. The allopathic medicines prescribed by the doctor in Uttarkashi town had not helped at all and the woman was getting weaker by the hour, her body not perspiring and the fever not breaking.

Using another one of Dr T's treatments, I told her brother (through Anil) to do 'the trunk pack'. This involves taking a sheet and placing it in the coldest water available. After thoroughly saturating it in the cold water and wringing it out just a little bit, one wraps the cold wet sheet around the trunk of the body from below the breast area fairly tightly but not enough to inhibit breathing. Next, a towel is wrapped on top of the wet sheet around the body, followed by a blanket wrapped on top of the towel. The patient is then put in bed and covered with several blankets. Normally, within twenty minutes, even a stubborn fever will break and the patient will start perspiring freely, thereby allowing the toxins causing the fever to be eliminated through the perspiration.

The following morning, the brother came by to thank us, saying that his sister's fever had indeed broken the previous night after he had applied the trunk pack. She had slept well through the night and was finally regaining her strength now that the fever was gone. Both Anil and I were thrilled to hear this welcome news.

Some years later, I had to use the trunk pack on Anil as well. He was suffering from a high fever ranging between 104 degrees to 106 degrees and was not perspiring at all. So, I applied the trunk path method. For the patient, being wrapped in an icy-cold, wet sheet is certainly not comfortable! Anil complained the entire time I was wrapping it around him! But as soon as he was in bed, in less than twenty minutes, he fell into a deep sleep, his body freely sweating out the toxins that had caused the fever, the fever completely broken and his temperature coming back to normal. I also had to use the same method on a dear friend who was suffering from dengue fever. It took longer for the fever to break and the sweating to begin, but within forty minutes, she too was sound asleep with her body's perspiration flowing freely marking the breaking of her fever.

By the time Anil and I had trekked to the third and last village of the Fold area, we were greeted by dozens of people suffering from various ailments. The *pradhan*, or mayor, of the village asked us to come to their village meeting room to meet and help the people gathered there.

The room was completely packed by the time we arrived. There were so many people in fact that I had to give healing techniques in bulk, asking, 'How many people have this problem. Please raise your hands.'

The emphasis on these healing sessions was not just to help the individual involved, but to remind the patient and everyone there how so many of their healing medicines were growing in their own kitchen gardens, how using water therapies in various ways could help them recover their health, and ultimately, how relying on Nature to help them get well was the quickest, most practical and least expensive healing method there is—and it was all right there for them to remember and use, the aim being to revive simple, reliable 'home remedies' that had simply been forgotten.

The extraordinary healing properties of onion and garlic were demonstrated many times over our years in the Himalayas on many different health problems. One example was with staph infections. To treat this, first the area infected would be coated with pure ghee followed by the application of a mixture of freshly cut onion and garlic on top of the ghee. Sometimes the onion/garlic mixture would be slightly boiled beforehand, sometimes left in its raw state. Then the area would be covered with a clean cloth to hold the healing poultice in place.

In the early 1990s, when a pneumonic plague broke out first in Surat, Gujarat, and then spread across the country, the people of the Uttarkashi region were agitating for their own state which was eventually formed, Uttarakhand being carved out of the original state of Uttar Pradesh. As a result, roads were blocked and no buses or other vehicles were being allowed through from the plains below.

This form of plague is transmitted via infected water droplets in the air through coughing. The drug of choice for treating it at that time was Tetracycline. But none of the pharmacies/chemist shops had any in stock in Uttarkashi.

Once again, the healing powers of garlic came to the rescue as I had researched several studies that proved its efficacy against the plague even when compared to Tetracycline. I advised everyone to start eating raw garlic with their food a few times a day—something I myself did as well. No one in our area fell victim to the plague, though it did infect others in the region.

The healing power of honey is another near-miraculous gift Mother Nature has given us. Two incidents in particular stand out. The first was with the two-year-old child of our local electricity lineman. His son had backed into the woodburning *chulha* (stove) causing a pot of boiling water on the stove to tip over on to him, deeply scalding the poor little boy's back and legs. As they lived in a different village some distance away, the father had to carry the screaming child for almost thirty minutes, before reaching our house.

Most unfortunately, the father had not immersed his son's scalded areas in cold water before coming, immersing in cold water being the very first thing to do with burns of this type—not applying ice as ice placed directly on any burn may stick to the skin, causing even more damage.

So, the first thing I had the father do was to put the poor child in the cold spring of fresh water on our land, immersing his entire body—clothes and all—since trying to remove the child's clothing may have also caused additional damage to the burnt skin. I told him to keep the child in the water until the skin was no longer warm to the touch.

As soon as the boy was put into the cold water, there was an immediate reduction of the child's crying and screams of pain. As soon as the skin was cooler, we stripped off the child's clothes. I then poured honey over his entire back and legs. Next, I wrapped him in a cold wet sheet and had his father take him to the government hospital about thirty minutes away in our car.

A day or two later, the boy's grateful father visited us to thank me for my help, adding that the doctors at the hospital had told him that my actions had saved the boy's life. Over the coming days and weeks, we supplied honey as well as vitamin E oil to be applied to the boy's burns to promote healing and to limit scarring of the skin. Thankfully, the young child made a full recovery.

The second honey incident involved a major fire started by arsonists in the mountains not far from our land. Three men had been caught in this fire, all being severely burned by this blaze. Two of the men died, but the family of the third man came to us to ask for help. While the man was in the hospital, the doctors had given up hope for his recovery. Once again, the use of honey on the burns coupled with the doses of vitamin E oil capsules we gave for him to take internally saved the man's life.

It is so necessary to spread the knowledge about the use of these simple yet effective natural remedies, especially for the poor, since money for doctors and medicines is always in short supply. However, it is also important to distinguish between these natural remedies that work versus the cruel use of animal-based, so-called 'remedies' that use tiger, bear, pangolin scales or body parts of other animals as mentioned in earlier chapters.

Mother Nature has given us a true cornucopia of pharmacology within the world of plants. Therefore, there is no reason or justification for the use of cruel methods that cause animals to suffer for the healing of humans. Even the honey used for burns should be honey that has been harvested humanely from the hive. There are other healing methods for burns that are just as effective, such as the use of curds or yogurt, aloe and potato peels.

There is no end to the healing powers of Nature. We just have to become aware and educate ourselves about her healing elements and use them correctly.

## International Repercussions and the Black Hole of Corruption

Our search for what would become our Himalayan home ended almost as soon as it began, short-circuited by the fallout from a series of international incidents that sounded more like they came from a spy novel, or the script for a *James Bond* or *Mission Impossible* movie, rather than real life!

Back in the 1960s, the Indian and the US governments joined forces to spy on China's nuclear programme. Their plan was to put nuclear-powered, surveillance devices across the Himalayas. The devices were to be used to track Chinese nuclear tests and missile firings, China having exploded its first nuclear bomb in 1964. This proposed monitoring project came on the heels of the Indo-China War ending in 1962, and at the height of the Cold War, America's suspicion and paranoia with any communist regime being at its peak. So, it's easy to see why the two governments teamed up for the project.[*]

In October 1965, an Indo–American mountaineering team made up of first-class climbers attempted to scale India's second highest peak—Nanda Devi, located near India's north-eastern border with China—while carrying seven capsules filled with plutonium along with other monitoring equipment. The 'spy packs' that each of them were carrying weighed 57 kg

---

[*]  Refer to the bibliography for source.

(125 pounds). This does not include the weight of the survival gear (food, oxygen, tents, etc.) they needed to carry with them as well. The surveillance equipment was to be placed at the very top of Nanda Devi's 7816-metre-high (25,643-foot-high) peak, the heavy loads making the task unbelievably difficult.

While the climbers were still well below the peak, a blizzard blew in, forcing them to descend as quickly as possible, the group leaving behind on the mountain two radio communication sets, a six-foot-long antenna, a power pack and all of the plutonium-packed capsules, the plutonium meant to be the energy source for the power pack.

The blizzard marked the start of winter, so any attempts to recover the equipment and place it on the mountain peak had to wait until the following spring. But when spring rolled around, a recovery expedition failed to find anything—the plutonium-packed capsules along with everything else had disappeared.

Over the past fifty years, several attempts to find the nuclear devices and other equipment have all ended in failure. To date, no one knows what happened to those capsules. One of the American climbers involved—Jim McCarthy—is quoted as saying:

> The device got avalanched and stuck in the glacier and God knows what effects that will have!

The dangerous implications of this nuclear mess should not be taken lightly. It may take centuries before the plutonium deteriorates. Until then, those capsules remain a radioactive hazard that could contaminate meltwater from the glacier and snowmelt that make their way into the headwaters of the Ganga, thereby poisoning one of the most important rivers of India that provides water for hundreds of millions.

This story about the Himalayan expeditions remained a secret until 1978 when the *Washington Post* reprinted facts originally appearing in the US magazine *Outside*, adding that at least one of the expeditions actually did succeed in putting nuclear-powered surveillance devices on the peak of Nanda Kot in 1967.

The accuracy of the reporting was acknowledged in India's Parliament by the then prime minister Morarji Desai, in April 1978. As a result of these disclosures, dozens of protesters demonstrated in front of the US Embassy in New Delhi in April 1978 chanting slogans like 'CIA quit India!' and 'CIA is poisoning our waters!'

When floods killed over fifty people in the Chamoli district of Uttarakhand in early February 2021, villagers began to believe that the nuclear devices had exploded, causing the deadly deluge specifically in the village of Raini. Indeed, a small station in this village is where water and sand from the river is regularly tested for radioactivity contamination, although no official word has come forth on whether or not contamination has ever been found.

The town of Chamoli is the halfway point in the journey to Uttarkashi. Hence, people across the entire state of Uttarakhand, including in the Uttarkashi region, were well aware of the nuclear fiasco and the involvement of America's CIA in it. It is understandable, then, how people could be wary and downright suspicious of anyone coming from the US when Anil and I showed up, just a few years after Morarji Desai's 'bombshell' disclosure to Parliament.

However, for one corrupt official, my American citizenship became an excuse to try and block our purchase of any lands in the area. This was in spite of us being cleared by officials from the Indian Central Bureau of Intelligence, who met with Anil for questioning.

Here again, divine protection came into play as a wonderful *leela* of divine drama unfolded during Anil's questioning. Almost as soon as Anil sat down, the official asked him, 'Aren't you Indira Devi's son from Sri Aurobindo's ashram in Pondicherry?'

A bit taken aback, Anil answered, 'Yes.'

The official then went on to say he recognized Anil from when he was a child decades earlier at the Aurobindo ashram, adding that Anil's resemblance to his mother was unmistakeable.

As it turned out, this official had been an ardent follower of Sri Aurobindo and would make a point of attending all of Dadaji's singing programmes and bhajan sessions at the ashram, Anil's mother always sitting alongside Dadaji during these events. Anil was at these sessions as well since he was a student at the Mother's School at the ashram, often singing with the children's choir that was taught by Dadaji. Hence, Anil's striking resemblance to his mother was instantly noticed by this man.

The gentleman then explained to Anil that there had been an incident involving nuclear material and the US CIA a few years ago in the Himalayas. This was the reason for the inquiry into our reasons for being in the area, especially since we had recently been in the US, and I was an American. Being fully satisfied with Anil's answers, he gave complete CBI clearance for both of us.

However, the CBI clearance did not stop the corrupt official from seizing upon my American citizenship as an excuse to block any purchase of land by us. When Anil met him and enquired why he was causing problems for us, his true motivation was then revealed: greed for money. Without a payoff, he would continue to block any and all attempts by Anil to purchase land in the district. Anil flatly refused, leaving our future in limbo until, what we can only call divine intervention, came to our rescue. The corrupt official was transferred shortly thereafter and demoted on another issue. He was forced to work at a desk job in a city far, far away.

Graft and corruption are a monstrous black hole. They suck dry the very heart of a democracy like India—or America—if they are not stopped. It matters not what form the corruption takes—payoffs or promotions, government contracts or funding politicians' campaigns for office—the result is the undermining of the fundamental foundation of a democratic republic that is based on the concept of 'government by the people, for the people'.

It matters not whether those engaging in this unscrupulous behaviour are 'suited booted' businessmen and lobbyists in America, or dishonest civil servants demanding bribes from even the poorest of the poor here in India. All are guilty of destabilizing the very fabric of the country that was originally woven with the threads of truth, justice, right action and accountability. Without these four pillars of good governance, a country will spiral downwards to the depths of depravity, portending its demise as a properly functioning human community, with chaos, civil unrest and violence being the inevitable and inescapable result.

While some may call it 'greasing the wheels', in truth graft and corruption are like tar poured into the government machinery, gumming it up and slowing it down, eventually stopping its ability to run properly and purposefully for the betterment of the society for which it was formed.

There is no justification for it, and the only solution is to expose it and stamp it out wherever it is found. All of us, each and every one of us who are blessed to live in a democracy have the duty to help in this exposure, shining the light of truth wherever and whenever needed to eliminate this despicable practice once and for all.

## The Assi Ganga

As a result of what the CBI official had told Anil, we decided that I should not go out in public, since fear and concern over the incident was still strong in the area. We were staying at the Uttarkashi Tourist Rest House (the 'UKI TRH' as we came to call it), overlooking the Bhagirathi River. So there I remained, in our room, in virtual isolation for quite some time—an extremely lonely period and low point for me in my life, cut off from friends and family abroad with no contact whatsoever for months.

My one bright spot during this lonely time was Prema. Prema was a tiny kitten I rescued from below the TRH. He was being terrorized by a group of children and mewling pathetically in fear. While I had no initial intention of keeping him, Anil said to do so as there was no one else around to take care of such a young kitten.

Our own beloved cats Sathi and Bandhu were still in Hawaii, being looked after by close friends. Only after we had found and bought our land, would they be able to come and join us here in India—a process that meant over two and a half years of separation. I missed their companionship, their playfulness and, most of all, their love.

This new little kitty helped to fill the void within—especially when it came to filling me up with his love. Hence, I called him 'Prema' meaning 'love'. He also filled my lonely days at the TRH with his antics, playing 'hide-and-seek' with me behind the curtains, chasing whatever little balls or toys I threw, racing after shoestrings I would twirl around on the floor or up in the air, giving me tremendous joy from morning to night.

Meanwhile, Anil continued his search for a suitable land for our home until he found some on the banks of the Assi Ganga River, north of the town of Uttarkashi. The Assi Ganga is a main tributary of the Bhagirathi River, its name stemming from the fact that eighty streams flow into this river on its way to meet the Bhagirathi, *assi*, meaning 'eighty' in Hindi.

We purchased a few acres of abandoned land from a local man who wanted to sell it. This was our first experience dealing with the often frustrating, convoluted state and union laws regarding acquisition of agricultural land.

First, Anil had to prove he was an agriculturalist, which he did through proof of his family's ownership of ancestral agricultural lands in the Kurukshetra area of the Punjab State in India. Then he had to secure 'No Objection Certificates' from every member of the seller's family since they were also on the original deed, the seller never having applied for or gotten a partition deed separating his own property from the rest of the family's lands. This is common in parts of rural India, tracts of family land never being legally partitioned amongst family members, even though the members agree between themselves which land is whose. Through the maze of legal twists and turns Anil prevailed, and we finally owned the land, free and clear.

Then came the question of building a house in such a remote area, where there were no professional engineers or architects available. We ended up seeking the help of a *sadhu* (monk) who had been a mechanical engineer before he had entered spiritual life. Brahmachariji (as we called him) told me to draw up a map or design of what I wanted the house to look like. It had to be very detailed with the various rooms, their sizes, electricity points, etc.

Thus began my crash course in architecture and engineering. I didn't have a clue about what to do, which was amply demonstrated by my plans for the first floor that contained a staircase going up with no way to come down!

My dearest Dad came to my rescue. Being a construction engineer himself, he had plenty of experience to share, which he did, in the form of a few *Build It Yourself* books he sent to me from the US.

I was fascinated by the whole task and learned such an incredible amount of invaluable information. Unless we build our own structure, few of us really think or know how much planning and design has to go into a building—doorways and windows, their sizes and which direction they are to open; pillars and columns to hold up the ceiling and for floors above; light switches, fixtures and outlets and where to put those two-way switches in staircases and rooms; plumbing fixtures and all the bathroom requirements from showers to sinks to toilets; and in the kitchen—counter heights and depths, cabinets and shelves, drawers and places for stoves, ovens and refrigerators; not to mention the staircases and how to measure and make steps and risers so one can comfortably walk up and down the stairs.

Then there was the foundation of the house and its plinth level, as well as thresholds on outside doorways to keep out rainfall and unwanted little critters. So much detail!

Of course, access to water is the most important consideration because we cannot live without it. Fortunately, we had two sources—the Assi Ganga River as well as the freshwater spring on the property. To tap these sources we would require electricity to work the pumps to lift the water to the overhead tanks on top of the house. And therein lay another challenge—getting access to electricity.

The village of Ravada, where we were located, was not connected to the state's electricity grid. In addition, back then, solar power was still in its infancy in India and not efficient at all. Importing equipment from the USA was prohibitively expensive, so this option was out too. In order to get power, we had to pay for the installation of a large transformer that would provide electricity not only for us, but for the entire village. We did have to install a 10 KVA backup generator for power as well, since government electricity was very unreliable, especially during the monsoon and winter seasons.

Finally, there was the question of heating our home during winter months. This was my first realization that many people in other parts of the world did not have central heating, which was so common and taken for granted in the USA. Heating had to be provided mainly through the burning of wood.

Thus began yet another lesson in designing the house with its south-facing windows and walls for sunlight to enter and warm the rooms, wooden shutters for insulation in winter and, most of all, building centrally located fireplaces to heat the entire home.

With my father's *Build It Yourself* books in hand, Brahmachariji designed our main fireplace in the middle of the building using cast-iron plates within the fireplace and air ducts below and above on its sides to bring in cool air, heat it as it passed by the hot plates and let the air rise to the top creating a natural air convection or circulation pattern. A ceiling fan would help distribute the warm air below so it could filter through the house. The fireplace was also fitted with cast-iron doors that closed, the hot doors radiating heat into the house as well.

Even with these sources of heat, it was still bitterly cold during the winter months, especially since the sun only rose above the mountain peaks between 9.30 and 10 a.m., warming our small valley for but a few hours, before it disappeared behind the western peaks short of 3 p.m. Long, cold nights were the norm, as we slept in long-sleeved and full-legged thermal tops and bottoms under as many as four 5 kg quilts and comforters at the height of winter.

## Frigid Oven: No Water, No Light

However, the situation at our home was far better and much warmer than what we had had to endure at the Uttarkashi Tourist Rest House, where we lived over the three years it took for us to find and purchase our land, and then to build our house on the Assi Ganga. The UKI TRH was a government run hotel on the banks of the Bhagirathi River in the town of Uttarkashi. The rooms we stayed in were like an oven in the summer and an ice box in the winter. For those freezing nights there, we had had to rely on an electric heating rod that produced heat no further than eighteen inches to two feet away from it!

The electricity at the TRH was off almost all of the time as the supply of electricity to the area was limited. It was also out so much because of the weak aluminium wiring used which burned out constantly, leaving us with no lights and no heat very, very often. This again was a real adjustment for me to make.

In the USA and other developed countries, we take a constant supply of electricity for granted. Even at our land in Hawaii, we had a continuous supply of electricity, although we certainly had to learn lessons in conserving it, especially during the cloudy and rainy periods. Still, electricity was the norm for me from childhood, as it was and is, for most living in developed countries – that too, safe electricity with proper wires and wiring according to sensible building codes.

India in general, and Uttarkashi in particular, was another story. As mentioned, many in rural areas had no electricity at all. If there happened to be a power grid, how well the supply was installed was another matter of concern. Over the years of living at the TRH, we rewired at least three units that we were renting with copper wiring with the help of a proper electrician and the management's approval.

We also helped them install solar hot-water tanks on the roof. Prior to this, heating water was another new and potentially dangerous daily undertaking at the TRH. Bucket baths were the order of the day and are still used extensively throughout India, especially in poorer and more rural areas. A bucket of water is heated with a heating rod—usually a long metal device on one end that is inserted into the water with an electric plug for electrical input at the other end. The device is immersed in the water and hooked to the side of the bucket so the bottom end of the contraption dangles above the bottom of the bucket. If one unthinkingly puts one's hand into the bucket of water without first turning off or unplugging the heating rod, one could end up with a fatally shocking experience!

Water itself was a precious and scarce resource. Piped water to the bathroom and to the outdoor kitchen areas was released for only an hour or so each in the morning and in the evening, not flowing during the rest of the day. This meant filling up plastic buckets with the precious liquid for use in bathing, cooking, cleaning, doing the laundry and dishes and even for flushing toilets.

Since the cooking area was outside and not connected directly to the main rooms, this meant braving both the cold and rain seasonally, going to and from the kitchen. It also meant hauling buckets of water from the bathroom to the kitchen as the single faucet in the kitchen was often without water.

It was while living in these conditions that I first truly began to appreciate the value and weight of water quite literally—water is extremely heavy! Lugging buckets of it is no joke! So, no water was ever wasted; each drop was precious and conserved as much as possible.

I was cooking food on a kerosene stove at the TRH. Anyone who has cooked on kerosene knows how difficult it is to clean the outside bottom of the pot which is blackened by the kerosene's fire. The only thing available then for me to use to clean the pot was wood ash. Scrubbing the bottom of the pot with ash is the perfect formula for permanently stained nails and cuticles!

I was also washing our clothes by hand in plastic buckets. This included our bed linen and towels. Anyone familiar with handwashing will understand the amount of strength one needs in one's hands, arms and upper body to wring things out before hanging them up to dry. Over the years, the practice of lifting buckets and wringing out laundry by hand made me much stronger than I was before. Indeed, three years after leaving the USA, when I returned to Hawaii to pack up our goods for shipping to India, I went to the massage therapist who had regularly given massages to both Anil and me when we had lived there on the Big Island.

As she started working on my back, she exclaimed, 'Oh my goodness! Your body has completely changed! Your shoulders and upper torso are totally developed in areas they never were before. What were you doing over there these past three years?!'

'The laundry,' was my wry reply with a smile.

## The Ultimate Goal of Life

While there certainly were many, many challenges and adjustments that I had to make in the way I was used to living my life, the years we lived in the holy Himalayas were an extraordinary period of our lives together. These magical, mystical mountains have been the fount from which innumerable spiritual masters have emerged, having performed their own *tapas* and *sadhana* (spiritual practices) to finally achieve the goal of conscious union with the Divine.

Being home to four 'dhams'—four of the holiest sacred sites in all of India—the vibrations emanating from these mountains are saturated with spirituality. Numerous ashrams have been established in the area; in some cases, many centuries ago. Pilgrimage locations of Gaumukh, Gangotri and Yamunotri consecrated to the feminine aspect of the Godhead on one side, with Kedarnath and Badrinath dedicated to the masculine aspect on the other, have drawn and continue to draw those seeking the highest purpose in life—conscious union with the Divine.

There is an abundance of individual mystics—both men and women—clad in ochre-coloured robes, walking through these holy hills. Many are not associated with any specific ashram or spiritual community. Instead, they are all on their own spiritual journey following the call of the Divine. We would meet them during our own treks into the hills, or sometimes they would come to the door of our home on their own. Each encounter with such a person was an inspiration for our own spiritual-seeking and growth.

The goal of individual God-realization is not pursued from a selfish motivation, but from the innate desire of the soul to merge once again into the ocean of Divine Love from which it has taken birth. Like the streams and rivers flowing to merge with the sea, each soul's pull towards reunification with the Supreme Absolute is as unmistakable and irresistible as that of an iron filing to a magnet.

To achieve that final reunion, the selfish and self-centred ego lost in the false illusion that we are separate from one another, from all facets and aspects of creation and from the Ultimate Supreme, must be effaced through various practices like prayer, repetition of the Lord's name (whichever name one feels closest to) and meditation.

The great God-realized mystic Shirdi Sai Baba once compared these various practices to the physical action of constantly rubbing two coins together. The coins are embossed with various designs imprinted on them. By continuously rubbing these coins together, that imprint is worn down to the point that it disappears altogether. All that is left is one smooth, uniform surface.

Spiritual practices do the same thing when the heart and mind are fully engaged in them focusing on the Divine. They wear down the ego, the mental impressions that have been 'embossed' or imprinted on each individual soul through the succession of various lives over countless ages.

The imprints of deceptive individuality erect barriers between one's self and others. The ego-centred negative thoughts and emotions of selfishness and greed are the primary forces deluding the mind. This leads to fear and suspicion of 'others', rather than to the recognition of one's own self in the eyes of another—that same spark of the Divine shining forth from within ourselves being reflected back to us from the eyes of someone else, thereby reuniting each one of us together in Oneness.

This recognition dissolves all fear, all sense of separation and separateness, the feeling of unity and love sweeping away all such negativities, leading to open, full-hearted compassion, cooperation and the experience of the intimacy of soul-sharing that only spiritual realization can bring.

When the veils of delusion dissolve in our mind and recognition awakens our soul once again, we are swept to the freedom of the Spirit on a wave of bliss, being lifted out of our restraining ego-cocoon on the wings of Universal Love to the experience of conscious union with the Godhead, the Divinity of all life, with all creation glowing and vibrating to the Primordial Chord of creation—the AUM. All is God, all is beauty, all is truth, compassion and love, as are we—all of us—seemingly individual sparks of light, but in reality and in essence, all tiny refractions of the diamond Godhead that is the Divine.

Therefore, within each and every one of us, indeed within each and every fragment and fraction of creation is the spark of that Divine Diamond, revealed within and without ever more brilliantly each and every time we strive for and surrender to the Divine in love.

Every spiritual practice we do is akin to polishing the diamond within, helping it to shine with ever greater brilliance while simultaneously weakening the grasp the ego has over us. Each repetition of the Divine Name helps to pull out the threads that make up the delusive ego-veil of separation. Each time our heart thrills to the thought of God, each longing we feel to be consciously in the Divine Presence attunes our heart and spirit more and more to the vibration of the Divine Heartbeat that animates us and all creation.

Each time we feel compassion or lend a helping hand to another being helps us to recognize the Divinity within that being and within everything, bringing in turn the awareness that all acts are meant to be acts of service to God, all we do to be done in awareness of the Divine Presence.

This then is the triune path of sadhana, of yoga that mystics and saints have trodden upon since time immemorial—work, worship and wisdom. Selfless service to others helps us to identify with them, while recognizing the Divine being reflected back to us in the eyes of those we serve. Each action we do dedicated to the Divine helps to enflame our heart and soul with deep feelings of devotion, surrendering all we do, all we have and all we are to the Supreme in unconditional love.

Eventually our sadhana ripens into the highest wisdom of conscious realization of the Divine—both within and without—transforming our lives to ones of harmony and balance, peace, truth and love, lived in full consciousness of the Divine Guidance both within and without at all times and in following that guidance, being one with that wisdom, we can never again err in our ways.

This is the path extolled by the rishis in the Vedas, by Lord Krishna to his closest disciple Arjuna in the Bhagavad Gita and exemplified by the lives of Lord Buddha and Jesus Christ, as well as other realized prophets, sages and saints, mystics and seers throughout the world, throughout time.

It is that spiritual path which, if followed in sincere earnestness, will most readily bring the soul to its full fruition in life. Thus do our lives, our beings become living instruments of the Divine, to be used in devotion and service to further His evolutionary plan—the goal of the revelation of the Divine on Earth.

Nature is the stage upon which this play of spiritual evolution is enacted. For it is through recognition of Nature as God's outer vesture that we are led most easily to the pinnacle of Divine Realization. For within the heart of Mother Nature is a secret doorway to higher consciousness and cosmic union with the Divine.

As the great spiritual mystic and God-realized master, Sri Aurobindo, states in his epic spiritual poem 'Savitri':

> *This world is GOD fulfilled in outwardness . . .*
> *On Nature's luminous tops, on the Spirit's Ground—*
> *Nature—the Hidden Godhead—recognize.*

# 15

# The Balding of Our Mother

Being in Nature is being in the beating heart of the living Lord, the Divine Mother. The ease of meditation when within that heart is extraordinary. I found this especially true while living in the holy Himalayas. The vibrations felt in these sacred mountains are surely the result of the spiritual tapas, penance and sadhana performed in single-minded devotion to the Supreme by countless saints and sages over many ages.

It is as the monk said to Anil in Gangotri—these mountains are not mere rocks, but the souls of great beings continuing to perform their spiritual oblations and absolutions to God, the intensity of their devotion uplifting the vibrations and therefore the consciousness of the entire earth to a higher level of be-ing.

Throughout our years of living in these holy hills, we trekked into Nature's heart again and again. One of our favourite places to go was above our house upstream on one of the many tributaries of the Assi Ganga. There is a series of spectacular waterfalls that cascade down the mountainside to the valley below. Over time, the various falls have created ponds beneath them, of differing depths and breadths.

We would spend our days here in deep meditation and reverie, usually after taking a purifying dip in the waters, those waters being quite cold even during the hottest months of the year. The waters were both refreshing and revitalizing, the sudden chill helping to clear extraneous thoughts from our minds while simultaneously cleansing our bodies.

These were years of deep self-inquiry, but also years of intense reflection on the state of the world around us. Disturbing signs from Nature signalled to us that things were not as they should be, that the balance of Nature was being disturbed on all levels and that this disturbance would eventually lead to readjustments by the Earth in her attempt to regain balance.

When we had originally started searching for land in the Himalayas, we had been shaken by how much deforestation had already taken place in the lower foothills and regions around Rishikesh and Mussoorie. Indeed, when we first visited Mussoorie back in September of 1986, staying at Anil's maternal grandfather's hotel—the Savoy—we were told an astonishing account of an earlier visit to the area by the then prime minister, Indira Gandhi.

The Nehru family, including Mrs Gandhi's father, Jawaharlal Nehru, had visited Mussoorie often over the decades, actually staying in the Savoy itself many times. At that time, the hills and Dehradun Valley were lush with forests, as was the case when Anil had attended school in the Doon Valley even earlier. But things had changed, with deforestation plaguing both the valley and the Mussoorie area.

As our car made its ascent up the roads leading to Mussoorie, I noticed that the big rocks on either side of the road had old green paint on them. Upon asking why the rocks had been painted green, we were told that officials in the area had done so prior to a planned visit to Mussoorie by then prime minister, Indira Gandhi, just a couple of years earlier. Mrs Gandhi loved Nature and wildlife. India owes the existence of the environmental laws it has had, as well as its earliest programmes to help save the tiger, in particular, to Mrs Gandhi.

Motivated by her love of wildlife, she framed the first true environment laws in the country—laws that were strict and absolutely essential to stop the wholesale destruction of India's forests and slaughter of its wildlife. Because the fundamental truth is that, without a healthy environment, without forests and the wildlife that sustains them, without the ecosystem services like water production and conservation that forests provide, no development of any true or lasting worth is possible.

The plundering of India's natural wealth had begun under the British but increased exponentially after independence had been won. By the late 1960s and early 1970s, many of India's iconic species, like the Bengal tiger, were in a perilous state, with their population so dangerously low that even with strict laws to protect them, it was doubtful they would survive. With the input from some of the country's leading wildlife experts and conservationists (like Anne Wright, founder of WWF and mother of tiger expert Belinda Wright), Mrs Gandhi fought for and achieved the passage of conservation laws necessary to give India's forests and wildlife at least a fighting chance to survive, thereby giving India and the Indian people a chance to survive as well.

While the laws when properly implemented surely had positive impacts, deforestation in the country still raged on unchecked in many areas. This was the case in much of the Himalayan region, especially around Mussoorie. So, when Mrs Gandhi announced her planned visit to the area, officials panicked, knowing what her reaction to the continuing deforestation would be.

Thinking they might be able to fool her into believing all was well, they painted large rocks green in the hope that she might mistake the green rocks for green trees from the helicopter that would be flying her in! Of course, she was not fooled at all and the officials involved reaped the karmic repercussions of their stupidity and attempted deception, the old green paint a testimony to the lengths some will go to, to try to cover up their mindless and continued looting of India's and the world's natural wealth at the expense of the present and future generations.

## Chir That Is No Cheer!

We witnessed the same sad tale of continuing deforestation throughout our journey in the Himalayas until we finally reached the Uttarkashi Valley. Here there were still forests and that too, forests filled with native tree species. Species like tun or red cedar, banj oak, angu, Himalayan elm, kail and burans (a type of rhododendron) as well as coniferous species like deodar cedar and picea spruce still covered the slopes of much of the areas beyond Uttarkashi town.

These wonderful native trees were however edged out in places and mixed with another pine called 'chir' (pronounced 'cheer'). Chir is a pine tree normally found in the lower elevations of the Himalayas. It was promoted by the British during their rule since it grew straight and tall relatively quickly, thereby being useful as a tree for 'lumber' . . . or so they thought.

In fact, while chir does indeed grow straight, it is a poor species to use for building, unlike the native trees of the region. Over the years, chir warps even when it is fully dried before use. In addition, it is prone to parasites like termites who have an easy time eating into its softer wood compared to the natural conifers and hardwoods of these mountains. Hence its true value as lumber is severely limited. But that did not stop the British from promoting its cultivation, planting it everywhere.

For the local people living there, the long needles of the chir tree are perilous to walk on, especially during the rainy season. Both Anil and I have experienced how horribly slippery the needles get when wet—something very dangerous to have to deal with when you are walking on sheer cliffs and mountain paths.

In addition, these same needles speed up rain runoff, the water sliding off the long needles with ease and picking up speed as it races down the mountain. This, in turn, lends itself to flash flooding, unlike the indigenous conifers whose short needles minimize rain runoff, helping to capture moisture on the hilly slopes. The deciduous trees are even more effective in this with their fallen leaves acting as sponges to soak up the rain, while also bringing valuable and vital nutrients to the forest soils that enhance future fertility and growth. The chir needles take many, many years to biodegrade, thereby merely robbing nutrients from the soil and not giving it back to the forest at all, unlike the endemic tree species.

Mira Behn (or Mirabehn)—the British daughter-disciple of Mahatma Gandhi—was one of the first people to ring the alarm bells regarding the steady upward spread of chir trees from lower altitudes to higher elevations and the devastating effects the chir had on flooding downstream. From childhood, she had been an enthusiastic lover of Nature, spending all the time she could in forests, enjoying the wildlife wherever she was. Hence, her ability to sense any imbalance in Nature was honed at an early age.

After Gandhiji was assassinated, she moved north, spending time in the Tehri region of the Garhwal Hills—an area you pass through on the way to Uttarkashi. While the Tehri Valley is lower in elevation than Uttarkashi, it still is home for most of the same tree species. She recorded the advance of the chir up the slopes, and the unwise practice back then of the forest department's policy of cutting down banj oak and planting chir pine instead. In an essay entitled 'Something Wrong in the Himalaya', that she wrote in 1952, Mira Behn noted the detrimental effect these trees had on the environment and on the local people, urging the forest department to change their policies.

The banj oak forests were the centre of the economy and environment of the area, she wrote, adding that cutting them down was equivalent to cutting out the very heart of the entire ecosystem which would inevitably bring about its deadly collapse. She surmised that their presence in Tehri was a warning signal that the Himalayas were warming up.

This was quite a remarkable observation to have made at that time during the late 1950s and was based on her knowledge of the local native fauna. Chir grows best in the warmer temperatures one finds at lower elevations. The fact that it was now spreading on its own, being seen at higher elevations could only mean that overall temperatures at higher altitudes were climbing as well.

The British were also responsible for deforesting the Himalayan slopes well up the major rivers. To get the felled trees down to the valley below, they floated them on the river itself, thereby bypassing the need to use the treacherous mountain roads. Teaching this technique to some of the local people further enhanced the speed with which the Himalayan forests were being destroyed.

## Ominous Changes and Prophetic Warnings

By the time we first came to the Himalayas in 1986, so much deforestation had taken place that we virtually gave up hope of finding any forested land. Fortunately, some good forest cover remained especially outside the town of Uttarkashi. Still, signs of future problems were evident for those attuned enough to the natural rhythms of the area to see, hear and feel. It was our encounters with some of the sadhus/holy people there that confirmed our own concerns for the region's environmental future, as well as the changes being seen in some of the local communities.

The people of these regions had long been known for their hospitality and humility, honesty and integrity, as well as for their reverence for Nature and respect for the holy men and women who frequented these sacred hills.

As one monk told us, 'Ten years ago [in the 1970s], if I dropped a purse full of money on the path and came back two weeks later, that purse would still be there, with all that money. Today, when I go to bathe in the mountain stream, I may well come back to find that my only cooking vessel has been stolen!'

He said the changes were the result of more people coming up from the plains to the hills, most of whom were not coming for spirituality and pilgrimage but to escape the summer heat, looking only for 'fun and amusement' in the mountains, as he put it. Contact with this type of individual along with the insidious influence of Bollywood cinema films that were promoting violence, greed, arrogance and other negative emotions were sowing 'bad seeds' into the minds of locals, he said—seeds that were sprouting and spreading throughout the formerly respectful and reverent local populace of these holy hills.

The monk also mentioned how lazy the men had become: 'They sit and drink chai and smoke beedis all day long, talking about nothing of value, while the women are left to do all the work. From before dawn until late at night, these women must work—cooking food, gathering firewood and fetching water from the river. Then they have to cut fodder for their cattle, putting their lives at risk, climbing these sheer cliffs with no ropes or support at all. Each year some of them plunge to their deaths.

'None of this was necessary in the past when our mountains were filled with the native trees that God had put here ages ago. All of this has come as a result of man's greed and his disrespect for Nature and the Creator. What arrogance to think that men know better than God what is meant to be grown where!

'These mountains have been sanctified by the Creator as the birthplace of the holiest of rivers—the Ganga and Yamuna,' he said, adding, 'they are the spiritual "training ground" for the saints and sages, the home of countless God-realized souls who have given up all worldly desires while joyfully offering their entire heart, mind and soul to the Divine. How can people do what they are doing now—destroying our Mother and the ageless spiritual refuge of the holiest members of humanity?!'

Referring to the rampant deforestation throughout the area, he lamented, 'They are shaving off our Mother's hair, making her bald—all for money! How can they escape their karma!' The monk warned, 'God is the **G**enerating, **O**rganizing *and* **D**estroying principles of the Supreme Absolute. Man will have to pay for his disrespect, his lack of humility toward the Creator and for his greed and corruption that is turning the holy Himalayas into denuded hills of trash.'

These prophetic words of the sage would indeed see fulfilment in the coming years . . .

## No Bridge for Troubled Waters

We ourselves witnessed the truth of his observations over the years in various ways. I have never seen such hardworking women in my life, toiling from before sunrise to long past sunset. One of the most shocking sights for me was seeing the unbelievably huge loads of grass and wood that the women would pile on their backs to carry home after hours spent in places where forests remained and grasses still grew. They would walk for kilometres in search of wood and fodder, the heavy burdens they carried on their backs forcing them to bend forward almost in half! Then they had to cross the icy-cold waters of the Assi Ganga, often flowing dangerously fast, in order to bring their huge burdens home as their villages were on the other side of the river.

The sight was so appalling to me that I asked Anil if we couldn't build a bridge for the women to use to cross the river by our land. He agreed and set out to see where a permanent bridge could be erected. In the meantime, a temporary wooden plank bridge was made and installed—something that the local women sincerely appreciated, even though this temporary bridge was lost every year during monsoon due to the swollen waters of the river rising and washing it away. Suitable land for a permanent bridge was found just upstream, going from government revenue land on one side to the other. Anil secured all the necessary permits and was about to start the work when he was stopped by one villager claiming 'possession' of the land on the opposite side.

When investigated, Anil found that the man did not have any legal claim to the land, nor was he even growing any crops on it. Still, Anil offered to pay the man for the small space the foot bridge would have required. But the man refused to agree—a refusal we could not comprehend since it was women of his own village who would be helped by this foot bridge.

Then some men from our own village of Ravada approached Anil and asked him not to build the permanent foot bridge. Their reason? They did not want the women from the other villages across the Assi to be able to cross the river on a year-round basis as it would mean less fodder and firewood for their village.

The people of these villages on both sides of the river were related to one another. They were cousins, aunts and uncles. Their communities had been there for generations, and for generations, they had cooperated with each other to help in various ways, whether in building homes or in ploughing fields. Now that spirit of cooperation and mutual aid was gone. The underlying cause of this—deforestation.

Deforestation had meant fewer resources of wood and fodder for all communities. As a result, the spirit of joint community and cooperation had been replaced by feuding and competition for the dwindling resources left after the plunder of the land.

This was one of the first examples we saw with our own eyes of the devastating effects deforestation causes to local people that get caught in the vice of conflict over dwindling resources as the forests and the ecosystem services they provide disappear. Centuries of cooperative living destroyed, replaced by anger,

competition and discord. While the forests and the wildlife that
sustains and regenerates them were alive and thriving, so was the
spirit of communal harmony, sharing and peaceful coexistence. As
the trees and wildlife disappeared, so did this spirit of camaraderie
and cooperation.

As a result of the opposition from our own village, coupled
with the lack of cooperation from the man who claimed 'possession'
from the other village, we were never able to build a permanent
foot bridge across the Assi. But we did erect temporary bridges
year after year, for as long as we lived there.

Of course, I have a hard time keeping quiet when I see
something that disturbs me and/or when I believe an action—or
inaction—is wrong. So, on more than one occasion, I spoke out
against the virtually tyrannical control that the men in the area had
over the women.

I remember one conversation I had with some of the men of
our village when we were giving them a ride home from Uttarkashi
town, thirty minutes away. I spoke frankly about how good the
men had it there, with the women doing all the hard work while
they drank chai, smoked and gossiped. They looked a bit surprised
by my candour—nothing new for me for sure!

Summarizing their situation vis-à-vis the women of the area
I said, 'So they do all the work while you relax, and yet they—the
women—have to pay dowry to your family when you are married!
How backwards is that!?'

Nervous laughter rippled through the car.

## Burning with Anger

The injustice of the dowry system is one of the remaining vestiges
of the severely patriarchal society that has held sway over India for
many centuries. While things are changing throughout India with
respect to women, and equality of women with men, the dowry

system is still in vogue in some of the more remote areas of the country, and even practised amongst some of the educated and well-to-do, despite its being made illegal in 1961. This is according to a new World Bank study published in 2021. It and other unjust traces of the past do still linger on in some communities.*

Another example would be the practice of animal sacrifice I was shocked to see being carried out on the banks of the Assi Ganga. The sacrifices had nothing to do with religious ceremonies, such as those done on certain Muslim festivals. These sacrifices on the banks of the Assi were being carried out to 'appease' so-called demonic spirits troubling someone with bad dreams or ill health, normally being done when Anil was not home in Ravada with me.

Anil had already been successful in getting a slaughterhouse closed, which was located on the banks of the Bhagirathi River, opposite the UKI TRH, while we were still living there. He petitioned the district magistrate about it, pointing out that dead carcasses and discarded body parts, blood and other pollutants were being thrown straight into the river without any kind of decontamination processing at all—that too, directly into a river that was considered one of the holiest of all India by Hindus.

In the end, newly passed water pollution control laws were the grounds whereby I was able to stop the sacrifices, but my 'interference' and outspokenness—while appreciated by some, especially the women—were not appreciated by others.

Another environmentally destructive activity we desperately tried to stop was the annual burning of the government forest lands around the region. These fires were the result of arson— not natural causes like lightning. Their purpose was two-fold: to burn dry grass areas before monsoon with the misconception that

---

*    Soutik Biswas, 'Indian Dowry Payments Remarkably Stable, Study Says', BBC, https://www.bbc.com/news/world-asia-india-57677253

new grass would grow back greener and fuller the following year, and to increase the speed with which the sap flowed in the chir trees. The sap or resin collected was used to make turpentine— another example of the negative impacts this human-introduced tree species had on the ecosystem of the area, the sap normally flowing during the warm weather in any case. It was nothing but greed that encouraged the use of fires to speed up the process.

The tradition of stubble burning was started by the British but has been carried on by the local people even after the British left. The practice is terrible for the ecosystem as it burns up the young saplings of the native trees trying to grow in the area. Also, the fire consumes whatever fodder still remains in the vicinity, forcing the women foraging for their herds of cattle to go further and further away to get it. The air would be thick with smoke, forcing us to close all windows at the height of summer, when cross-ventilation was so badly needed. The impact of the heavy smoke in the air, especially on the lungs of the young and elderly, is devastating.

Using our own lands as living laboratories, we demonstrated how lush green grass would indeed grow back with monsoon rains, without burning the old first. At times, only the grass on our land was green for kilometres around. Hence, we let the local women harvest it for their cattle to help them out.

One of the projects we sponsored was the planting of native fruit trees both in people's private properties as well as on government forest lands securing the approval of the forest department to do so. Between the example of our green grasses growing without first being burnt on the one hand, and the distribution and planting of native fruit trees on the other, we hoped to help stop the burning of the slopes around us.

Many did indeed embrace the 'no burn' concept along with the native fruit trees, helping to protect the forest lands and put out unnatural fires. But there always seems to be a small percentage of individuals who apparently live for causing trouble for others—even for those whose sole motivation is to help them. Thus, we became a target for these dastardly few.

On one occasion during the burning season, while we were at the bottom of a ravine by a stream, fires were deliberately started, both up and downstream of where we were blocking our escape. Simultaneously, someone started throwing rocks down from the cliff above us. Taking refuge under a ledge from the rocks, we made our way downstream and out of sight of the rock-pelting men. We then clambered up the ledge to safety using only the tree roots that dangled over the ledge. Mother Nature surely did protect us, providing us both with cover and a safe way to escape.

## Of Vedas, Tigers and Temples

Another extraordinary incident of grace and protection from Mother Nature came a few years later. I had been showing some of my films on Nature, wildlife, and some of the great spiritual sages of India to the children from the local government village school as well as to the three Nepali sisters who worked for us for years. For some perverse reason, these same few troublemakers complained against my activities, saying I was a threat to their Vedic culture.

Nothing could have been further from the truth since the very roots of Vedic culture come from the teachings of sages and mystics, whose highest personal spiritual experiences have very often occurred in Nature. These spiritual experiences in Nature form the base for their teachings.

In addition, the Vedas and the wisdom stemming from them are filled with observations of Nature, her natural cycles and balance, the process of creation through the evolution of the five elements, as well as the oft-repeated declarations that Nature is indeed the outer vesture of the Divine—the hidden Godhead that must be recognized. But these truths were ignored by the troublemakers, and they had vowed to stop me.

While Anil had initially been at home with me in Uttarkashi at the start of this controversy, he had to leave unexpectedly due to the passing of his Uncle Noti in Pune. As a result, I was again alone. I must admit that I was concerned since our house was quite isolated below the village of Ravada; there was no telephone or mobile connectivity, no driver on site and hence, no way to contact the police if there was trouble of any sort. Still, I had had many experiences already where Mother Nature had protected me in the past, and so I put my faith in the Divine.

It was about 10.30 at night when I first heard strange sounds below my house. It sounded somewhat like someone sawing wood, but the sounds soon changed into low growls. Tigers! Two tigers were directly below the house in the tall grass! They seemed to be 'talking' to each other, which was what I had heard. Occasionally, they would let out a louder, longer roar that reverberated on the surrounding hills. Mother Nature had sent not one but two tigers apparently to protect me! Who could ask for better 'watchdogs' than a pair of tigers by your house!

For a full week, the tigers returned each night, making sure those nearby knew they were there. Clearly, no one would venture out with tigers close by. My security was assured.

When Anil returned, the real reason behind these false accusations and threats was revealed. These same troublemakers approached Anil for money, saying that they would make sure I was protected when Anil was not around, if he paid up. Needless to say, Anil did not give in to this extortion, nor did I fear for my safety again. Mother Nature was always there in every way to help, even when Anil had to be absent for one reason or another.

The whole threatening approach of these few was so unnecessary. All one had to do was ask for help and we were only too willing to give it, whether in the form of employment, healing, or the use of our vehicle for emergencies, especially with regard to accidents or other health problems, transporting people either to the hospital or to Swami Akandanand, also known as 'Homeopathic Swami'.

This wonderful sadhu lived outside Uttarkashi town and had dedicated his life to the Divine and to *seva*, or selfless service, in the form of providing homeopathic remedies to those who sought his help. Some of his remedies were a result of observing animals, seeing which plants they would go to eat or rub against when ill, the holy man making medicines out of the flora for similar ailments afflicting humans. We supported his efforts both through donations and purchases of homeopathic remedies for his seva whenever we went to the cities of the plains where such medicines were more readily available.

Our help to the people of the area also included funding the rebuilding of the main *mandir*, or temple, there. The old mandir had been built back in the 1800s, according to some accounts. It was dilapidated and desperately in need of repairs. An auction was held to help raise money for the project with bids being given to buy the old wood from the original structure. The highest bidder would get whatever wood that was there to take away for their own personal use.

Unfortunately, the bidding didn't come anywhere near the amount of money needed for the project. So, the villagers approached Anil, asking him to bid on the wood himself. When told how much was needed, Anil bid a bit more just to give a little extra cushion for the temple budget. As a result, he won the auction. Now enough money was guaranteed for completion of the temple.

When someone helps out another person when asked, there is certainly a positive karmic effect for the giver in one way or another. In this instance, the positive effect was almost instantaneous. For, when the walls of the old temple were broken down, they revealed plank after plank of two-hundred-year-old, seasoned, deodar wood—one of the best and strongest woods in the entire Himalayas! For just a little bit of charity, what a bonanza was received!

We ended up using those beautiful planks as shutters on our large windows to help ward off the cold during winter nights. In honour of the temple and the long time the wood had stayed in such a holy place, we had various spiritual symbols carved into them when making the window shutters—the Sanskrit Om (ॐ), the Buddhist chakra or wheel, the Christian cross, the Hindu heart chakra which is also the Jewish Star of David, Islam's crescent moon and star, the Taoist Yin-Yang, the flaming fire urn of the Parsees and the sacred symbol of the Native American Great Plains people that represented their holy 'four corners' area of the American Continent—the cross within a circle with four smaller circles in each quadrant.

These eight symbols represent eight of the great cultures and faiths of humanity, all of which teach peace, tolerance, compassion and love above all else. They also stress respect and reverence for the natural world the Creator has made, including the need to keep Nature's balance and purity intact for the benefit of the present and future generations. Indeed, it is everyone's duty, honour and privilege to do so as a sign of our gratitude to the Divine Creator of us all for all that we have been given.

These spiritual guidelines had protected these sacred mountains, generation after generation, with the local people living the tenets of 'need—not greed' with respect to their relationship with Nature, helping to ensure a year-long bounty not only for themselves but for all of Nature's other children, i.e., the other species as well.

But all of that was changing, and that too at an incredibly fast pace. As greed was replacing respect, deforestation was escalating at a horrific pace with species disappearing for lack of habitat and food as well as due to poaching for the illegal wildlife trade in skins, furs and body parts.

More and more frequent extreme weather events were occurring—high winds, sudden cloudbursts causing landslides and flooding, and hotter, dry summers meaning less crops harvested and less grass and other fodder for the family cattle. For us, the signs were becoming very clear—Nature's balance was being severely stressed.

## Sacred Lands be Damned

These desecrations of the holy Himalayas were compounded by the growing demand for energy. One can certainly understand the difficult position for the government in this issue. It was trying to provide energy for everyone across this vast nation—urban and rural areas alike. But unfortunately, in some instances, it followed the disastrous examples of the developed world in building huge dams. This often meant ancient villages and sacred places, as well as large tracts of forest, submerged under the new dam's waters.

A huge dam project at Tehri had been opposed for years by local people and activists combined; the fight was led for decades by the late great Sunderlal Bahuguna. A genuine activist of the Gandhian tradition, Bahuguna fasted many times over the years to bring the plight of the people and the environment to the attention of the general population as well as to the government officials making the decisions.

The massive dam was to be downstream of the confluence of two tributaries of the Bhagirathi River. Beyond the fact that thousands of hectares of forests would be submerged, the entire Tehri Valley including the homes, temples, and ancestral lands of the local community would be inundated as well, displacing over 100,000 people. The dam itself would put tremendous stress on the joints of fault lines where the tectonic plates meet below ground since water is extremely heavy.

The surface of the Earth is made up of these tectonic plates that sit or 'float' on the molten liquid core of the planet. As a result of sitting on the liquid core, the plates are in subtle, almost constant motion all the time. Where these plates meet is where both volcanoes and mountain chains have risen over geologic time spans, the two plates pushing against each other in the process of their movement raising the ground upward as a result, forming mountain ranges over time.

The Himalayas is the youngest mountain chain on the planet, much younger in comparison to others like the Rocky Mountains. They have been formed by the Indian plate (formerly an island) moving northward and colliding with the Eurasian plate. This ongoing collision has raised these mighty mountains to staggering heights over time, the Himalayas being the tallest mountain chain on Earth.

With both plates still actively moving, earthquakes are inevitable throughout the Himalayan mountain region. This is particularly true in the Garhwal region, where both Tehri and our land were located, as this is the actual boundary where the two plates meet, the Indian plate continuing to move toward the northeast at a rate of 5 centimetres (two inches) annually.

Storing thousands of millions of litres (hundreds of millions of gallons) of heavy, standing water on the fault lines or 'seams' where these plates meet is a recipe for disaster. The added stress from the additional weight will ultimately lead to shifts of the plates triggering massive and highly destructive earthquakes, along with the risk of either a full or partial collapse of the dam.

Any collapse would release huge amounts of water that would rush down the valleys of these mountains, wiping out everything in its path like an 'inland tsunami' or tidal wave, putting over one million people in direct danger of the dam's floodwaters. These waters would potentially go all the way to the city of Meerut near New Delhi before stopping.

Catastrophic collapses of dams have indeed happened in other parts of the planet in the past, including in Japan, the USA and China, leading to massive devastation and loss of life in the wake of the dam's floodwaters. The Chinese dam catastrophe in 1975 killed over 171,000 people, leaving over 11 million more homeless, for instance. Dam disasters in India include those at Gwalior, Morbi and Pune where thousands lost their lives and property.

In addition, the area where the dam was to be built is the central Himalayan seismic gap, which is a major geologic fault zone and also one of the zones with the highest number of earthquakes in the world—zone number five. Zones are determined by the risk factor of earthquakes associated with tectonic plate movements, the scale going from one (least likely to have an earthquake) to the highest zone of five (an area where two or more tectonic plates meet and where movements of those plates thereby bring the highest risk of massive earthquakes). Almost the entire Himalayan region is zone five—the highest risk. In this situation, it is not a question of *if* an earthquake occurs, but *when*.

Environmental activists tried in vain to explain all of these geological and scientific facts to the successive governments pushing for the dam. They even drew up alternative dam designs, proposing that two smaller and, therefore, less dangerous dams be built before the confluence of the two branches of the Bhagirathi, that would provide plenty of electricity and cost almost the same amount of money to construct as the single mega-dam.

But the government chose to build the mega-dam instead.

Mega-dams are mega-disasters wherever they are built. While hydroelectricity is labelled an alternative 'green source' for power versus fossil fuels, in fact, large dams produce ten times more GHGs (GreenHouse Gas emissions) in their first decade of operation than fossil fuel plants, releasing 25 to 38 per cent higher amounts of methane than coal-fired plants. This is due to the submergence of forest areas that inevitably comes with the construction of large dams. The submerged vegetation starts to decompose, releasing massive, concentrated quantities of methane into the air.

As mentioned earlier, methane has over 21 per cent higher heat-capturing abilities than does carbon dioxide, with another dam-released GHG—nitrous oxide—having over 219 per cent higher heat trapping capacity compared to carbon dioxide.* Clearly, this 'green' alternative is not green at all, even if the forests are cut down before submersion.

In addition, water in dams is stagnant, making the water unable to cleanse or revitalize itself with oxygen, the static waters becoming low in oxygen as a result. This, coupled with additional silt settling on the bottom of the dam, means additional vegetation growing in the water that depletes the oxygen level even further. Consequently, the stage is set for production of heavy metals, one of the most dangerous being mercury.

While mercury exists in an inert form in dry soil, when it is submerged under the oxygen-deficient waters of a dam, it undergoes a chemical change and turns into methylmercury—the most toxic and deadly form of mercury. Mercury then enters the food chain by poisoning fish in the water, which in turn poisons the creatures that eat the fish, the toxins going up the food chain, ultimately reaching humans as well; mercury-poisoning causing birth defects, kidney disease and neurological diseases, to name a few of its deadly effects.

Without any movement, the still water collected in dams heats up, adding to higher air temperatures and adversely affecting aquatic reproduction of different species that are unable to tolerate the water's warmth—fish species like salmon, especially juvenile fish, as well as several species of amphibians and others.

---

* Refer to the bibliography for source.

Recently, the disastrous effects of warmer waters have been demonstrated by the massive die-off of salmon in the American state of Alaska. With temperatures at all-time highs, even the moving waters in rivers are becoming lethally warm for the annual salmon run, salmon dying in their attempt to head upstream to spawn due to the lack of oxygen in the warm river waters. This, in turn, is leading to a decrease in food for larger predators, impacting their ability to survive too.

Finally, large dams submerge and cut off traditional biological corridors for great landscape animals like elephants as well as drowning food and habitat for innumerable other species that have relied on these areas for survival for countless generations. Whether elephant or tiger, deer or guar, river otters or birds, they all must search for new habitat, new food sources and new migration routes, inevitably bringing them into contact with human populations, thereby increasing human-animal conflicts.

Another problem is the silting that happens with dams, the build-up of soil and sand underneath the dam's waters meaning less electricity output very quickly. But due to financial assistance and technical expertise promised by the former USSR, the building of the dam was approved.

As it turned out, the government of the former USSR pulled out of the dam project even before it was built, due to its own political instability. That left the costs for the dam to be borne by the union and state governments jointly.

## Seismic Waves: Divine Grace

The seismic repercussions of building the Tehri Dam and others in these geologically fragile and fractured hills were underscored by the powerful earthquake that struck the Uttarkashi region in1991. I was not in India at the time of the quake, having gone back to the USA to visit family, and to typeset and publish our second book on prophecies and comparative philosophy, *The Scriptures Are Fulfilled.*

It was early in the morning of 20 October 1991. Our cat, Prema, was sleeping with Anil upstairs in our home on the banks of the Assi Ganga. At about 2.45 a.m., Prema woke up quite agitated, waking up Anil as well. A few minutes later, at 2.53 a.m., the entire house started shaking violently. The house was made of stone with its foundation on bedrock, hence, its violent movement was unbelievable.

Having lived on the Big Island of Hawaii, we had both become used to earthquakes which were usually magmatic in nature there—the quakes occurring due to the movement of magma beneath the earth's surface and not due to the movement of tectonic plates, as was the case here in Uttarkashi. This quake was the destructive aftermath of two tectonic plates pressing on each other, with one, or both, giving way and snapping into new positions, the resultant shaking of the earth being far more powerful and dangerous.

Anil quickly sat up and started repeating God's name. A dear, American friend of ours who was visiting rushed into Anil's room from the adjoining bedroom, his face as white as a sheet. Seeing Anil repeating the name of God, he followed suit, both praying intensely throughout the forty-five seconds that the quake lasted.

Two different scales are applied to a quake's strength and effects—the Richter scale, which registers the 'magnitude' or energy released by a quake according to the seismic waves it produces, and the Mercalli scale which measures the intensity and effects/destruction caused by the quake. While only 6.8 on the Richter scale, this quake measured IX or 'violent' on the Mercalli scale—a measurement of destruction that normally occurs with quakes of magnitude 8.0 or higher on the Richter scale.

Part of the reason for this may have been because the epicentre of the quake was only seven miles (11.6 km) deep—a very shallow quake—with the land shifting almost five feet (1.5 metres) at the main landslip area.

It wasn't until the sun rose a few hours after the quake struck, that the full extent of its devastation could be seen. Collapsed buildings—homes and *goshalas* (or cowsheds)—littered the landscape. Those that didn't collapse had huge cracks in the walls, with some homes shifted out of place like toys. Stone tiles from roofs lay strewn everywhere. No building in our village of Ravada (Rawada) was spared. With the epicentre of this violent quake just 33 kilometres (20 miles) away, it is easy to understand why there was so much destruction. This was true for the other villages around us and on the opposite side of the Assi Ganga—not one building had been left untouched. Virtually all had suffered major damage.

It was the same story throughout the region. In fact, one village only a few kilometres away from our home had been completely buried by the quake, swallowed by the earth. It took relief workers four days to just reach the roofs of the buildings of this ill-fated village.

According to local sources, this village had been a centre for the illicit alcohol business in the region—a business that had already cost the lives of countless individuals who had drunk the illegal and deadly brew, including one of the carpenters who had worked on our own house at the Assi.

A sadhu had visited the village just two months before the quake and warned the people that karmic repercussions would befall them if they did not mend their ways. Rather than taking his warning seriously and stopping their poisonous activities, they drove the sadhu out of the village, telling him to stop interfering in their 'business' and not to come back. Two months later, there was no village left to come back to, precisely as the monk had warned.

Over 300,000 people in at least 1294 villages were affected by the violent quake. While the government's official death toll was between 768 to 2000, with 1800 injured, local people claim that both figures are much, much higher—thousands more had lost their lives, their relatives, their families and/or had been injured.

With government figures stating 42,400 houses severely damaged or destroyed, that figure was also much higher since the loss of goshalas/cowsheds and other buildings that were used seasonally by local people were not counted.

Roads to the district were blocked everywhere due to landslides triggered by the quake's force, cutting off relief efforts in the forms of supplies and materials as well as man- and machine-power to help the survivors. Aftershocks continued for several days, causing additional road blockages and new slides, as well as more damage to structures already weakened by the major quake.

Sitting in the middle of this scene of catastrophic devastation, stood our home—virtually unscathed by the quake. There were thirty-eight large plate glass windows in the house. Despite the violent shaking the house went through, not a single window was cracked or broken. Indeed, there was no damage at all in the entire house except for a small crack on one of the columns holding up our water tank—something that was easily and quickly repaired.

The house was filled with statues and photos of Nature and various saints, mystics and aspects of Divinity revered by various faiths from around the world. Not a single photo or statue fell down or was damaged. Astonishing as it was, our house was the only habitable building within a ten-kilometre radius, even though the quake's epicentre had been so close. Truly, Divine Protection had spared not just our home and property, but far more importantly, the lives of Anil, our dear American friend and our beloved cats as well.

## Photos That Speak a Thousand Words

This amazing situation was not just about having a house that was well built. Other structures made with similar materials had not fared well at all, including some of the buildings in the Gangotri region, where they were either severely damaged or had collapsed, killing the occupants inside.

This fact was verified by another sadhu we had met years earlier at the TRH. Swami Sunderanand had travelled across the Himalayan region for many years when he first began his spiritual journey. He has come to be known across India and around the world for his stunning photographs of the holy mountains, earning him the nicknames 'photographic swami' and 'the sadhu who clicks'. His photos have appeared in articles, with 425 gleaned from over 100,000 photos he has taken throughout his lifetime appearing in his own book called *Himalaya: Through the Lens of a Sadhu*.

A few years after starting his spiritual quest, Swamiji began questioning whether he was on the right path or not, discouraged by what he perceived to be a lack of spiritual progress. High in the Himalayas surrounded by its snow-capped peaks under a thick, grey cloud cover that obscured the sky, he prayed in all sincerity to the Divine, asking God to give him a sign that he was indeed on the right path, that he should have faith and continue his spiritual journey.

Deep within he heard that still, soft Voice saying, 'Look up!' Turning his gaze towards the heavens, he watched as the thick clouds parted to form a distinct Om (ॐ) in the exquisite azure vault above him. God had heard him, giving an immediate answer to the heartfelt prayer of this genuine seeker of the divine.

Always with a camera close by, Swamiji quickly clicked a photo of the sacred symbol—ॐ—the symbol that is said to be the Voice of the Divine—the holy link between the manifest and unmanifest, the vibration from which all creation has come forth. As it says in the Bible, 'In the beginning was the Word, and the Word was God.*'

---

* John 1:1 New Testament, the Holy Bible, King James version.

Meditation on the sacred 'Om' is said to pierce the veil of separation between manifest creation and the Unmanifest Absolute, the Holy Ghost, or Spirit, of Christ's teachings, the key to reaching beyond the 'Void' in Buddhism and other faiths. Years later, we were blessed not only to see this photo, but to be given a copy of it by Swamiji as a birthday gift for Anil. It is one of the most treasured memories we carry with us from our years of living among the Himalayan masters. Like us, Swamiji believes that God is to be found in the heart of Mother Nature.

During his travels, Swamiji documented, via his photographs, the great devastation being wreaked in the sacred mountains through rampant deforestation, before settling down near Gangotri. He also photographically recorded the continuing recession of the great Gangotri glacier over the years due to deforestation, drop in rain and snowfall, and the rise in temperatures across the region.

Taking this photographic evidence to government authorities, he desperately tried to get them to stop the unbridled tree cutting, demanding action against those involved in these illegal activities. His pleas mainly fell on deaf ears, but those engaged in the deforestation vowed to put an end to his campaign to save the forests of his hallowed hills.

Being a lover of the Divine, Swamiji was keenly attuned to Nature, taking his cues from her as the outer vesture of the Divine in manifest form. One day, while returning to his small kutia/hut, he was surprised to see a chipmunk on the path, constantly trying to block him from going forward, the little squirrel looking directly into Swamiji's eyes while incessantly chattering in a panicky manner. Taking seriously the chipmunk's warning that something was wrong, Swamiji stopped, spending the night under the open sky, instead of returning home.

The next morning, the little chipmunk had disappeared, so Swamiji continued to his kutia. Upon arrival, he realized why Mother Nature had sent him a warning—his hut had been broken into and ransacked, most likely by those involved in the illegal timber industry who were looking for his photos and negatives documenting their criminal deeds. Fortunately, all that evidence happened to be with Swamiji and not at his hut. Had Swamiji been there, he surely would have been assaulted and possibly killed.

Such are the dangers that environmentalists around the world still face today, their only 'crime' being their dedication to protect and preserve the planet for present and future generations of all beings, all species that call Mother Earth 'home'.

During the earthquake, Swamiji was in his kutia, lying on the floor. Putting his ear to the ground, he said the thundering rumbles of the quake sounded like Lord Shiva doing his 'Rudra Tandav' dance—Shiva's dance of anger and destruction.

This most recognized pose of Lord Shiva symbolizes the cosmic cycles of creation and destruction and the daily rhythm of birth and death. Standing in the middle of a circle, representing Maya or the material world, Shiva is depicted crushing underfoot the demon of ignorance—the ego.

In one of his four hands, he holds the *damaru*—a drum representing the cycles of creation and dissolution, life and death. In his rear left hand he holds a flame, symbolizing the purification of Maya and burning of illusion. With his front left hand, Shiva points to his left foot that is raised off the ground, symbolizing spiritual liberation through meditation on the Divine. His front right hand is upheld in the traditional 'blessing pose', signifying his attribute of safeguarding the universe and meant to reassure all those who sincerely seek spiritual liberation of his protection and guidance, leading ultimately to their spiritual liberation.

On the left side of his head is the sacred visionary datura flower, whose blossoms are woven throughout his flowing locks of hair, demonstrating Shiva's ability to transform poison into purity, parts of the purified datura plant still used today in certain Ayurvedic preparations.

This one extraordinary pose summarizes the entire purpose of life in the material world—spiritual liberation—simultaneously pointing to the path to achieve that liberation. The back of the ego must be broken; the ego, as the source of all ignorance and delusion that leads us astray must be crushed. Simultaneously, to gain the freedom of spiritual liberation, we must raise our consciousness through contemplation and meditation on the Divine. Simply put: no meditation, no liberation. But Shiva reassures us as the personification of the Divine teacher and guide, that he will bless, protect and guide all those truly striving for the goal.

## Sadhus and Science Agree

Meeting us a few weeks after the quake, Swamiji informed us that many of those engaged in these unlawful and nefarious pursuits had died during the earthquake, buried under the rubble of collapsed buildings in Gangotri. No one can escape their karma . . .

With our own house being the only one standing, it quickly became a relief centre for food, clothing, blankets, medicines and other essentials. The ashrams of the area sent their monks out to help the local people cope with the utter ruin and desolation surrounding them. Anil accompanied them to some of the more far-flung villages to gauge the situation and set up a system for those in the greatest need to get urgent relief.

Tokens or chits with numbers on them were given first to those in greatest need—like the elderly, the widows and those with young children—and then to others. Notations were made in a book, registering the name of the individual, village and primary goods needed, be they blankets, medicine, food, clothes, plastic tents, etc. Fortunately, the freshwater springs, streams and Assi Ganga in our area were free of debris, so good drinking water was not a major problem, as it so often is in earthquakes elsewhere in the world.

Men from the village would bring the chits to our home to pick up the goods listed for each individual, packing them on their backs to carry home since all vehicular travel was impossible due to landslides cutting off the roads. Help for the roads, however, was close at hand.

Since Uttarkashi was the headquarters for the border security force of the Indian army, troops began clearing roads to and from the main Uttarkashi–Gangotri route quickly. Clearing of other roads took several weeks and even months, in many cases.

I was not in Uttarkashi or even India at the time of the earthquake and was therefore desperate for news of his well-being. It was through Indian army personnel that we first got news that he was alive and well. One of the devotees of Anil's mother was a retired Indian army general with many friends still with the armed forces. He was kind enough to ask his friends to check on Anil and his situation, since all telecommunications in and out of the region had been cut off by the quake. Only the wireless system of the border security force was functioning.

I cannot even describe how copious was the flood of tears of relief unleashed when I finally got word from Anil's mother, via a telephone call from Pune to where I was in Hawaii, that Anil was safe, as was our dear friend and even all our cats.

Although I had planned to be back in India already, my return had been delayed due to an operation I had had to undergo while in the USA. In late August, a malignant tumour had been discovered on my scalp below my hair that required immediate removal. Only two locations in the USA could perform the type of surgery needed, at that time. I was fortunate to be in New Jersey when the tumour was found, as the New York University Medical Centre in New York City was one of those places where the surgery could be performed.

Since the surgery was on the top of my head, I was unable to fly for several weeks during the healing process which could be affected by the changes in cabin air pressure that take place during take-off and landing of aircraft. I had only just reached Hawaii the previous day from New Jersey to pack up and return home to India within the next week, when the quake struck.

It took months for the Uttarkashi area to limp back to any semblance of normalcy. What is so very sad is how prophetic the warnings were that the mystics and sages had given to the local people regarding this very type of karmic repercussion as Mother Nature attempted to regain her balance which had been thrown off by human activity in the region. It is true that areas like the Himalayas are seismically active because of continuous tectonic movement beneath the Earth's crust. But recent scientific research has shown that deforestation, wherever it takes place, does indeed increase the risk of earthquakes, including in high seismic activity zones.

When deforestation takes place, especially in hilly areas, the subsequent erosion during rainy periods is increased, the trees no longer there to help hold soil in place or mitigate heavy rainfall before it hits the ground. The mass of eroded material washed into valleys below increases the weight, bearing down on geological faults, thereby increasing the stress on those faults over a period of three months to three years. This, in turn, triggers a destructive earthquake of 6.0 magnitude or higher, as the tectonic plates readjust.

The destabilizing process of deforestation followed by major rainstorm events triggering earthquakes has been statistically correlated by scientists looking back over the past sixty years. This includes an analysis of quakes in the Himalayas, the quakes usually occurring during the dry winter season after heavy monsoon rains have caused extensive erosion of denuded hillsides in the mountains, the extra mass of soil and ground cover washed into valleys adding pressure on fault lines throughout the Himalayan range.

So, as it turns out, the sages were both karmically and scientifically correct. Clearly, deforestation is having massive repercussions on the Earth's stability and delicate balance, compromising her ability to provide the very foundations upon which all species, including humans, depend for survival.

The warnings of the sages continue, amplified by those of scientists. Both are desperate to wake people up to the guaranteed intensification of the horrific disasters if the 'balding' of our Mother—dear Mother Earth—does not stop. If disrespect for her as a living being continues, with disregard for her laws of balance carrying on, karmic boomerangs will surely come back to haunt humanity in the not-so-distant future—something we are already witnessing in the Himalayas and around the world.

# 16

# The Final Transplantation

Over a year before the violent earthquake shook the Uttarkashi region, Anil had received a warning from a sage living in southern India. He had gone to see the sage to check on the validity of claims made in a book that the sage had written regarding a group of eleven yogis living high in the Himalayas not far from us.

It was claimed that they had been sent there to practise intense spiritual tapas to help protect the Earth by raising the consciousness of humanity as a whole. As mentioned in Chapter 15, the high spiritual vibrations emanating from great sages, engaged in deep meditation and spiritual union with the Divine, radiate outwards to uplift not only the immediate area, but the entire Earth.

The planned fifteen-minute meeting of Anil with the sage unexpectedly turned into a three-hour marathon of spiritual discussions and sharing. Amazingly, the sage had read our first book regarding prophecies and predictions of our times, finding it remarkably accurate. He told Anil that it paralleled his own insights and warnings that he had received through meditation, study of ancient scriptures and from the words of great mystics he himself knew. It was he—Swami Maheshwarananda—who first warned Anil about looming upheavals and problems in the

Himalayan region, urging Anil to consider relocating to the southern Indian peninsula.

Anil and I had already discussed the need to relocate, not only due to the deforestation and destruction of Nature that we had witnessed all around us, but also due to the land-ceiling laws which limited purchase by any one family to just twelve acres. Twelve acres was nowhere near enough land for us to create the forest and wildlife sanctuary we had hoped to establish there, especially in such a hilly terrain where one needs to protect both sides of a water source from deforestation to ensure its continued flow as a lifeline for the area's wildlife.

As the environmental situation in the mountains continued to deteriorate due to deforestation, with the incidence and severity of landslides, cloudbursts and flooding, drought and fires escalating, Anil headed south to search for enough appropriate lands to purchase to transform my dream—our dream—into a reality. To establish a living legacy—'of life' and 'for 'life'—would be our gift back to Mother Nature and all her children for the abundant gifts of grace she had showered on us throughout our lives.

## Coming Full Circle

It was April of 1992 when Anil first saw the land that would become the very heart of our forest sanctuary. For months, he had searched high and low throughout the southern Indian peninsula for just the right piece that had all the natural elements needed to transform our dream to reality. From Andhra Pradesh to Tamil Nadu, from Kerala and throughout Karnataka he searched, trekking through scores of properties for sale, but being disappointed with each one he found.

Something was always missing. Sometimes it was the lack of a perennial source of freshwater. At other times it was the lack of privacy with a piece hemmed in by other properties that were far too close, or properties on steep slopes where the lands on the opposite side were not for sale, being owned by someone else.

The different governments ruling the various states also came into play, as each state had its own sets of laws, rules and restrictions about how much land someone could buy, what could and could not be done with the lands, and how much non-agricultural income an individual could already have to still qualify to purchase agricultural lands.

Quite discouraged by what he had been able to find from his travels all over the south, Anil returned to our small house in Andhra Pradesh which we had purchased some years earlier. He happened to mention his disappointment to our neighbour there. This neighbour suggested Anil check the Coorg/Kodagu district of Karnataka to see what was available. The neighbour had relatives who lived in Mysore and, as a result, had been to Kodagu himself over the years.

So, Anil made one last attempt to find suitable land to buy in the south where we could hopefully make our dreams come true, this time visiting Coorg/Kodagu. He had not been there since our visit back in January of 1986, when the then-wildlife warden of Nagarhole National Park had requested us to set up our sanctuary in the district that was his own home. Perhaps his prophetic words then would be fulfilled after all.

Anil started his search in the north, near the district capital Madikeri (also known as Mercara), but again could not find suitable land. Finally, a broker he met there thought he might have the right piece in the south of the district and introduced Anil to a close friend of the seller. The bank was foreclosing on the property as the current owner was not able to make his loan payments, the seller being in danger of losing not only this property, but virtually all his assets to the bank. Here then, was an opportunity for Anil to not only purchase land, but to aid someone who was in dire need of financial help as well.

Thus began a process that would become the pattern of almost all lands that would eventually make up our sanctuary—helping sellers in financial need, with lands in turn becoming part of our sanctuary, this first piece indeed going on to become the very heart of our sanctuary.

It was a fifty-five-acre parcel that had been used as a coffee and cardamom plantation. Where cardamom had been grown, there were still tall grandmother trees high overhead. But where coffee had been planted, the area had been quite denuded, with only a few native trees left to shade the growing coffee plants.

One of the land's borders was a flowing river that had its origin in the national Brahmagiri Wildlife Sanctuary, the confluence of two freshwater streams that made up the river being within the property's boundaries on one side. This was critically important since a perennial water source was essential for living on the land fulltime and for reforestation and rewilding efforts, the confluence forming a small pond from which the larger river continued flowing.

Further downstream was a much larger, wider and deeper pond, stunning in its beauty, surrounded principally by bamboo as well as various water-loving native trees. This larger pond would become an absolute magnet for wildlife in the future, including Asian elephants and Bengal tigers.

Just upstream from this magnificent large pond was another extraordinary feature of this part of the land—a grove of huge 'great-grandmother' trees towering overhead, reaching for the heavens. The exquisite trees were later identified as *Lophopetalum wightianum* by an Oxford professor who also stated that they were over 700 years old. He went on to explain that each of these giants was a micro-ecosystem for at least fifty other species of both flora and fauna—from orchids, ferns and creepers, to birds, squirrels and civets, to snakes, frogs and other amphibians.

The professor also pointed out that the loss of just one of these magnificent trees would adversely affect numerous other species critical to the overall balance of life in the area. He dubbed our sanctuary 'Noah's Ark' due to its very high level of biodiversity, which included many endemic species found only in the Western Ghats region, most if not all of which were highly threatened with extinction, as were these lofty giants themselves.

While this very special piece of land had virtually all the elements we needed to transform it into the living paradise of 'life' as we had envisioned, it did not span both sides of the river. It also bordered some other lands that protruded into key areas along the banks of the river and various-sized ponds which the river formed on it journey. Additionally, except for one natural meadow, it lacked large areas of wetlands and grassy meadows so vital for grazers and grass-eaters like species of deer and gaur, whose presence would, in turn, attract larger predators.

So, Anil asked the owner of the fifty-five-acre parcel to put us in touch with the owners of the neighbouring lands we were interested in purchasing along with his. He agreed, and soon, Anil was negotiating with the two additional landowners who had also abandoned their lands in question, moving out of the area many years earlier to other lands they owned elsewhere in the district. Both owners were keen to sell what were to them their 'useless' tracts of land, but which were to us vital to piece together the heart of our sanctuary.

Negotiations took several months, not only with the three landowners and their families, but also with the bank which had been in foreclosure proceedings with the original owner of the fifty-five acres. Drawing on all his negotiating skills, Anil travelled to Mangalore to meet the bank officials at their regional office on behalf of the owner. The result was that the outstanding interest owed on the loan was capped, and all outstanding liens on all properties at risk were removed, as our payment for the purchase of the fifty-five-acre parcel covered the entire loan amount plus interest due, with some cash left over for the original owner as well.

Hence, the New Year of 1993 began with the promise that our dreams were about to be fulfilled. We became the new owners of the properties needed to create the heart of our forest sanctuary, while the previous owners received the cash they needed for their own personal plans in life.

We decided to name our sanctuary SAI Sanctuary, SAI being an acronym for **S**ave **A**nimals **I**nitiative. But there is a deeper spiritual meaning behind that name as well—the roots of the word 'sai' are 'sa', meaning 'all, universal, divine', and 'ai', meaning 'mother'. Hence, the sanctuary was dedicated to the Universal Divine Mother—Mother Nature—Mother of us all.

Now began the process of building our house.

The first step was to identify where to build it. We had originally chosen a site uphill away from the river, even though we could not hear the sound of the river—something that both of us greatly missed having lived in our home on the Assi Ganga in the Himalayas and our house in Hawaii overlooking the Wailuku River with its many waterfalls.

We had chosen the area because we decided we would not cut down any living trees in order to build, just like we had done in the Himalayas and in Hawaii. This original site had no trees on it but did have adequate space to build. However, I was disappointed, and in my heart still hoped that somehow, in some way we might be able to at least hear the river if not see it.

Pre-monsoon showers had already begun when I decided to take one last look around the property along the river to see if I could find anything, anywhere, suitable to build upon that would have the sound of rushing water nearby. With only three areas along the river with rapids, I knew it would be difficult.

I had checked both sides of the river's length and was on my way back, quite disheartened at finding nothing appropriate, when I realized that the waters of the river had risen too high and were travelling too swiftly for me to cross over at the usual spot. So, I went downstream to try and find another place to cross.

The place I found took me from a flat area of the river to a small hill on the other side that was covered with bamboo. I climbed the hill as quickly as I could knowing full well that I would probably end up covered with leeches!

When I reached the top, I was stopped in my tracks by the view—there it was! The view straight from my dream—looking out from the top of a small hill, overlooking a pond with the river flowing past in the heart of a small valley, with whitecapped mountains all around, the mountaintops shrouded in pure, white mist from the monsoon showers.

This was it! And to make things even better, there were absolutely no large trees at the top of the hill that would have to be cut down to build—only bamboo. The nearest trees were far enough that I could incorporate their positions into the floorplan of the house to avoid them and their root systems.

I was both stunned and absolutely elated at what I had seen, and ever thankful to Mother Nature for having forced me to cross the river at this precise spot, since it was impossible to cross anywhere else. I couldn't wait to show Anil! After seeing the location, he was as excited as I was. The view was more beautiful than anything we had had in Hawaii or in the Himalayas. My dream—our dream—was actually coming true!

Once the area was cleared of bamboo, I set out to draw up the design for our home, making sure to take into account the current locations of any nearby trees. As a result, the floorplan looked like a giant old fashion number one (1) with the position of the exterior walls moving in and out, depending on the location of the trees.

Using the engineering knowledge gleaned from Brahmachariji while building our house in the Himalayas, I placed columns and pillars along with the beams and crossbeams to carry the load of the different storeys and the weight of the water tanks accordingly.

The roofs were flat but sloped enough to help direct rainwater into the gutters and pipes connected to our water-catchment system. As with our home in Hawaii, the rainwater harvested would provide all our freshwater requirements during monsoon season. But water would have to be pumped from the river during the dry season through the use of a solar-battery-powered pump.

To make sure that my engineering plans were sound, I visited Brahmachariji at his ashram near Uttarkashi town to ask for his advice. He approved them, adding that, if anything, I seemed to have 'erred' on the side of caution.

With the floorplans complete, construction for our sanctuary house began in early June 1993. With monsoon rains looming in the very near future, it was a race against time to finish digging and laying the foundation on the solid bedrock below.

However, before any work could begin, the last four or five kilometres of dirt road of the village had to be repaired, so that materials could be transported to the building site. The terrible condition of this road had been one of the reasons that the land had not been sold before Anil saw it. Most people were unwilling to trek the long distance to even see the parcel, especially during the rainy season. But Anil was undeterred. He knew all too well with our experience in our land in Hawaii, that if you want to have the blessing and beauty of Nature all around you, you may have to accept and adapt to the lack of an easy access.

Our repair of the village road was a boon for the local people in the area as well, who had had to deal with long treks—often through knee-high mud—especially during the prolonged monsoon season, even four-wheel-drive vehicles being unable to manoeuvre through the soft, deep mush.

When the heavy rains did arrive, the foundation of the house had just been completed—another 'gift' of grace from dear Mother Nature. Now it would be at least four months before we could begin construction again. In all, it took over three years to finish the house, although we moved into it in October 1995, just before Dussehra celebrations, finishing the upstairs as we lived below on the ground floor.

It was hard to leave the holy Himalayas when it finally came time to depart. We had had such wonderful spiritual experiences in those majestic mountains, met such extraordinary individuals and witnessed so many amazing things while living in the lap of Nature on the edge of the holy Assi Ganga—our years there had changed us forever.

And yet, it was clearly the right thing to do, not only because of the restrictions on the amount of land one could purchase there, but also due to the environmental destruction taking place that was sure to have even greater impacts in future years.

We got a reminder of this during the very last days of our living there. An overnight cloudburst sent a wall of water down the canyon of one of the smaller tributaries that emptied into the Assi Ganga just upstream from our home. We had walked up this canyon into the mountains many times to see the series of exquisite waterfalls there, often meditating near them.

The cloudburst hit at night, catching everyone in the village above us by surprise as most of the village homes got swamped with a massive mudslide that moved incredibly fast from the hills above. While our house was once again left unscathed, many homes and cowsheds were lost in the tidal wave of muddy water.

This was the second major warning Mother Nature was giving that things were getting worse as her balance was increasingly disturbed due to ceaseless deforestation 'cutting her hair and making her bald.' We were surely leaving at the right time . . .

## Sustainable Living off the Grid

As with our home in the Himalayas, this area of Kodagu was also without electricity, the last connection to state-supplied electricity being several kilometres away. With no quick way to get connected, we had an important decision to make, i.e., to live solely on diesel-run generators, or to design an adequate, alternative-energy system that could supply enough electricity throughout the year. Naturally, we chose the latter, not only because of our experience of living off-the-grid with green power in Hawaii, but also because of the terrible environmental pollution that total reliance on diesel generators would cause, not to mention the noise that the generators would make!

It was another challenging situation for me as I had to design the system myself, relying on the research I could get from America, mainly in the form of books and catalogues on 'green energy'. Except for solar hot-water-heating panels, India's alternative, green-energy industry was still in its infancy, both in terms of supply and especially technological expertise, so reliance on information from the USA was essential.

Solar-photovoltaic panels became the very heart of our system for energy supply. Here in India, the potential for use of solar power, in general, is massive considering how much of the year the country is bathed in sunlight. Even in our rainy area, where the monsoons rage on for three to four months in the year, the sun shines brightly and often enough to both heat our water and to supply electricity to our home, the extra electricity being stored in a large battery bank for use at night and during cloudy days.

Two small windmills along with three micro hydro-generators were the other two elements of the design. Both the wind and hydro power would help during the monsoon season, when rain and heavy cloud cover would block out the sun's rays.

While I may have designed our energy system, I lacked both the technological and mechanical expertise to install the system and link its pieces together into a coherent, uninterrupted supply of green power. We had to turn to help from America once again for that, actually flying in two engineers whose expertise and creativity turned my thoughts and design on paper into a practical, working system.

Mounting the solar panels on our flat roof was not difficult. But aluminium-and-steel stands had to be specially fashioned to hold the panels and give them the proper elevated pitch to catch the maximum hours of sunlight. Mounting the two small windmills on the highest point on the roof also was not hard. But while we have not had a single incident with birds or bats being killed by the windmills' propellers, it is a problem with the use of windmills in general—one that can make their use in power generation on a large scale a genuine concern.

The greatest challenge was figuring out how to get the three micro hydro-generators in place in the river. Since the bottom of the river was hard granite, it was almost impossible to securely attach them on pillars anchored into the ground. The answer was to mount them on a pontoon built out of aluminium and large plastic pipes. The pontoon floated on the water's surface, while the propellers of the generator were lowered into the water.

Ropes and a heavy-duty guy-wire attached to trees on opposite sides of the river kept the pontoon in place despite the swift currents when the river was in full spate. The trees were protected from damage by the guy-wire by placing old tyre tubing between the trees' bark and the wire. Precautions were also taken to keep fish and other aquatic life from getting caught in the propellers, using aluminium mesh on the front of the pontoon.

While not a perennial source of energy as the river was too low to use them except during the monsoons, the micro hydro-generators have indeed helped generate electricity, especially at the height of the rainy season when there was virtually no sunlight for the solar panels. During the rest of the year, the pontoon is pulled out of the river until the rains return.

We did install two backup diesel generators for emergency use if and when needed, such as during rainy spells lasting as long as thirty days without a break. However, with the green power systems in place along with the large battery bank for electricity storage, our need to rely solely on these diesel gensets was thankfully gone.

It was March 1997 by the time the energy system was fully up and running. The building work on the rest of the house had been completed a little earlier, including the construction of a storage basement and a small greenhouse directly connected to the main house, as well as a much larger greenhouse close by. A nearby grassy area with no trees opposite the larger greenhouse was cleared for use as an outdoor organic garden, where all kinds of vegetables, herbs, spices and various fruits were grown. We shared whatever excess produce there was with our workforce, too.

As time went by, more and more people approached us to buy their lands. Virtually all the lands involved had been abandoned by their owners as 'unproductive'. The funds we gave them for their parcels, in many cases, were reinvested in agricultural lands in drier, more productive areas of the district. Some former owners faced dire financial problems—a mountain of debt from healthcare expenses for serious illnesses, the need to finance a daughter's wedding, school fees for their children, repairing or rebuilding homes or goshalas/cowsheds, etc. Whatever the reasons, the money given helped each of the previous landowners in their hour of need, while we were able to add more lands to our sanctuary for protection and preservation.

In some cases, we gave individuals money for them to leave government lands they had illegally encroached upon, thereby giving them adequate funds to legally purchase land elsewhere. We never did anything to these newly liberated government lands, other than to protect them from fires, poachers, loggers, or any other illegal encroachers. In this way, Nature could take her natural course in reforesting and rewilding them on her own, most of these lands being contiguous to our sanctuary and/or the Brahmagiri Wildlife Sanctuary.

We had always believed in sustainable living, which included growing one's own food whenever possible. Hence, our greenhouses and organic gardens. But we also wanted and needed a crop to see us through monsoon periods and last at least a year or two in storage. Rice was the logical choice.

On the four corners of our sanctuary are natural wetlands where rice had been previously grown. So, we grew rice on two of these wetlands for several years, receiving bountiful harvests each year despite a certain amount of so-called 'crop raiding' by the wildlife.

It should be remembered that every acre of land that humanity uses to grow its crops, is land that used to be part of the natural ecosystem which provided food for the native wildlife living there. The loss of these natural 'food stores' for wildlife puts them in dire straits where they need to choose between relocating to another wooded area, or come into conflict with humans while taking some of the crops humans have sown on what had been wildlife's own natural food stores.

Our wetlands were no different. They had once provided lush grasses to grazers like deer and gaur, the cornucopias of flowers and seeds produced by the native grasses giving a wonderfully rich and varied diet to different birds, bees and butterflies as well as to other species, including both small mammals and the largest land-dwelling mammal in India—the Asian elephant.

While elephants love eating fruits, leaves, even twigs and branches, they also eat vast quantities of native grasses whenever and wherever they can, particularly after the monsoon season when the lush grasses are rich in nutrients. It is essential for them to eat as much as they can of this post-monsoon bounty to get into peak physical condition to help see them through the lean months of the dry season that lie ahead. So, it was only just and right for us to share some of the rice we were cultivating in these wetlands with the elephants in particular.

As in Hawaii, we had entered into a 'silent agreement' with the elephants. Our 'nursery beds' located in the middle of the large wetlands were the natural dividing line for this agreement. We left all the rice fields cultivated above these 'nursery beds' to them, silently asking them to leave the lower fields to us. As with the wild boar in Hawaii, the silent agreement was clearly accepted by the elephants, as they ate all they wanted of the upper rice fields, leaving the lower ones to us.

One animal that kept pulling out our newly sprouting rice was, surprisingly, the crow. As with the birds in Hawaii, we felt it was our obligation to provide a small offering to the crows as well. So, we started putting out small amounts of cooked rice every day on top of some rocks at the edge of the lowest rice field for them. The offering was immediately accepted by the crows and they completely stopped pulling out the newly sprouted rice thereafter.

The rice crop not only fed us, but also our workers and our cattle. We had decided shortly after relocating to the sanctuary that we would raise a few cows and water buffaloes to provide milk for ourselves, our workers and our cats. The cattle were taken out daily to graze in other wetlands and natural meadows within our sanctuary. The dung from the cattle became the main organic fertilizer we used in our greenhouses and garden, as well as in our rice fields, with the dry straw becoming food for the cattle, supplementing their diet especially in the dry season, when grass was not as plentiful as during other times of the year.

Their dung also became the principal cooking fuel in our home after we built a small *gobar* (dung) gas plant at one end of the garden. We also built a small plant for our workers near their quarters, which was located next to our goshalas/barns. The dung is mixed with small amounts of water and poured into one part of the plant. Through the natural fermentation process that follows, methane gas is released, captured and piped into our kitchen, where it is used for cooking. These plants have been a real boon to all of us over the years, providing almost all of our cooking fuel, the process producing a carbon-neutral energy source. I prefer cooking on methane gas from the plant versus the natural gas of LPG cylinders as it is a 'cooler' flame, heating things more slowly—something I believe enhances the taste of food.

The dung itself is transformed into a nitrogen-enriched slurry once it has passed through the plant. This slurry is then dried, powdered and used in our organic growing. It forms the base of our food-growing fertilizing process and is combined with compost made up of decomposed leaves and straw, with inputs from the kitchen like vegetable peels and crushed eggshells, the eggshells provided by the chickens we keep.

## Cats and Dogs

Anil and I have been vegetarians for decades, as mentioned earlier, and while we were living in the Himalayas, we had given up eating eggs, too. But the various domestic cats that have been a part of our family have their own dietary needs.

Cats have evolved as true predatory carnivores in accordance with Nature's own law of balance. Many, if not most feline species, are nocturnal. As a result, they need certain nutrients particularly for their night vision. One of these nutrients in Taurine—something that is found in abundance in animal-based foods like meat but is almost non-existent in the vegetable world, with the exception of seaweed. Without adequate amounts of taurine in their daily diet, cats are in danger of losing their night vision. Hence, we were faced with the dilemma of how to provide proper nutrition to our cats while they lived in our vegetarian home.

Initially, we solved the problem by importing the essential nutrient in a powdered form from the USA and making our own dry cat food with it as one of the ingredients, since no such products were then available in India. But getting the supplement was always a problem as the powder had to go through Indian customs, often finally reaching us only after months, with the containers opened and left only half-full.

In addition, several studies linked the use of dry cat food with the incidence of blockages in the urinary tract, especially that of male cats as well as feline diabetes. So, we decided to raise some chickens in order to provide fresh eggs to our cats along with dairy products from our cattle. Today, we feed them high quality wet food that we are finally able to purchase here, as well along with fresh eggs and dairy/curds.

Over the years, we have had many domestic cats and some dogs that have been given to us by people who have either found them abandoned or injured. In all cases, we have accepted the animals and done what we could to help them. Those that have survived have become part of our family, with all the cats and dogs being inoculated against rabies, as well as neutered and spayed in order to keep feral populations from growing and disturbing wildlife.

Our own domestic cattle and chickens have been similarly inoculated against various diseases to safeguard both them and the wild species of the area. Encouraging our neighbours to follow suit, we have been paying for inoculations and sterilization operations for all domestic animals for years now.

Feral dog populations in India and elsewhere in the world continue to grow, posing an increasing danger to wildlife, both in terms of spreading deadly diseases like rabies and distemper, and in killing prey species like deer. I have personally had to come between domestic dogs and deer like sambar, many times over the years, to keep the dogs from killing them.

This is yet again another problem humans have created. It is we who domesticated wild wolves and then bred them to get the present domestic dogs we have today. Hence, it is we who have the responsibility to limit their numbers through compassionate means such as sterilization. It is we who have the responsibility to restrict their movements when they are a part of our household and to make sure they are inoculated against deadly diseases for their sake, for the sake of nearby wildlife and for our own safety as well.

India has the highest number of rabies cases in the world. We have a responsibility to take this seriously and right yet another wrong for which we are responsible.

Domestic cats are less of a problem here in India compared to some other parts of the world. While cats are true predators, they do not hunt in packs like dogs. As a result, the prey species they can hunt are smaller. Still, we have a responsibility to limit their impact on wildlife, too, again in terms of sterilization, inoculations and in terms of their ability to roam. While our cats are free to roam during the day, they are kept inside at night, thereby keeping them safe from larger predators and giving smaller wildlife a break from them as well.

Collars with bells that make enough noise to warn birds in particular of a cat's presence is another way cat lovers can help limit the impact of cats on wildlife. However, only 'tear away' cat collars should ever be used, so that if the collar gets caught on something while the cat is outside, the collar easily comes off when the cat tries to free itself so he or she is not strangled in the process.

These are just some of the issues we have had to think about and deal with over the years, trying our very best to be as aware, compassionate and responsible as possible, always keeping in mind that the goal of our life and purpose of the sanctuary has been and continues to be the protection and preservation of Mother Nature and her 'children' in all the wonderful and diverse forms they are found.

## The Impact of Cattle

It had never been our intention to breed cattle. We had only wanted to have enough dairy for our own use and the use of our workers. But that is not what happened over the years. With both local and jersey cows plus water buffalo of breeding age, it wasn't long before we had several calves and more milk than we or our workers needed daily. From just one bull and cow each of water buffalo, jersey and local cattle, we eventually ended up with twenty-eight! That's a lot of cattle that needed a lot of loving care, including names to keep them all straight!

It was my task—and joy—to name each of them. I separated them along 'family lines'. Since the original jersey cows had been named Ram and Sita, all their offspring got their names from the characters in the Ramayana—Laxman, Urmila, Lav, Kush and Bharat were some of the names given. The local cows were named after the various Hindu demigods and their consorts—Shiva and Parvati being the first two, their 'children' including Karthikeya, Ganesha and Subramaniam. The water buffalo were given the names of the holy rivers of India—Ganga and Cauvery, Krishna and Godavari, Saraswati and Yamuna being some examples.

The goshalas/cowbarns in which they were kept at night, needed good daily cleaning to keep disease at bay. Access to fresh water for them to drink was essential, with availability of plenty of good green grass to graze upon equally important. The addition of feed to supplement their diets during certain seasons was also part of their dietary requirement. Fresh water, abundant grass and green foliage were not hard to find in our sanctuary since there were wetlands on all four of its corners where nutritious grasses grew year-round, along with natural meadows interspersed within forest areas throughout the grounds.

But to get the cattle to and from those areas every day required employing staff to take them there, even though Anil and I did our own fair share of driving the cattle whenever necessary. Still, it was not possible for us to look after them by ourselves all the time, so more help was hired to do so.

Hiring outside help can be a double-edged sword. While the work needing to be done can now be delegated to others, it can be very difficult to find help that will treat the animals you love and who are ultimately in your care, with the same affection, respect, or compassion as you. There can also be the problem of drunkenness, especially among the men, coupled with physical abuse of wives and children.

Abuse of women is a global problem that exists in India as well. While both tobacco and alcohol use are banned within our sanctuary grounds as well as at our workers' quarters, that didn't stop some of the men from flouting that ban and bringing liquor packets to their rooms to drink, and/or going out, getting drunk and then returning in an inebriated state. In most cases, neither their wives nor their children scolded the men, as to do so would mean risking getting hit. Even saying nothing was no guarantee that the man wouldn't end up beating his wife anyway, often demanding whatever was left of their family money to go out and get more booze. If the woman tried to refuse to give more of their hard-earned income to him, explaining that the funds were needed for clothes for the children, books for school, or other family necessities, she was silenced more often than not by her husband's fist in her face or other parts of her body until she stopped her protests and handed over whatever was left of their earnings.

Both Anil and I have had to intervene to put a stop to this abhorrent activity physically, as well as having the police come to arrest the abusive husband and lock him up. In some cases, where the women wanted to leave the husband altogether, we would give her funds for herself and her children to return to their home village, where her own family members would protect them. In other cases, where she wanted to stay with us, we would help her financially to start a new life for herself and her children while remaining in our employ.

Setting up bank accounts for her and her children, where she alone controlled the account meant her earnings would finally be protected from being snatched by the husband, who had no access to the accounts. This simple action meant that she could finally begin to save a good portion of her income for future use, be it for a daughter's future wedding or for higher education, helping her children and especially her daughters go to college, making them the first generation in their family to get a college degree.

Beyond the difficulty of finding good people who were stable and who would not cause problems from liquor and/or spousal abuse, there was the challenge of instilling an awareness of the environmental hazards of polluting the land and water both around their quarters, and especially throughout the sanctuary and goshalas, where the cattle were kept at night.

We experienced first-hand the tragedy of plastic taking the life of an animal that eats it with the very first calf we had. The calf ate a plastic bag discarded by the very same worker entrusted with her care. It was heart wrenching watching the mother mourn the death of her baby, refusing to leave the dead calf's body. Such a waste of life! And all due to the lazy carelessness of thoughtless humans!

It is not only domestic animals that are suffering from our thoughtless actions, as mentioned in earlier chapters. Wildlife is being drowned in a sea of plastic and being buried under mountains of refuse that we humans generate every day. Even rocks on the shores of oceans and other water bodies are getting coated in a dangerous plastic slime that is inhibiting or dangerously mixing with the natural growth of moss and lichens that are essential food sources for various species of wildlife.

In India's forests, even elephants are falling victims to our plastic garbage, the plastic in the stomachs consumed by desperately hungry elephants killing off these gravely endangered gentle giants. What does it take to shock us into action to do something to end this man-caused assault on the very fabric of 'life' on the planet?!

Most unfortunately, changing this mindless behaviour of just dropping and dumping anything anywhere is extremely difficult. While our house was being built, it was even worse with construction crews leaving materials everywhere—tiles, cement bags, plastic, paint cans, old brushes, bottles—just horrific!

In one instance, I severely scolded a couple who were continuing to throw litter everywhere, despite warning after warning, including throwing the husband's alcohol bottles into our river. I got to the point of threatening to fire them as a result, saying they would have to leave our site the following morning. That night I was a bit concerned that the husband might take revenge for my actions. Anil was not here, having to be away for other work in Bangalore.

Lying in bed on the ground floor of our yet-unfinished house with no security of any kind around, unable to sleep, I was suddenly startled to hear the roar of a tiger next to my bedroom window! The roar came yet again . . . and again, as the tiger seemed to be circling our home while calling.

Instantly, I felt so relieved—Mother Nature had once again sent a tiger to protect me, the tiger staying near the house and roaring every now and then, right up to sunrise. Clearly, no one would dare to venture near with the tiger here!

A few hours later, when the workforce arrived, I asked one of our permanent workers who was staying in the same building as the couple, if he had heard the tiger. He answered that not only he, but all in the house had heard it, adding that he had spent the night under his bed being so frightened by the tiger's incessant roaring! The couple had left our land quickly in the morning, never to return!

This is just one example of how hard it is to uproot humanity's laziness when it comes to dumping trash. Even today, we have to pick up trash mainly brought downstream from neighbours and their workers upstream, who just toss empty bottles, in particular, into the river during monsoon.

We now collect the trash and take it to each and every neighbour upstream to show them what they and/or their workers have done. This exercise in shaming them for their lack of consciousness is having an effect, the number of bottles and amount of trash having diminished considerably over the years.

However, this was still a major problem years ago, and one of the main reasons that we seriously questioned keeping our cattle as their number grew. More cattle meant more people to care for them, which also meant more trash generated by the increased number of workers—trash that might be discarded anywhere in the sanctuary as they took the cattle out to graze, in spite of the containers given to them for garbage, composting and recycling—containers that were routinely collected and disposed of properly.

For me, the main problem with keeping a larger staff was that it inhibited the free movement of wildlife through the sanctuary grounds, the constant daytime presence of humans in various areas of the sanctuary meaning wildlife usually venturing out only between dusk and dawn. This sanctuary was, after all, meant for wildlife, for any and all species to have freedom from the fear of human presence and to have full and free movement to any part of the sanctuary during the night or day.

In addition, the growing number of cattle meant less grass and other flora for wild grazers to eat, especially during the dry season—again, the opposite of our initial intentions for setting up the sanctuary. Hence, it was clear that our beloved cattle would have to go. But where? We had a responsibility to them to make sure they were loved and cared for during their entire lifetime.

Anil came up with the solution: gifting the cattle to economically disadvantaged neighbours living on the borders of our sanctuary. In this way, our neighbours would gain a valuable asset in the form of those cows and buffaloes given to them, as we would buy back any excess milk as well as dung to continue using in our biogas plant for our own cooking.

Because the neighbours would be caring for the cattle themselves rather than using outside workers, the cattle too would receive better and more direct attention and care. In all cases, the neighbours chosen to receive the cattle had ample fresh water and land of their own for grazing, so the cattle would stay healthy and happy.

There were only two stipulations to which the neighbours would have to agree: first, no animal would be slaughtered, and second, if they did not want the cows or buffaloes in the future, they would give them back to us. In this way, we were ensuring the best future for the animals we had come to know and love and from whom we had received so much over the years.

# 17

# Weaving Together the Tapestry of Life

With the cattle settled in their new homes, the sanctuary was finally fully dedicated to wildlife. We had already stopped harvesting any cardamom or coffee years earlier, keeping only a small area for growing organic food near our home. We had also stopped growing our own rice, opting instead to purchase organically grown rice from our neighbours, giving yet another source of income to them.

All of these actions were taken intentionally to be able to limit staff and intrusive human movement through the sanctuary grounds for the benefit of wildlife, so that they could be at peace and live their lives without human presence and activities disturbing them. The only exception to this would be the continued planting of native trees during monsoon season in any areas that were still degraded from past human use.

Virtually all the various parcels bought that end up as a part of our sanctuary had been abandoned many years earlier by their former owners, as mentioned before. Hence, Nature had already started to 'reclaim' the lands by sowing her own seeds of grasses, bushes and even small trees, in some cases, depending on how long the lands had been abandoned, Mother Nature using wind, rain and wildlife to disperse the seeds for future growth.

But the natural process of land reclamation takes Nature a long time, even in a rainforest. After all, Mother Nature is not in a hurry. She has all the time she needs to do what she wants to do, which is why no matter what we humans do to the Earth, eventually she will recover, albeit extremely slowly and in an evolutionary manner that may see the extinction of most of the present species of life on the planet, including humans.

If we want to avoid that disastrous prospect, then we must give her a helping hand, helping to speed up the recovery process, but in an informed, intelligent and scientific manner. We need to observe what Nature herself has grown in the area to understand what has already evolved over time in this particular ecosystem with its own parameters of temperature, sunlight and rainfall, type of soil and flora, tree cover and wildlife, all of which have worked together over millennia to rejuvenate and sustain the proper balance and functioning of the existing ecosystem. Through keen observation, we can help replicate the conditions under which the original ecosystem evolved, thereby speeding up Nature's own reclamation process.

This is exactly what we did at our sanctuary—first, allowing the land to breathe and recover somewhat from decades and even centuries of human use and abuse by leaving it alone, then intervening in the recovery process through planting only native trees and flora originally found in the area. To know what to plant required observation, research and help from those far more knowledgeable than we were.

We turned first to the local people for advice and guidance— especially to those members of the older generation who had grown up living in a far closer and intimate manner with the surrounding forests and wildlife. This was especially true of the tribal community there, whose invaluable ancient knowledge is fast disappearing due to lack of support for their way of life on the one hand, and, on the other, a lack of interest in their own cultural heritage by the younger generation. The insidious influence of commercialization, coupled with ridicule and lack of respect heaped upon indigenous communities has helped to erode the faith and confidence of many of the younger indigenous peoples in the wisdom of their forefathers and their way of life. For, it has been the indigenous peoples who have lived in forests for generations, living off the land in sustainable manners, not overexploiting Nature of her wealth of species, both flora and fauna.

Many indigenous peoples know that trees do not grow independently, but as one part of a community that is made of various other species of flora—different ferns, grasses, bushes, fungi, flowers and other plants, all of which contribute to the overall health and wellbeing of their own ecological community. The same is true of the different types of animals of a particular area, whether large species like elephants who pass through on their daily migrations, helping to sow the very seeds needed for the ecosystem to regenerate, leaving ample fertilizer in the form of their dung to help the process along, or birds overhead whose eliminations also spread seeds far and wide.

Other creatures have their own niche as well, from amphibians to insects and small tree-dwelling mammals to larger grass-eating herds, with various predators at each level of the food chain helping to keep the 'web of life' healthy and strong, its various filaments of species woven together into a coherent community far richer than any that humans have ever tried to plan or plant.

Therefore, it is essential to use every bit of wisdom and knowledge we can glean from the humans who have been a living part of this community as well, in order to help Nature re-weave this delicate and exquisite tapestry of life as quickly as she can.

## The Wood Wide Web

The use of scientific studies and techniques is also essential in this day and age, where scientists versed in the intimate and intricate workings of the varied, interconnected strands of the tapestry of life can help guide our choices of plants and trees to reintroduce, to create that living community once again.

For example, the discovery of the incredibly elaborate and complex underground networks of mycelium/fungi in forests by American researcher Suzanne Simard revolutionized the way we look at trees and forests in general. These fungi enter into a symbiotic relationship with the trees of the forest, binding to tree roots to form a 'wood wide web' (as she dubbed it) through which trees communicate with each other.[*]

The results from her observations and scientific studies, as well as those of others like Peter Wohlleben and Monica Gagliano, have also helped to explain why two or more species of trees are found growing close to one another, while other species stand alone. The reason is that certain species cooperate with one another, sharing water and nutrients, including sugars and carbon during the different seasons of the year using this intricate mycelium network. Without this underground connection through the 'wood wide web', both species of trees would suffer lack of these nutrients at different times during the year.

Again, without the ground-breaking observations of scientists and naturalists, we would not be aware of the care which mother and grandmother trees give to their offspring, helping them to stay alive and continue to grow at the most vulnerable times of their life, when they're just starting out as a young sapling, providing them with extra nutrients through this fungal web to help them stay strong, or recover when they are ill.

Not just mother trees but tree 'neighbours' also help out their 'friends' and 'siblings' at times when an individual tree is ill, sending them nutrients via the fungal network in order to help them survive. This is a mark of evolutionary 'intelligence' as the

---

[*]    Refer to the bibliography for source.

survival of the whole group is based on the good health of the individuals that are a part of it.

Indeed, forests are a symbiotic community where virtually all plant species including trees 'communicate' with each other to 'spread news' using chemical compounds and electrical impulses over the fungal wood wide web. They also communicate via scent, releasing certain odours and aromas into the air in order to warn others of any kind of danger to the community—from leaf-eating pests to humans with chainsaws. Studies of plant bioacoustics demonstrate that the roots of plants react to soundwaves, too.

Hence, 'dumb' trees are not dumb at all, being neither silent nor non-thinking! The woods are humming and buzzing with information, news and alerts with the aim of protecting the entire forest community in ways we could never have guessed, using systems and techniques that seem to have come straight from the movie *Avatar*.

When trees are not connected through this fungal internet, they suffer immensely. It could be compared to a person who has lost the use of their senses. They are without the ability to 'get the news' of impending dangers, unable to share nutrients with others or receive them when ill, cut off from the rest of the community that would have helped ensure their health and survival.

This is the tragedy of deforestation and of the fallacious delusion that we humans can rebuild the forest we have destroyed just by planting some trees. When lands have been bulldozed or ploughed for agriculture, the mycelium net is destroyed in the process. With this vital link gone, newly planted trees become isolated individuals, unable to connect or communicate with one another as they need to and do in a normal forest environment.

The notion that we can continue to denotify forest lands for other purposes like roads, mining, or dams and then 'make up' for the loss of carbon sequestration, water production and conservation, or other ecosystem services that natural forests provide simply by planting rows of unconnected saplings in another area is a ludicrous misdirection tactic used by those wanting to financially benefit from these projects.

It takes many, many years for the mycelium network to grow, and even when it does, the newly planted saplings are 'handicapped' with no knowledge of how to connect and communicate with those around them. It is akin to immigrants coming to a new land with no ability to speak its language. They lack the ability to communicate with others. Their children born in the new country may be able to communicate in the future, but it will take a generation or more for genuine sharing through the language of the new region to be possible.

So it is with newly planted trees and tree plantations, in general. It will take years, decades, generations for the fungal network to grow and for trees to learn the intercommunicative 'language' for proper communication and cooperation to be established—something that may only be possible for their own offspring in the future.

Other recent studies have underscored the critical importance of plant biodiversity. Results show that biodiversity-rich areas have fewer pests and parasites. This is one of Mother Nature's insurance strategies to inhibit the outbreak of infectious disease in both plants and animals, including humans. The increase in different species of plants effectively 'dilutes' the chances of disease.

Hence, human-induced losses of biodiversity through deforestation and fragmentation of forest areas pose a public-health threat by causing and exacerbating disease outbreaks. The loss of the closed forest canopy means additional sunlight and heat that negatively affects forest species, while creating open-spaced 'barriers' that both plants and animals hesitate to cross, impacting their ability to propagate and survive.

Forest fragmentation also poses a serious threat to national and global food security as essential pollinators are unable to bridge the gaps between forest fragments, pollination being one of the most essential ecosystem services that Nature provides. The population of wild pollinators like bees, wasps, butterflies, moths, beetles and other insects is in sharp decline, having dropped 45 per cent over the last few decades, this human-caused, precipitous drop due to loss of habitat and chemical pesticides. The disappearance of insects is already having severe effects on food production, as 75 per cent of all crops require insects for pollination, as do forest trees and flowers.

The loss of insects not only means loss of pollinators, but also lack of food for larger animals as well, the decimation of insect numbers affecting the entire food chain from the smallest to the largest, ultimately leading to cascading ecosystem collapse—an ecological Armageddon. If we lose the insects, we lose everything since they form the base of the web of life.

Anthropogenic climate change is the other major factor in the loss of insects. While protecting forests for their carbon-soaking trees is vital, so is protecting the biodiversity of wildlife as well. In this case, the larger animals are even more crucial.

Current research has documented the highest concentration of carbon in forest soils where vertebrate wildlife has gathered, such as below fruit-bearing forest trees or where predators have caught prey. Organic matter remnants of the meals consumed cause an increase in microbial activity in the soil as microbes convert the remains to stored carbon—carbon which then becomes available for the benefit of the surrounding trees, helping to keep them healthy as well, this wonderful cycle helping to mitigate climate change.

This is especially true in tropical locations like the equatorial rainforest belt into which most of India falls. Loss of India's wildlife is equivalent to emitting millions of tons of carbon directly into the atmosphere without cutting a single tree. That amount of carbon is equal to cutting down millions of acres of trees—comparable to 150 per cent of the entire deforestation that took place in the Amazon region between the years 2000 to 2013.

These dramatic results underscore the crucial need to protect all wildlife, but particularly larger species like elephants. Only large herbivores like elephants can swallow the seeds of the large native trees that are the best carbon-absorbing trees in the forest. Without these large herbivores, the forest becomes bereft of these carbon-soaking giants, and therefore, less effective in carbon sequestration and storage, in turn, limits its climate change mitigation abilities.

Hence, it is critical not only to protect and preserve our forests, but also all species of wildlife. From the smallest insects for their ecosystem services of pollination and as food for larger animals, to the largest elephants for the vital role they play in spreading the forest and keeping it full of the lofty leafy giants we desperately need to cushion the effects of climate change for the entire planet, biodiversity is the beating heart of this circle of life upon which we too depend for survival.

## From Thought to Action: From Dream to Reality

Many of the scientific findings mentioned before are confirmations of the teachings and wisdom of indigenous peoples including Native Americans who have always viewed the Earth as a living being and recognized that every species is a member of Mother Nature's global environmental community. This is one of the principal reasons that they have spoken out against the wholesale destruction of the natural world—from forests to oceans, from waterways to deserts—each ecosystem having its own unique species which play vital roles in the overall health of its biological community.

Since our own reforestation and restoration efforts started long before many of these scientific studies were conducted, we employed all the knowledge and understanding we were given from every source available—indigenous, local and scientific, coupled with our own observations, plus what tree seeds and saplings were available for us to use.

Because part of the lands we had bought had been used to grow cardamom, some areas still had large mother trees towering overhead. So, while we initially grew many saplings from whatever tree seeds we could find within our grounds, we also used 'excess' saplings from these great mother trees, gently uprooting some of the smallest ones growing around her, taking care not to damage their delicate roots. These saplings were either directly transplanted in appropriate areas of the sanctuary or put into pots where they were cared for in our greenhouse for a year or two until they had grown larger and stronger, thereby better able to survive once planted outside in the future. The process has taken decades and is still ongoing.

Over the years, we have welcomed many scientists and naturalists to the sanctuary to do studies and give us guidance as well. But today, the most crucial thing for us to do is to protect the sanctuary's existing forest areas, letting Mother Nature continue her own natural regenerative process in her slow but sure manner.

It is important to note that some areas of the sanctuary will never be forests as their natural geological structure inhibits the growth of most trees. These areas are the wetlands and meadows that have been created by Nature to remain rich sources of food for the consumption of so many different species of deer and birds, gaur, elephants and others that feed upon the nutritious feast of grasses, ferns, seeds, flowers, small fruits and berries. Very few species of trees can find their way through the granite rock that exists below most of the natural meadows, while the standing water and saturated soil of the wetlands rots the roots of most trees that try to sprout there. So, the wetlands and meadows remain open areas that are encircled by heavy forest on their edges.

This is, of course, as it should be. Nature is the exquisite reflection of the Creator, the heart of our Mother God, perfect in every way, with every distinct ecosystem having its special place and purpose in the overall Divine plan and programme of life on the planet, each an essential 'thread' woven with intelligent, loving care into the tapestry of life.

With the cattle gone, our labour force reduced and no longer going through our grounds on a regular basis, it did not take long for wildlife to come out of their daytime 'hiding' and start enjoying the sanctuary during daylight hours as well as at night. The only person now going through the sanctuary on any regular basis was me, sometimes accompanied by Anil. As a result, I have been thrilled every day to come upon different animals in various parts of the sanctuary going about their daily lives unafraid and uninhibited.

Whether it is sambar bucks or does with fawns, cheetal/spotted deer in small groups, or the mostly solitary muntjac/barking deer cautiously crossing a path, the different species of deer are everywhere to see.

The family herd of gaur/Indian bison, usually with fifteen to twenty members, regularly spends much of the day in one of our largest wetlands, the alpha bull being accompanied by his several cows, many of whom are mothers with calves of various ages and sizes. The older adolescent bulls periodically spar with one another, testing their strength and skills in order to determine their 'ranking' among the males. It is always a great delight coming upon them when they have a newborn or very young calf with them, the young calf romping around, running up and down the slopes of the hilly edges of the wetlands, occasionally jumping into the air just for the sheer joy of life while its tolerant dad, mom and aunts look on. You could almost see them smiling at the antics of the youngster, as am I!

My favourite time to watch the gaur is during the afternoon, when most of them lie down for a nap in the long grasses covering the wetlands, frequently sprawled out completely on their sides, with heads down and necks extended—a wonderful indication of and testimony to their feelings of complete safety and security within our sanctuary grounds.

While the alpha male may seem to be the leader of the group, it is the alpha female/cow who takes great care in guarding her family from harm, relying principally on her sense of hearing. Being exceedingly alert to any sound her sharp ears may detect, she puts the rest of the group on notice when something is close by. If she senses any sign of danger, she will immediately rally the group, heading out of open areas into the safety of the forest. I have often sat quite close to the herd to observe and film them on my camera. As long as I sit very still and make no sound, my presence usually goes undetected.

I love all the different species that have come to call our sanctuary 'home', be they permanent residents or those who come and go depending on the seasons. What is particularly gratifying and exciting is that our sanctuary has become a veritable crèche with all kinds of species migrating to give birth and raise their young here. I have been privileged to see a number of different animal mothers with their newborns with them, our camera traps catching even more species of mothers with their young.

Open-billed storks fly in at the close of monsoon to nest and bring up their chicks, as do several other birds, while many more stay year-round. Mammals of all shapes and sizes are either permanent residents or travel here specifically to give birth—from porcupine, mongoose and civets to both small and giant flying squirrels; from various deer and gaur to other smaller mammals like wild hare and the diminutive mousedeer/chevrotain; from monitor lizards and snakes to frogs and tree-dwelling shrews; from Nilgiri martens and Malabar giant squirrels to Asian leopards and Bengal tigers—all are here, having turned our sanctuary into a biodiversity-rich sanctuary of life!

Many of these wonderful animals are found nowhere else, being endemic to the region and very, very rare. As deforestation continues unabated here in India and in the Western Ghats, in particular, wildlife is being squeezed into smaller and smaller areas of forest that are left, increasing the number of species under threat of extinction as their population numbers dwindle due to loss of food and good habitat for raising their young.

I remember one heart-breaking scene almost fifteen years or so ago, that brought tears to my eyes. It was after the mania for growing coffee had gripped virtually all the planters in our area, as it had throughout the rest of the Kodagu district years earlier. The big, native shade trees that had once stood cooling the air, protecting the cardamom crops from the scorching sunlight while ensuring the ground stayed moist and nearby freshwater sources still flowed through the long dry season, had been felled everywhere— victims of the insanity that greed and lack of foresight can cause in humans.

The wisdom of the Kodava elders had also fallen victim to this same 'illness' as their wise teaching of keeping 25 per cent of their private lands forested to ensure proper rainfall and rich soil nutrients for their crops, ensuring a living future for their own family and community, was completely ignored. The avarice of many members of the younger generations of Kodava had translated into the total destruction of these private forest areas to make way for more 'cash crops' like coffee.

Gone too are the thousands of Devarakadu that the Kodava ancestors established throughout the district, these special forests dedicated to the Creator who had blessed this community of people with so much abundance. These sacred groves were the sacred treasures of this land—emerald gems of beauty and spirit, the direct connection of the people to their Creator, from which the echoes and spiritual vibrations of the prayers of previous generations had risen to the heavens in humility and gratitude for all they had received. An insatiable desire for money and complete lack of respect for the elders and their wisdom has destroyed them.

These private forested lands, along with the sacred groves, had been critical habitat for many different species that once lived and nested in the great towering trees found there. Nilgiri marten, Indian giant squirrel and other mammals including primates like the lion-tailed and bonnet macaques had all lived there, along with different species of hornbill, including the great Indian hornbill and the Malabar grey hornbill—the 'laughing hornbills' whose call sounds just like someone laughing.

One afternoon, as I stood near one of the edges of our sanctuary, surveying the destruction of the lands nearby, the area once filled with towering giants now devoid of trees, I was startled by the continuous calling of hornbills overhead. I watched as wave after wave of hornbills flew into the mother trees within our grounds. At least three dozen or more flew in, seeking refuge in our trees.

While exhilarated by the sight, my eyes filled with tears as I realized their numbers were so many here because they had nowhere else to go. The other great trees—the mothers, grandmothers and great-grandmothers—that had supported and been responsible for so much 'life' in this area were gone . . . lost to a human wave of madness that, in but a moment, had destroyed what took Mother Nature many, many centuries to create.

Today, our great mother trees continue to provide homes and nesting sites for all those animals that need the support and protection that these ancient and very special 'mothers' give them. In addition to the common grey and Malabar hornbills, these wonderful 'mothers' are homes not only for martens, squirrel and civets, but also for a family troop of lion-tailed macaques and a nesting pair of great Indian hornbills—a bird not seen in the area for over thirty years.

## Barbie and the Lovebirds

Living at the sanctuary full-time, it wasn't long before we were involved with the rescue, rehabilitation and release of wildlife as well—from amphibians, lizards and snakes to squirrels, moles and wild hare, to turtles, jungle cats and deer. But one of the most numerous of all have certainly been the different species of birds which have been in our care and called the sanctuary 'home' over the years.

It all started with 'Barbie'—a small green barbet found with a broken wing. While we did all we could for Barbie, his wing never healed well enough for him to be released back into the wild. His ability to fly was too compromised. When we contacted the forest department about him, they told us to keep him in our care at the sanctuary with the hope he may recover well enough to be released. Since it was clear that Barbie's stay was going to be a long one, we decided to build a large aviary for him so that he could be outside in Nature even if he had to be screened in.

The large enclosure also gave him the opportunity to practise his flying and to catch insects blown inside by the wind in his direction wherever he chose to perch on the bushes and branches of the small trees within the aviary. We of course supplemented his diet with proper food as well as the live insects we caught for him, releasing them alive in the compound for him to continue practising his own skills catching them.

Over time, various rescued birds came and went from the aviary with Barbie being left behind alone. Then our vet, Dr P informed us of some African lovebirds being kept in terrible conditions by a breeder in Bangalore, suggesting that we rescue them and make them permanent residents in the aviary with Barbie. This way he would always have company, even if they weren't the same species.

Although the lovebirds were born in India, they were not native to India. Hence, they could not be released back into the wild since their presence might adversely impact native/endemic species. They would have to live out their lives within the aviary.

With this in mind, we expanded the enclosure, making new sections with interconnecting doors between all three areas that could be opened or closed, depending on different situations. The new sections were made with elevated screened domes so all the birds would be at the height of some branches in surrounding trees. For the rescued birds, going from tiny cages in which they could barely turn around, to this expansive aviary with its trees and bushes, branches and natural swings everywhere must have seemed like 'bird paradise' even if they were still enclosed behind steel fencing mesh.

We also made two four-by-four-by-six-foot 'feed and sleep' cages like Barbie's with bird-boxes and 'hammocks' in them. This was where their main food and water was kept for the night, although birdbaths and strands of rice dhan/seeds along with lettuce and other goodies were hung outside as well. They quickly learned to go into the smaller cages at sunset to have their last meal for the night and for a warm, cosy night's sleep, either in the straw-filled bird-boxes or in the cloth hammocks filled with cotton wool. The doors of these smaller cages made with window screen mesh were then closed, for extra safety, in case any small snakes or rats managed to get inside the aviary at night somehow.

In just a few days, the change in the behaviour of the lovebirds from the time they were rescued was dramatic. From terrified, shy and soundless birds, they quickly transformed into some of the happiest birds I have ever seen—flying free and easy, swinging inside and out, enjoying their treetop views while singing and chirping so much and so loudly, that Anil dubbed the group 'the racket-teers' as in 'making a racket!'

It wasn't long before the lovebirds started pairing off to have their own families. While this had never been part of the rescue plan, it was certainly a sign of their happiness and contentment.

Two couples quickly paired off—Ivy and Halo, along with Angel and Holly—laying tiny eggs in the nests of straw made by the females within two of the wooden bird-boxes. Incubation of the eggs followed, with the females gently shifting the position of the eggs from time to time before carefully sitting on the clutch of eggs again.

The chicks hatched within twenty-three days or so—tiny featherless babies totally dependent on their moms and dads for food. The males would eat food outside and regurgitate it to the moms, the moms, in turn, regurgitating it to each chick waiting with wide open mouths to receive it. It was truly remarkable watching the dedication of the dads to bring food and the tenderness with which the mothers cared for their little babies.

As the days passed, the chicks grew, eventually sprouting tiny feathers everywhere. Soon the chicks were standing on the perches at the hole that was the doorway of the box, begging their fathers to feed them directly. It was interesting to see the shift of parental care from mother to father as the chicks got older. Indeed, once the babies were old enough to start flying, they followed their dads everywhere in the aviary to be fed, learning directly by watching their dad about what was good to eat and what was not.

We had never intended to breed the lovebirds at all. But once they did start to breed, we needed to think about how to keep their population down. Population control was done in part naturally as the couples that were from different species of lovebirds lay infertile eggs. Though the eggs never hatched, they could be used to serve a very important purpose. To control the population of the couples of the same species, infertile eggs of cross species parents were substituted for their own eggs. This avoided the need to remove eggs from their nests, thereby eliminating the distress the parents felt at returning home to an empty nest. The mother would still dutifully incubate the substitute eggs, but after twenty-eight days or so, when they did not hatch, she abandoned them on her own.

Dr P had told us that the average lifespan of the lovebirds raised in captivity in tiny cages, like the ones we had rescued, was no more than five to six years. Our lovebirds lived on an average of at least twice that amount of time, with our oldest original lovebird named 'Pixie' living to the ripe old age of sixteen! It demonstrates how critical natural surroundings are for the happiness, health and longevity of animals in general. Barbie, too, lived for many years with us, his soul finally flying free of his body one quiet, sunny morning.

Whenever an animal in our care dies, we always bury them and plant a tree where they have been buried, the trees being a living symbol of the love and life they shared with us. In Barbie's case, we had decided to bury him under the highest dome of the aviary, as it had always been one of his favourite places to stay, perching on the top of one of the trees enclosed within the dome.

After his grave was dug, but before we put him inside it to say prayers and bid him goodbye, an extraordinary thing happened. The small green barbets outside the aviary flocked around the dome, perhaps wondering why they were not hearing his customary response to their calls, as they had done for so many years. As we watched, several barbets landed on the trees around the dome, peering down inside to see where he was. I lifted his little body which was lying on a small gold cloth to show them that he had passed on. Amazingly the group stayed on and watched as we placed his body in the grave and said prayers for his soul. Indeed, they did not fly away until after the ceremony was over and the tree had been planted, marking his resting place from where his soul had taken its flight into the Infinite. It was a truly remarkable and moving experience, demonstrating that, although he had had to live out his life separated from the rest of his flock by wire fencing, Barbie had still been a part of their family group.

People often say that one of the things that distinguishes animals from humans are human emotions like love, pain and grief. I completely disagree. I have personally seen, experienced and witnessed, time after time, the deep emotions that animals feel, be it the joy of living exhibited by a bird flying high or a fawn jumping and frolicking in happy play, or the deep pain and grief of separation from a loved one, no matter what the relationship with the departed one may have been. Mothers who have lost their offspring, partners who grieve for the death of their beloved, members of a flock or herd that gather around the body of one of their own to grieve and bid 'goodbye' to the departed soul— be it lovebirds, or barbets, or parrots, or larger animals like deer, elephants, or big cats—they *feel* the same emotions that we all feel and express them in undeniable ways to those watching, to those close and sensitive enough to see.

Anyone who has had animals as part of their family can testify to the depth and purity of emotions felt and conveyed by their beloved animal family member. This is one of the reasons, too, that I am so against the raising of animals for meat that inevitably entails the heartless separation of members of a flock or herd. It is also one of the reasons that hunting is so abhorrent to me— gaining pleasure by killing another living being, not to defend one's self, but for the perverse 'pleasure' derived from doing so.

Yet, the hunter virtually never sees the grief and pain he has caused to a child and family left without a mother, sister, father, son, or friend. The same is true of those who raise animals for slaughter—a practice I just cannot comprehend; a vocation that must involve some type of emotional disconnect for those engaged in this heartless industry—a disconnect that I find hard to believe does not adversely affect them on some unconscious level over time.

## Jasper and Tulsi: Holly and Clover

Soon after Barbie's departure, we were given different groups of Alexandrine parrots by the forest department for rehabilitation and release into the wild. Most of the parrots had been rescued as chicks from unscrupulous men involved in the illegal wildlife trade, thieves robbing the nests of wild parents when the chicks were very young, often killing the parents in the process. As a result, the chicks lacked proper nutrition and the immunities passed on from the mom to her young when regurgitating their food for them and feeding them. Hence, most chicks die. In fact, in one group of thirty-six Alexandrine chicks initially rescued by the forest department, only eleven had survived by the time they were brought to our sanctuary.

Alexandrine parrots are the largest parrots found in India. They are very curious, highly intelligent and quick to learn, with researchers saying that they, as well as some of the other parrots and parakeets, have about the same intelligence as a six to eight-year-old human child. They are also extremely loving and playful. It is these very traits that make them targets for the poachers of the illegal, wild-bird trade as they are in high demand on the black market and can fetch a handsome price for the sellers. The high demand for these beautiful parrots has decimated their numbers in the wild so much that they are now threatened with extinction.

Each parrot has its own distinct personality, physical features and call, again reminding us that individuality and uniqueness is yet another thing that members of the animal world share with humanity.

Whenever new parrots arrived, the presence of the happy and relaxed lovebirds in another part of the same enclosure was somehow reassuring to the new arrivals, not to mention seeing how much they trusted us. Considering the trauma they had undergone, since virtually the time of their birth, it was quite remarkable how quickly the parrots too came to trust us.

Earning their trust was very necessary in order to teach them what they needed to learn before they could be released in the wild, one of the most important being the recognition of natural food found in the forests. To do this, we would cut small branches from the surrounding trees and introduce the fruits attached to them, to the parrots. Chewing bark and leaves is also part of their natural behaviour and diet.

While some of the parrots were able to fly, others could not and therefore had to learn by watching those that could, as well as the lovebirds. The aviary sections were large enough for the birds to learn and to practise short flights back and forth in safety with plenty of tree branches suspended from the wire mesh roof of the aviary to give them ample safe perches to land on.

Another important thing for the parrots to learn was to live in a flock, recognizing the flock as extended family members. Members of a flock take cues from one another, especially when it comes to approaching dangers. Learning to respond to these dangers, alerting each other and acting together to avoid it is a necessary survival strategy for all flock members.

Finally, one of the most critical things that the parrots needed to learn was to fear humans, since they had 'imprinted' on humans, having been raised from 'chickhood' by humans. In the natural world, chicks or any newborn animal baby would see their adult parents upon birth, thereafter 'imprinting' or identifying themselves with that species as their own. But when human poachers intervene, the newborns see humans as their 'parents' and begin to identify with humans instead, losing all fear of humans as a result.

To reverse this imprinting was not an easy task, since on the other hand, they needed to trust me and Anil. It was important for them to learn to distinguish between human beings, recognizing those who were 'safe' and avoiding the rest. For, if they trusted all humans, they would quickly fall prey to poachers once again, who would be looking to either kill and eat them, or more likely, capture them for sale into a life of captivity once again.

One parrot, in particular, had a very hard time being on his own when he and his partner arrived. Jasper and Tulsi had been kept by one individual from the time they were chicks before being given to the forest department. Under India's Wildlife Protection Act (WPA) of 1972, it is illegal for anyone to keep any species of wildlife native to India in captivity. Unfortunately, that does not stop people from doing so.

Both parrots were exceptionally affectionate, especially the male Jasper who found it very difficult to stay in the aviary with the others, rather than with humans. He would cling to me in the evenings after being fed, hiding under my shirt, in the hope that I would not leave, or would take him with me wherever I was going. It was heart-breaking having to literally peel him off of me and place him in the sleep cage at night.

To ease his transition, I stayed in the aviary well past sunset until he had fallen asleep in my lap. Then gently lifting him up, I would carefully place him in the food cage near Tulsi. This routine went on for weeks, until Jasper had adapted enough to his new life with the others. Although he would still stay with me until sunset, he started voluntarily going into the sleep cage at night, whenever I would get up to leave. By the time he was released with the others, he and Tulsi had become the 'leaders' of the flock.

While in some instances it took a good deal of time for the parrots to learn what they needed to, in order to have a good chance of surviving in the wild, all of them eventually did and were successfully released. But before any of them could be set free, they had to be inoculated against any and all illnesses that they may be carrying, so that there was no threat to other birds and animals in the wild. This is a critical practice to follow when doing rescue, rehabilitation and release of wildlife in the wild again. Coming in contact with humans and domestic animals and/or being kept in enclosures with a number of other members of the same or other species can sow the seeds of illness, with the newly released individuals unwittingly spreading that illness to wild populations.

In the case of birds, Newcastle disease is one of the most dangerous and virulent, spreading among a flock of birds from a single ill individual in just a few days, killing the entire flock. There have been several instances where this type of 'contamination' in the wild has occurred, severely impacting various species of wildlife.

In each and every case, we ensured that all animals brought to us were protected through proper inoculations, no matter what the species. Close observation of rescued individuals is extremely important, noting any signs of illness such as lethargy, lack of appetite, or changes in their eliminations—all warning signs that something is wrong and that the individual in question is not ready for release, that its abilities to survive in the wild are very doubtful, plus it being a potential carrier of illness that could infect the wild population as well.

Most unfortunately, we did receive two parrots that were indeed ill upon arrival. I suspected something was wrong shortly after they were brought to the sanctuary. One of the two died within just a day or so of its arrival, with the other one starting to show similar signs of illness within a few days. We quickly isolated the second individual from the rest of the group and called Dr P for help. Upon examination, Dr P verified that the parrot was suffering from Newcastle disease.

· Thus began an intensive effort to save the parrot's life, involving injections, oral medicines and flushing of the infected eyes. It took seven weeks for the parrot to finally start getting better, losing eyesight in one eye as a result of the disease. But finally, he did recover fully. I named him 'Clover', as in a four-leaf clover, because he was lucky to have survived. Clover was able to return to the aviary to join another parrot we had been unable to release thus far—Holly.

Holly had no signs of Newcastle disease but could not fly due to his flight feathers constantly dropping from his wings. Dr P thought the reason might be the fault of the poachers, who routinely cut the flight feathers of the birds they caught so they could not fly away. Cutting these feathers too deeply and/or when the birds are too young can permanently disable birds, flight feathers never growing back properly or strongly enough to stay attached to the wing. This appeared to be the case with Holly.

It took months of good nutrition to reverse Holly's condition, but eventually, his flight feathers grew, and stayed! What a joy it was to see Holly finally able to learn to fly like the other parrots instead of falling each time he tried.

Soon, he even became an expert flyer, as did Clover who learned to adjust his depth perception while flying and landing, despite only having one healthy eye. Clover's success in flying was, in large part, due to Tulsi, who was by far the best flyer among the group, helping to show others like Clover how to manoeuvre and land with ease. She and Clover became very close, both while in the aviary and once released—something that helped Clover adapt to his own disability. So, when it was time for the next group of parrots to fly free, both Holly and Clover were able to join Jasper, Tulsi and the others. Once freed, Holly was one of the first to fly out with confidence.

However, most were still a bit unsure of what to do with their newfound freedom, especially at night, when darkness normally meant sleeping in food cages or under the top of the aviary's covered eaves. This is where their trust in Anil and me once again came into play, as we coaxed them to follow us up to the roof of our main house where food and water was waiting for them, along with plenty of safe sleeping areas in the tall trees surrounding the building. Reassured by our presence and the food and water offered—all of them taking their day's last bites and drinks—they quickly relaxed and found spots to sleep in the nearby trees.

At dawn's approach, we could hear their individual calls outside our bedroom windows beckoning us to come up and reassure them again. Encouraging them to explore close by, while still providing food and water for them if and when they needed it, was important, especially during those first few weeks. The wild parrots of the area were also helpful, since seeing and interacting with them calmed and uplifted our parrots.

As the weeks went by and their self-confidence grew, each member of our 'family flock' gained their full independence, eventually flying off to join the others, including dear Jasper and Tulsi and Clover—the last one to go. Finally, they all were free to live the life they were meant to live, as part of the flying jewels that sparkle overhead in the Indian skies. Occasionally, they still visit, calling to us from the sky, thrilling us with their aerial displays, singing their songs of sheer delight as they soar in the heavens above.

## Terri the Terrapin

Another example of the amazing ability of animals to adapt to their disabilities if just given a chance, was a turtle we called 'Terri the Terrapin', the word 'terrapin' being a Native American word meaning 'little turtle'. Terri had come with another turtle for immediate release in the wild. Both were taken to a slow-moving part of the river and released along the grassy shallows.

A few days later, while checking to be sure all was well and both turtles had entered the river to swim downstream, I found one in the exact same spot where we had left them both, the second one having apparently successfully swum away. What was wrong with this one?

Upon examination, I found that all the digits on her left front foot were gone! Later, I heard the story of how Terri had been an illegal 'pet' in someone's home, where their dog had caught her and chewed off her digits! How can people be so careless, cold-hearted and cruel! As mentioned earlier, keeping any native Indian wildlife species as pets is illegal to begin with. But illegal or not, how can anyone not protect those gentle animal souls who are in their care?!

Terri had apparently suffered either a blow to her back, or been dropped as well, since a bubble had formed under her shell, inhibiting her ability to dive underwater. Without being able to dive, she could neither feed herself properly nor dive underwater to escape danger. Frail and weak from lack of food for many days, there was no way Terri was going to be able survive on her own. At least, not yet.

Taking her back to stay in one of the elevated lotus ponds we had built, I started feeding her by hand to build up her strength. Within a few weeks, she weighed more and was able to finally eat on her own. Within a few more weeks, the bubble underneath her shell miraculously disappeared; she was now able to dive! But she was still relatively inactive, not moving around much, principally due to the lack of claws on one of her front feet. Turtles use the claws on their front feet to pull themselves up onto whatever pieces of wood or logs there may be in the waterways that are their home. Sunbathing is essential for them, being coldblooded animals like reptiles. But Terri's digits and claws never regrew.

In order to let her sunbathe and to encourage her to move around more to tone her muscles and gain more strength, we put thin, flat pieces of wood in the lotus pond for her to use—the flat surface being necessary, so she wouldn't fall off since she couldn't hold herself in place easily with just one set of front claws.

Slowly but surely, Terri gained enough strength that she was able to climb up on to the wood on her own using her one set of front claws to pull herself, with both back feet pushing her up. The cement walls of the lotus pond were about a metre above the ground. So we put a wooden plank from the top of the pond's wall to the ground, to encourage her to explore grassy areas below. Amazingly, she did precisely that, climbing out of the pond and going down the plank, spending time in grassy outcroppings and under various bushes.

With this tremendous improvement in her overall physical condition, it was time to put Terri back into the river to see if she could at last survive on her own. We chose a shallow pool where she would be restricted from going downstream until we were sure she was able to survive in the wild. While I still left some food for her, I reduced the amounts and frequency of feeding to see if she would lose weight or be able to feed herself. It didn't take long before Terri was actually gaining weight! Clearly she had a healthy appetite and was feeding herself on the natural food sources that surrounded her in the shallow pool.

At last, Terri had gained the skills she needed to survive on her own. So, with the forest department's approval, she was allowed to swim downstream to full freedom with the flow of the sacred waters all around her.

Rescuing and rehabilitating wildlife is a wonderful experience, with releasing them back into the wild, healthy and happy being the greatest 'reward' one can receive. But it is a lot of work, requiring medical expertise and great dedication, as the animal in question is totally dependent on you while he or she is in your care. The other essential elements in helping and healing are patience, compassion and love, with the full realization that the care may end in a joyous release back into the arms of Mother Nature or end with the painful sadness of loss.

As humanity continues to destroy the natural world, more and more members of the wild kingdom are being orphaned and injured, more and more individual animals need help from humans to survive. I honour all those heroic and noble people and groups who take up this calling to help the helpless in their hour of need.

Further, I ask us all to help through making our voices heard in the halls of power around the world, demanding preservation for the natural world everywhere, demanding protection for the wild kingdom across the planet. If we do not speak up now and demand that the destruction of Mother Nature be stopped, there will be little chance of avoiding the annihilation of humans that will surely follow.

# 18

# Living within the Heart of the Mother

Over the years here at our sanctuary, Anil and I have had the joy and privilege of seeing and experiencing so much beauty, so many wonders and so many members of Mother Nature's family—her other 'children' who live here in her heart with us. My favourite times to walk through her heart are early in the morning and early in the evening, when wildlife is most active and the sun's rays light up the forest in very special ways.

Hours before any workers arrive and long before anyone else is moving about, I take my morning walks, savouring my solitude and the hushed silence all around me. It's as if the forest is holding its breath as it waits for the first rays of the sun to bathe it in a golden hue, the silence eventually broken by the melodious tunes of the Malabar whistling thrush—always the first to greet the coming dawn with its joyous song.

A fine mist lifts in answer to the sunrise, leaving behind a thin coat of dew on everything. Little by little, the dewdrops merge together as they slide down the forest leaves. They mingle with the remnants of raindrops from the light shower an hour earlier to become crystal spheres of diamonds, edged in rainbow colours, sparkling everywhere as the sun slowly rises in the sky, each crystal drop finally falling to the earth. Drip, drip, drip . . .

An explosion of blossoms of a special native bush line the forest path—colourful balls ranging from deep purple to lilac to silver-white. They are the blossoms of one of the forty-six different species of the Neelakurinji found in the Western Ghats. This rare floral pageant only happens every twelve years, the bush normally adorned with simple green leaves. But this year (2018), unlike some of the other species that blossom in the open mountain shola grasslands, its flowers fill every nook and corner of the sanctuary's forests.

The buds begin as perfectly round spheres of deep purple that gradually elongate, some putting forth a tiny trumpet-shaped bloom, its opening accented in deep blue. Others continue to elongate, looking like small, closed pinecones, their tones varying from deep pink to different shades of mauve, violet and lavender. The single glittering drop of dew gathered at the base of each bud mirrors the surrounding foliage, capturing it perfectly. This remarkably unusual and fantastic spectacle lasts an astonishing fifteen months or more!

The sun's beams shining through the mist create exquisite shafts of light amidst the towering trees in all directions. Glistening off the pearls of water gathered on the spiders' webs, they transform them into delicate twinkling necklaces, more beautiful than any wrought by human hand.

As they filter through the trees, the rays highlight sprays of small white orchids growing in clusters on the deep emerald-green moss covering the trees, the tiny orchids virtually glowing in the beams of light. Cascades of violet morning glory flowers with deep pink-purple centres add to the enchanting scene.

The wind stirs the treetops causing more crystal drops to fall to earth, the breeze filling the air with the heady aroma of fragrant flowers. I breathe in deeply . . . and nearly swoon from the intoxicating scent to which no artificial perfume could ever compare. Flowers fallen from the blossoming tree canopy overhead carpet the forest path.

Innumerable butterflies hover around the treetops, as buzzing bees swarm the profuse blooms to sip the sugary nectar within. Both creatures pollinate the trees that make up the forest helping to ensure its future, the continuous humming of the bees sounding like the primordial chord of creation itself—AUM—the sound of the Eternal's whispering echoing in the sky, sounding like 'Oooooommmmmm . . .'

Two of the canopy's most spectacular trees are the flame of the forest and the tiger claw tree, or Indian coral, resplendent with their bright, crimson-orange flowers. Considered sacred by many different communities in India, parts of both trees are beneficial for treating all kinds of ailments, often being used in ayurvedic and traditional remedies—from joint pain and arthritis to skin diseases, cataracts and night blindness; from wounds, cuts and infections to dysentery and the treatment of worm infestation.

Perhaps this is one of the reasons that birds flock to these natural 'medicine trees', despite the massive thorns on the tiger claw trees. Birds are their principal pollinator, deftly manoeuvring around the huge thorns. Another must be the rich stores of sweet nectar found inside the blossoms of each. Countless bird species fill both trees when in bloom to enjoy the syrupy delight.

The morning chorus of birds is now in full swing—a harmonic symphony of coos and cries, whistles and chirps, sometimes punctuated by the drumming of the woodpeckers. The song and 'rat-a-tat-tat' of one of the largest woodpeckers in the world—the large, endangered, white-bellied woodpecker with its topknot of bright red feathers—complements those of the greater flame-back and little golden-backs as they listen for the tell-tale sounds of insects moving underneath the bark of a tree. The tiny heart-spotted woodpeckers, decorated with their sweet little heart-shaped spots enhance the performance with their own rhythmic drumming. A special feature of the percussion session is the tabla-like call of the Malabar giant squirrel as it races through the 'skyway highway' above, with the continuous calls of the large cicada ringing in the background.

Some of the more numerous members lending their voices to the choir include the white-bellied treepies, with their beautiful long black and white tail feathers and raucous cry, flocks of yellow-browed bulbuls and scimitar babblers babbling away, scissor-tail and racket-tail drongos with their amazing repertoire of fifty-one different sounds, mimicking at least forty other birds species, two mammals, two frogs and one insect, as well as their own unique songs!

Close by sits the large coucal or crow pheasant with its rust-coloured wings, adding its distinctive melody to the chorus. The sighting of this beautiful bird is said to be an auspicious sign among the local people. The hornbill joins in, his laughter going up a note on the scale with each laugh, until he reaches the top with a crescendo before going down the scale again: 'Ha! Ha! Ha! Ha! Hahahahahahahaha!' It is impossible to hear these morning songs of glory to Mother Nature and not feel exhilarated and blessed!

As I head toward the river for my morning prayers and meditation, the small male sunbird breaks into song, the brilliant, iridescent colours of his feathers flashing forth as he displays to his mate in the sunlight—maroons and purples, greens and yellows—taking my breath away! His mate flies in quick succession back and forth, bringing building materials in her beak to the low-hanging branch where she is making her swinging pouch-nest of lichen and moss, cleverly using sticky spider webs to glue it all together. Sitting on a branch close by is one of my favourite birds—the male Malabar trogon. His resplendent colours of vibrant crimson body, black chest and head separated by a pearly white 'necklace' are radiant in the dawn's rays.

Native bushes and trees near the river are filled with a kaleidoscope of butterflies. Our sanctuary is both a haven for permanent resident species and a resting place for the travellers of India's butterfly migration. While most are blue tigers, dozens of other species are also present, many extremely rare. They have gathered in such huge numbers that the leaves and branches of the bushes and trees are completely covered. As I slowly approach, I am greeted by a cloud of colour flying all around me, my heart fluttering and my soul uplifted with joy, soaring on the wings of these exquisite, mystical creatures—the symbols of spiritual rebirth.

At the river's edge I find the large, brown-headed, stork-billed kingfisher perched on a bamboo arching over the water, his enormous, dark red bill almost as long as his whole body! His plaintive call reassures his hungry child perched on the bamboo next to him. He spots a fish and quickly plunges bill-first into the water, catching his prey with that huge beak, then takes his prize back to feed his hungry chick. For many years, a pair of these giant kingfishers have nested in the same hole in one of the trees next to our house, affording us the privilege of watching them care for and teach their little ones all they need to learn to thrive here within Nature's heart.

Further upstream are two of the most gorgeous kingfishers at the sanctuary—the dazzling three-toed kingfisher with its stunning colours of vivid amethyst-blue, orange-yellow and deep lilac head offsetting his coral-coloured bill, along with the small blue kingfisher with his own striking colours of blue/green back and wings with deep rust-coloured chest. This sweet little kingfisher periodically bobs his head and body up and down as he searches for prey in the river below, his short tail abruptly flicking upwards in seeming response to his little dance. As quick as lightning, he dives into the water, re-emerging with a small fish in his mouth, then races downstream with his catch calling gaily as he goes.

Reaching the river to make my small offering of cooked organic rice, the white-breasted waterhen with its long, dark-yellow legs and dot of red at his bill's bridge walks downstream to meet me. Normally a shy bird, he has come to trust my presence every morning, continuing his own morning rounds for food. Quickly raising his stubby tail with each step, he reveals a flash of beautiful reddish orange feathers underneath.

A school of fish gather in the water below me, while the colourful grey jungle fowl cock comes out of the underbrush on to the open rock above me, his long, blue tail feathers gleaming in the morning light. Silently, I recite a Native American prayer:

To the East which is Illumination,
To the South which is Healing and Growth,
To the West which is Introspection and Understanding,
To the North which is Wisdom,
To Mother Earth Who nourishes and sustains us,
To Father Sky Who watches over and protects us,
And to the Great Spirit Who binds us all together in His Circle
of Harmony and Concord,
I offer these prayers and this offering from You back to You
In gratitude and thanks for everything You do for us each and
every day in every way.

Placing some rice on the rock behind me, I put the rest into the river. The fish promptly accept my gift, their whirling bodies glistening with different colours, highlighted by a sunbeam shining through clear water. The beautiful jungle cock is joined by his gentle lady-friend, flanked by some of their adolescent chicks. It is she who first started coming every morning to greet me and partake of this little offering of rice, along with the jungle crows. A couple of emerald doves fly down for a bite, too, as the little yellow wagtail picks up a morsel here and there, his tail beating in time to his own inner song.

After prayers and meditation by the river, my morning walk continues through the enchanted woodland. Very often, I meet other denizens of the forest out for a morning stroll as well—mongoose or wild boar, the Nilgiri marten couple emerging from their nesting hole in one of the giant trees overhead, or a unique 'family' that has made the sanctuary their home for the last few years—a primate family whose members are two different species of langur.

About four years ago, a common grey langur mom showed up with her very tiny, newborn baby clinging to her body. We don't know why the mom and newborn were all alone, without their family troupe. Perhaps the mom had been 'exiled' by the alpha male for having been with another male, and the baby was not his offspring. It is also possible that the alpha female forced her out because she saw her as a threat to her own position as 'head of the ladies' of the group. We'll never really know the answer, but she and her baby were now in the sanctuary to stay, having found here a safe haven away from harassment by both her previous family members and humans, along with plenty of the food and water that they would need to survive.

As the months passed, the baby grew bigger and stronger. Soon, the little one began jumping from tree to tree and swinging on branches following 'mom' wherever she went, making sure to stay close to her at all times. With the wide range of native trees in our sanctuary, there were always some fruits and fresh green leaves to eat, the diverse trees putting forth flowers and fruits at different times of the year.

But it was still a lonely life for both the mother and her child. Langurs normally live in large family groups, with plenty of 'aunts and sisters' to help raise babies, and lots of 'friends and cousins' for the youngsters to play with, helping them to strengthen their muscles and hone their skills in coordination as well. So I couldn't help but feel sorry for them both, having to live with no other companions and no 'dad' to protect them, if it became necessary.

Fortunately, that was going to change, at least somewhat, in the near future . . .

One day, about eighteen months or so after the mom and baby first came to the sanctuary, I heard an unusual sound coming from the tall trees next to our house. Listening closely, I realized it was some type of primate 'talking' to me from above. Then I saw him—a large, male langur—but not a common grey. It was an endangered Nilgiri langur! Found only in the Nilgiri areas of the Western Ghats, it is estimated that only 4000 or so remain in the wild.

His dark body gleamed in the sunlight, the long fur encircling his pitch-black face looking like a reddish halo, highlighted by the sun. He was in the very top branches of the trees but kept leaning over to try and get a better look at this 'strange' human he was seeing, no doubt the first non-Indian he had ever glimpsed! Getting my camera, I took some photos of him and then went into the house again—something he apparently didn't like! He started calling even more vigorously, standing up and swaying from side to side, making the whole tree sway with him.

I came out again, this time onto the encircling veranda outside my bedroom which is almost at treetop level. As I talked to him to try and calm him down, he stopped swaying and chattering, finally sitting quietly on the juncture of several branches. Staying with him for a little more time seemed to reassure him enough that he began to eat some of the leaves and small, white flower blossoms in the trees around him. After taking some more videos of this truly beautiful creature, I gently waved 'goodbye' and went inside, my new 'friend' spending the rest of the daylight hours in the trees surrounding the house. He stayed with us for the next five days or so, getting used to our presence, while exploring the jungle all around our house and then disappeared.

A few weeks later, he was back again, but this time he was not alone. The grey mother langur and her child were with him. They had obviously met somewhere in the sanctuary's forests and had become a 'family', the black langur becoming the 'dad' the little child didn't have and the male 'protector' that both the mother and child needed. Bolstered with the presence of the big black male, who had already recognized me as a 'friend', both mom and her young child came much closer to both me and Anil, than they had before.

Now, whenever the little 'family' was near, the youngster would squeal in delight and climb down the branches to get as close as he could to us, 'posing' for photos and videos, playing 'run and jump' in sync with my walking from tree to tree, almost like a game of 'tag!' It was great fun for us both!

The three members of this little family became inseparable—something that brought me great happiness! They had more than enough food within the sanctuary grounds and so never ventured past our borders.

And now there is a new addition to the family—the mother has given birth to another baby! This new little one is a cross-species, and unlike its grey mother, the baby is black—just like the dad! The mother holds her newborn close to her heart at all times, the infant tightly clinging to her mom as she moves slowly from tree to tree. Their arrival came a month after the mother disappeared, she and her teeny tiny babe coming to our house area for the first time the day after I had returned from Bangalore. I had to undergo yet another operation there to remove two malignant lymph nodes—not good news at all.

So their visit was such an uplifting 'welcome home' present for me! I had been very worried about the absence of the pregnant mom prior to my departure, wondering if she was okay. With their arrival, all my worries melted away, being replaced by the contented reassurance that, yes, Mother Nature was looking after them, as she looks after me as well, and that life does indeed carry on no matter what! Now this wonderful quartet is always a delight to see anytime, including during my morning walks.

As mentioned before, I meet many different dwellers of our forests during my walks, but my most common encounter is certainly with sambar deer, whether the majestic buck with his huge rack of antlers, or a protective mother doe with her little fawn in tow. The many encounters with one particular sambar doe will always remain precious memories, as she filled my heart with joy and touched my soul with her love. Her name was Sita.

## Sita

No one knew how she had lost her mother, but the tiny sambar fawn was clearly an orphan. Found wandering aimlessly through the woods of the Brahmagiri Wildlife Sanctuary by the forest department personnel, she was raised by hand, using cow milk as her main source of nutrition, until she was old enough to start eating solid food.

Lacking her own mother's nutritious milk that was far thicker and full of the fat and nutrients she had needed as a fawn, she remained smaller than other sambar does, but was nevertheless healthy and strong. However, it was obvious she had suffered an injury, perhaps during birth, as her muzzle/nose and mouth area were not perfectly straight as they should be, but slightly bent to the right. Fortunately, this bend did not affect her ability to nurse or drink or eat.

She was called Sita, named after the consort of Lord Rama. 'Sita' means 'furrow' as in a furrow tilled in the ground, the original Sita said to have been the daughter of Mother Earth herself.

Sita stayed with the kind and attentive forest department guards who cared for and protected her from harm. As a result, she imprinted on humans, her group of forest guards being her own special family 'herd'. Over time, she got old enough to accompany them on their routine rounds through the surrounding government forests, which included regular visits to our sanctuary as well. It was a special privilege meeting Sita with them the first time. She was calm and relaxed, seeing that her 'family' trusted us, allowing us to approach her slowly and gently stroke her beautiful body, her long ears feeling like velvet to the touch. And so it was that Sita became our friend, while we became part of her extended family.

As the years went by and Sita got old enough, she started visiting us on her own. Each time she came was very special, her calm and gentle demeanour staying the same, always allowing us the joy of caressing her while talking quietly to her. She took great interest in meeting our three cats whenever she visited, especially seeking out the male in our group—Shanti. At first frightened by her size and overt interest in him, Shanti shied away from her, hiding underneath a bush whenever she came near. But soon, they became friends, both Sita and Shanti accompanying me on my walks near our house and along the river, while our lady kitties, Leela and Shradha looked on from a distance.

Sita was very inquisitive of any new creature that crossed her path, be it bird or otter, mongoose or squirrel. She seemed to be fascinated by my camera traps as well, following me to them and watching intently as I opened them to change memory cards, her nose often getting both me and the camera's lens wet as she sniffed these strange boxes to try and figure out what they were. The camera traps helped to keep track of her travels around the sanctuary, capturing her crossing the river or following some of the wild sambar that make our sanctuary their home, too.

When Sita was between four and five years old, she came into season or heat (oestrus), the camera traps showing her with various interested sambar bucks following her. It was about this time that she paid us a visit, spending the entire day with us, foraging around the forest encircling our home for tasty leaves and fruits to eat. It was on this occasion that Anil took the photo of Sita and me that has become the cover of this book.

A few months later, during another of her frequent visits, I noticed that she had put on a lot of weight and was very filled out. I immediately suspected that she might be pregnant, although her udder was not swollen with milk, nor were her nipples distended. But it is often the case in many mammal species that these tell-tale signs are initially absent in a first-time mother, until right before or immediately after the birth of their child. So it was with Sita.

A few more months went by and monsoon broke, bringing torrents of rainfall to our area, the rains falling relentlessly for weeks on end. It had become Sita's pattern to take shelter from the heaviest rains by staying in covered areas around our house or within the dry warmth of one of our old goshalas (barns). We always left the barn door open for her, spreading dry straw on the ground for her to lie down on, if she wanted to rest.

It was early morning on 7 September, when Sita finally gave birth to a little girl in the dry warmth of our barn. The tiny fawn was very small, which was a good thing, considering Sita was so small herself. I had been concerned that Sita might have trouble delivering her baby if the fawn was too large. But Mother Nature had clearly helped her through this first delivery, both Sita and the baby coming through the birth with no problems at all.

Light greyish white in colour, the little one was healthy in every regard, standing up quite quickly and taking her first drink of Sita's warm, nutritious milk which was now flowing abundantly. Over time, the fawn's colour would darken, first to a pale yellow and greyish-brown, then to darker shades of golden grey-brown, until she would match the darker colours of her mother. But that would take many more months.

About four weeks later, Sita brought her little fawn from the goshala area to our house for the first time. While Sita was as friendly as ever, her little fawn was not so sure whether or not to trust these strange-looking, two-legged 'animals'. Sita had been raised by humans, but now she was raising her little one as a natural mother would, which meant having a very wary attitude towards humans, with little or no contact at all.

In the epic Ramayana, it is written that Mother Sita gave birth to two children in the wilderness. Their names were Kush and Lav—*Kush* meaning 'happy' and also referring to the sacred kusha grass, and *Lav* in its original Sanskrit meaning 'a little piece of something'. I chose to call Sita's fawn 'Lav'—a little piece of Sita, the daughter of Mother Earth and therefore, a little piece of Mother Earth herself.

For several months, Sita and Lav stayed close to our house, giving us the opportunity to watch little Lav grow. During one very special encounter, Sita gave Anil and me the great privilege of watching her nurse little Lav—a touching and heart-warming scene which I was able to film as well.

From nursing to nibbling her first blades of grass and ferns, Lav's adventures with her mother Sita unfolded before our eyes. One especially comical and yet tender experience was watching them down at the river below our home. I was out with my video camera when Sita turned her head to look to the right. Lav's two long ears and eyes popped up from behind the small diversion wall on the river and then disappeared again. It was as if Lav was playing 'hide-and-seek' with her mom and me.

Suddenly, Lav jumped on to the large rock to the right of her mom in one big wet leap, spraying water on herself and her mom, Sita lovingly licking off the excess water from Lav's lower neck to dry her. It was this kind of tender, intimate moment we were so very fortunate to witness up close.

More months went by with Lav growing and learning about life in the forest from mother Sita. My camera traps would show photos and videos of them in various parts of the sanctuary. In one very funny sequence, Lav scared herself by seeing her own reflection in the very same camera trap her mother had 'helped' me to install at the river crossing below our kitchen a year earlier, Lav, first looking intently into the camera and then quickly jumping backwards upon seeing her own image peering back at her from the camera lens.

## A Daytime Drama

I regularly met Sita on my walks, Lav now accompanying her. One morning, as I returned to our house from my walk, I could hear Sita constantly calling from the other side of the river. This was unusual behaviour for her, as she was normally so quiet. Her constant calling concerned me, fearing that she and Lav might be in danger, perhaps being harassed by feral dogs. So I crossed the river to investigate.

Quickly but cautiously approaching the patch of jungle on the river's edge from where I could hear Sita frantically calling, I listened for the sound of dogs barking as they usually do when chasing any wild animal. There was no barking. I also listened for the whistles of the *dhole* (Indian wild dogs), the whistles being the means of communication used by pack members to coordinate their attacks on prey. But there were no dhole whistles either—only the sound of Sita's hooves nervously moving on the ground inside the forest.

Swiftly searching the ground around me for any tell-tale prints to shed some light on the cause of Sita's panic was no help either. There were no large paw prints or pugmarks of any kind to explain her behaviour.

Suddenly, out of the forest little Lav bounded at full speed heading straight for the river. Right behind Lav was Sita, both running as fast as they could, galloping across the river in seconds. Once on the other side, Sita turned around and looking directly at me, started calling again, as if to warn me of imminent danger nearby. I paused, listening and looking for any sounds or signs of an animal moving close by. I couldn't detect anything.

Going into the forest patch slowly and on guard, I inspected the ground again for some clue as to the cause of the panic both Sita and Lav had just displayed. All I could see were the scattered hoof prints Sita had left behind during her panicky calling and swift departure. Stumped, I crossed the river to see if Sita and Lav were okay, which they were, having moved deeper into the forest away from the river, Sita still calling but less often and softer than she had before.

The entire incident remained a mystery until I collected the memory cards from the several camera traps positioned around the sanctuary. One of the cameras, located at a ten-minute-walk downstream above the elephant pond, but on the same side of the river where Sita and Lav had been, solved the mystery. While reviewing its memory card to see what animals it had captured, my heart skipped a beat. 'Tiger!' I softly gasped, watching the footage, 'Tiger!'

The camera had caught the still profile of a beautiful, full-grown, male tiger, the video showing him strolling through the woods heading further downstream. The photo and video were astonishing because they were daytime footage—not night-time, which is when the cameras have captured leopards and tigers before.

The tiger was absolutely stunning, in peak condition and completely relaxed—something that was extremely gratifying to see, as it meant he felt totally secure within our sanctuary grounds. I quickly looked at the time and date of the recordings: it was the same date and just ten minutes after my encounter with Sita and Lav, the time recorded as 8.45 a.m.

*This* was what she had been so panicked about—she had seen the tiger walk past her and her fawn in the open meadow only a few metres away. This is why she was so concerned and continued to try to warn me as well of the tiger's presence. I, too, was only a few metres from where he had been—less than one hundred feet away. And yet, he had had no interest in me at all, leaving me totally alone, continuing to travel calmly and confidently through our sanctuary grounds. What a thrilling and extraordinary experience!

Unlike the resident tiger of the Brahmagiri Wildlife Sanctuary, who mostly stays deep in the forest there, or the adolescent male tiger we had captured on camera the previous year almost on the exact same date, this older, larger, male tiger had decided to visit our sanctuary far more often, being caught on camera again one month later, during early morning hours in yet another part of our sanctuary.

Coincidentally, Sita and Lav had visited the same wetland about six hours later. The videos show Sita on full alert, sniffing the earth exactly where the tiger had previously passed just a few hours earlier, Sita stomping on the ground in warning to her fawn, Lav, and any other wildlife in the area that a tiger was on the prowl.

Later that day, we received the news that the tiger had been spotted killing a cheetal or spotted deer in the government forest bordering our sanctuary. He was clearly frequenting the area and doing precisely what he was supposed to do—keeping Nature's balance by killing the various prey species around so they did not overpopulate and denude the forest of its flora and ground cover.

Some weeks later, the tiger visited our sanctuary again. Anil had gone for a quick dip in the smaller pond opposite our house, meeting the small-clawed river otter family as he came out of the water. About twenty minutes later, he sat outside our house in a location that overlooks this same pond. Within a few minutes of Anil sitting down, the tiger crossed the river precisely where Anil and the otters had been, precisely the area where Sita and Lav had bolted across the river a few months earlier. Halfway across, the tiger stopped, turned his head to look at Anil, then calmly continued on his way. It was late afternoon when this encounter took place.

Clearly, our sanctuary has become a living micro ecosystem of Nature's balance of predator and prey, as it should be. We are both humbled and gratified to see and experience this balance in action.

One day, when Sita and Lav arrived below our house, I noticed Sita limping badly. She had scraped the skin off the back of her knee joint on her right hind leg, leaving an open gash. Left unattended, the wound could become infected. Trusting as ever, Sita allowed me to examine and put medicine on her wound, lying down close by to rest and recover. Though it took a couple of weeks to heal, Sita did recover fully from the injury.

It was a few weeks afterwards that we noticed Lav was straying further and further away from her mom. She had been weaned many months earlier and had grown quite tall, rivalling her mom in height. She increasingly spent time following the wild sambar herd around where she was clearly accepted as a family member.

This was as it should be. While Sita's 'family' had been human, it was only right that her daughter Lav's family should be sambars. After all, Lav's future lay with them, thanks to their acceptance of her as a group member.

Several weeks later, when I was in America for the first time in many years, Anil told me that Sita had not been seen by anyone in the past ten days. This was not that unusual since, now that her daughter was grown and on her own, Sita would be coming into season again—a time when sambar doe do wander in search of a suitable buck.

Sita's daughter, on the other hand, had been seen several times with the wild sambar herd. In addition, she had come to the back of our house to browse, as she had so many times with her mother, closely followed by a sambar stag who foraged with her—perhaps an indication that yet another 'little part of Sita' will soon arrive. However, our dearest Sita has not been seen again.

I still hold on to the hope that we will meet one day, that I will be able to stroke her neck and talk quietly to her again, exchanging breaths with her in greeting as I always did when we would first meet. But if she is gone, if she has fallen prey to the tiger she so desperately tried to warn me about, it is both moving and reassuring to know that her gentle spirit of love lives on through her own daughter Lav.

## Cats and Cameras

It's the day of our weekly fast—a practice we have followed for decades, abstaining from solid food, consuming only liquids like water and juice. Started as a spiritual discipline, fasting has helped us immensely on the physical plane as well. Once-a-week abstinence from solid food is highly recommended by many in the medical field today, not to mention its positive effects on lowering demands on the environment that go into the production of solid foods. As a spiritual practice, it reminds us of the truth of Christ's words:

> Man shall not live by bread alone, but by every word that proceedeth out of the mouth of God.
>
> Matthew 4:4

Another bonus for me is more free time, since I don't have to prepare any meals—free time that is spent outside in the Mother's heart, this time with Anil. After attending to any necessary work, we are off. Our destination—the large elephant pond downstream.

On our way, I tend to any camera traps we come across, changing memory cards and rechargeable batteries that are weak. Checking the first we come to, on the edge of one of our meadows, I am thrilled to see that the leopard has visited. We were first made aware of his presence several years ago through one of the naturalists doing a study here. Naturalist A and his colleagues had found claw marks on a tree not far from the other side of this large meadow.

Big cats, like little cats, often sharpen and clean their front claws on a tree, standing on their hind legs and scratching as high as they can reach on the tree. The resultant claw marks they leave 'advertise' their presence to other big cats. A gland between the digits of their paws secretes a scent when they scratch, further aiding in 'staking their claim' to an area.

They also mark their territory by spraying urine mixed with scent-gland secretions on surrounding foliage, other big cats being able to 'read' the markings to distinguish the species, gender and sexual maturity of the one who has sprayed. The fresh spray of tigers has a strong odour to it—an odour I have smelled several times while going through our sanctuary.

It was CCF MK—Kodagu district's chief conservator of forests—who excitedly identified that odour for me some years ago while visiting here. As we trekked through some jungle opposite our house on the other side of the river in the early evening hours, he immediately recognized it. A pre-dawn rain shower had taken place earlier and yet the scent was exceedingly strong, therefore very fresh.

A couple of weeks after naturalist A alerted us to the leopard's presence, he was caught on film for the first time in another part of our sanctuary—a large, handsome male, the black rosette pattern of his beautiful fur gleaming in the photos and videos from the infrared night light of the camera. Like the stripes of tigers, each rosette pattern of leopards is individually unique. Now a regular visitor, he moves about our grounds not only at night, but in early evening and morning hours, too, having been joined recently by a second leopard, this one a much rarer black panther.

At the rocky edge of the large meadow, I find the droppings of both sambar and cheetal deer. It is easy to see why they are here. The monsoon rains have transformed the dry straw of summer into a rich carpet of nutritious grass—an exquisite patchwork quilt of varying textures and hues—from deep purples and reds to lighter shades of softer pinks, with silvery-white patches glistening in the sun. A breath of air passes through the multi-hued carpet causing the colourful thigh-high grasses to undulate like waves of the sea, the patches of silver particularly looking like ocean waves, the moving carpet of colour gleaming in the sunlight. We are mesmerized by the sight, the movement of the waves being almost hypnotic.

The grass has been compressed in a circular pattern in some places—a sure sign of deer having slept there, the soft grass making a perfect bed. Some larger circles have much smaller ones right next to them, indicating where a mother doe has slept with her tiny fawn next to her. Then in the distance, I see them—some sambar does with fawns enjoying the bountiful feast. We quietly enter the forest so they can continue eating in peace.

The next camera is positioned at a junction of paths wildlife have made coming from every direction through the jungle. This location is a particularly active site for the movement of wildlife since the jungle paths connect the big meadow to the large wetland below the hill.

In addition, several of the native trees at this crossroads produce luscious fruits, nuts and seeds loved by many different species. Hence, the camera not only records who has visited, but documents longer-term species behaviour as well. Elephants, Nilgiri martens, various deer, small leopard cats, jungle fowl and other birds, wild hare, mongoose, porcupine, gaur and dhole—this camera watches them all.

The heavy monsoon rains have washed the leaf litter and loose soil off some parts of the small hill into the wetland valley below enriching its soil and adding nutrients to the wetland's flora—a definite benefit for the wildlife gathered to eat there. Now, the jungle's own 'wood wide web' is revealed—an incredibly intricate tangle of fungi connections linking the roots of all these native trees together. In some areas, there are larger species of fungi growing on pieces of dead wood, helping to break down and recycle nutrients of the dead wood back to the soil. Their small, saucer-like shapes hold some water from the light pre-dawn shower, the water enhancing their beautiful colours of browns, tans, reds and black.

Reaching the wetland, we find the gaur family already settled for their afternoon siesta. Not wanting to disturb their rest, we retreat into the forest again. Soon, we have reached the bamboo-lined edge of the large elephant pond.

The pond is filled with life. Black clouds of tadpoles from various species are everywhere, each individual at a slightly different stage of development, some already losing their tails, having sprouted their legs and feet while others still looking like fish with oversized heads. The fingerlings of endemic species of fish along with snails and mussels move about in shallow pools downstream of the pond with crabs occasionally venturing out of their hiding places in the rocks to search for titbits of food. Seeing them reminds me of an amazing little crab who became my friend, Crabby.

## Crabby

Crabs are usually very shy creatures, understandably so as they are prey for many species as well as hunted persistently by humans. When cornered, they will defend themselves as best they can, using their pincer-like claws to inflict pain on the attacker, giving them the reputation of being angry and ill-tempered. This, in turn, has given rise to humans labelling quarrelsome or grouchy people as 'crabby'. But this little crab was certainly not grouchy at all. Rather, he was exceedingly curious, gentle and sweet.

I first met Crabby shortly after the monsoon rains had ceased. Anil and I were at one of our favourite meditation spots, sitting on rocks at the edge of the river, when I felt something crawling on to my lap. I looked down to see this little crab calmly sitting there, looking back at me with his strangely elevated eyes. The eyes of crabs and most other crustaceans are mounted on the end of 'eye-stalks'—a special protruding tentacle that lifts and separates the eyes to give them a better field of vision.

Crabby wasn't aggressive in the least, seeming exceedingly curious about me. Though certainly surprised, I could not help but smile at this sweet little guy who seemed determined to be my friend. After sitting in my lap for quite some time, Crabby finally climbed down and started to move sideways (as all crabs do) towards the back of the rock I had been sitting on, watching me the whole time. It was as if he wanted to show me something. Getting up, I followed him to a spot where he showed me a small hole in the ground next to the rock. After looking at me again, Crabby went inside the hole and disappeared, the hole obviously the entrance to the underground 'home' Crabby had made for himself.

From that day onwards, Crabby was my friend, always coming out to visit when I was there, even responding to my calls to him when I would arrive to say, 'Hi!' The friendship lasted for many months—right up to the start of the next monsoon season, when the rain-swollen river covered our meditation rocks and Crabby's home. What happened to Crabby after that, I will never know. Perhaps he is still out there somewhere, since land crabs can live for eleven years or more! So if I hear someone describing someone else as 'crabby', I can't help but smile, remembering my dear, sweet, little friend.

There are a lot of land crabs here, particularly in one softer, wetter meadow area of the sanctuary, their presence clearly evidenced by the many mounds of soil pebbles left behind from their eating process of taking in bits of earth, filtering it for particles of food and then expelling it as small pellets, piles of which can often be found beside the burrows they have dug in the ground for homes. Crabs have a high amount of phosphorus in their bodies, which may be the reason why these pebble mounds literally glow in the moonlight—a truly extraordinary and almost otherworldly thing to see at night!

The elephant pond where I met Crabby is our favourite place to take a dip and swim, with its wonderfully 'layered' water temperatures. The surface layer is nice and warm, having been warmed by the sun, while the deeper waters remain quite cool throughout the year. After our refreshing swim, we cross the river to settle down on the rocks to relax and enjoy being within Nature's heart. But a sad sight awaits us . . .

Unusually heavy monsoon winds have brought down one of the mother trees on the side of the river, her prone body lying in the water, her leaves slowly withering away, her root ball exposed, revealing that she had lived all these years without a firm roothold in the soil, having grown on top of the great granite rock below. A silent victim of climate change and the extreme climate events that are becoming all too common, her death speaks volumes of the injury humanity's lack of care and foresight have wrought and continue to bring to the Earth as a whole. I cannot help but shed a tear, for she has been our constant companion over the years whenever we have visited this area.

Looking at the pond calms my heart, its surface like glass perfectly mirroring the blue sky and white clouds above, as well as the tree-lined shore encircling it. A deep peace descends upon my soul . . .

A small family flock of open-bill storks flies above the pond, landing in the upper branches of a huge wild mango tree near us, using their graceful black and white wings to help them balance on the top branches of the tree. A light puff of wind follows them, setting off a wave of ripples across the pond, transforming its mirrored surface to infinite sparkling diamonds reflecting the sun's light, dazzling in their brilliance, filling us with awe and wonder at the beauty of Nature's many faces.

The cormorant has come along with the darter or snake bird, both drying their outstretched wings, the black and silver-white wings of the darter gleaming in the sunshine. Both are perched on branches of a submerged tree in the pond, turtles sunbathing on the trunk of the same tree. A familiar call announces the presence of the bee-eater family, all sitting together in a row on a branch above, each one taking his or her rounds in the air catching insects on the wing.

Drongos arrive to take their afternoon bath, first doing 'loop-de-loops' in the air before dropping feet first and wings open with a 'plop!' on the water's surface before flying up again. They are soon joined by another very special bird that is the logo for our non-profit charitable trust—the paradise flycatcher. The male's long white tail streamers quiver in the air as he shakes the excess water from his strikingly beautiful body.

Suddenly, Anil sees something else in the pond. 'Otters!' he whispers to me. Yes! An otter family is here—mom, dad and two pups. The high-pitched, almost bird-like chirps of the two little ones are now audible, clearly showing their excitement at being here. Mom and dad take turns diving for food, their movements looking so much like those of porpoises and dolphins as they swim and dive. Of all the different species of wildlife we have known throughout our lives, otters are certainly one of my most beloved 'friends'.

## The Otter Side of Life: Part Two

My encounters with small-clawed river otters go back to our very first years here at the sanctuary. My first encounter came one evening at dusk. I had already bathed and was wearing a pair of bright, pink pyjamas for the night, when I heard the sound of crunching outside near the river below the house. *Otters!* I quickly went out and walked down the steps to the river, trying to be as quiet and unobtrusive as possible, so as to not startle the feasting otter.

Bending down on a large rock at the edge of the river, I could see the otter sitting on the opposite shore eating his meal of crab. I immediately froze, not wanting any movement to disturb him, but it was too late. I had already been spotted, the otter looking straight into my eyes. And yet, he continued with his meal, until he was finished.

Afterwards, he entered the river and swam directly over to me, circling in the water in front of me less than two feet away, as if to say, 'Are you kidding me?! You really think I couldn't see you in *that* outfit?! I mean, really—how could I miss you? Hot pink, at that!'

Another special encounter came a few years later. Anil and I were sitting next to each other meditating on rocks in the river, below the kitchen. Two friends visiting us were sitting a little further upstream. At one point, I was prompted from within to open my eyes. As I did so, I saw a head pop out of the water directly in front of us. It was an otter looking right at us! He began swimming in circles all the while looking towards us before disappearing below the surface. All of us were thrilled to have seen him but were somewhat disappointed that he had not stayed around a bit longer.

In another few minutes, we saw his head pop out of the water again. He was back! And then . . . a second head popped out of the water right next to him! Both of them stared intently at us for several seconds and then swam to the edge of the river and climbed out. Standing up next to a tree holding on to it for support, they alternated looking directly at us and then at each other.

It was as if you could 'hear' the conversation going on between them, the first otter saying to the second one, 'See! I told you they were humans—humans who are giving us love vibes!' The second otter seeming to reply, 'Love vibes instead of trying to catch and kill us! How amazing!'

This intense communication continued for a couple of minutes before they both went back in the water and started nonchalantly swimming in front of us completely relaxed, knowing we meant them no harm and were no danger to them at all. The pair of them stayed with us for at least twenty minutes before heading off together, slowly swimming further downstream. What an extraordinary experience we had all been privileged to share!

I had a very touching and intimate encounter in the same area some years later, when I was alone. Late afternoon sunlight filtered through the trees at an angle that lit up a rocky area of the shore in front of me. I was sitting on a large rock in the river, my cat, Leela, having joined me, now sleeping peacefully in my lap. I had brought my camera equipment just in case any wildlife happened to come by.

Suddenly a head emerged from below the water in front of me. Otter! I immediately turned on my video camera, but within a second or two, the head was gone. 'Missed him,' I thought while still scanning the water in front of me for tell-tale ripples that might indicate the otter's whereabouts.

Disappointed, I kept the camera running just in case . . . and then I spotted him. He was right in front of me, having climbed up out of the water on to that very ledge being illuminated by the late afternoon sun. Zooming in on him, I was then given the most wonderful and intimate encounter I had ever had.

Though the otter knew full well I was there, having looked me straight in the eye when he had first seen me, he was totally relaxed, feeling comfortable and safe enough to give himself a complete grooming in front of me. From head to tail, he carefully cleaned his thick fine fur, making sure to remove every last speck of debris in it and taking great care that it was finely 'combed' with his teeth, twisting backwards as far as he could to make sure he reached his spine area as well. Then it was time for his webbed feet, toes and claws and finally his tail, afterwards stretching out on the rock to enjoy the last warm rays of the sun.

The entire grooming session took several minutes. As the sunlight started to fade, my little friend slipped back into the water, heading downstream, climbing out on to the shore again at one point to hunt for mussels in the sand, which he did indeed find, happily eating them before going further downstream and out of sight.

The whole episode filled me with joy, moving me to tears at the same time. How lucky I was to have witnessed this at such close range and filmed it on top of that! But more importantly, how blessed I was to have been trusted by this sweet innocent creature—a creature whose life has been made a deadly hell by other humans who have hunted them relentlessly to the point of extinction for their pelts, as mentioned earlier in Chapter 11.

And yet, this beautiful, gentle being had allowed me to witness him in such an intimate and special way, to honour me with his trust and faith, sharing with me a snapshot of his life in the wild in our sanctuary, which was his home. How deeply humbled and grateful I was to him and Mother Nature for this rare and precious gift!

For a few years after this experience, we did not see otters directly again, although I found their eliminations or 'spraint' here and there along the river's edge. I was always so happy to find this evidence that at least one or more were alive and well. My deep concern for their safety was due to the terrible revelations coming from Delhi. During a raid on poachers there, huge quantities of otter pelts were found. At least sixty-eight otter pelts were discovered with just one poaching ring, with the poachers admitting that many of the pelts had come from the south, specifically the Cauvery–Kodagu area.

Hearing this horrible news made my heart weep for all the sweet, innocent and playful otters we had come to love so much. Poaching of otters here in India has been so rampant that they are now listed as a Schedule-I species by India's Wildlife Protection Act—the same category as the Bengal tiger.

In August of 2019, additional international protection was given to them as well, when the Convention on International Trade in Endangered Species (CITES) also listed them in Appendix-I, with their inclusion in the red list of the International Union for the Conservation of Nature (IUCN), all underscoring the high risk of extinction of these wonderful creatures.

River otters are an important part of the ecosystem, being a keystone species and the top predator of their aquatic habitat in many areas. Their presence, or lack thereof, is a major indication of the purity and health of the river systems where they are normally found. As rivers become polluted, otters find it difficult to find food since toxins have killed off their prey.

In addition, otters often dig their dens or burrows under the tree roots of large trees on the banks of rivers and other waterways. As riverbanks become devoid of trees due to logging by humans, otters disappear as they cannot find suitable den sites to live in and raise their young—a dangerous sign foreshadowing both the drying up of the river, as well as severe erosion and future flooding. Trees are critical for water regulation, absorbing excess water and releasing it back into the river system in the dry season. Their roots also purify water while holding soil in place, thereby stopping erosion of riverbanks. The disappearance of trees translates into ecosystem collapse—a collapse portended by the departure of the otters.

Simply put, the absence of otters indicates a river or water system that is in peril, whereas their presence is a positive sign of water purity and ecological balance. Therefore, as a keystone and indicator species for critical freshwater ecosystems that we depend on for survival, it is in our own self-interest to protect them and their habitats from destruction.

## Northern Cousins

Ironically enough, the next time Anil and I saw otters was in December 2010 in northern India. We had gone to Corbett National Park and Tiger Reserve, and had been exceedingly blessed, seeing a tiger on the very first day, the tiger approaching us around noon, her beautiful fur glistening in the sunlight. It was truly a very special encounter for us both.

The following day, we decided to go to a different area of Corbett, along the Ramganga River. While the likelihood of seeing tigers was less there, the tremendous bird life in the forests near the river, coupled with the chance to see otters, certainly made the trip worth taking.

It was early December and very cold. But the sun was shining brightly by the time we arrived at the river's shore. Leaving the jeep behind, we walked downstream a bit until we came to some large rocks, Anil and I each sitting on separate rocks, a few metres apart. The river water was crystal clear, flowing full and fast past us. Small birds were using the rocks as perches for both catching insects as well as bathing in the cool, clean spray being created by the river's tumbling over rocks as it rushed by.

While filming a few of the birds, I noticed some movement on the opposite shore. Otters! It was a family of smooth-coated otters—a much larger species than our small-clawed otters in the sanctuary, but also endangered. They were making their way across a large rock outcropping towards the river. I was so excited I almost dropped my camera!

Within seconds, the family of four had entered the icy cold water and were swimming towards us, getting out of the river on to a sandy bank exactly opposite where I was sitting. Mom and dad looked in my direction and continued to climb up the sandy bank, followed by their youngsters, who were almost as large as they were. Our presence was not inhibiting them at all.

Then all four of them started rolling on the fine white sand, enjoying themselves immensely. The sand was clean and warm, having been baked in the morning sun for at least an hour or more before their arrival. What a wonderful way to greet the day—rolling around in the warm sand, cleaning their fur in the process. Their joy was so evident it was almost as if you could hear an audible 'Aaaaahhhhhhh!' from them.

I could not believe how fortunate we were, first, to see otters at all, and then to have them trust us enough to watch them in their carefree glee of their morning sand bath, completely unperturbed in our company. How utterly privileged we were!

Our joy and the otters' playfulness continued for several minutes. Then suddenly, first one and then the second adult looked across to the right from where we were sitting, standing up on their hind legs to get a better look. In an instant, there was an entire change in their behaviour—from being fully at ease, joyfully playing and rolling in the warm sand, they were now alert and tense, undoubtedly concerned by what they were seeing. Humans—some other humans had arrived and the otters obviously did not feel at all comfortable by their appearance.

Quickly, the family group headed for the river, slipping into the water, where they felt safe. Swimming close to us and looking directly at us as they swam past, it was almost as if they were saying, 'Goodbye—we are sorry we cannot stay,' disappearing downstream, carried away by the river's rapid current.

While this incident did not take place at our sanctuary, it illustrates how critically important calm, peaceful and loving vibrations are whenever one is in the presence of wildlife. One might argue that the otters at our sanctuary know us, and therefore trust us, allowing us to be close to them whenever they are around—a justifiable theory. But here were otters who did not know us at all, since Anil and I had never visited Corbett National Park before this. The acceptance of our presence by the otters was solely based on the loving feelings and vibrations emanating from us towards them.

In addition, the two larger otters were parents with two younger pups or 'kits' (as in 'kittens'). They trusted us enough to witness such an intimate and playful moment in their family life. Considering the abuse humans have inflicted on otters for their pelts and/or the illegal pet trade, it was truly amazing and an honour that they decided to trust us as they did.

Over the years, the camera traps throughout our sanctuary have helped us keep track of the otters living and visiting here, as well as documenting the various other species that visit and/or make our sanctuary their home full-time. The cameras have also become a helpful tool against poachers and illegal loggers, leading to arrests and prosecutions of offenders—necessary actions to stamp out the killing and deforestation so rampant in the district and entire country.

The year 2017 was a true 'banner year' for the otters at our sanctuary. It was the end of February when I first heard the high-pitched call of young otters swimming in the elephant pond. I had gone there to change the memory cards in the camera traps as I was leaving in a couple of days to go to New Delhi.

I was to receive the Nari Shakti Puruskar (Women's Empowerment Award) from the president of India in the presidential palace of Rashtrapathi Bhawan on International Women's Day— 8 March—also 'coincidentally' my birthday. I had been nominated for the award by the union minister for women and child development Maneka Gandhi for my environmental work at our sanctuary, Mrs Gandhi recognizing and understanding fully that women and children suffer the most due to environmental degradation.

It was already early evening by the time I arrived at the elephant pond. The high chirping calls of the young were unmistakable, and I was very excited that I may be able to glimpse a family swimming, hunting for food and frolicking about in the water. Bending down behind a stand of tall river grass, looking out on the pond, I was delighted to see four otters—two parents and two kits. However, one of the parents spotted me and quickly sounded the alarm to the rest of the group. The others responded by swimming further upstream in the pond.

Taking this opportunity when they had their backs turned toward me, I quickly moved to some rocks lined with overhanging bamboo, the bamboo helping to conceal me from view. Within a minute or two of getting settled with camera ready, I was given one of the most wonderful 'shows' by the otters that I have ever seen. The parents were taking turns swimming and diving into the water, while the two little ones followed behind. Within a few minutes, the whole group had moved downstream towards me again, the father being right in front of me. I held my breath as he came even closer until he suddenly disappeared behind the tall river grass. In an instant, he was by my feet! Only then did he realize that I was there.

Scurrying off the rock and back into the water, he disappeared behind the grass again, reappearing just a metre away from me. He then stood up in the water on his hind legs and started scolding me, as if to say, 'You scared me! I forgot you were here! Don't do that again!'

Diving back into the water after scolding me, he swam upstream to join the rest of his family group. But they continued to dive and hunt, and frolic and play, very close to me again, despite the scare, accepting my presence and going back to enjoying their evening fun. I continued to watch and film until it became too dark, finally leaving as night began to fall.

I was absolutely exhilarated with this wonderful 'close encounter of the otter kind' and couldn't wait to share it with Anil. Little did I realize then that this would be the first of many more close encounters through the coming months, the next one being just a few days after my return from the awards ceremony in New Delhi.

However, this time there were not just four otters—there were ten! It was a large family group of adults and babies, youngsters and adolescents of various ages and sizes—an extended family that was to spend every day in our sanctuary right up to the beginning of the monsoon.

Much of their time was spent directly below our house, hunting and playing, giving us the delight of watching them from the comfort of our own home. I was thrilled to also get fantastic camera trap footage, especially from the camera placed on the end of the island in the middle of the river. One sequence captured the entire family as they came on shore, the little ones begging the parents to give them some of the fish that they had caught and carried on to the land, the sounds of their begging recorded as well.

Otters display the sheer joy of life, their captivating playfulness helping to bring joy to all who, like me, are lucky enough to watch them up-close. I remember one day when I was able to watch one of the youngsters exhibit this joy in such a sweet and endearing manner.

I was sitting on the edge of an elevated riverbank, when a youngster swam upstream on his own. He was just casually swimming around in the river right below me, not hunting or diving, just lazing around; sometimes floating on his back paddling past; other times having fun just blowing bubbles in the water, lowering his head below the surface every so often just to make bubbles for the sheer fun of it, then watching them pop up and burst. There is no way anyone can observe such behaviour without a giant smile on their face!

This, however, is in sharp contrast to the bravery and strength they can exhibit if they feel any sense of danger to a member of their family group. One afternoon, while the whole extended family was swimming near the island below our house, one of our cats, Shradha, decided to investigate this raucous group.

Crouching down and moving ever closer, she was stopped in her tracks by the two largest otters, first scolding and then chasing her. The rest of the adults joined in the pursuit, chasing Shradha clear off the island. She was so intimidated by them that she didn't stop running until she reached me where I was filming the entire encounter, hiding behind me for safety, totally deflated of all her predatory bravado!

On another occasion, when our cats Shanti and Leela accompanied me to the end of the island to change the memory card in the camera, the mother and father of the family swam in the river in front of us the entire time we were there, even standing up close to shore, scolding me, as if to say, 'Why have you brought these two cats with you? You may be welcome to watch us in peace, but they are not welcome so close to our family!'

Like virtually all parents, otters are very protective of their young, their strong defence of their family earning them the reputation of being fierce in their efforts to ward off any predator's attempts to attack a family member. Having witnessed this protective behaviour myself, I can certainly testify to the bravery and dedication to family that these loyal creatures have for each other.

Beneath their wonderfully playful demeanour lies a strength and courage, fuelled by love and devotion for each other. I am very grateful to have been able to witness this spirit and affection first-hand, and to have been given the privilege of being trusted enough by these intelligent and playful creatures for them to share some of their most intimate and touching moments with me. For me, they are a wonderful reminder to live life to the fullest, infusing every single day with joy!

# 19

# From Love-Posts and Bears to the Gentle Giants of SAI

As time slips away watching the antics of the otters, we reluctantly leave the elephant pond and head into another section of the forest to check more cameras. Colourful arrays of flowers greet us inside. Long strands of the critically endangered bi-colour clock vine dangle down from branches above. Their deep orange-red blossoms open to reveal their bright yellow hearts within, their tubular centres filled with sweet nectar, attracting butterflies large and small to enjoy the sugary treat. Stunning deep-purple funnels bloom closer to the forest floor.

Garlands of orchids of every shape and size decorate the trees, their various hues spanning the colour spectrum from white to deep lavenders and blues, from greens to soft pinks and reds. They and other succulent plants with long tendrils of flowers cascading down, perfume the air with their sweet scent.

Adding to this bouquet of beauty is the red of new leaves on various trees all over. This is one of Nature's ways of protecting the newly unfurled leaves from the damaging effects of the ultraviolet rays of the sun, the red pigment in the new leaf acting like a sunscreen, reflecting red light while the leaf is still young and its 'internal organs' for photosynthesis are still developing. It may also be a bit of 'plant camouflage', making the new leaves less perceptible to leaf-eating insects.

It is like a reverse autumn here with the canopy of trees coloured by this brilliant new growth, the deep maroon of new leaves eventually becoming lighter shades of red, orange, pink and light green, finally darkening to rich, deep green once mature—a process that takes weeks to complete.

While looking at the tiny white orchids covering the lower trunk of a tree, I suddenly see some large scat on the ground. First, I mistake it for that of a tiger. I have seen tiger scat before, even taking photos of it to share with colleagues far more knowledgeable than myself for help with its identification. The bones and hair or fur of the prey animal that the tiger had consumed were clearly visible, embedded in the scat.

But this is different—there are seeds in it. Big cats (and small) rarely eat fruit, doing so only for digestion purposes or due to lack of regular prey.

'Bear!' I think to myself. Being omnivorous and eating almost anything they find, bears love fruits. Hence, their eliminations are usually full of small seeds from the berries or fruit they have eaten.

It was again CCF MK, who had identified the smell of the tiger spray, that later verified that the scat was indeed that of sloth bears. He confirmed that this region of the Western Ghats had been their natural habitat in the past. But no sloth bear had been seen in the area for several decades, having been killed off by poachers. He went on to explain that the bear was named thus due to the error of a European zoologist, who thought it was related to the sloths of Central and South America.

CCF MK then proceeded to give me a wonderful lesson in identification of bear scat. It was the presence of small, hard, white balls in their scat that truly confirmed it as being that of a bear. As he explained, in addition to fruit, bears love to eat large black ants. While the rest of the ants' bodies are dissolved by digestive juices in the bear's stomach, the skulls do not dissolve and hence are eliminated in the bear's scat as small white balls.

Looking around the hilly meadow where the scat was discovered, CCF MK found more scat and more evidence of bears—not just one, but several. While normally solitary animals, sloth bears will tolerate each other's company when abundant food is available. This is true of grizzlies and black bears in the northern hemisphere of the Americas during the annual salmon run. Here, at our sanctuary, it was the fruits of the few trees in the meadow that drew the bears in numbers, these fruits being one of their favourite treats to eat.

Inspecting the trees, CCF MK showed me the tell-tale claw marks of bears hoisting themselves up the large tree branches to try and reach the delicious fruit. While some ripe fruit had fallen from the trees on to the ground, there was still plenty more on the branches. So, our sanctuary was providing refuge and food for yet another threatened animal species—the sloth bears—who were finally returning to their former range, now that they had a safe place to stay, with plenty of food and water to sustain them.

As Anil and I near the next meadow, the breeze brings yet another familiar scent. 'Elephants!' I whisper to Anil, excitedly. Proceeding cautiously, we see their moist dung all over the meadow. This meadow, too, is dressed in its own colourful carpet of grasses which the elephants have clearly been enjoying. But the family herd is not here right now, so we enter the meadow climbing up the hill, checking cameras as we go.

At the top, we are enthralled by the magnificent view—the Brahmagiri mountains in all their glory rise peak after peak toward the southeast, the hills coloured in green splendour, including the shola meadows on the tallest peaks. Forests fill the landscape from base to summit, creating a breathtaking scene of green. We drink in the beauty, while noticing a band of heavy white clouds starting to move across the peaks, shrouding them in white. Soon, we, too, are engulfed in a fine fog, everything taking on an etheric quality.

Heading down the meadow back to the jungle, our senses are acutely alert to detect the presence of the elephant herd. We cross our footbridge that spans the river connecting both sides of our sanctuary—a location I have used many times to observe and film the elephant family, since they cross the river below the bridge quite often.

The bridge brings us to the grove of those magnificent 700-year-old great-great-grandmother trees. With their crowns hidden in the misty white clouds, they look like gigantic stairways linking Earth to Heaven, their trunks and limbs decorated with feathery ferns and garlands of orchids and other flowering plants. Their enormous roots are the size of mature trees of other species.

Standing next to them is truly humbling, as one feels so tiny in comparison. Their girth is so wide it would take many people to enfold them in a loving 'group hug'. Stroking and hugging trees or 'love-posts', as Anil likes to call them, is something we do frequently, the benefits of tree-hugging now having scientific facts to back up those good feelings when we hug one. When hugging a tree, its electromagnetic field intermingles with our own and their grounding vibration helps us to feel more peaceful, calm, grounded and yes, loved.

In addition, research has shown that the electromagnetic fields of large forests help to strengthen Earth's protective magnetosphere. Earth's magnetic field deflects charged particles from the sun and cosmos that would otherwise destroy the ozone layer, which is our main shield for protecting the Earth from harmful UV rays (ultraviolet radiation). Unfortunately, the magnetosphere has weakened by at least 10 per cent since measurements first started in 1838, this decrease coinciding with the onset of massive global deforestation.

Scientific facts aside, these ancient orchid-laden lofty 'love-posts' are unique. Their presence here has created a very sacred place. While all of Nature is sacred, areas like this that have ancient forms of life still living on them have a very special spiritual vibration that uplifts the heart and soul effortlessly to heavenly realms.

Perhaps it is because these trees have lived so long, seeing countless generations of other plants, animals and humans come and go, while they have remained, continuing to give to many generations of the more ephemeral creatures of the Earth, like humans, the water and oxygen they produce, the shade they impart and the carbon they sequester, and the food and homes they provide for countless other species of plants and animals, that they produce such an exceptional spiritual vibration that enfolds one in an aura of deep peace just by being near them.

To quote Alexander von Humboldt, the first person to recognize human-induced climate change back in 1800, and whose scientific and visionary work helped inspire the view of the universe as one interacting living being:

Reverence the tree, it is one great miracle, and it was holy to your ancestors.
The enmity against the tree is a sign of the inferiority of a people and the low-mindedness of the individual.

Overhead, innumerable species of birds merrily sing away while butterflies flit past our faces, having descended from the blossoms above after sipping their sweet treat of nectar. The civet has been here recently, its seed-laden scat sitting on a huge root of one of these majestic giants. Nearby, huge woody creepers—also hundreds of years old—encircle some trees in a gentle embrace before climbing up the trees to help stitch together the canopy's skyway highway.

Close to this grove of woody creepers and ancient trees is one of the best camera locations in the sanctuary. Situated near an elephants' river crossing, the elephants' weight has compressed the soil to create easy access to the river for other wildlife. The camera captures photos and videos of numerous species that come primarily to drink water here. Night or day, the camera clicks away.

One amazing three-hour series involved the Nilgiri marten couple—the sequence started with what looked like pieces of paper falling in front of the camera's lens. The 'paper' was actually part of a wild wasps' hive that the marten was dislodging above the camera on the same tree. Once down, this persistent fellow was determined to pull apart the hive to get at the sweet honeycomb inside, no matter what. He continued to tear apart the paper-like hive despite being stung, rolling in the loose soil and leaves by the tree to dislodge any wasps stinging him.

He finally succeeded and the wasps gave up, he and his mate thoroughly relishing the sweet reward for his unbelievable persistence and tenacity. But what was equally amazing was the number of other animals that got to share his sweet reward—cheetal, sambar, gaur, barking deer, birds, chipmunks, mouse deer, mongoose and more, all took turns eating delicious pieces of the honeycomb, the act of one benefitting so many others as well.

Another very special night-time series was that of a tiger. Starting with his arrival, it showed him drinking for several minutes before getting halfway into the river, then backing out to look straight into the camera, William Blake's poem, 'The Tyger'(tiger) perfectly describing his huge luminous eyes:

*Tyger Tyger, burning bright,*
*In the forests of the night . . .*

A second tiger video at the same location is quite extraordinary as it captured the curious behaviour exhibited one day by our semi-resident tiger. One morning, around 4 a.m., I was awakened by a loud, strange sound right below my bedroom window. It took me a minute or so of listening before I recognized what it was—the roar of a tiger! But it was not just one roar—the tiger kept roaring almost constantly for a full hour or more! This was highly unusual as he was normally very quiet.

His roaring continued off and on from different parts of our sanctuary until 8.30 a.m. and then started again around 8 p.m., this time closer to the Brahmagiri Wildlife Sanctuary. I still have no idea what provoked the roaring spree, but his roar was caught on camera at this location as he started walking away from the river, after having had a refreshing drink of water. For me, listening to his roar has definitely been one of the highlights of his regular visits.

However, the most amazing series of the tiger so far was filmed on our camera trap right below our house. Located at one of the major river crossings used by virtually all wildlife species, it has captured a number of wonderful wildlife behavioural videos over the years.

In this series, it shows the tiger coming to the river, first to drink, and then fully immersing himself in the water. He continued to lie down in the water for almost twenty minutes, relishing its liquid coolness, both for his body as well as for drinking, shifting his position periodically from time to time, often looking straight into the camera lens, before finally climbing out. An absolutely incredible and exceptional series, it was a wonderful birthday present from Mother Nature to me since I collected the memory card on my birthday! What a fantastic and breathtaking gift!

## Gentle Giants of SAI

Back at the towering love-posts, I find it so poetically appropriate that the giants of the canopy are one of the main meeting and eating places for the gentle giants of SAI's forests—the elephants. The river's bamboo-lined edge, as well as the abundance of jack, wild mango and other fruits promise them a banquet of delicacies, along with easy access to cool, clear water. And sure enough, the family herd has indeed been here, their huge footprints in the sandy soil evidence of where they have recently crossed the river to reach here, the prints being quite fresh.

More signs are the countless bamboo pieces snapped and bent along the river's bank. The area is right above the elephant crossing and in line with the same camera. So, the camera has captured plenty of elephants, too. I call this place the 'bamboo salad bar' because of the way the elephants eat here—the entire family group in a perfect line, heads and trunks buried in the bamboo, happily eating, with the rest of their bodies sticking out, tails swishing away as a youngster runs about in play, the whole scene reminiscent of a human family at a salad bar.

Another funny video captured two young tuskers getting ready to cross the river. The first hesitates to go in, like a reluctant human swimmer not wanting to get into the cold water. As the second tusker's patience wears thin, he starts pushing the first—gently but firmly—into the water with his head and tusks, as if saying, 'Come on already! Move, would you?! Enough is enough!'

Besides camera trap photos and videos, Anil and I have been very fortunate to have seen the elephants up close and personal on many occasions ourselves as well. They are such extraordinary beings and we owe them a lot for their help in reforesting the sanctuary grounds. While our reforestation efforts have certainly been fruitful, the reforestation by these elephants has been extremely important, since their travels through the grounds have sown seeds of different species of grasses and shrubs as well as those of the most important canopy trees—the living giants and other large trees whose ecosystem services of rain production and conservation, soil enrichment and carbon sequestration are so critical to us all.

Without elephants, the wetlands and meadows would not be so rich in biodiversity. Without elephants, the number of tree species here would be far less, too, the seeds of these trees carried, planted and fertilized by the elephants and their dung. While elephants have benefitted from our protection, we have benefitted far more from their presence here, both environmentally and spiritually.

This is one of the many reasons that I just love them. I love everything about them—their huge size, wonderful long trunk and enormous ears that even look a little bit like India! I love the way they flap their ears back and forth, which is one of Nature's ways of helping them cool themselves—as their ears are full of blood vessels, their continuous flapping helps to cool the blood in the ears, thereby cooling themselves. They also have incredible hearing, their large funnel-shaped ears are able to hear storms that are between 160 to 240 kilometres (100 to 150 miles) away!

I love the way they communicate using a complex language of trumpet calls, roars, squeaks, chirps, snorts, cries and low frequency rolling rumbles that fall well below the threshold of human hearing. Called 'seismic communication', these sounds create vibrations or waves that travel through the earth and can be felt and understood by other elephants almost 16 kilometres (6 to 10 miles) away! The low frequency vibrations are detected through their padded feet by a huge ball of fat called a 'digital cushion'. The dozens of touch receptors in the elephant's foot feel the vibrations, sending a signal to the elephant's brain. These vibrations also travel through the elephant's skeleton directly to the ear, transforming what has been 'felt' into something that is now 'heard'.

Their trunks also add to this system of communication through the sense of touch. Elephants often put the tips of their trunk into the mouths of others to comfort and reassure one another, as well as to caress each other, sometimes hanging their trunks on one another or putting their heads close to each other in a tête-à-tête, these actions being signs of affection, love and care. Not surprisingly, these trunks also provide elephants with an excellent sense of smell—one of the best in the animal kingdom—having more smell receptors on its tip than those of any other mammal. They can detect water almost 20 kilometres (12 miles) away and are able to distinguish between different people just through testing the air for their scent.

The way they eat is also extraordinary, using the tip of their enormous trunk as a 'hand' to grab whatever it is they want to eat, either stripping off leaves from branches or grabbing large quantities of grass with amazing dexterity or swatting the grass on the ground to dislodge any dirt that may be clinging to it, before shovelling it into their huge mouths to swallow.

I love the way elephants walk at a slow measured pace and how extremely observant they are, noticing the slightest change around them. I have seen examples of this many times on videos caught on our camera traps. The elephants approaching the cameras immediately notice them, no matter how well camouflaged they may be, using their long trunks to investigate, sniffing around the cameras to determine just what kind of a strange thing I have put up there. And yet, not once have they purposely disturbed or damaged any of our cameras, thus demonstrating a remarkable degree of gentleness as well as faith in us and the safety they find within our sanctuary grounds.

On several occasions, colleagues as well as forest department personnel have remarked on how calm and peaceful the elephants appear on videos that we have shown them, in comparison to footage they have seen elsewhere, including footage filmed inside government protected forests. One naturalist even told me that the elephants in her area consistently use their dexterous trunks to take down whatever camera traps have been installed.

This curiosity that elephants display is a sign of how very intelligent they are; they are considered to be one of the most intelligent species on the planet, their long memories being another indication of how smart they are. Examples of their amazing memory abound, particularly when it comes to finding water sources during the long dry season. An elephant may have only been to a certain water source once as a young calf during its long lifetime, and yet it will remember how to get there if the need arises, even decades later.

The way elephants drink is truly unique, drinking as much as ten gallons a minute, using their trunks to draw up to 2 gallons (over 7.5 litres) of the precious liquid at a time and then spraying it into their open mouths, consuming up to 50 gallons (over 189 litres) of water on a daily basis! That's approximately the amount of water held by a standard Western bathtub!

As mentioned earlier, elephants love to bathe in water, taking great delight in spraying it on their backs or dunking their whole bodies underwater like they do in our large elephant pond. They do this not only to get clean, but even more to cool off. Having very few sweat glands, they are always keen to take an invigorating dip. This is where the many wrinkles of their skin also come into play. They help to spread and hold five to ten times more water for far longer against the elephant's skin, than if they were not there. This helps the elephant to regulate her body temperature through evaporative cooling in the same way human sweat glands help us cool down.

After a cool bath, elephant skin care often calls for a dusting of fine dirt thrown all over the body, again by their trunks. The many wrinkles keep the dust in place, thus protecting the skin from scorching sunlight as well as from biting pests. For elephants, the more wrinkles, the better!

Scientists now agree that elephants have a sense of 'self' just like humans, being able to recognize themselves in a mirror and even using the mirror in the same way we do to be able to see parts of our body we normally cannot see. This sense of self is another indication of their great intelligence.

Self-awareness is also considered the basis for the creation of 'communities' and even the concept of 'Divinity'. It leads to the recognition of the need to cooperate with others. Cooperation with others benefits an individual in many ways—from safety and security, to learning skills and talents, to additional opportunities for finding food and water—all important elements for survival.

Cooperation with others leads to loving others as well. And this is the most important reason that I love elephants. Put simply, I love the way elephants love each other.

The family is the centre around which all of elephant life is lived, and 'women power' is what keeps their families strong, the extended family group usually being led by the oldest and wisest of all its members—the matriarch. It is she who guides the family and keeps them from harm. It is she who helps them find food and water and it is she who passes on to the younger generation all she has learned over her long life of fifty to sixty years, sharing everything she knows about surviving and thriving in the wild.

Thus, within the heart of Mother Nature beats the great heart of the grandest mother elephant who showers love and comfort on all the rest of her family members, love being almost literally the glue that binds these very special creatures together.

## Elephant Tales

I have been privileged to witness this love and devotion upfront and personal on several occasions over the years. And it has been the matriarch's trust in me and tolerance of my presence that has made these close encounters possible.

The family group that regularly visits our sanctuary is led by the largest female Asian elephant I have ever seen. And yet, the most recognizable of the group is another older female who had lost over half of her tail. We have no idea how or when that half was lost, but it makes her easy to spot and distinguish from others. Naturally we call her 'Cut-tail', her presence in her own smaller family group making it easy to distinguish them from others whenever large numbers of elephants happen to be in the sanctuary at one time—something that has happened on a regular basis over the years, especially during the dry season when water and food are scarce in drier forests elsewhere.

Smaller family groups searching for adequate water and food will converge within our sanctuary grounds at these times, the smaller units being parts of the larger extended family gathering. Most of the elephants are related to one another—mothers and aunts, sisters and daughters with young male elephants as well.

Older males stop staying exclusively with their family group once they are in their early teens. For the next several years, they wander between their own and other family herds. They also eventually join groups of other bachelor males, where they test their strength and establish their place in the male hierarchy through mutual sparring. As youngsters, they will seek out older males to learn more about the 'male way of life', older bulls often play-fighting with younger males as well, actually getting down on their knees to spar with the youngster—a wonderful display of empathy and just plain fun on the part of the big bulls.

Males reach full maturity at about the age of thirty, with the onset of 'musth'—the time when bulls can be aggressive due to their bodies being filled with hormones which drive them to seek out females in season, in order to mate. But they visit family herds, especially their own, periodically in any case, and not just during musth. They, like male tigers, are not necessarily the 'loners' we humans mistakenly thought they were.

We do have regular visits from solitary males, but they also join the group visits of Cut-tail's extended family from time to time.

It was during one such convergence that the love and dedication for their family members was dramatically illustrated right below our home.

The elephants had been with us all day spending much of their time down at the river eating bamboo and drinking the fresh cool water. It was my birthday—8 March—which coincided with Holi that year—the festival of colours that celebrates the coming of spring, with Nature displaying her own myriad hues in the blossoms that burst forth in the forest. Even as night fell, the elephants continued to stay on, giving Anil and me the opportunity to enjoy their presence that much longer until we went to sleep around 11 p.m.

It was after midnight when I was awakened by several elephants trumpeting away just below my bedroom window. It was clear that they were very upset about something, but what? I woke up Anil and the two of us went out on to the upstairs balcony to see if we could figure out what was wrong. The full moon was shining brightly overhead in a cloudless sky, illuminating the entire area with its radiant silver light. But to see even better, we switched on the powerful outside search lamps that shine on the grounds below and around the house.

Elephants were everywhere, trumpeting away and clearly very upset. Then we saw what was causing their distraught behaviour. One of the younger elephants had fallen into a pit and could not get out, the pit being part of our septic system.

When building the house, we purposely separated 'grey water' generated from the kitchen and bathing areas from toilet water, the water from the toilet being piped into a series of pits that isolates solid matter from liquids for further decomposition to avoid polluting the surrounding land.

The original system had been further enhanced with two more pits that lay outside our boundary wall. Initially, there was no wall around the house area. But when the aviary was built and the rescued lovebirds became permanent residents, I had to go out every night to cover their sleep cages to insulate them from the cold winter temperatures that are normal during that time of year—low temperatures that the lovebirds would not be able to survive being left uncovered and exposed. On very cold nights, I even put hot water bottles on the bottom of the sleep cages to ensure extra warmth.

As a result of this nightly ritual, I was often walking very close to any elephants that happened to be around the house, without even realizing it. As strange as it may sound, these huge creatures blend in perfectly with their surroundings, especially at night, due to their grey colour. They also walk so quietly that you could come very close to literally bumping into one, if not careful, and/ or could find yourself walking between a mother and her baby—a potentially dangerous situation.

Unlike cattle, who make a lot of noise when they move about, elephants are extraordinarily quiet when walking. Like ballerinas, elephants literally walk on their toes. In addition, the feet of elephants are heavily padded, that same huge ball of fat—the digital cushion that lets them hear subterranean sounds—being the source of that padding. This elastic spongy cushion not only acts as a shock absorber as elephants walk over terrain, it also expands when they walk, muffling the sound of their footsteps, even when walking on branches and leaves.

To avoid the elephants or myself any potential problems caused by an unexpected close encounter, we built a four-foot-high wall around approximately two acres of land, enclosing our house, the aviary, our two greenhouses, vegetable garden and a series of storage rooms. This way, any night-time excursion by me or them would not lead to an unanticipated crossing of paths.

The two pit extensions of the septic system were dug outside this wall a year or so after the wall's completion. Initially, there was no question of an elephant walking over of these pits, since they are very wary about standing on any fresh dirt they may come across. This avoidance of fresh dirt goes back to the historical human practice used to capture elephants, the captured elephants turned into beasts of burden or vehicles for warfare, like horses. A large pit would be dug and then lightly covered over with dirt. An unsuspecting elephant would walk on top of the pit and fall inside, becoming trapped and unable to climb out. Hence, the tell-tale sign of freshly dug dirt was a 'danger signal' for elephants saying, 'Don't walk here!' But as the years rolled by, rainfall and fallen leaves had worked together to cover any sign of fresh dirt and the pits' existence.

There still should have been no problem, even if the elephants had walked on the covers of the pits as they did with other covers, when they had been able to walk right next to our house in the past. But unfortunately, the mason had not properly secured the cement and steel covering for one of the new pits. When the young elephant walked on top of it, the cover gave way under its weight, cracking in two and sending the poor elephant to the bottom of the pit.

This was the cause of all the panic being exhibited by the rest of the elephants and not just close family members. Elephants from every direction converged on the area, some even scaling the four-foot stone wall around the house in order to see what had happened and try to help, some also breaking through the fencing surrounding the vegetable garden.

Others used their incredible might to try and break down the ten-foot-tall double-door heavy steel gate to gain access, bending both sides of the gate in the middle. The gate held but is permanently bent even now—a testimony not only to the physical strength of elephants, but even more to the amazing strength of their family bonds—bonds of love and affection, and their complete dedication and devotion to each other and to their entire family group.

Anil and I watched from above as elephants from every direction converged on our house. One large female came up from the river stood below us and then violently shook one of our hibiscus plants, looking us in the eyes as if to say, 'What have you done to my little sister?'

Looking down at her, I said out loud in English, 'Your family is not here. You need to turn around, cross the river and go to the back of the house to find them and help,' using my hand to point to the direction she needed to go. Instantly, she turned around, crossed the river in front of us and headed to the back of the house, precisely as I had told her. While it is doubtful she understood my English, she clearly understood where I was showing her to go.

Meanwhile, an astonishing demonstration of love, loyalty and intelligence was unfolding. First, one of the elephants picked up half of the cement cover and threw it to the side. Next, the other half which was protruding from the pit was manoeuvred so that it became a slanted ramp coming up to the top of the pit. Then, with interlocking trunks to help pull out the trapped 'sister' amid a cacophony of calls of direction and encouragement, the elephants worked together to pull out their sister from the pit—an almost unbelievable feat of strength, thinking and cooperation fuelled through the power of love.

The entire event lasted about ninety minutes. During the whole time, not one elephant left the scene before their sister had been rescued and freed. By God's grace, she was unharmed and able to walk normally with the rest of her beloved family back into the jungle of our sanctuary home.

Had the elephants not been able to get her out, it is highly questionable whether humans could have succeeded, without her being severely injured or killed, since there was no heavy equipment available in the region at that time to hoist her out, not to mention she would have had to be tranquilized in order to put any kind of harness on her to even attempt it.

Tranquilizing any animal is always a risk, especially one as large as an elephant. Too much tranquilizer and the elephant could easily go into a coma, especially having been under such stress for several hours, as elephants can suffer from PTSD (Post Traumatic Stress Disorder), just like humans. Not enough sedative would mean no human could approach her to put any harness on, as it would be too dangerous to try.

Needless to say, the septic system extension pits have been walled in and the new cover securely installed. We also raised the entire rock boundary wall to five feet since elephants demonstrated that they could still scale it at four feet.

Both Anil and I were concerned that this incident may have broken the faith and trust the elephants had for us. Fortunately, it did not, the entire family group demonstrating their intact faith in us not long thereafter.

## Chorus Line for the Christmas Parade

Anil and I were sitting on our favourite large rocks in the middle of the river one afternoon, meditating and simply soaking in the peace and beauty of the forest all around us when the tell-tale sound of bamboo being broken alerted us to the arrival of the elephants. It was Cut-tail's family, the group numbering at least eight or more individuals including young babies.

We continued sitting on the rocks while the family herd moved closer and closer, spreading out up and down the river's edge, coming within just a few metres of us. They were certainly aware that we were there as we were sitting elevated in the open and therefore were easy to see, not to mention smell since their wonderful trunks give them one of the keenest senses of smell in the animal kingdom. Yet, they were not in the least perturbed by our presence, continuing to enjoy eating the abundant bamboo and river grasses everywhere, occasionally drinking large trunkfuls of water to wash it all down.

We enjoyed their company for almost an hour before the matriarch signalled quite literally that it was time to go. Picking up a piece of bamboo about a metre or so long with her trunk, she proceeded to lift it horizontally above her head, raising it up and down three times. Immediately the others stopped eating. What followed reminded me of old films with scenes of a chorus line moving as one. Turning in absolute unison with the matriarch towards the right, the entire group moved back into the forest, quickly vanishing from sight as if they had melted away. What an amazing scene!

Over the years, we have continued to be privileged to observe the elephants at close quarters, whether below our house at the river or from the two bridges that span it, or while sitting on the boundary wall while they eat the lush greenery all around them. On every occasion, they have accepted our presence near them, never threatening us in any way. But we are also always careful to respect their space, not going too close and being sure to never come between family members, especially a mother and her child.

Christmas of 2013 was particularly wonderful as the entire extended elephant family shared the holiday with us, even giving us a 'Christmas Parade' caught on camera with the newest addition to their family—appropriately enough a very young little boy less than a month old, making his debut on Christmas Day. He was accompanied by his mother and at least fifteen others—aunts, brothers, sisters and cousins and, perhaps, even his father, as a large tusker was also with the group, the entire family staying within the sanctuary for many weeks thereafter.

As mentioned earlier, our sanctuary has become a veritable crèche of life with various animal species coming here to give birth and care for their newborns. The elephants have been no exception. Over the years, we know of the births of at least six elephant calves to have taken place.

Whether born within the sanctuary or not, elephants have brought the youngest of their young here for many years—truly a testimony to how safe and secure they feel. On one occasion, the herd has even left a young adolescent behind in our sanctuary for almost two weeks, the rest of the family disappearing during that time period for whatever reason. During the family's absence, this adolescent female of about six years of age stayed within the sanctuary, moving from one area to another to eat, never straying outside our borders, ultimately reuniting with the rest of the family when they returned.

Another incident again underscores both the intelligence and dedication that elephants have for each other, especially their young. The elephant family regularly crosses the river from time to time and has certain crossing points they particularly like to use. One such crossing is close to one of our bridges, which affords me a great vantage point to observe and film them. At this locale, the banks of the river are not very low. Indeed, the elephants literally slide into the river from one side—the well-worn slide area easy to spot—climbing out on the other.

While sliding into the river may be fun, trying to climb up the steeper bank on the other side certainly isn't for a young calf. So it was on one occasion that a little one just could not reach up high enough with her feet to climb onto the opposite bank, the little girl venting her frustration with high-pitched crying.

Meanwhile, her mother and aunts were becoming increasingly concerned about the situation, trumpeting and calling between themselves to try and figure out what to do. Once again, elephants from all directions converged on the spot to see what the problem was and help out, if they could.

Their solution was quite ingenious. Using their own feet, they carved out 'steps' in the soft clay bank so the little one could have a foothold, the mother helping to lift her up from below, using her head and trunk, while others on top of the bank pulled her upwards using their own trunks for support. The 'rescue' operation took about forty-five minutes, with all the elephants remaining until the little girl was up on dry land, safe and sound by her mother's side.

In May 2021, at this same bridge, Anil and I had one of the most memorable encounters with the elephants we have ever had. Cut-tail and one of her grown daughters had been in the sanctuary continuously for over two months. Anil and I had gone to the elephant pond for a swim, accompanied by our kitty Shanti. Upon our return, I could hear bamboo being crunched, as well as the sound of water moving. As we neared the bridge, we could see Cut-tail's daughter in the river, diving and bobbing up and down in the water, just having a great time. Cut-tail was further upstream on the island, but eventually joined her daughter in the river.

I decided to try and film them, so went to the middle of the bridge and sat down. Cut-tail first saw Anil and Shanti sitting on the riverbank, lifting her trunk to 'test the air' for their scent. Then she saw me on the bridge. Unperturbed, she started swimming downstream towards the bridge, her daughter right behind her. As I quietly filmed them both, Cut-tail swam towards me, testing the air once again to verify that it was really me. She then proceeded to swim directly beneath me under the bridge to the other side, her upraised trunk nearly touching the bridge precisely where I was sitting. Then her daughter followed, swimming right beneath me as well, both of them being close enough to touch me! I could barely believe it!

With the camera still filming, I quickly shifted to the other side as Cut-tail and her daughter continued swimming in the river, occasionally grabbing bamboo along the way, her daughter, in particular, still diving in the river to fully immerse herself in its cool waters.

I cannot fully describe the awe and joy that this experience brought to both Anil and me. At no time did Cut-tail or her daughter exhibit any aggression whatsoever—no rumbling, no trumpeting, no nervous behaviour at all—just an extraordinary display of complete trust, with tangible vibrations of love and affection.

Unfortunately, not all stories have a happy ending. A few years ago, one of the newborn calves did not make it—a little boy who became increasingly weak until he finally died, an autopsy revealing the cause of his death to be natural, as no sign of injuries or poisoning was found. As with human society, the death of a family member in elephant society is a tragic event, especially if the one who has died is young. The grief displayed, especially by the mother, is heart-wrenching, with all members of the family exhibiting signs of stress and grief, often touching the body of the one who has died; the entire group refusing to leave the body of the deceased loved one for days.

The depth of emotion displayed by elephants at the time of death of one of their own clearly shows how similar they really are to us. Both elephants and humans exhibit great excitement and joy at the birth of a child. Both humans and elephants show profound grief at the passing of someone dear, both emotional reactions springing forth from the deep well of love within each heart and soul.

That love is the fount of our being, the language beyond words that links us all together, binds us heart to heart, soul to soul, to each other and to the Divine. It is from the heart of the Mother—Mother Nature—that this divine light of love shines forth to light up creation and beyond. It can be seen, felt and heard whenever we are within her heart, filling us with the joy of being, expressing itself visually in the beauty that surrounds us, calling to us with the breath of the wind, singing in the sky as the birds fly by and resonating as the Soundless Sound within and without us.

## As Evening Falls . . .

Knowing the elephants are very close, Anil and I head back to our house. As we get near, we hear the tell-tale 'snap, crack and pop' of elephants eating bamboo. And here they are—the whole family—below our house once again, and that too with a delightful and heart-warming surprise—not one but two babies! We are thrilled beyond words at witnessing the continued turning of the circle of life!

Settling down on the steps to our river to watch them, we are reminded of how incredibly blessed we are to be here, to be able to be a part of their lives and to share in their joy. As evening falls, we take our leave, the snapping of bamboo continuing into the night.

Going to the flat roof of our home, we await the sunset knowing it will be exceptionally beautiful due to the light cloud cover above. Birds are everywhere, busy eating their last bites before the sun goes down. Bulbuls and jungle mynahs, pigeons and doves, sunbirds and honey creepers, all twittering while flitting to and fro to get last minute titbits to see them through till tomorrow's dawn.

The strange croaking of egrets perched on the tall trees next to our house sounds more like frogs and toads than birds, the flock taking off in waves circling in front of us, before landing in trees upstream, looking like so many Christmas ornaments.

A pair of hornbills laugh to each other as one and then the second fly in their peculiar flap, up-glide, flap, up-glide flight mode, the brilliant white tips on their grey wings and tail glistening in a ray of the setting sun. Meanwhile, a flock of parrots call as they land in the canopy. Our beloved Clover is with them. He has come to view the sunset with us, as he has done so many times before.

As the huge ball of orange starts slipping behind the peaks of the western hills, the clouds begin their colour transformation. Gleaming strips of yellow blend with those of orange, gold and scarlet, some clouds glowing pale pink to lavender, all contrasting with the different hues of the blue sky, its own colours spanning light angel-blue to azure, darkening to navy, deep sapphire, indigo and violet. Reds become crimson and maroon, finally fading to deep greys across the midnight blue sky.

As the sunset colours fade away in the west, replaced by twinkling stars, the full moon slowly rises in the east, casting its lustrous glow below. Thin layers of cloud create rainbow rings encircling it as they pass over its face. The sound of the flowing river adds to the hushed silence filling the air, broken only by the continued snapping of bamboo and the occasional low rumbles of the elephants.

Then, in the distance, a second set of rumbles begins, this brought by the heavy clouds forming in the south-west, the rumbles punctuated sporadically by loud claps of thunder. Continuous flashes illuminate the dark clouds. Bolts of lightning streak across the western sky like the writings of the ancients etched into the heavens. Another rainstorm is coming . . .

It is time to leave this wondrous display of Mother Nature, thanking her for yet another glorious day of beauty, awe and communion within her heart of love.

# Epilogue: Reflections from the Past, Visions of the Future

*'A human being is part of a whole, called by us the "Universe", a part limited in time and space. He experiences himself, his thoughts and feelings, as something separated from the rest—a kind of optical delusion of his consciousness. This delusion is a kind of prison for us, restricting us to our personal desires and to affection for a few persons nearest us. Our task must be to free ourselves from this prison by widening our circles of compassion to embrace all living creatures and the whole of Nature in its beauty.'*

—Albert Einstein

After years of searching, learning and hard work, my dream has finally become Reality—I really do live in a house on top of a hill, overlooking a pond, with a river flowing past, in a wooded valley, surrounded by white-capped mountains, the entire area being full of wildlife.

To transform this dream into reality has taken many, many years—years filled with obstacles and struggles, as well as tremendous joy and fun! Writing this book—my memoirs, as it were—has caused me to reflect deeply on that journey, the memories visited while strolling down 'Memory Lane' being seen through the lens of 'Time'.

While Time may dim the recollections of some things, it can bring others into focus, helping one see certain events, people and places in sharper relief, against the backdrop of an entire lifetime. The 'distance' that time brings can help objectivity as well, viewing things not as a current participant, caught up in the emotions and thoughts of the moment, but as a hopefully more objective observer or witness to the event.

It has helped me to stand back and see the common threads that have run through my life from childhood to the present. Looking back, I can say without a doubt that I am very grateful I was born when and where I was. It was a time when children were still allowed to be 'children', when 'innocence' was still very much alive, living in a place where playing outside in the woods was the norm, not the exception.

I was extremely fortunate and blessed to be born into a family with two responsible and caring parents who loved me and my siblings, and each other, to the end. Having a 'wild bunch' of brothers and sisters to play with was, and remains, yet another blessing—all five of us still living and able to depend on each other for love, help and support when needed.

I am thankful that Love and Faith in God were instilled in me at a very early age by my mom and dad. The presence, throughout my childhood and adolescence, of a compassionate minister— Father Best, a true man of God—reinforced that faith and love, while helping me to connect the dots linking Nature and God at such an early age.

My mom's own love of animals and forests, the river and the sea, planted the seeds of that same love for Nature in me. Her encouragement to follow my own heart and to believe in my dreams helped me to make those dreams come true.

My mother's Native American ancestry has been a very special gift. Their culture, sustainable lifestyle and beliefs have been an inspiration for me in all facets of my life. Their wisdom of living within the limits that Nature can provide, their respect for all living creatures and recognition that every aspect of Creation is part of their 'family', all born from the same Mother, all gifted with special talents and attributes, each with its own important and unique role to play in the Mother's Drama of Life, helping to keep the Balance of Nature that ensures the continuation of 'life' on Mother Earth—all are echoed by India's ancient Vedantic philosophy as well.

Both stress the responsibility humanity has to protect and preserve the Earth for future generations, pointing out the ephemeral, transitory nature of individual life in manifest form, reminding us that it is the soul within each form that is eternal, the Spirit that animates 'life', the 'Screen' upon which the Drama of Life is projected, which alone remains when the projected images cease to be.

As Lord Krishna puts it so simply in the Bhagavad Gita (excerpts from 2:18 to 2:23 and 2:28):

> Only the material form assumed by the Soul,
> Which is fathomless and eternal, comes to an end . . .
>
> One is never born nor dies at any time
> Nor once he comes to be, ever cease to be.
> The Soul is unborn, immutable, eternal, ageless . . .
>
> Even as a man discards his worn-out robe
> For a new one, so a worn-out body is
> Left by the Soul for a new one after death . . .

One is unmanifest at the beginning,
Manifest in the middle and becomes
Unmanifest in the end once more. So what
Is there so tragic about this law of life?

However, while on Earth, we have a duty, a responsibility to care for Mother Earth, for the benefit of generations to come. As mentioned before, this is the principle of the Seventh Generation—the recognition that each decision we make and each action we take impacts not only the present but the future as well. Hence, we must keep that Seventh Generation in our minds, when deciding what should and should not be done right now.

We must live with the consciousness that we are 'borrowing' the Earth from future generations of all species on the planet, including our children's children's children, and we therefore have the duty to give it to them in at least the same, if not better, condition that our parents gave the Earth to us.

This must become humanity's living creed, our mission on Earth, for the sake of the yet unborn generations of the future, and for the spiritual growth of our own souls. For, each selfless action we take, each sacrifice we make for others, helps erase our own karmic debts, raising the spiritual vibration of our entire being. With each uptick in vibration, we come closer and closer to full Realization and Conscious Mergence with the Divine, in the ecstatic bliss of God-Love.

## Twin Souls, One Goal

Recently, someone wrote that Anil and I are 'twin flames' or 'twin souls', here on Earth to unite in accomplishing a particular mission—originally one soul that has become two, like a single cell dividing to become two cells. Driven by their spiritual ideal to give back to the world from the abundance and grace they have received, twin souls unite to make a positive difference for the Earth and all her children.

Other indications of twin soul incarnation include the two souls being born a great physical distance apart from each other, eventually meeting, as if drawn one to the other. Their relationship is often quite difficult, working together harmoniously being a challenge.

However, for the greater good of their soul, and in order to accomplish the mission they are so intent on completing, cooperation replaces competition, their cooperative efforts enhancing and accelerating their spiritual evolution, effacing the ego that is keeping them apart from each other, and from the Divine. Finally, surrendering in love, the two souls come together to merge in unity with the Divine.

Clearly certain aspects of our life together coincide with the distinctive signs of 'twin souls', including the last mentioned. For, many of my most blissful and extraordinary spiritual experiences have come through surrender and soul-mergence with Anil, including glimpses of the Goal—Union with the Divine.

This is not the first time I have heard of this concept. It was actually Swami M (Swami Maheshwarananda) who first mentioned it back in the early 1990s, stating that twin souls or flames are like mirrors for one another, helping each to see where he or she can improve spiritually, as well as balancing each other's energy. Thereby, they achieve the ultimate goal of Conscious Union with the Divine, this ultimate goal facilitated through the merging of the two souls in Unified Oneness with one another—a process that can take several lifetimes to achieve.

The concept is part of many cultures and faiths. One example from the West is the assertion made by renowned American psychic Edgar Cayce, who stated that Jesus Christ and his Mother Mary were 'twin souls'.

In Hinduism, this concept is symbolized by the composite androgynous form of Shiva with his consort Parvati, known as

Ardhanarishvara—one body containing the masculine form of Shiva on the right side representing 'Spirit', and the feminine form of Parvati on the left representing 'Nature'. It illustrates that they are inseparable, the fusion of these two being the root and base of Creation, as all of Creation is born from this union of Nature and Spirit.

It also signifies the equality of both forms. The feminine is equal to the masculine in every way, the two uniting in the crown chakra to initiate spiritual enlightenment, represented on the forehead by the presence of the single 'Third Eye of Wisdom' shared by both. This equal balance between the feminine and masculine is essential for each individual as well—balancing intellect, logic and reason (masculine) with intuition, nurturing and feeling (feminine).

Perhaps it is no coincidence that our sanctuary grounds are filled with trees associated with this form of Divinity—the Rudraksha. The seeds of this tree are said to be a link from Earth to Heaven, its name meaning 'Eye of Rudra', 'Rudra' being another name for Lord Shiva. Thus, its seeds are used for prayer beads.*

When relaying his information about twin souls, Swami M was unaware of the Suka Nadi reading we had had several years earlier, in 1986, when we first arrived in India. These readings are based on the ancient writings of certain gifted sages who could see

---

* The fruit of our Rudraksha trees are relished treats for huge bats—the flying fox—who devour them in great quantities, dropping the seeds everywhere, the flying fox being a principal pollinator and propagator for this and many other native trees. These giant fruit bats search for food using keen eyesight, as well as a rudimentary but unique form of echolocation/sonar not witnessed in any other animal to navigate through the dark nights. Rather than using their vocal cords to send out sounds to find their way, they use wing 'clicks' to steer in the dark, bats being the only mammal with the gift of true flight. Other mammals, like 'flying squirrels', only glide from tree to tree, but bats have evolved actual wings like birds—truly amazing creatures of Nature in so many ways.

the past, present and future of various individual souls incarnating on the Earth, their prophetic visions being recorded on palm leaves and the bark of trees.

According to our reading, Anil and I have been together for three lifetimes: the first in China, where Anil was my spiritual preceptor and I, his student; the second in south India, where again Anil was my spiritual guru, but I was both his student and wife; and the present lifetime.

Some years after Swami M mentioned this concept of twin souls to us, we hosted another sage named Swami Sai Charan here at our sanctuary for several months while he did various spiritual cleansings and purification ceremonies. During his stay, he relayed to us some of the apparitional visitations he received from the Mother, he himself being a devotee of the feminine aspect of the Godhead.

In one such visitation, the Mother told him that he, Anil, and I had lived a previous life in contact with one another—he as a monk, and we as husband and wife. Anil and I had been living near Mysuru (Mysore), where we too worshipped the feminine form of the Divine, and the Mother directed us to this very land in Kodagu, where the sanctuary stands today, to continue our spiritual sadhana/practices with his help and guidance.

Our help to him in the present lifetime was a repayment of the karmic debt we owed him for his help then. Swami Sai Charan had no knowledge of our Suka Nadi reading almost fifteen years earlier, so the mention of our previous life in Mysuru (Mysore) in southern India is quite amazing.

True or not, I do indeed believe in both Karma and Reincarnation. In India, it is often said that the only thing we take with us into the afterlife is our karmic balance sheet of the good and wrong acts we have done in our present life, with those acts extending to our thoughts and words, as well as actions or deeds.

Each incarnation on Earth is another lifetime chance for Realization and Conscious Union with the Divine by working off karmic debts we owe to other souls, either because they have helped us in past lives or because we have wronged them in another lifetime. This is why it makes sense to me that we meet certain souls repeatedly during the course of different lifetimes, even though the relationship between the souls may change from lifetime to lifetime.

Regardless of who we or they were in our past lives, the important thing is to concentrate on our present, and to deal with everyone who crosses our path with integrity, compassion and love, helping each in whatever ways we can. Doing so brings us a deep sense of self-satisfaction, but also helps to shift the balance sheet in our favour, bringing us that much closer to Spiritual Liberation.

## A Sacred Perspective

The one other thing that can tip those scales, cushioning, mitigating or even wiping out negative karmic debt, is Divine Grace. But to be eligible for that Grace requires sincere regret for the past errors, coupled with acts of selfless service—acts of service done not for name or fame, but solely for benefiting others, especially those in the greatest need.

I would count wildlife and our forests as a whole, in that category. Our forests and wildlife nationally and across the planet are in dire straits, being under constant, unrelenting assault by humanity, which has forgotten that we cannot survive if the environment is destroyed. This unquenchable greed, causing destruction on a global scale, is robbing future generations, and many living today, of the ecosystem services needed for survival.

Herein lies the crux of the problem—perspective. The problem of perspective is very evident when comparing Western development versus sustainable living practices of Native

Americans and indigenous people in general globally. As the great Native American Chief Oren Lyons has summed up so perfectly, 'What you call "natural resources" our people call our relatives.'

That's it! If we perceive wildlife as an extension of our own family, we cannot inflict the cruelty upon them that we do. We cannot blame them for simply trying to survive. On the contrary, we would treat them with kindness and understanding, helping to insure they have the adequate natural space they need to continue to live and play their role in maintaining Nature's balance.

Even from the perspective of self-interest, our future existence is intertwined with the future existence of our forests. For, what we exhale ($CO_2$, carbon dioxide), trees inhale, and what trees exhale ($O_2$, oxygen) we inhale.

Can we not see the perfection and wisdom with which Creation has been designed, has evolved over millennia? Can we not see that we are also part of Creation's family? Can we not see how sacred our Mother Earth truly is—that 'pale blue dot', as Carl Sagan called her, floating in the great cosmic sea of space.

And yet, Earth is the chosen place where life has evolved into a coherent combination of interconnected elements that, when left untouched and undisturbed by humanity's destructive interference, retain their perfect balance according to Nature's Laws, ever evolving and changing, and yet promoting the principle of Life at all times.

As the great spiritual master Sri Aurobindo states in his epic poem 'Savitri':

The cosmos is no accident in Time . . .
This world is not built with random bricks of chance,
A blind god is not destiny's architect;
A conscious power has drawn the plan of Life;
There is meaning in each curve and line.

Decades before James Lovelock promoted his Gaia theory, Sri Aurobindo wrote to Dilip Kumar Roy (Dadaji) saying that the Earth is indeed a conscious being. Again, as he put it in 'Savitri':

> Earth is the chosen place of mightiest souls,
> Earth is the heroic spirit's battleground,
> The forge where the Arch-mason shapes his works.
> All Earth shall be the Spirit's manifest home,
> Hidden no more by the mind's ignorance . . .

The sacred nature of Mother Earth, and of all beings on Earth, was underscored by the visitation of the Divine to Native Americans as the White Buffalo Cow Woman. It was She who gave them the sacred peace pipe—the symbol of their connection to the Earth and to all living beings, as all Creation 'breathes' together in this vast Circle of Life, protected and supported by the Great Spirit. She said,

> Remember that the Earth is your Mother and Grandmother.
> Every step you take upon her must be as a prayer.

The name of our sanctuary is SAI Sanctuary. SAI is an acronym for Save Animals Initiative. But the roots of the term 'SAI' show a deeper meaning—'Sa' means 'Universal Divine' and 'Ai' means 'Mother'. Hence, the sanctuary is dedicated to the Universal Divine Mother—Mother Nature.

Its second name is Butterfly Haven, not only due to the countless butterflies found here but also as a symbolic reference to the transformation of consciousness from material bondage to spiritual freedom—the soul flying on the wings of Spirit into the Higher Realms of Being, after its metamorphic change in the chrysalis of the body, conscious at last of the Divine both within and without through the Secret Door of Nature.

## Seeing All with an Equal Eye

When we first came here, most people thought we were crazy, putting money into what they thought was 'useless' land, with no expectation of financial returns. Some were downright hostile since our presence here meant curtailment of the illegal activities that were looting the forests of their natural wealth, the curse of the timber mafia and wild bush meat trade being rampant in the Brahmagiri and surrounding Reserve Forests.

Since the border to Kerala is only four to five kilometres away when travelling through the jungle, 'cut, kill and carry' was the reality at that time, denuding the forests of sandalwood, rosewood and other hardwoods, while trading in the meat and body parts of numerous wildlife species, decimating their numbers, with valuable timber species disappearing completely as well.

From Day One of our arrival, we worked in every way we could to stop this, thereby causing a great deal of resentment among those whose illegal income was being affected. This has translated into a number of problems over the years. Once, I was severely assaulted by a group of men who were poaching and polluting the river at the border of our sanctuary.

There is no question that discrimination has played a part in these and other unpleasant encounters, including lies and slander spread about us. Discrimination is ugly. It reveals the darkness covering the soul, the smallness of the heart and pettiness of the minds of those who discriminate against others on any basis—race, religion, gender, sexual orientation, national origin or any other irrelevant and extraneous excuses.

These experiences have helped me to further understand and appreciate what my maternal ancestors suffered, as well as empathize with black African Americans and other groups who have been the target of discrimination and continue to experience this in the USA and elsewhere.

In India, there is a saying about this: 'All cows, no matter their colour, give the same milk.' Similarly, all human beings, no matter their faith, race, disabilities, gender, etc., are members of the same family of humanity. Indeed, we are all part of Creation's family, all children of the same Mother, as those who realize the divinity underlying and within all, see. As Lord Krishna put it (Gita, 5:18–19),

> The sage views all with an equal eye, a learned
> And humble Brahmin (priest), a dog,
> A cow, an 'outsider,' or an elephant.
> God who is flawless is the same in all.

Therefore, it is our duty to continue fighting evil and protecting the innocent, especially those who cannot protect themselves. Hence, warriors for Mother Earth must balance their forgiveness and understanding of humans with their commitment and compassion for the denizens of what is left of Nature's wild places.

The present condition of Earth is encapsulated in the following three equations:

- IPAT: The *Impact* of humanity on the environment is equal to human *Population* plus its *Affluence* plus *Technology*

Humanity's massive impact on the Earth today is the result of human avarice, magnified exponentially by human overpopulation, and our misuse of technology, from bulldozers to bombs.

The second equation points out the link between trees and water:

- No trees = no forests; no forests = no rainfall; no rainfall = no water; no water = no life

The presence of liquid water on this planet was the defining element for 'life' to take root here, for complex-celled creatures to evolve here, for biodiversity to bloom here. Without our forests, life as we know it would not be possible, since they are the 'arks' that create, hold and carry water across the globe.

The third equation explains the link between trees and climate change:

- No trees = no photosynthesis = no carbon sequestration = higher temperatures = Hot House Earth = loss of species and complete catastrophic collapse of the biosphere of Earth = ELE (Extinction Level Event)

Sri Aurobindo's *Savitri* summarizes things well:

> An idiot hour destroys what centuries made . . .
> He calls heaven's retribution on his head,
> A growing register of calamities
> Is the past's account, the future's book of Fate:
> The centuries pile man's follies and man's crimes
> Upon the countless crowd of Nature's ills;
> He walks by his own choice into Hell's trap;
> This mortal creature is his own worst foe.

In January 1986, right after we arrived in India, I saw a large billboard on a road. It was a drawing of a man balanced on the limb of a tree, sawing the trunk of the tree *below* the limb he was on. A bird sitting behind him was 'tweeting', 'Oh, you foolish human! If you cut the tree, you will kill yourself!'

It really is that simple: cut the forests, we destroy ourselves; protect, preserve and expand the forests, and we help ourselves in every area, including climate change. As scientific studies have illustrated, tropical forests in particular can provide one-quarter of the efforts needed for climate mitigation.

While scientific research can provide the facts and figures about the state of the planet and the dangerous future we face, it cannot change hearts and minds. Only spiritual power can do that. Mankind needs to quite literally repent—go in the opposite direction to that where we are currently headed. After all, humanity was meant to be the Earth's steward, her caretaker—not her undertaker!

This is why it is essential for all religious and spiritual leaders of every faith, across the Earth, to come together, to help bring about this repentance; to awaken the conscience and consciousness of their followers; to teach, preach and practise the Divine Tenet of the Sacredness of the Earth, and all life upon Her; to start that spiritual revolution that is fundamentally crucial, if we are to survive, and some of them are doing precisely that, thank God!

As the Vietnamese Buddhist monk Thich Nhat Hanh has said, 'We need a Revolution: It starts with falling in love with the Earth.' And as the Dalai Lama put it, 'People must go back to Nature, back to sunshine!'

The appropriately named Pope Francis writes very clearly that it is humanity that has caused the disasters we face today, as we continue to destroy Nature. In his encyclical *On Care of Our Common Home*, he writes, 'Because of us, thousands of species will no longer give glory to God by their very existence, nor convey their message to us. We have no right.'

The Interfaith Rainforest Initiative (IRI) is yet another example where religious leaders from different faiths, cultures and countries are stepping up to the moral, ethical and spiritual imperative to ACT NOW in Unity to save the Earth. Joining hands to preserve what is left of the planet's rainforests, Christian, Muslim, Jewish, Buddhist, Hindu and Taoist religious leaders are working with indigenous peoples to protect and preserve the forests, while holding government officials and politicians accountable to the people for the state of the Earth.

The IRI's 'Faiths for Forests Declaration' states:

Tropical deforestation is a crisis of existential proportions . . .
We either deal with it or leave future generations a planet in
ecological collapse.

Almost 1000 religious leaders have endorsed the declaration,
pledging to preach and promote a change of heart and conscience,
for the sake of conserving God's Creation—the most sacred goal
humanity can have at this critical juncture of Time.

As Native American Chief Oren Lyons explains: 'We've got
to get back to Spiritual Law, if we are to survive.'

Their efforts to raise the consciousness of humanity, by
awakening the recognition of the sacredness and sanctity of Mother
Nature, instilling respect, reverence and love for our Mother, give
me hope for the future. So does the growing global movement of
conscious children.

## The Mirrors of Our Eyes

Whether it's business or the corporate sector or government
officials, all of us need to change. Otherwise, how can we look into
the eyes of our children and not feel guilty? How do we look into
the eyes of Earth's other species—our relatives—without guilt?
One of the most poignant encounters I have ever had was with
the matriarch of the elephant family here. It was not long after
the little baby boy had died, so the whole family was still grieving.
Her older ten-year-old daughter had gone to the river to drink,
walking by the wall where I was sitting, on her return. A brief
moment of concern was quickly replaced by recognition and trust
as she passed by me.

Then her mother emerged from the forest of bamboo. Seeing
me, she stopped, bending the bamboo down in front of her with

her trunk to have a clearer view, looking directly into my eyes. In that moment, all the pain and grief she had felt for the loss of her son washed over me, followed by a deep feeling of calm surrender and acceptance, coupled with trust and love, touched with hope. It was a sharing of souls and hearts, an extraordinary experience of conscious Oneness as time stood still.

Then, with a subtle nod of her head, she continued walking towards me, eating bamboo along the way, only turning to leave when she was just a few feet away, disappearing behind the bamboo screen, to join the rest of her family. The precious memory of that moment remains so vivid in my mind, heart and soul. What an honour to be trusted so much! What a privilege to have shared such an intimate moment with her!

But I was curious about her nod. Was she conveying something to me that would explain the transformation of feelings from grief, to love and hope? Indeed, she was, as time would reveal. She was pregnant again, as was one of her daughters, bringing new hope and joy to the family, and to me.

It is magical moments like these—mystical, enchanted, transcendental moments like this—that are the cherished memories I will carry with me for the rest of my life—touching the heart of another being, gazing into their eyes to see their soul revealed. For, the eyes truly are the windows of the soul.

Our mission has always been to protect and preserve Mother Nature throughout the world. The goal of this book is to help spread more awareness and inspire others to return to Nature, to protect and preserve Mother Earth, and to live by the Spiritual Law of Balance, based on Love, Gratitude, Humility, Sharing and Caring, so that we can look into the eyes of the children of all species without guilt, knowing we have done all we could to pass on a 'Living Legacy' to them—an Earth alive and thriving, throbbing with the pulse of 'Life' everywhere, with abundant clean waterways, unpolluted living oceans, skies of blue, free of dirty brown clouds, fertile soils capable of producing more than adequate food for humanity, while leaving the rest of the planet 'WILD' for the millions of other species with whom we share our H-OM-E.

It has been over two years since the original manuscript of this book was completed. So much has happened during these years, with new challenges and changes, while so much has, unfortunately, stayed the same. Personally, I had to go through another operation to remove two cancerous lymph nodes from under my arm. Follow-up therapy for me now is taking medicines from a Tibetan Buddhist doctor—the medicines are made from healing plants found in the Himalayas—instead of doing radiation or hormone therapy as I did after the first surgery. With the cancer resurfacing in less than two years, I thought it best to turn to Mother Nature for help physically, and also to develop a deeper communion with the Divine to calm my mind and uplift my spirit.

However, far more devastating than the cancer has been the sudden and completely unexpected loss of my beloved husband and partner in life, Anil. He had no physical complaints and showed no signs of any illness. Indeed, just a few days before his passing we had walked throughout the sanctuary together. The day before his departure, he spent hours discussing various environmental issues with a visiting film crew, expressing eloquently his deep love and concern for Mother Nature.

That fateful morning of 22 November 2021, he rose early from sleep, did his prayers and meditation, bathed and dressed in clean clothes, and did his 'aarti', offering a small lit candle to the Divine, fully immersed in humility and devotion. He then lay in a prone position on his bed to continue doing 'japa' (repetition of the Lord's Name) which was part of his regular worship practices. He passed away with God's Name on his lips from a sudden heart attack, his soul leaving the chrysalis of his body to rise into the Heavenly Regions of the true lovers of the Almighty, not to be brought back into his body again, in spite of all efforts performed. He is now in bliss in the heart of God. I look forward to the day in the not-so-distant-future when I may join him in that bliss, peace and love within God's Heart.

None of us knows when the last grain of sand will fall through the hourglass of our life, but that moment is certain to come to us all. Hence, we must prepare ourselves by seeking a closer communion with our Creator and doing all we can to preserve and protect His outer form as Mother Nature.

## Visions of the Future

Of the countless mails I receive, the ones that touch me the most are those sent by members of the younger generations asking for help and guidance, telling me their fears and real concerns for the future, since they are the ones who will be most affected by the inaction of the older generations. Often, they share with me their own hopes and dreams of creating a sanctuary like ours wherever they live.

This has always been one of our own greatest hopes—that our sanctuary would help inspire others to take up the cause, the quest to defend Mother Nature, and to help her other species by preserving, protecting and creating the forests and ecosystems needed by them to survive; that others would be inspired enough to replicate what we have done here, across the country and around the world.

For, I have another dream, and in that dream I see private sanctuaries linking government forest together to recreate the biological corridors needed for great migratory animals to use. I see these corridors acting as 'green highways' for the monsoon rains to follow, so they may shower the blessing of their life-giving moisture across the country.

I see the transformation of agriculture, from deadly chemicals to organically alive, from monocropped 'deserts' to havens of life, with many different crops growing together, all bordered by these corridors of great native trees providing the crops with the proper balance of sun and shade, moisture and nutrients, as well as the pollinators necessary for the crops to thrive.

I see the great waterways finally released from the massive dams that have unnaturally hemmed them in, flowing freely once again, their waters filled with life, their banks green with the diverse grasses, bushes and trees that help keep them 'alive' and flowing.

I see these green biological corridors of life connecting to go beyond manmade borders of states and nations, these corridors and the expansion of Peace Parks helping to end hostilities between neighbours, sowing the seeds of cooperation and harmony between peoples, and the nations of the Earth.

I see the resurrection of Life on the planet, a reversal of the extinctions taking place, species after species being helped to recover, helped to return to where they belong—in the forests, rivers, lakes and seas now cleansed of man's pollution, where they may once again play their role in this great Drama of Life, helping to keep Nature's Balance, so all of Earth may be the beautiful Paradise of Peace and Plenty the Creator gave to us so many generations ago.

I call upon all who read these words to heed this Clarion Call, to step up and be counted among the 'Healers' of the Earth, among the Warriors for Nature, among the Guardians of our Mother. Each one of us must do whatever we can to turn this dream into reality. Whether as individuals or families, groups of friends or communities, schools and colleges, or businesses and government agencies, along with NGOs and Trusts—all of us must work together NOW to start this transformation of the Earth, so that it becomes the living, breathing, exquisite Home she once was—our sacred Mother of Life.

And it all starts with the transformation of ourselves. We must stand before a mirror, look ourselves in the eyes and ask, 'Am I doing enough? Am I helping to ensure a bountiful future for my children and their children by helping Nature and her children today? Can I really look into the eyes of my children, my grandchildren and into the eyes of the "children" of other species as well and say, "Yes – I am doing my best?"'

If the answer is 'no', then there is no better time than the present to start.

Come! Join us in the revival of the Earth, the rewilding of Nature and the restoration of our Soul. Anil and I will be with each and every one of you in Spirit, asking for God's blessings and guidance for us all.

## The New Day . . .

Dusk has come. The sun has set. I look out on to the sanctuary's canopy as the egrets fly by, their white wings illuminated by a last hint of daylight. As they head north, they cross paths with huge bats flying south—the giant flying fox, coming to the sanctuary to feast on the ripe fruit of the Rudraksha trees.

Hundreds of bats, wave upon wave, fly by. Suddenly, a single bat and single egret break off from the rest of their group and begin circling each other, like two dancing ballerinas pirouetting in the sky. Round and round they circle together, keeping perfect distance from each other, two species using two different senses to 'see'—the graceful egret using sight, the agile bat using both sight and sound—as the skies continue to darken.

Their movements remind me of the Taoist symbol for balance—the yin–yang, dark and light, night and day—complementary opposites whose interaction gives rise to 'life'.

After several revolutions, they each return to their family groups in flight—two beings that evolved to fly, and yet so different in other ways.

A change of Nature's guard is taking place. The high-pitched cry of the critically endangered slender loris fills the air; the call of the tiny nocturnal primate is like that of the town crier of old, announcing the end of day and beginning of night— 'Eeeeeeeeeeeeeeee!'

A cool, brisk breeze blows from the south-west, bringing dark clouds with it that hug the green peaks of the Brahmagiri Hills in an ethereal embrace. Light mists move quickly across their face, wisps of grey curls rising into the sky. All is silent . . . all is calm . . .

The overwhelming beauty moves me to tears . . . and to prayer . . . How long will these hills remain green? How long will these skies be the stage for aerial ballets? How long will it take for us to be the children of the Divine that we are meant to be?

Yet, despite all that has passed, all the destruction that has taken place and continues to rage on, I must believe that life on this blue-and-white pearl will survive. For love is stronger than evil. Somehow, in some way, it will prevail. For there is nothing more powerful, nothing more healing than Love.

I awake the next morning in a state of love-filled peaceful bliss—the result of a lucid visionary dream of the Divine Mother. Standing like a Living Flame in the heavens, Her entire being luminous in golden light, Her exquisite brilliance emanates a golden aura everywhere, as She radiates compassion, peace and love. With Her open arms, She beckons my soul to mergence. 'Immaculate, immaculate . . .' the only words I receive.

Dawn has come with the Promise of a New Day . . .

# Acknowledgements

This book would not have been possible without the love, help and support of several people. First and foremost, my love and thanks to my husband, Anil—it is due to his love and perseverance that my dream of SAI Sanctuary became a reality at all. His encouragement and help with the details were a tremendous aid while writing this book.

My love and gratitude to my family and especially to the other 'four Ps in the pod'—Peter Gale, Patty Bryer, Pris Gettis and Paul Gale—along with my cousins Robert and Hunter McKee, for their help with childhood memories. Special thanks to my sister Patty, the 'family historian', for all the time she spent digging up diaries, letters, newspaper clippings and other pieces of family history, especially about the McKees; and to Lynn Gale, for her help with the Gales. Thanks also to Anil's relatives Bim Bissell and Arun Nanda, who helped with information about Anil's family.

My special thanks and love also to Karen Esposito, Tara Chander, Catherine Dammeyer Lehman and Bruce Cook, for their valuable feedback and encouragement throughout the writing of this book.

Finally, my gratitude to my publishers, Penguin Random House India, and especially to their publisher, Indian languages, Vaishali Mathur, who asked me to write this book, and whose patience, support and understanding have transformed my thoughts and reflections into the pages of this book.

# Bibliography, Notes and References

## Introduction: My Childhood Dream

1. https://www.un.org/sustainabledevelopment/blog/2019/05/nature-decline-unprecedented-report/
2. https://now.tufts.edu/articles/extinction-crisis
3. https://www.worldwildlife.org/threats/deforestation-and-forest-degradation
4. https://ypte.org.uk/factsheets/rainforests/what-are-the-threats-to-the-rainforests
5. https://www.theguardian.com/global-development-professionals-network/2017/jan/23/destroying-rainforests-quickly-gone-100-years-deforestation
6. https://www.theguardian.com/environment/2019/sep/12/deforestation-world-losing-area-forest-size-of-uk-each-year-report-finds
7. https://www.conservation.org/blog/nature-now%E2%80%99-in-new-film-climate-heavyweights-make-plea-for-the-planet
8. https://www.conservation.org/video/nature-now-video-with-greta-thunberg
9. https://www.nationalgeographic.com/science/article/why-climate-change-is-still-the-greatest-threat-to-human-health
10. https://www.nationalgeographic.com/environment/article/heat-related-deaths-attributed-to-climate-change

11. https://www.nature.com/articles/s41558-021-01058-x
12. https://www.firstpost.com/tech/science/end-of-humanity-begins-in-2050-most-climate-change-models-too-conservative-report-6768451.html
13. https://edition.cnn.com/2019/06/04/health/climate-change-existential-threat-report-intl/index.html
14. https://www-vox-com.cdn.ampproject.org/c/s/www.vox.com/platform/amp/future-perfect/22643358/social-cost-of-carbon-mortality-biden-discounting?fbclid=IwAR3LQRX00K5GZFfUsAh7xhrsdSvsfQIZuUrFH1G4qPxhO7x9T33BXhYcrJc
15. https://www.nature.com/articles/s41467-021-24487-w

## Part I: The Seeds Are Sown
## Chapter One: Childhoods in Nature

1. 'The Peace of Wild Things', Wendell Berry, Penguin Publishing, 2018.
2. Quotes by Wangari Maathai are from a live interview on Indian national TV channel in early 2006, when Maathai came to India to receive the Indira Gandhi Prize for Peace, Disarmament and Development.
3. https://www.defense.gov/Explore/News/Article/Article/603440/
4. https://www.youtube.com/watch?v=dA0qGlnc-30
5. https://www.youtube.com/watch?v=psynAbgdA5o
6. https://theowp.org/one-billion-climate-refugees-by-2050/
7. https://reliefweb.int/report/world/climate-migrants-might-reach-one-billion-2050
8. 'The Bonhoeffer Legacy', *Australasian Journal of Bonhoeffer Studies*, volume 2, ATF Press, 2013.

## Chapter Two: Deep Roots

1. Information on Native Americans, the Osage tribe and Buck McKee's connection with Will Rogers comes from family diaries, letters, family documents, photos and Grandpa Leo McKee's stories. Confirmations can be found in *The Collected Writings of Will Rogers*, with copies of some actual letters between Buck McKee and his second wife available at the California State Library. 'Guide to the Buck McKee Letters, 1906–1909', http://www.library.ca.gov/

2.  'Guide to the Buck McKee Letters', 1906–1909 (cdlib.org).
3.  https://www.westernhorseman.com/article/flashbacks/2845-flashback-will-rogers-and-his-horses?start=3
4.  https://www.democracyandme.org/learning-from-history-pandemics-are-nothing-new-in-native-communities/
5.  http://nativeamericannetroots.net/diary/252
6.  https://www.nationalgeographic.com/news/2011/12/111205-native-americans-europeans-population-dna-genetics-science/
7.  https://www.cairn.info/revue-annales-de-demographie-historique-2005-2-page-17.htm#
8.  https://www.historynet.com/smallpox-in-the-blankets.htm#:~:text=Smallpox%20had%20broken%20out%20among,militia%20wrote%20in%20his%20journal
9.  https://web.stanford.edu/dept/HPS/MayorSmallpox.pdf
10. https://www.history.com/news/colonists-native-americans-smallpox-blankets
11. https://hsp.org/sites/default/files/legacy_files/migrated/excerptsfromwilliamtrent.pdf
12. https://academic.udayton.edu/health/syllabi/Bioterrorism/00intro02.htm
13. https://www.straightdope.com/columns/read/1088/did-whites-ever-give-native-americans-blankets-infected-with-smallpox/
14. https://www.pri.org/stories/2019-01-31/european-colonization-americas-killed-10-percent-world-population-and-caused
15. https://www.britannica.com/topic/Native-American/Native-American-history
16. https://www.businessinsider.in/science/european-colonizers-killed-so-many-indigenous-americans-that-the-planet-cooled-down-a-new-study-reveals/articleshow/67917478.cms
17. http://www.tahtonka.com/apology.html
18. https://www.pbs.org/buffalowar/buffalo.html; additional quote from same article: 'By the middle of the 19th century, even train passengers were shooting bison for sport. "Buffalo" Bill Cody, who was hired to kill bison, slaughtered more than 4,000 bison in two years. To make matters worse for wild buffalo, some U.S. government officials actively destroyed bison to defeat their Native American enemies who resisted the takeover of their lands by white settlers. American military commanders ordered troops to kill buffalo to deny Native Americans an important source of

food.' PBS is the US Public Broadcasting Society and is a highly respected source.

19. https://www.theatlantic.com/national/archive/2016/05/the-buffalo-killers/482349/

20. Esther Wagner Stearn and Allen Edsin Stearn, *Effect of Smallpox on the Destiny of the* Amerindian, University of Minnesota; 1945, pp. 13–20, 73–94, 97.

21. https://indiancountrytoday.com/archive/scalping-in-america

22. http://www.danielnpaul.com/BritishScalpProclamation-1756.html

23. https://revolutionaryfrontlines.wordpress.com/2010/03/26/native-blood-the-myth-of-thanksgiving/

24. https://academic.oup.com/ahr/article/120/1/98/47185?login=true

25. https://www.pbs.org/kenburns/the-west/

26. On scalping: https://en.wikipedia.org/wiki/Scalping. 'The scalper firmly grasped the hair of a subdued adversary, made several quick semi-circular cuts with a sharp instrument on either side of the area to be taken, and then vigorously yanked at the nearly-severed scalp. The scalp separated from the skull along the plane of the areolar connective tissue, the fourth (and least substantial) of the five layers of the human scalp. Scalping was not in itself fatal, though it was most commonly inflicted on the gravely wounded or the dead . . . The Connecticut and Massachusetts colonies offered bounties for the heads of killed hostile Indians, and later for just their scalps . . . During the French and Indian War, as of June 12, 1755, Massachusetts governor William Shirley was offering a bounty of £40 for a male Indian scalp, and £20 for scalps of females or of children under 12 years old. In 1756, Pennsylvania Lieutenant Governor Robert Morris, in his Declaration of War against the Lenni Lenape (Delaware) people, offered "130 Pieces of Eight, for the Scalp of Every Male Indian Enemy, above the Age of Twelve Years," and "50 Pieces of Eight for the Scalp of Every Indian Woman, produced as evidence of their being killed." It was a "uniquely American" innovation that the use of scalp bounties in the wars against indigenous societies "became an indiscriminate killing process that deliberately targeted Indian non-combatants (including women, children, and infants), as well as warriors."'

27. https://indiancountrytoday.com/archive/indian-killer-andrew-jackson-deserves-top-spot-on-list-of-worst-us-presidents

28. http://www.pbs.org/wgbh/aia/part4/4p2959.html

29. 'The Legend of Pine Ridge: FBI History: "The Reign of Terror" in the Osage Hills'.

30. Dennis McAuliffe, *The Deaths of Sybil Bolton: An American History*, Times Books, republished in 1994 as *Bloodland: A Family Story of Oil, Greed and Murder on the Osage Reservation*, Council Oak Books.

31. David Grann, *Killers of the Flower Moon: The Osage Murders and the Birth of the FBI*, Vintage Press, 2018.

32. 'Leonardo DiCaprio, Martin Scorsese Team on "Killers of the Flower Moon"', *Variety*.

33. http://www.markedbyteachers.com/gcse/history/the-only-good-indian-is-a-dead-one-to-what-extent-can-this-statement-be-seen-as-an-accurate-summary-of-the-philosophy-of-the-white-american-in-the-second-half-of-the-century.html https://www.britannica.com/event/Trail-of-Tears

34. https://www.nps.gov/trte/learn/historyculture/what-happened-on-the-trail-of-tears.htm

35. https://history.howstuffworks.com/historical-events/trail-of-tears.htm

36. https://www.merriam-webster.com/dictionary/m%C3%A9tis

37. https://www.smithsonianmag.com/smart-news/751-unmarked-graves-discovered-near-former-indigenous-school-canada-180978064/#:~:text=In%20late%20May%2C%20Chief%20Roseanne,Residential%20School%20in%20British%20Columbia.

38. https://indigenousfoundations.arts.ubc.ca/the_residential_school_system/https://indigenousfoundations.arts.ubc.ca/the_residential_school_system/

39. *Survey of Conditions of Indians in the United States*, Google Books.

40. https://www.theatlantic.com/education/archive/2019/03/traumatic-legacy-indian-boarding-schools/584293/

41. https://www.reuters.com/world/us/native-americans-decry-unmarked-graves-untold-history-boarding-schools-2021-06-22/

42. https://www.dailymail.co.uk/news/article-9712255/Native-Americans-decry-unmarked-graves-untold-history-boarding-schools.html

43. https://www.inquirer.com/news/rosebud-sioux-claim-remains-their-children-who-died-former-carlisle-indian-school-20210626.html

44. https://www.nationalgeographic.com/history/article/a-century-of-trauma-at-boarding-schools-for-native-american-children-in-the-united-states
45. https://www.cbsnews.com/news/canada-indigenous-children-school-bodies-unmarked-graves-2021-06-30/#:~:text=From%20the%2019th%20century%20until,never%20returned%20to%20their%20families.
46. https://www.bbc.com/news/world-us-canada-57592243
47. https://www.livescience.com/childrens-graves-residential-schools-canada.html
48. https://www.washingtonpost.com/world/2021/06/25/canada-schools-unmarked-graves/
49. https://www.thehindu.com/news/international/over-750-graves-found-at-former-canada-school/article34955692.ece
50. https://www.narf.org/nill/documents/nlr/nlr7-1.pdf
51. https://www.nytimes.com/2020/07/11/us/muscogee-creek-nation-oklahoma.html?action=click&module=RelatedLinks&pgtype=Article
52. http://archive.boston.com/news/nation/articles/2009/12/27/indian_tribes_buy_back_thousands_of_acres_of_land/
53. Information on the Gale Family as well as its connection with George Washington comes from family diaries, letters, family documents, photos, and stories from my father and mother.

## Chapter Three: Barefoot and Free

1. Richard Louv, *Last Child in the Woods: Saving our children from Nature Deficit Disorder*, Algonquin Books, 2008.
2. http://www.childrenandnature.org/
3. https://www.montessorinature.com/quotes-on-nature/
4. https://www.goodreads.com/author/quotes/90594.Richard_Louv
5. https://www.outsideonline.com/1928266/we-dont-need-no-education
6. https://www.whitehutchinson.com/children/articles/childrennature.shtml
7. http://richardlouv.com/blog/what-is-nature-deficit-disorder
8. http://www.bbc.com/news/science-environment-38094186
9. https://greatergood.berkeley.edu/article/item/how_to_protect_kids_from_nature_deficit_disorder

10. h t t p s : / / s p e e d - o p e n 2 . c o m / r / ? t o k e n = e b d 9 a 9 7 fdfa8ffcaaaa24985447b3b241facbaf6&q=is%20nature% 20a%20cure%20for%20bullying?,bullying%20 prevention,children%20outdoors,environment,sierra%20 club,education,huffpost,children,outdoors,bullying,nature&-ref=https://www.huffingtonpost.com/jackie-ostfeld/nature-cure-for-bullying_b_1987758.html
11. https://peacefulplaygrounds.com/nature-deficit-disorder/
12. https://www.nationalgeographic.com/magazine/2016/01/call-to-wild/
13. http://blog.childrenandnature.org/2013/01/10/restoring-peace-six-ways-nature-in-our-lives-can-reduce-the-violence-in-our-world/
14. http://blog.childrenandnature.org/2013/04/01/peace-like-a-river-theres-a-time-for-hyper-vigilance-and-theres-a-time-to-pay-a-different-kind-of-attention/
15. https://qz.com/804022/health-benefits-japanese-forest-bathing/
16. https://www.mamanatural.com/forest-bathing/
17. https://www.ted.com/talks/suzanne_simard_how_trees_talk_to_each_other?language=en#t-406905
18. 'Nature Makes You Happy', BBC Earth, YouTube.

## Chapter Four: Suds in the Water, Tar on the Beach

1. http://www.adfg.alaska.gov/index.cfm?adfg=wildlifenews.view_article&articles_id=407
2. https://www.nationalgeographic.com/animals/2018/08/beavers-climate-change-conservation-news/
3. https://www.hakaimagazine.com/features/salmon-trees/
4. Library, Beaver Institute.
5. http://sustainablefootprint.org/trees-grow-on-salmon/
6. https://www.nature.com/news/2001/011001/full/news011004-4.html
7. h t t p s : / / b m c e c o l . b i o m e d c e n t r a l . c o m / articles/10.1186/1472-6785-13-38
8. https://www.speakingtree.in/allslides/10-little-known-facts-about-ganga/111576
9. https://www.speakingtree.in/allslides/10-little-known-facts-about-ganga/111594
10. https://www.npr.org/templates/story/story.php?storyId=17134270

11. https://indianexpress.com/article/india/india-news-india/imtech-microbiologists-find-healing-properties-in-ganga-water-3047654/
12. https://www.thehindu.com/news/national/Testing-the-waters-Labs-study-healing-powers-of-Ganga/article14416817.ece
13. https://www.ndtv.com/india-news/scientists-to-study-ganga-water-to-find-x-factor-that-purifies-it-1244041
14. https://www.ncbi.nlm.nih.gov/pmc/articles/PMC4946093/
15. https://www.newindianexpress.com/lifestyle/2016/sep/24/It's-scientifically-validated-now-Ganga-water-is-'holy'-1524518.html?pm=331
16. https://www.cntraveler.com/story/the-healing-power-of-indias-ganges-river
17. https://www.dailymail.co.uk/sciencetech/article-4758188/Largest-dead-zone-Gulf-Mexico.html
18. https://www.nationalgeographic.com/environment/article/dead-zones
19. https://www.scientificamerican.com/article/ocean-dead-zones/
20. https://www.noaa.gov/media-release/gulf-of-mexico-dead-zone-is-largest-ever-measured
21. https://www.noaa.gov/media-release/noaa-forecasts-very-large-dead-zone-for-gulf-of-mexico
22. https://www.nola.com/news/environment/article_31a00b4d-0a10-56cd-b5ba-f30141966512.html#:~:text=%22The%20Arabian%20Sea%20is%20the,and%20the%20study's%20lead%20author.
23. https://oceanservice.noaa.gov/facts/deadzone.html#:~:text=%22Dead%20zone%22%20is%20a%20more,of%20oxygen%20in%20the%20water.&text=Less%20oxygen%20dissolved%20in%20the,as%20fish%2C%20leave%20the%20area.
24. https://www.epa.gov/sites/production/files/2015-03/documents/facts_about_nutrient_pollution_what_is_hypoxia.pdf
25. https://www.epa.gov/ms-htf/hypoxia-101
26. 'Obama Rejects TransCanada's Keystone XL Pipeline', *The Globe and Mail* (archive.org).
27. https://www.nrdc.org/stories/what-keystone-pipeline
28. https://www.bbc.com/news/world-us-canada-30103078
29. https://www.narf.org/cases/keystone/
30. https://www.tcenergy.com/announcements/2021-06-09-tc-energy-confirms-termination-of-keystone-xl-pipeline-project/

31. https://www.nytimes.com/2019/10/31/us/keystone-pipeline-leak.
    html#:~:text=The%20Keystone%20pipeline%20system%2C%20
    an,wetland%2C%20state%20environmental%20regulators%20said.

32. https://www.dw.com/en/with-a-pen-stroke-president-joe-biden-
    cancels-keystone-xl-pipeline-project/a-56285371

33. https://www.nbcnews.com/politics/joe-biden/biden-reversed-
    trump-keystone-xl-pipeline-native-american-groups-
    want-n1265025

34. https://theoceancleanup.com/great-pacific-garbage-patch/

35. https://www.forbes.com/sites/scottsnowden/2019/05/30/300-mile-
    swim-through-the-great-pacific-garbage-patch-will-collect-data-on-
    plastic-pollution/?sh=6a2cdd06489f

36. https://theoceancleanup.com/great-pacific-garbage-
    patch/#:~:text=A%20total%20of%201.8%20trillion,every%20
    human%20in%20the%20world.

37. https://www.bloombergquint.com/charts/worlds-plastic-burden-
    weight-of-a-billion-african-elephants

38. https://www.theguardian.com/environment/2019/mar/19/
    shocking-autopsy-photos-show-toll-of-plastic-waste-on-dead-
    whale

39. https://www.nationalgeographic.com/environment/2018/11/dead-
    sperm-whale-filled-with-plastic-trash-indonesia/

40. https://www.sciencealert.com/rescuers-couldn-t-save-this-pilot-
    whale-after-it-ate-over-7-kilograms-of-plastic-bags

41. https://www.thenewsminute.com/article/elephant-dies-kerala-
    after-eating-plastic-who-blame-76467

42. https://www.indiatimes.com/news/india/images-of-elephant-
    leopard-eating-plastic-shows-how-pollution-is-killing-the-
    wildlife-371319.html

43. https://journals.plos.org/plosone/article?id=10.1371/journal.
    pone.0111913

44. https://www.nationalgeographic.com/magazine/2018/06/plastic-
    planet-health-pollution-waste-microplastics/

45. https://orbmedia.org/stories/Invisibles_plastics/

46. https://www.earthday.org/the-invisible-plastic-particles-in-our-
    drinking-water/

47. https://www.indiatoday.in/education-today/gk-current-affairs/
    story/microplastic-tap-water-1039104-2017-09-06

48. https://www.iaea.org/newscenter/news/new-research-on-the-possible-effects-of-micro-and-nano-plastics-on-marine-animals
49. https://www.nature.com/articles/s41565-019-0437-7
50. https://www.theguardian.com/environment/2020/dec/22/microplastics-revealed-in-placentas-unborn-babies
51. https://www.eco-business.com/news/great-concern-as-new-study-finds-microplastics-in-human-placentas/
52. https://www.scientificamerican.com/article/earth-talks-breast-feeding/
53. https://www.earthdecks.net/plastic-water-salt-milk/
54. http://news.bbc.co.uk/2/shared/bsp/hi/pdfs/14_03_13_finalbottled.pdf
55. http://environmentalthinker.blogspot.com/2009/02/purpose-and-importance-of-trees.html
56. https://www.carbonbrief.org/deforestation-in-the-tropics-affects-climate-around-the-world-study-finds
57. https://www.sciencemag.org/news/2017/08/trees-amazon-make-their-own-rain
58. https://www.weforum.org/agenda/2017/08/how-trees-in-the-amazon-make-their-own-rain/
59. https://rainforests.mongabay.com/amazon/rainforest_ecology.html
60. https://www.cifor.org/library/4454/how-plants-water-our-planet-advances-and-imperatives/?pub=4454
61. http://www.nature.com/nature/journal/v496/n7445/abs/nature11983.html
62. https://forestsnews.cifor.org/20789/best-of-2013-forests-as-rainmakers#.UxY0V4WZ55h
63. http://adsabs.harvard.edu/abs/2012JHyd..416..182M
64. https://www.cifor.org/library/2770/how-forests-attract-rain-an-examination-of-a-new-hypothesis/?pub=2770
65. http://www.pnas.org/content/114/32/8481.abstract
66. http://www.sciencemag.org/news/2012/08/amazon-seeds-its-own-rain
67. https://global.nature.org/initiatives/natural-climate-solutions/natures-make-or-break-potential-for-climate-change?src=social.multiple.site_globsol.cam_ncs.link_initative.d_oct2017.info_ncs3
68. https://www.weforum.org/agenda/2017/10/tropical-forests-used-to-absorb-carbon-not-any-more?utm_content=buffer17a4e&utm_medium=social&utm_source=twitter.com&utm_campaign=buffer

69. https://www.newyorker.com/tech/elements/the-fate-of-earth
70. https://economictimes.indiatimes.com/news/politics-and-nation/indias-natural-forests-half-of-what-ministry-claims/articleshow/38504925.cms
71. http://indiaclimatedialogue.net/2016/03/21/varying-rainfall-threatens-biodiversity-western-ghats/
72. https://news.mongabay.com/2018/06/nature-retention-not-just-protection-crucial-to-maintaining-biodiversity-and-ecosystems-scientists/
73. https://thewire.in/65037/deforestation-reducing-monsoon-rainfall-in-india-new-study/
74. https://sandrp.wordpress.com/2013/07/26/climate-change-in-western-ghats-4x4-report-and-beyond/
75. http://www.deccanherald.com/content/565499/reduction-forest-area-has-led.html
76. http://www.downtoearth.org.in/news/is-this-a-sign--56018
77. https://www.leeds.ac.uk/news/article/3284/loss_of_tropical_forests_reduces_rain
78. http://www.nature.com/nature/journal/v489/n7415/full/nature11390.html
79. http://www.dailymail.co.uk/sciencetech/article-2198809/Cutting-rainforests-dramatically-impact-rainfall-researchers-find.html#ixzz2u2kQeaBk
80. http://www.insightsonindia.com/2016/10/29/1-rainfall-western-ghats-steadily-declining-triggering-fears-drought-one-worlds-water-rich-regions-impact-declining-rainfall-region-analy/
81. http://www.firstpost.com/india/drought-in-the-western-ghats-part-2-how-deforestation-saved-ecologically-sensitive-hills-in-kerala-3432708.html
82. http://indiaclimatedialogue.net/2016/03/21/varying-rainfall-threatens-biodiversity-western-ghats/
83. https://news.stanford.edu/2017/10/09/animal-biodiversity-important-part-carbon-cycle/
84. https://www.nature.com/articles/s41559-017-0334-0
85. https://blog.conservation.org/2016/04/wildlife-loss-in-tropical-forests-is-bad-news-and-not-just-for-animals/
86. https://www.nature.com/articles/ncomms11351; Anand Osuri, National Centre for Biological Sciences in Bangalore, Research Scientist, Earth Institute, Columbia University.

87. http://www.nature.com/news/social-cost-of-carbon-emissions-in-spotlight-1.18789
88. http://economictimes.indiatimes.com/news/politics-and-nation/asian-elephants-play-key-role-in-spreading-green-cover/articleshow/49214437.cms
89. http://www.sciencedaily.com/releases/2015/06/150615094309.htm
90. 10.1073/pnas.1506279112
91. http://science.sciencemag.org/content/345/6195/401
92. http://www.bbc.com/news/science-environment-11418033
93. http://phys.org/news/2014-06-forest-loss-starves-fish.html
94. http://e360.yale.edu/features/dying-waters-india-struggles-to-clean-up-its-polluted-urban-rivers
95. http://www.tenmilliontrees.org/trees/
96. https://www.treehugger.com/process-of-using-water-by-trees-1343505

## Chapter Five: Dreams Beyond the Rainbow: A Collision of Worlds

1. Wangari Maathai quotes are from a live interview on Indian National TV channel in early 2006, when Maathai came to India to receive the Indira Gandhi Prize for Peace, Disarmament and Development.
2. https://www.defense.gov/Explore/News/Article/Article/603440/
3. https://www.youtube.com/watch?v=dA0qGlnc-30
4. https://www.youtube.com/watch?v=psynAbgdA5o
5. https://mountainscholar.org/bitstream/handle/10217/83877/Anderson_colostate_0053N_12391.pdf?sequence=1
6. https://www.brainyquote.com/authors/wangari-maathai-quotes
7. http://www.ecology.com/2011/10/24/wangari-maathai-quotes/
8. https://www.indiatoday.in/elections/karnataka-election-2018/story/all-you-need-to-know-about-the-cauvery-dispute-between-karnataka-and-tamil-nadu-1228138-2018-05-07
9. https://timesofindia.indiatimes.com/topic/Cauvery-water-dispute
10. https://bangaloremirror.indiatimes.com/bangalore/cover-story/after-cauvery-karnataka-and-tamil-nadu-in-a-new-river-dispute/articleshow/72078902.cms
11. https://www.nationalgeographic.com/magazine/2018/03/drying-lakes-climate-change-global-warming-drought/
12. https://www.nationalgeographic.com/news/2016/01/160121-lake-poopo-bolivia-dried-out-el-nino-climate-change-water/

13. https://www.wilsoncenter.org/sites/default/files/Duffy.pdf
14. http://peace.maripo.com/p_parks.htm
15. https://neoiascap.com/2019/10/26/india-nepal-bhutan-trans-border-conservation-area/environment/protected-areas/
16. https://www.worldwildlife.org/stories/what-does-transboundary-conservation-mean-and-why-does-it-matter
17. Global Transboundary Protected Areas Network (tbpa.net)
18. https://peacetourism.org/peace-parks-project/
19. Air Marshal K.C.(Nanda) Cariappa (retired) and Kent Biringer, senior researcher at the Sandia National Laboratories, Albuquerque, NM, *Peace Parks: Conservation and Conflict Resolution*, edited by Saleem H. Ali, associate professor of environmental planning, Rubenstein School, University of Vermont, Burlington, MIT Press, 2007.
20. *Peace Parks: Conservation and Conflict Resolution* (eBook), WorldCat.org, 2007.
21. https://neoiascap.com/2019/10/26/india-nepal-bhutan-trans-border-conservation-area/environment/protected-areas/
22. 'India, Nepal, Bhutan Plan Trans-Border Conservation Area', Downtoearth.org.in.
23. http://www.ngopulse.org/organisation/peace-parks-foundation
24. http://iipti.in/entries/general/blog-post
25. http://www.iipt.org/newsletter/2015/october.html
26. https://thesmetimes.com/women-spirit-gets-accolades-in-mitm-2015-international-institute-for-peace-through-tourism-iitp-commemorates-women-for-their-contribution-in-promotion-of-tourism/
27. https://www.nytimes.com/2013/09/29/books/review/the-blood-telegram-by-gary-j-bass.html
28. https://www.thedailystar.net/opinion/peripherally-yours/archer-blood-americans-sacrifice-bangladesh-1332442
29. https://www.thedailystar.net/the-blood-telegram-52771
30. https://www.economist.com/news/books-and-arts/21586514-new-history-sheds-fresh-light-shameful-moment-american-foreign-policy-blood
31. http://www.docstrangelove.com/2007/12/02/bangladesh-genocide-archives-foreign-newspaper-reports/
32. http://www.bbc.com/news/world-asia-16207201
33. Bangladesh profile, Timeline, BBC News.

34. 9780521861748_frontmatter.pdf, cambridge.org.
35. 'The History of Bangladesh', History of Bangladesh.
36. 'History of Bangladesh', Britannica
37. https://www.youtube.com/watch?v=2nc8ZNlWgwE
38. Jack Anderson with George Clifford, *The Anderson Papers*, Random House, 1973.
39. W. Norman Brown, *The United States and India, Pakistan, and Bangladesh*, Harvard University Press, 1972.
40. *The Blood Telegram: Nixon, Kissinger and a Forgotten Genocide*, Penguin Random House, 2013.
41. *The Blood Telegram: India's Secret War in East Pakistan*, Penguin India, 2014.
42. Sumit Ganguly, *Conflict Unending: India-Pakistan Tensions since 1947*, Oxford University Press, 2001.
43. Richard Sisson and Leo E. Rose, *War and Secession: India, Pakistan, the United States, and the Creation of Bangladesh*, University of California Press, 1990.
44. Daniel Ellsberg, *The Doomsday Machine: Confessions of a Nuclear War Planner*, Bloomsbury Publishing, 2017.
45. http://www.nytimes.com/2016/12/31/opinion/sunday/nixons-vietnam-treachery.html
46. https://library.usask.ca/vietnam/index.php
47. https://www.archives.gov/research/pentagon-papers
48. https://www.nytimes.com/2021/01/07/us/pentagon-papers-neil-sheehan.html
49. https://www.thehindu.com/news/international/the-hindu-explains-the-pentagon-papers-saga/article26805135.ece
50. https://www.npr.org/2018/01/19/579101965/daniel-ellsberg-explains-why-he-leaked-the-pentagon-papers
51. https://www.thehindu.com/books/books-reviews/the-doomsday-machine-confessions-of-a-nuclear-war-planner-review-brink-of-annihilation/article23626290.ece
52. https://www.washingtonpost.com/outlook/how-us-nuclear-weapons-strategy-only-makes-us-more-vulnerable-to-catastrophe/2018/01/12/13817c30-d91a-11e7-b1a8-62589434a581_story.html
53. https://www.britannica.com/event/Vietnam-War
54. 'Vietnam War US Military Fatal Casualty Statistics', National Archives.

55. 'Was My Lai Just One of Many Massacres in Vietnam War?', BBC News.
56. 'Vietnam's Forgotten Cambodian War', BBC News.

**PART TWO: The Tree Takes Root**
**Chapter Six: Rocky Mountain Highs: Finding the Divine in Nature**

1. https://www.ncbi.nlm.nih.gov/pmc/articles/PMC4813425/
2. https://insideclimatenews.org/news/28082017/southern-pine-beetles-spreading-climate-change-northern-canada-new-jersey-maine/#:~:text=Southern%20pine%20beetles%20are%20among,kill%20the%20trees%20they%20infest.
3. https://www.fs.usda.gov/ccrc/topics/bark-beetles-and-climate-change-united-states
4. https://www.nationalgeographic.com/science/article/bark-beetles-helped-stoke-2020-devastating-wildfires
5. https://academic.oup.com/bioscience/article/60/8/602/305152
6. https://www.cabi.org/cabreviews/FullTextPDF/2021/20210064841.pdf
7. https://link.springer.com/article/10.1007/s40725-018-0075-6
8. https://pubmed.ncbi.nlm.nih.gov/522165/
9. https://www.youtube.com/watch?v=Q3hQrac_oFM
10. https://www.humansandnature.org/stephan-harding
11. https://improvisedlife.com/2017/10/24/move-beyond-intellect-to-poetic-encounter/
12. Albert Hofmann and Richard Evan Shultz, *Plants of the Gods*, McGraw-Hill, 1979.
13. https://aeon.co/essays/is-psychedelics-research-closer-to-theology-than-to-science

**Chapter Seven: From Pills to Plants: A Life in Healthcare**

1. https://www.legendsofamerica.com/na-herbs/
2. https://lib.dr.iastate.edu/cgi/viewcontent.cgi?referer=https://www.google.com/&httpsredir=1&article=5837&context=etd
3. https://www.arcgis.com/apps/Cascade/index.html?appid=1806faa8349048c891576d4a83a7a8ac
4. https://www.offthegridnews.com/alternative-health/31-long-forgotten-native-american-medical-cures/

5. https://defenders.org/wildlife/bison
6. https://www.ncbi.nlm.nih.gov/pmc/articles/PMC2746847/
7. https://www.crueltyfreeinternational.org/why-we-do-it/arguments-against-animal-testing#:~:text=Unreliable%20animal%20testing&text=Using%20dogs%2C%20rats%2C%20mice%20and,predicting%20the%20effects%20on%20humans.
8. https://www.peta.org/issues/animals-used-for-experimentation/animal-testing-bad-science/
9. https://www.hsi.org/news-media/limitations-of-animal-tests/
10. https://www.petaindia.com/blog/mahatma-gandhi-quotes-on-animals/
11. https://www.goodreads.com/quotes/340-the-greatness-of-a-nation-and-its-moral-progress-can
12. https://www.gutenberg.org/files/44929/44929-h/44929-h.htm
13. https://en.wikipedia.org/wiki/Arthur_Schopenhauer%27s_view_on_animal_rights#:~:text=According%20to%20Schopenhauer%3A%20%22Since%20compassion,Buddhist%20views%20on%20animal%20ethics.
14. https://ivu.org/history/europe19b/schopenhauer.html - *From The Ethics of Diet, a Catena, by Howard Williams, 1892*
15. A Critique of Kant, by Arthur Schopenhauer (animal-rights-library.com)
16. https://www.azquotes.com/author/4399-Albert_Einstein/tag/animal-cruelty#:~:text=The%20indifference%2C%20callousness%20and%20contempt,impoverishment%20of%20the%20human%20spirit.
17. https://www.inspiringquotes.us/author/3804-albert-einstein/about-animal-cruelty
18. https://www.nytimes.com/2018/04/07/health/antidepressants-withdrawal-prozac-cymbalta.html
19. https://timesofindia.indiatimes.com/life-style/health-fitness/health-news/one-in-every-20-indians-suffers-from-depression/articleshow/56867750.cms
20. https://timesofindia.indiatimes.com/life-style/health-fitness/health-news/Anti-depressants-easily-available/articleshow/50652120.cms
21. https://www.firstpost.com/living/dont-pop-that-prozac-the-rise-of-anti-depressant-abuse-913007.html
22. https://www.huffpost.com/archive/in/entry/good-mental-healthcare-in-india_in_5c19d1d6e4b08db99058d6b7

23. https://www.independent.co.uk/voices/antidepressants-study-new-research-depression-medication-a8223801.html
24. https://www.sciencedirect.com/science/article/pii/S0920996418301786
25. http://sciencenordic.com/schizophrenia-more-prevalent-away-green-spaces
26. https://www.theguardian.com/commentisfree/2017/mar/13/warning-living-city-seriously-damage-health?CMP=Share_iOSApp_Other
27. https://www.thehindu.com/society/how-urban-design-impacts-mental-health/article31693107.ece#:~:text=According%20to%20the%20Centre%20for,to%20loneliness%2C%20isolation%20and%20stress.
28. https://www.ncbi.nlm.nih.gov/pmc/articles/PMC2996208/
29. https://www.urbandesignmentalhealth.com/facts-and-figures.html
30. https://www.un.org/development/desa/en/news/population/2018-revision-of-world-urbanization-prospects.html.
31. https://www.sciencedirect.com/science/article/abs/pii/S0920996418301786
32. http://sciencenordic.com/schizophrenia-more-prevalent-away-green-spaces
33. https://sciencenordic.com/denmark-environment-schizophrenia/schizophrenia-more-prevalent-away-from-green-spaces/1455850
34. https://www.pnas.org/content/116/11/5188
35. https://www.ncbi.nlm.nih.gov/pmc/articles/PMC4813425/
36. http://www.indiatimes.com/news/india/union-minister-maneka-gandhi-wants-medical-marijuana-legalised-in-india-326867.html
37. https://www.marijuana.com/news/2017/08/the-future-of-cannabis-in-india/
38. http://www.financialexpress.com/india-news/maneka-gandhi-suggests-legalising-marijuana-for-medical-purposes/786555/
39. State Medical Marijuana Laws, ncsl.org.
40. https://www.healtheuropa.eu/health-benefits-of-cannabis/92499/
41. https://www.health.harvard.edu/blog/medical-marijuana-2018011513085
42. 'Pfizer, Eli Lilly Were the Original Medical Marijuana Sellers', Forbes.com.
43. 'All Info - H.R.4498 - 97th Congress (1981-1982): A bill to provide for the therapeutic use of marijuana in situations involving life-threatening

illnesses and to provide adequate supplies of marijuana for such use.'
Congress.gov, Library of Congress.

44. 'Congressional Funding Bill Restores Financial Aid for Students
    with Drug Convictions, and Has Other Marijuana Provisions',
    Marijuana Moment.

45. Doctor Robin L. Carhart-Harris, PhD, et. al., 'Psylocibin with
    Psychological Support for Treatment-Resistant Depression: An
    Open Label Feasibility Study', *Lancet*, volume 3, issue 7, 1 July 2016,
    pp.  619–27,  https://www.thelancet.com/journals/lanpsy/article/
    PIIS2215-0366(16)30065-7/fulltext

46. https://www.vice.com/en/article/g5ppe7/this-drug-designer-is-
    creating-a-new-psychedelic-to-treat-anxiety-and-depression

47. https://www.nature.com/articles/s41591-021-01336-3

48. https://www.thelancet.com/journals/lanpsy/article/PIIS2215-
    0366(16)30065-7/fulltext

49. https://www.sciencenews.org/article/psilocybin-treat-depression-
    mushrooms-psychedelic

50. https://www.independent.co.uk/voices/antidepressants-drugs-pills-
    opioids-addiction-mental-health-a9131901.html

51. https://sapiensoup.com/serotonin

52. http://psychedelicsociety.at/

53. https://aeon.co/essays/is-psychedelics-research-closer-to-theology-
    than-to-science

54. https://www.ncbi.nlm.nih.gov/pmc/articles/PMC4813425/

55. https://www.cbsnews.com/news/psychedelic-drugs-lsd-active-
    agent-in-magic-mushrooms-to-treat-addiction-depression-
    anxiety-60-minutes-2020-08-16/?intcid=CNM-00-10abd1h

56. https://www.cbsnews.com/news/magic-mushroom-psychedelic-
    may-ease-depression-anxiety/?intcid=CNM-00-10abd1h

57. https://www.cbsnews.com/news/psychedelic-therapy-
    tried-by-patients-for-mental-health-psychological-
    conditions/?intcid=CNM-00-10abd1h

58. https://icpr2020.net/europes-psychedelic-science-renaissance/;   scroll
    down to video from the Centre for Psychedelic Research of London's
    Imperial College on their research and its purposes and goals.

59. https://icpr2020.net/psilocybin-and-mystical-experiences/;    scroll
    down to video of Johns Hopkins research.

60. https://www.independent.co.uk/voices/antidepressants-drugs-pills-
    opioids-addiction-mental-health-a9131901.html

61. https://www.apa.org/monitor/2020/04/stop-antidepressants
62. https://www.ncbi.nlm.nih.gov/pmc/articles/PMC4813425/
63. https://www.cbsnews.com/news/magic-mushroom-psychedelic-may-ease-depression-anxiety/?intcid=CNM-00-10abd1h
64. https://www.cbsnews.com/news/psychedelic-therapy-tried-by-patients-for-mental-health-psychological-conditions/?intcid=CNM-00-10abd1h
65. https://www.outlookindia.com/website/story/is-limited-research-why-psychedelic-drugs-are-not-an-option-for-treating-mental-/302539
66. https://www.ncbi.nlm.nih.gov/pmc/articles/PMC5857492/
67. https://gizmodo.com/new-lsd-research-may-help-explain-the-brain-chemistry-o-1823901901
68. https://gizmodo.com/magic-mushroom-chemical-appears-to-physically-change-de-1819447096
69. https://sapiensoup.com/medical-benefits-of-psychedelic-drugs
70. https://www.nytimes.com/2021/05/03/health/mdma-approval.html
71. https://www.nature.com/articles/s41591-021-01336-3
72. https://www.scientificamerican.com/article/mdma-shows-new-promise-for-trauma-but-the-drug-alone-is-not-a-cure/
73. https://www.healtheuropa.eu/mdma-assisted-psychotherapy-for-ptsd-approved-by-fda/96931/
74. https://www.nytimes.com/2016/11/29/us/ptsd-mdma-ecstasy.html
75. https://www.psychiatryadvisor.com/home/conference-highlights/us-psych-congress-2019/psychedelic-assisted-therapy-how-mdma-is-changing-treatment-for-ptsd/
76. Meditation has been shown to be very useful here at stopping the 'round and round' of the mind/DMN: https://medium.com/swlh/the-brains-default-mode-what-is-it-and-why-meditation-is-the-antidote-d0408ab989d6
77. https://www.cbsnews.com/news/psychedelic-therapy-tried-by-patients-for-mental-health-psychological-conditions/?intcid=CNM-00-10abd1h
78. https://www.cbsnews.com/news/michael-pollan-on-testing-psychedelics-as-a-treatment-for-depression/?intcid=CNM-00-10abd1h
79. https://www.cbsnews.com/news/magic-mushroom-psychedelic-may-ease-depression-anxiety/?intcid=CNM-00-10abd1h

80. https://www.newsweek.com/fluoxetine-and-antibiotic-resistance-key-ingredient-antidepressants-linked-1113596#:~:text=Newsweek-,Fluoxetine%20and%20Antibiotic%20Resistance%3A%20Key%20Ingredient%20in,Linked%20to%20Rise%20of%20Superbugs&text=An%20ingredient%20in%20many%20commonly,in%20the%20journal%20Environment%20International.
81. https://www.uq.edu.au/news/article/2018/09/antidepressant-may-cause-antibiotic-resistance   https://www.intelligentliving.co/antidepressants-antibiotic-resistance/
82. https://www.epa.gov/sites/default/files/2015-08/documents/mgwc-gwc1.pdf
83. https://www.groundwater.org/get-informed/groundwater/contamination.html
84. https://www.nature.com/articles/s41598-020-75236-w
85. https://www.nytimes.com/2020/10/21/climate/beef-cattle-methane.html
86. https://www.smithsonianmag.com/smart-news/seaweed-fed-cows-burp-less-planet-warming-methane-180977296/
87. https://www.ecowatch.com/biomass-humans-animals-2571413930.html
88. https://www.ecowatch.com/human-production-mass-nature-biomass-2649441047.html
89. https://www.vox.com/2014/8/21/6053187/cropland-map-food-fuel-animal-feed
90. https://www.theguardian.com/environment/2018/may/21/human-race-just-001-of-all-life-but-has-destroyed-over-80-of-wild-mammals-study#

## Chapter Eight: Colorado Rocky Lows: Missing Peaks for Uranium Tails

1. https://www.youtube.com/watch?v=7XIrI6K-HcQ
2. https://www.britannica.com/place/Rocky-Flats
3. https://www.westword.com/news/rocky-flats-nuclear-plant-shut-down-thirty-years-ago-but-is-still-a-hot-topic-11437949
4. https://cumulis.epa.gov/supercpad/cursites/csitinfo.cfm?id=0800360
5. https://coloradoencyclopedia.org/article/rocky-flats-nuclear-facility

6.  https://www.nytimes.com/1971/10/31/archives/-dear-sir-your-house-is-built-on-radioactive-uranium-waste.html
7.  https://www.energy.gov/lm/grand-junction-colorado-disposal-and-processing-sites
8.  https://coloradosun.com/2020/12/29/grand-junction-cold-war-nuclear-waste-dump/
9.  https://durangogov.org/DocumentCenter/View/16139/Uranium-Mill-Tailings-Fact-Sheet
10. https://www.nrc.gov/reading-rm/doc-collections/fact-sheets/3mile-isle.html
11. https://www.history.com/this-day-in-history/nuclear-accident-at-three-mile-island
12. https://www.britannica.com/event/Three-Mile-Island-accident
13. https://www.britannica.com/technology/nuclear-reactor/Three-Mile-Island-and-Chernobyl
14. https://www.aip.org/history-programs/niels-bohr-library/ex-libris-universum/three-mile-island-1979-accident-and-its
15. https://world-nuclear.org/information-library/safety-and-security/safety-of-plants/chernobyl-accident.aspx
16. https://www.nationalgeographic.com/culture/article/chernobyl-disaster
17. https://www.britannica.com/event/Chernobyl-disaster
18. https://www.nrc.gov/reading-rm/doc-collections/fact-sheets/chernobyl-bg.html
19. https://www.youtube.com/watch?v=roltJzTUTdM
20. https://www.youtube.com/watch?v=kbwSwUMNyPU
21. https://www.youtube.com/watch?v=-e50MBBCwLE
22. https://www.thegreatpeacemakers.com/iroquois-great-law-of-peace.html
23. http://www.ganienkeh.net/thelaw.html
24. https://www.researchgate.net/publication/304593087_Christopher_Buck_Deganawida_the_Peacemaker_American_Writers_A_Collection_of_Literary_Biographies_Supplement_XXVI_Edited_by_Jay_Parini_Farmington_Hills_MI_Scribner's_ReferenceThe_Gale_Group_2015_Pp_81-
25. https://www.7genfoundation.org/7th-generation/
26. https://www.theglobeandmail.com/news/politics/ottawa-notebook/jimmy-neutron-ex-president-carter-recalls-role-in-chalk-river-meltdown/article614379/

27. 'FOCUS: Goodbye Nuclear Power. Construction of Two of Four Remaining Planned US Plants Just Canceled', Readersupportednews.org.
28. https://www.indiatvnews.com/news/world/co2-emissions-at-record-high-despite-covid19-pandemic-710164
29. https://www.indiatimes.com/technology/science-and-future/earth-carbon-dioxide-levels-542275.html
30. https://research.noaa.gov/article/ArtMID/587/ArticleID/2764/Coronavirus-response-barely-slows-rising-carbon-dioxide
31. https://www.greenpeace.org/usa/harvard-study-500-billion-full-cost-of-coal/
32. https://pubmed.ncbi.nlm.nih.gov/21332493/
33. https://chge.hsph.harvard.edu/files/chge/files/MiningCoalMountingCosts.pdf
34. https://www.reuters.com/article/idINIndia-46684920100305
35. https://energy.economictimes.indiatimes.com/news/coal/india-australia-china-russia-pushing-massive-coal-expansion/83248723
36. https://scroll.in/article/989859/in-indias-oldest-coalfield-mining-has-caused-irreparable-damage-to-the-environment
37. https://india.mongabay.com/2020/11/indias-largest-coalfield-to-expand-green-cover-under-threat/
38. https://www.nsenergybusiness.com/features/states-india-largest-coal-reserves/
39. https://mnre.gov.in/solar/current-status/
40. https://mnre.gov.in/
41. https://mnre.gov.in/solar/current-status/
42. https://www.investindia.gov.in/sector/renewable-energy
43. https://energy.economictimes.indiatimes.com/news/renewable/solar-and-wind-power-costs-in-india-will-be-comparable-to-coal-in-2025-moodys/79300584
44. https://www.wsj.com/articles/solar-power-is-beginning-to-eclipse-fossil-fuels-11581964338
45. https://mercomindia.com/renewable-cost-drop-leaves-coal-plants-uneconomical/
46. https://www.bloomberg.com/news/articles/2018-08-06/negative-prices-in-power-market-as-wind-solar-cut-electricity
47. https://www.amnesty.org/en/latest/news/2013/04/india-landmark-supreme-court-ruling-great-victory-indigenous-rights/

48. https://www.indiaspend.com/government-industries-nationwide-dodge-law-take-over-forest-land-without-consent-of-tribal-communities/

49. https://india.mongabay.com/2021/03/pesa-the-wait-for-reforms-on-the-ground-continues-even-after-25-years/

50. https://economictimes.indiatimes.com/industry/indl-goods/svs/metals-mining/theres-no-mine-but-is-it-all-fine-on-niyam-hills/articleshow/63763978.cms?from=mdr

51. https://www.thehindu.com/society/dongria-kondhs-continue-to-fight-bauxite-mining-in-odishas-niyamgiri-forests/article26544621.ece

52. https://accessinitiative.org/blog/india%E2%80%99s-supreme-court-directs-mining-company-seek-approval-gram-sabha-village-assembly

53. https://thewire.in/government/supreme-court-must-safeguard-tribal-rights-over-niyamgiri-hills-in-odisha

54. https://apnews.com/article/ap-top-news-tokyo-japan-science-business-d1b8322355f3f31109dd925900dff200

55. https://www.bbc.com/news/world-asia-38131248

56. https://cleantechnica.com/2019/04/16/fukushimas-final-costs-will-approach-one-trillion-dollars-just-for-nuclear-disaster/

57. https://www.climateforesight.eu/energy/nuclear-power-feeling-the-heat/

58. https://thebulletin.org/2019/08/the-false-promise-of-nuclear-power-in-an-age-of-climate-change/

59. https://www.nature.com/articles/s41467-020-16012-2

60. https://www.utilitydive.com/news/for-nuclear-plants-operating-on-thin-margins-growing-climate-risks-prompt/584883/

61. https://www.spglobal.com/marketintelligence/en/news-insights/latest-news-headlines/climate-change-poses-big-water-risks-for-nuclear-fossil-fueled-plants-60669992

62. https://www.nrdc.org/experts/christina-chen/nuclear-vs-climate-change-feeling-heat-0

63. https://mediaindia.eu/business/jaitapur-nuclear-france/

64. https://www.livemint.com/companies/news/edf-submits-binding-techno-commercial-offer-for-jaitapur-nuclear-plant-to-npcil-11619168867867.html

65. https://mediaindia.eu/business/jaitapur-nuclear-france/

66. https://www.theguardian.com/environment/2011/jun/23/thorium-nuclear-uranium
67. https://news.climate.columbia.edu/2020/11/23/nuclear-power-today-future/
68. https://saplnh.org/wp-content/uploads/2016/12/Ages-of-US-Nuclear-Power-Plants-at-Closure.pdf
69. http://www.animatedsoftware.com/environm/no_nukes/nukelist1.htm
70. https://www.eia.gov/energyexplained/nuclear/us-nuclear-industry.php
71. https://cen.acs.org/environment/pollution/nuclear-waste-pilesscientists-seek-best/98/i12
72. https://cen.acs.org/energy/nuclear-power/Proposed-nuclear-waste-storage-materials/98/i5
73. https://www.thehindu.com/news/international/japan-to-start-releasing-fukushima-water-to-sea-in-2-years/article34307815.ece
74. https://www.bbc.com/news/world-asia-56728068
75. https://www.preventionweb.net/news/view/76583
76. https://www.dianuke.org/accidents-at-nuclear-power-plants-in-india/
77. https://www.rediff.com/news/2000/nov/22nuke.htm
78. https://tribune.com.pk/article/97109/the-alarming-safety-record-of-indias-nuclear-power-plants
79. https://timesofindia.indiatimes.com/india/11-nuclear-scientists-died-in-mysterious-circumstances-in-4-years/articleshow/49272275.cms
80. https://www.dnaindia.com/india/report-nuclear-radiation-impact-being-ignored-1815210
81. https://economictimes.indiatimes.com/news/science/kakrapar-plant-leak-exposes-mysterious-chink-in-armour/articleshow/51479467.cms
82. https://www.theleaflet.in/silence-on-fukushima-disaster-exposes-our-approach-to-nuclear-safety-and-why-india-must-oppose-dumping-of-radioactive-water-into-the-pacific/
83. https://www.hindustantimes.com/india-news/scientists-probe-mysterious-leaks-as-gujarat-s-nuclear-plant-contracts-small-pox/story-ppWAXn8YENbH0W0rBhpXsK.html

## Chapter Nine: To the Land of Rainbows and Angels of the Sea

1.  https://uk.whales.org/2018/07/25/why-whale-and-dolphin-captivity-is-cruel-the-science/
2.  https://www.worldanimalprotection.org/news/thousands-captive-whales-dolphins-and-other-marine-mammals-still-suffering-2019
3.  https://www.humanesociety.org/resources/marine-mammals-captivity#:~:text=Life%20in%20captivity&text=Because%20tanks%20are%20shallow%2C%20the,cause%20of%20dorsal%20fin%20collapse.
4.  https://uk.whales.org/our-4-goals/end-captivity/
5.  https://www.worldanimalprotection.ca/dolphins-captivity
6.  https://www.pbs.org/wgbh/pages/frontline/shows/whales/debate/ethics.html
7.  https://awionline.org/content/wild-vs-captivity
8.  https://uk.whales.org/2018/07/25/why-whale-and-dolphin-captivity-is-cruel-the-science/
9.  https://truthout.org/articles/with-food-source-endangered-southern-resident-killer-whales-face-extinction/
10. https://thenarwhal.ca/grieving-mother-highlights-crisis-for-southern-resident-killer-whales/
11. https://thenarwhal.ca/grieving-with-the-worlds-whale/
12. https://www.cmaquarium.org/winters-inspiration/winter-and-hope/
13. https://www.cmaquarium.org/winters-inspiration/dolphin-tale/
14. https://www.cmaquarium.org/dive-360/
15. https://hawaiihumpbackwhale.noaa.gov/#:~:text=Every%20winter%2C%20thousands%20of%20humpback,these%20whales%20and%20their%20habitat.
16. https://marinesanctuary.org/sanctuary/hawaiian-islands/
17. https://www.nationalgeographic.com/podcasts/overheard/article/episode-1-humpback-whale-song
18. https://www.frontiersin.org/articles/10.3389/fmars.2021.669748/full
19. https://www.youtube.com/watch?v=W5Trznre92c
20. https://wwf.panda.org/wwf_news/?1171341/Antarctic-Wildlife-to-Benefit-from-Fishing-Ban
21. https://thefishsite.com/articles/in-for-the-krill
22. https://www.bbc.com/future/article/20210119-why-saving-whales-can-help-fight-climate-change

23. https://www.nationalgeographic.com/environment/article/how-much-is-a-whale-worth
24. https://www.climateforesight.eu/oceans/whales-carbon-sequestration/
25. https://news.mongabay.com/2021/03/to-fight-climate-change-save-the-whales-some-scientists-say/
26. https://www.weforum.org/agenda/2019/11/whales-carbon-capture-climate-change/
27. https://time.com/5733954/climate-change-whale-trees/
28. https://www.imf.org/external/pubs/ft/fandd/2019/12/natures-solution-to-climate-change-chami.htm#:~:text=Whales%20accumulate%20carbon%20in%20their,of%20CO2%20a%20year.
29. https://www.pbs.org/newshour/science/koalas-may-be-functionally-extinct-but-what-does-that-mean
30. https://www.theguardian.com/environment/2021/apr/03/north-atlantic-right-whales-most-calves-since-2015
31. https://www.researchgate.net/publication/317821328_Widely_used_marine_seismic_survey_air_gun_operations_negatively_impact_zooplankton
32. https://www.floridatoday.com/story/news/local/environment/2017/06/22/study-airgun-blasts-search-oil-kill-plankton/421411001/
33. https://www.thejournal.ie/readme/do-we-want-our-beaches-strewn-with-stranded-dolphins-4107401-Jul2018/
34. https://www.nytimes.com/2019/01/22/science/oceans-whales-noise-offshore-drilling.html
35. https://www.reuters.com/article/us-whales/human-rights-urged-for-whales-and-dolphins-idUSTRE64M0UC20100523
36. https://uk.whales.org/blog/2010/05/next-stage-in-evolution-of-our-relationship-with-whales
37. https://www.youtube.com/watch?v=NTw8MR67xv8
38. https://www.dolphins-for-kids.com/do-dolphins-really-save-humans
39. https://savethewhales.org/dolphins-and-porpoises/
40. https://www.underwatertimes.com/news.php?article_id=51079184603
41. https://blog.nationalgeographic.org/2014/05/29/dolphins-guide-scientists-to-rescue-suicidal-girl/
42. https://www.youtube.com/watch?v=NTw8MR67xv8
43. https://www.youtube.com/watch?v=0NtBqnKg1Ms

## Chapter Ten: Awakening Compassion and Conscience

1. https://www.nrdc.org/stories/story-silent-spring
2. https://www.britannica.com/topic/Silent-Spring
3. http://www.rachelcarson.org/SilentSpring.aspx
4. Rachel Carson, *Silent Spring*, Houghton Mifflin, 22 October 2002.
5. https://abcbirds.org/program/hawaii/#:~:text=But%20look%20a%20 little%20closer,become%20extinct%20on%20Hawai'i.
6. https://www.dhakatribune.com/climate-change/2020/07/25/ bangladesh-trapped-in-a-bad-marriage-with-eucalyptus-trees
7. https://www.telegraphindia.com/west-bengal/when-greenery-is-harmful-eucalyptus-a-wrong-choice/cid/1695173
8. https://blog.invasive-species.org/2020/01/21/eucalyptus-the-thirsty-trees-threatening-to-drink-south-africa-dry/
9. http://www.janegoodall.org.nz/jgi-nz-campaigns/compassion-in-conservation/
10. https://www.psychologytoday.com/us/blog/animal-emotions/201902/accusations-invasive-species-denialism-are-flawed
11. https://www.psychologytoday.com/us/blog/animal-emotions/201901/what-if-new-zealands-war-wildlife-included-primates
12. https://link.springer.com/article/10.1007/s10806-020-09825-0
13. https://www.psychologytoday.com/us/blog/animal-emotions/202003/the-effects-imprinting-kids-kill-animals
14. https://www.frontiersin.org/articles/10.3389/fpsyg.2020.01277/full
15. https://www.psychologytoday.com/us/blog/animal-emotions/202003/the-effects-imprinting-kids-kill-animals
16. https://www.frontiersin.org/articles/10.3389/fpsyg.2020.01277/full
17. https://www.hsi.org/news-media/yougov-poll-reveals-vast-majority-of-brits-support-furfreebritain/
18. https://www.peta.org.uk/blog/brits-against-fur-poll/
19. https://www.rfa.org/english/news/tibet/animal-03042015170302.html
20. https://www.dalailama.com/news/2006/animal-skin-clothes-burned-in-tibet-after-dalai-lamas-call
21. https://www.dalailama.com/news/2006/tibetans-burn-wild-animal-skins-in-tibet-to-encourage-wildlife-preservation
22. http://www.shabkar.org/teachers/tibetanbuddhism/dalai_lama.htm
23. https://abcnews.go.com/International/story?id=1695717&page=1

24. http://www.wpsi-india.org/wpsi/index.php
25. https://grist.org/article/youre-looking-swell-dalai/
26. https://www.fws.gov/pacific/news/2000/2000-98.htm
27. https://www.npr.org/sections/thetwo-way/2017/11/16/564597936/why-did-the-passenger-pigeon-go-extinct-the-answer-might-lie-in-their-toes
28. https://www.audubon.org/magazine/may-june-2014/why-passenger-pigeon-went-extinct
29. https://www.smithsonianmag.com/science-nature/how-two-women-ended-the-deadly-feather-trade-23187277/
30. https://usfws.medium.com/love-birds-thank-harriet-hemenway-8928dae21737
31. https://blogs.massaudubon.org/yourgreatoutdoors/the-mothers-of-conservation/
32. http://todayinconservation.com/2018/05/may-25-lacey-act-created-1900/
33. https://www.trcp.org/2010/03/18/john-f-lacey-theodore-roosevelts-right-hand-man/
34. http://todayinconservation.com/2018/05/may-25-lacey-act-created-1900/
35. https://www.nrdc.org/onearth/serendipitous-villainy-gave-america-its-first-wildlife-law
36. https://archive.org/stream/majorjohnflaceym00iowa/majorjohnflaceym00iowa_djvu.txt
37. https://www.inhf.org/blog/blog/iowa-conservationists-john-f-lacey/
38. https://www.worldwildlife.org/stories/in-a-blow-to-wildlife-china-lifts-a-ban-on-the-use-of-tiger-and-rhino-parts
39. https://indianexpress.com/article/world/china-lifts-ban-on-trade-of-rhino-horn-tiger-parts-all-you-need-to-know-5430734/
40. https://www.theseahorsetrust.org/conservation/traditional-medicine-trade/
41. https://www.nationalgeographic.com/animals/mammals/facts/pangolins#:~:text=Tens%20of%20thousands%20of%20pangolins,are%20eight%20species%20of%20pangolins.
42. https://www.theguardian.com/environment/2020/jun/09/china-protect-pangolins-removing-scales-medicine-list-aoe

**Chapter Eleven: Keystone Species: Cornerstones of Life**

1. https://futurism.com/losing-biodiversity-extinction-cascades/
2. https://www.nationalgeographic.com/animals/2018/08/beavers-climate-change-conservation-news/
3. https://phys.org/news/2016-02-beavers-environmental-benefits.html
4. https://www.sciencedirect.com/science/article/pii/S0048969717315929
5. Library, Beaver Institute.
6. https://www.beaverinstitute.org/why-give-a-damn-biodiversity/
7. http://www.ontarioparks.com/parksblog/the-beaver-architect-of-biodiversity/
8. Ben Goldfarb, *Eager: The Surprising Secret Life of Beavers and Why They Matter*, Chelsea Green Publishing, 8 March 2019.
9. https://onlinelibrary.wiley.com/doi/epdf/10.1111/mam.12220
10. 'Could Beavers Have Saved Paradise?', Animals 24-7.
11. 'The Tulalip Tribes', tulaliptribes-nsn.gov
12. https://www.unep.org/news-and-stories/story/wetlands-and-biodiversity-theme-world-wetlands-day-2020
13. https://www.neefusa.org/nature/land/wetlands-united-states#California
14. https://edition.cnn.com/2021/07/21/weather/us-western-wildfires-wednesday/index.html
15. https://www.iii.org/fact-statistic/facts-statistics-wildfires
16. https://www.carbonbrief.org/analysis-why-scientists-think-100-of-global-warming-is-due-to-humans
17. https://www.usatoday.com/story/news/weather/2021/07/12/western-united-states-wildfires-heat-waves-temperatures/7945217002/
18. https://www.nationalgeographic.com/animals/article/yellowstone-wolves-reintroduction-helped-stabilize-ecosystem
19. https://www.yellowstonepark.com/park/conservation/yellowstone-wolves-reintroduction/
20. https://www.yellowstonepark.com/things-to-do/wildlife/wolf-reintroduction-changes-ecosystem/
21. https://www.bbc.com/future/article/20140128-how-wolves-saved-a-famous-park
22. https://www.nps.gov/yell/learn/nature/wolf-restoration.htm

23. http://sustainablefootprint.org/trees-grow-on-salmon/
24. https://www.nature.com/articles/s41598-021-82004-x
25. https://www.climate-policy-watcher.org/plate-tectonics/siberian-taiga-forest-and-global-carbon-sink.html
26. https://www.internetgeography.net/topics/what-is-taiga/
27. https://www.natureunited.ca/what-we-do/our-priorities/innovating-for-climate-change/primer-on-forest-carbon-in-canada-s-boreal-forest/
28. https://www.britannica.com/art/totem-pole
29. https://www.humanesociety.org/resources/about-canadian-seal-hunt#:~:text=And%20with%20nearly%20one%20million,seal%20population%20in%20coming%20years
30. https://www.bbc.com/news/science-environment-44155592
31. https://www.theguardian.com/environment/2016/jul/10/sea-otters-global-warming-trophic-cascades-food-chain-kelp
32. James A. Estes, *Serendipity: An Ecologist's Quest to Understand Nature*, University of California Press, May 2016.
33. https://www.britannica.com/video/162778/keystone-species-parts-coast-kelp-forest-ecosystem#:~:text=The%20presence%20of%20sea%20otters,species%20of%20the%20coastline%20ecosystem
34. https://www.sciencefocus.com/news/green-pawed-sea-otters-are-saving-californias-kelp-forests/
35. https://theprint.in/environment/how-otters-love-for-eating-purple-sea-urchins-is-protecting-fragile-ecosystems/636343/
36. https://defenders.org/wildlife/sea-otter
37. https://www.nationalgeographic.com/environment/article/oil-spills-30-years-after-exxon-valdez
38. https://www.britannica.com/event/Exxon-Valdez-oil-spill
39. https://www.history.com/topics/1980s/exxon-valdez-oil-spill
40. https://www.britannica.com/explore/savingearth/the-canadian-seal-hunt
41. https://www.hsi.org/news-media/hsi-canada-demands-cancellation-of-2021-commercial-seal-hunt/
42. https://www.ifaw.org/eu/press-releases/2021-canada-commercial-seal-hunt-begins
43. https://www.bbc.com/future/article/20140121-sea-otters-our-ocean-protectors
44. https://economictimes.indiatimes.com/news/politics-and-nation/lesser-known-species-like-otter-pangolin-form-a-large-part-of-wildlife-trade/articleshow/53458633.cms?from=mdr

45. https://www.otter.org/documents/IOSF_Illegal_Trade_in_Otters_Report_2014.pdf

46. https://indianexpress.com/article/express-sunday-eye/in-otter-news-6062456/

47. https://india.wcs.org/Newsroom/Blog/ID/12563/The-tigers-of-the-rivers

48. https://www.wwfindia.org/?19722/TRAFFIC-urges-not-to-wear-fur-or-other-products-made-from--protected-otter-species

49. https://news.mongabay.com/2016/07/india-at-heart-of-illegal-otter-trade/

50. https://awionline.org/content/shark-finning#:~:text=Continued%20demand%20for%20shark%20fin,year%20for%20their%20fins%20alone.

51. https://www.greenpeace.org/international/story/46967/100-million-dead-sharks-its-not-all-about-shark-fin-soup/

52. https://sharkstewards.org/shark-finning/shark-finning-fin-facts/

53. https://college.unc.edu/2017/03/predatory-fish/

54. https://www.weforum.org/agenda/2018/07/fish-stocks-are-used-up-fisheries-subsidies-must-stop/

55. https://www.cbsnews.com/news/sushi-eaters-pushing-pacific-bluefin-tuna-to-brink-of-extinction/#:~:text=The%20never%2Dending%20demand%20for,extinction%2C%20a%20conservation%20group%20said.&text=The%20list%20assesses%2076%2C199%20species,22%2C413%20are%20threatened%20with%20extinction.

56. https://www.cbsnews.com/news/sushi-eaters-pushing-pacific-bluefin-tuna-to-brink-of-extinction/#:~:text=The%20never%2Dending%20demand%20for,extinction%2C%20a%20conservation%20group%20said.&text=The%20list%20assesses%2076%2C199%20species,22%2C413%20are%20threatened%20with%20extinction.

57. https://www.biologicaldiversity.org/species/fish/Atlantic_bluefin_tuna/bluefin_boycott/faq.html

58. http://yafm.co.zw/vxqt/bluefin-tuna-population-2021

59. https://www.theanimalreader.com/2021/03/09/tuna-could-disappear-from-indian-ocean-as-demand-for-sushi-rises/

60. https://draxe.com/nutrition/is-sushi-healthy/

61. https://www.rokaakor.com/a-brief-history-of-sushi-and-why-its-so-popular-today/

62. https://health.clevelandclinic.org/get-the-scoop-on-sushi-safety/

63. https://livejapan.com/en/in-hokkaido/in-pref-hokkaido/in-sapporo_chitose/article-a0001909/
64. https://uk.whales.org/2018/07/25/why-whale-and-dolphin-captivity-is-cruel-the-science/

**Chapter Twelve: From Europe to Alaska: Signs of Grace during Terrifying Encounters**

1. https://e360.yale.edu/features/small-pests-big-problems-the-global-spread-of-bark-beetles
2. https://efi.int/sites/default/files/files/publication-bank/2019/efi_fstp_8_2019.pdf
3. https://phys.org/news/2019-09-germany-climate-stressed-trees-catastrophe-bugs.html
4. https://www.britannica.com/science/acid-rain/Effects-on-forested-and-mountainous-regions
5. https://www.nationalgeographic.com/environment/article/acid-rain
6. http://nadp.slh.wisc.edu/educ/acidrain.aspx
7. https://www.economist.com/1843/2015/01/05/what-is-the-opium-of-the-people
8. https://www.theguardian.com/commentisfree/belief/2009/jun/26/religion-philosophy
9. https://www.kommunismusgeschichte.de/jhk/jhk-2005/article/detail/the-atheist-civil-religion-in-communist-yugoslavia-the-broken-covenant-of-titos-people
10. https://www.medjugorje.ws/en/articles/medjugorje-visionaries.vicka-ivankovic/
11. https://medjugorjetoday.wordpress.com/background-7/the-visionaries/vicka-ivankovic-mijatovic/: 'Most of her suffering has been mysterious and redemptive suffering – voluntarily undertaken at the Virgin Mary's request. One example was the mysterious comas she suffered from in the second part of the 1980s. Another example was a brain tumour, delicately placed so the doctors could not remove it. Yet Vicka told everyone not to worry about her, and to her confessor she wrote down the date when the tumour would be gone. She sealed the date in two envelopes, and when the date she had prophesied arrived, the doctors found Vicka's tumour gone. She revealed that her sacrifice had been for the salvation of souls. In the same way and

again for the Virgin's purposes, Vicka also voluntarily accepted several discontinuations of her daily apparitions, for periods of up to 50 days.'

12. https://www.tektonministries.org/the-story-of-medjugorje/
13. https://www.medjugorje.org/
14. https://cruxnow.com/church-in-europe/2019/07/vatican-turning-more-benevolent-eye-to-medjugorje-apparitions/
15. https://www.catholicnewsagency.com/news/43898/medjugorje-visionary-says-monthly-apparitions-have-come-to-an-end
16. Theresa M. Karminkski, 'Are the Apparitions in Yugoslavia for Real?', *Catholic Standard and Times*, 2/2/84 issue.
17. Francis Johnston, *Fatima: The Great Sign*, Ami Press, 1980.
18. https://www.lyrics.com/lyric/3622952/Galt+MacDermot/Manchester+England
19. https://www.youtube.com/watch?v=yjZZITvtZHI scene from movie version of *HAIR*, 1979
20. https://www.michigandaily.com/michigan-in-color/machismo-culture-must-go/
21. https://www.bostonglobe.com/metro/2016/05/26/murray-straus-unh-researcher-who-led-groundbreaking-studies-corporal-punishment-domestic-violence-dies/RlmWltvNGe5I5TfUQFq1NM/story.html
22. https://faunalytics.org/wp-content/uploads/2015/05/Citation1729.pdf
23. https://www.feelguide.com/2016/11/07/hunting-linked-to-psychosexual-inadequacy-the-5-phases-of-a-hunters-life-of-sexual-frustration/?fbclid=IwAR33n1BFJIKZOQ6NQzgPcr9Ci0fgEoo7i-mUpzLkp8ISOuuL48yp-IUZrHo
24. https://www.idausa.org/campaign/wild-animals-and-habitats/hunting/
25. https://www.hsph.harvard.edu/magazine/magazine_article/guns-suicide/
26. https://www.rand.org/research/gun-policy/analysis/essays/firearm-availability-suicide.html
27. https://www.researchgate.net/publication/233599184_Hunting_and_Illegal_Violence_Against_Humans_and_Other_Animals_Exploring_the_Relationship
28. https://www.animallaw.info/article/link-cruelty-animals-and-violence-towards-people
29. https://www.humanesociety.org/sites/default/files/docs/first-strike-connection-resource-webinar.pdf

30. https://www.humanesociety.org/news/hsus-hsi-and-hslf-release-terrible-ten-trophy-hunting-stories-2019

31. https://www.dailymaverick.co.za/article/2019-12-11-outrage-over-unethical-botswana-elephant-hunt/

32. https://www.humanesociety.org/news/undercover-investigation-exposes-illegal-wildlife-items-including-elephant-skin-furniture

33. https://www.humanesociety.org/resources/animal-cruelty-and-human-violence-faq#connection

34. http://www.dailynebraskan.com/opinion/simon-hunting-perpetuates-cruelty-teaches-violence/article_ba32788c-5583-11e3-8816-001a4bcf6878.html

35. https://www.nature.com/articles/nature02177#a1

36. https://faunalytics.org/the-missing-link-hunting-and-child-abuse-are-correlated/#:~:text=This%20study%20found%20that%20areas,levels%20of%20crimes%20against%20children.&text=In%2021%20of%2022%20similar,for%20sexual%20abuse%20of%20children.

37. https://www.animallaw.info/article/link-among-animal-abuse-child-abuse-and-domestic-violence

38. https://medcraveonline.com/FRCIJ/animal-cruelty-pet-abuse-amp-violence-the-missed-dangerous-connection.html

39. https://www.independent.co.uk/news/long_reads/domestic-violence-animal-cruelty-abuse-neglect-murder-children-dogs-a9018071.html

40. https://english.mathrubhumi.com/news/columns/faunaforum/children-learn-animal-cruelty-from-adults--1.4462155

41. https://www.prnewswire.com/news-releases/hypothesis-put-forward-by-genetic-economic-analytics-suggests-premature-orgasm-and-buck-fever-linked-272135571.html

42. https://www.facebook.com/AELLA.ORG/posts/sports-hunting-is-a-form-of-sexual-sadismrenowned-psychiatrist-dr-karl-menninger/3534640303251499/

43. https://www.facebook.com/136918922995288/posts/sadism-may-take-a-socially-acceptable-form-such-as-deer-hunting-and-deer-stalkin/2159436704076823/

44. https://www.unh.edu/unhtoday/2016/05/passing-professor-murray-straus-1926-2016

45. https://www.animals24-7.org/2020/08/14/killing-the-female-the-psychology-of-the-hunt/

46. https://www.outdoorlife.com/why-we-are-losing-hunters-and-how-to-fix-it/

47. Thoughts on "Killing the Female" & Pennsylvania hunting memories by Karen Davis | Animals 24-7

48. https://animals24-7.us3.list-manage.com/track/click?u=49fddb776d9fb54a64b4f5569&id=aa2d4041ac&e=de09b6899f

49. https://www.animals24-7.org/1994/03/17/new-york-state-statistics-show-link-hunters-and-molesters/

50. https://www.animals24-7.org/1994/11/17/ohio-data-confirms-huntingchild-abuse-link-stronger-than-link-to-rural-poverty/

51. https://www.animals24-7.org/1995/10/17/michigan-stats-confirm-hunting-child-abuse-link/

52. https://www.animals24-7.org/2014/10/25/marysville-school-shooter-loved-hunting-pit-bulls/

53. https://wmpuk.home.blog/2020/11/09/respect-for-the-quarry/

54. https://www.researchgate.net/publication/231834742_Sadistic_cruelty_and_unempathic_evil_Psychobiological_and_evolutionary_considerations

55. https://www.nytimes.com/1989/11/21/us/vermont-journal-the-rite-of-autumn-is-the-song-of-the-rifle.html

56. https://www.motherearthnews.com/homesteading-and-livestock/deer-hunting-beginners-zmaz89ndzshe

57. 'Why Hunters Hunt—And Why Far More Men Quit Hunting Now Than Take It Up', Animals 24-7.

58. https://www.post-gazette.com/life/outdoors/2019/10/10/Why-Women-Hunt-author-K-J-Houtman-Pennsylvania-Coraopolis-new-book/stories/201910100115

59. https://www.nationalgeographic.com/animals/article/cecil-african-lion-anniversary-death-trophy-hunting-zimbabwe

60. https://www.nationalgeographic.com/pages/article/150728-cecil-lion-killing-trophy-hunting-conservation-animals

61. https://naturalresources.house.gov/imo/media/doc/Missing%20the%20Mark.pdf

62. https://www.nationalgeographic.com/animals/article/wildlife-watch-cecil-trophy-hunting-andrew-loveridge

63. http://www.takepart.com/article/2015/07/29/big-game-hunters-and-cecil-lion

64. https://www.washingtonpost.com/news/animalia/wp/2017/07/20/cecil-the-lions-son-shot-dead-by-trophy-hunter-officials-say/

65. https://www.four-paws.org.uk/our-stories/blog-news/cecil-the-lion-anniversary#:~:text=Cecil%20was%20made%20famous%20 as,complicit%20in%20this%20barbaric%20sport.

66. https://www.scottramsay.africa/wp-content/uploads/2020/03/ Loveridge-et-al-2007-impact-of-trophy-hunting-on-lion-population-dynamics-in-Hwange.pdf

67. https://africageographic.com/stories/trophy-hunting-wild-lions-big-lie-sustainability/

68. https://africageographic.com/stories/lion-trophy-hunting-we-interview-craig-packer/

69. https://www.animalmatters.org/facts/wildlife/

70. https://www.idausa.org/campaign/wild-animals-and-habitats/ hunting/

71. https://www.downtoearth.org.in/news/wildlife-biodiversity/some-200-wild-animals-killed-in-annual-tribal-hunting-season-in-bengal-last-month-76486

72. https://www.wcs.org/96-elephants

73. https://worldelephantday.org/about/elephants

74. https://www.worldanimalfoundation.com/advocate/wild-earth/ params/post/1286260/an-elephant-killed-every-15-minut

75. https://extension.okstate.edu/fact-sheets/impacts-of-lead-ammunition-and-sinkers-on-wildlife.html

76. https://www.biologicaldiversity.org/campaigns/get_the_lead_out/

77. https://wwf.panda.org/discover/our_focus/wildlife_practice/ problems/illegal_trade/

78. https://www.bornfreeusa.org/2020/07/28/follow-the-money-trophy-hunting-does-not-help-communities/

79. https://bantrophyhunting.org/about/

80. https://howtoconserve.org/2015/08/21/trophy-hunting-myths/

81. https://earth.org/what-is-trophy-hunting/

82. https://www.iccaconsortium.org/index.php/2019/12/05/ productive-retreat-the-four-moose-and-indigenous-led-conservation-in-canada/

## Chapter Thirteen: Embracing the Sun amidst a Poisoned Paradise

1. Doctor Ross Trattler, *Better Health through Natural Healing: How to Get Well without Drugs or Surgery*, McGraw Hill Book Company, 1985.

2. *The Phoenix Returns: Aquarius Dawns, Liberation Begins*, Cardinal Enterprises, 1983 (written under the pen name Kristina Gale-Kumar).

3. https://www.nytimes.com/1982/03/20/us/hawaii-recalls-pesticide-laced-milk-from-stores-and-schools.html

4. https://www.hawaiinewsnow.com/story/30709369/pesticide-that-prompted-hawaii-milk-scandal-linked-to-parkinsons/#:~:text=A%20team%20of%20researchers%20focused,pesticide%20commonly%20used%20on%20pineapples.

5. https://journals.lww.com/neurotodayonline/fulltext/2016/01210/Pesticide_in_Milk_May_Have_Caused_PD_Like_Damage.2.aspx

6. https://www.centerforfoodsafety.org/files/pesticidereportfull_86476.pdf

7. https://www.economist.com/united-states/2016/04/07/paradise-sprayed

8. https://earthjustice.org/features/pesticides-in-paradise

9. https://www.beyondpesticides.org/resources/pesticide-induced-diseases-database/brain-and-nervous-system-disorders

10. https://scroll.in/article/877049/eight-terrifying-things-we-found-about-pesticide-regulation-and-use-in-india

11. https://www.scientificamerican.com/article/pesticide-drift/

12. https://www.smithsonianmag.com/smithsonian-institution/heart-hawaiian-people-arguments-arguments-against-telescope-mauna-kea-180955057/#:~:text=Mauna%20Kea%20is%20the%20highest,of%20the%20Hawaiian%20deity%20W%C4%81kea.

13. https://religionlab.virginia.edu/projects/ku-kia%CA%BBi-mauna-mauna-kea-protecting-the-sacred-and-the-thirty-meter-telescope/

14. https://sites.coloradocollege.edu/indigenoustraditions/sacred-lands/sacred-lands-mauna-kea/

15. https://www.usgs.gov/volcanoes/kilauea

16. https://www.usgs.gov/center-news/photo-and-video-chronology-k-lauea-august-10-2021

17. https://www.nature.com/articles/d41586-021-01363-7

18. https://www.npr.org/sections/pictureshow/2020/12/31/951512509/hawaiis-kilauea-volcano-eruption-creates-600-foot-deep-lava-lake

19. https://www.bizjournals.com/pacific/news/2018/07/09/number-of-homes-destroyed-by-kilauea-eruption.html

20. https://www.nps.gov/havo/learn/nature/2018-eruption.htm
21. https://www.hawaiitribune-herald.com/2017/03/23/hawaii-news/big-island-population-rises-census-estimates-show-hawaii-county-making-biggest-gains/
22. https://www.census.gov/programs-surveys/decennial-census.html
23. https://www.livinginhawaii.com/hawaii/moving-to-hawaii/hawaiis-high-cost-of-living/
24. https://weather.com/science/environment/news/pearl-harbor-halawa-gate-navy-bunker-oil-plume
25. https://www.huffpost.com/entry/massive-oil-plume-pearl-harbor_n_55fc63d8e4b08820d91891ed
26. https://www.epa.gov/superfund/search-superfund-sites-where-you-live
27. https://www.hawaiinewsnow.com/story/30060416/exclusive-5-m-gallon-oil-plume-beneath-pearl-harbor/
28. https://www.hawaiinewsnow.com/story/4326275/federal-agency-warns-against-eating-fish-from-pearl-harbor/
29. https://www.nationalgeographic.org/encyclopedia/keeling-curve/#:~:text=The%20Keeling%20Curve%20is%20a%20graph%20that%20represents%20the%20concentration,in%20Earth's%20atmosphere%20since%201958.&text=Charles%20David%20Keeling.,of%20CO2%20they%20contained.
30. https://keelingcurve.ucsd.edu/
31. https://www.britannica.com/science/Keeling-Curve
32. Al Gore, *An Inconvenient Truth,* Rodale Inc., 2006.
33. https://www.algore.com/library/an-inconvenient-truth-dvd
34. https://www.britannica.com/topic/An-Inconvenient-Truth
35. https://news.un.org/en/story/2021/08/1097362
36. https://www.ipcc.ch/report/ar6/wg1/
37. https://www.ipcc.ch/2021/08/09/ar6-wg1-20210809-pr/
38. https://www.theguardian.com/environment/2021/aug/10/code-red-for-humanity-what-the-papers-say-about-the-ipcc-report-on-the-climate-crisis
39. https://www.bbc.com/news/science-environment-58130705
40. https://globalecoguy.org/the-three-most-important-graphs-in-climate-change-e64d3f4ed76?gi=e9bc61bcc61c
41. https://www.climatecouncil.org.au/deforestation/
42. https://www.rainforest-alliance.org/insights/what-is-the-relationship-between-deforestation-and-climate-change/

43. https://www.scientificamerican.com/article/deforestation-and-global-warming/
44. https://wwf.panda.org/discover/our_focus/wildlife_practice/problems/habitat_loss_degradation/
45. https://courses.lumenlearning.com/boundless-biology/chapter/threats-to-biodiversity/
46. https://www.nationalgeographic.com/environment/article/deforestation
47. https://www.globalforestwatch.org/blog/data-and-research/four-species-that-went-extinct-this-century-because-of-forest-loss/
48. https://www.theworldcounts.com/stories/causes-of-extinction-of-species
49. https://www.theworldcounts.com/stories/deforestation-facts-and-statistics

**Part Three: The Canopy Spreads**
**Chapter Fourteen: The Holy Himalayas**

1. https://www.bbc.com/news/world-asia-india-56102459
2. timesofindia.indiatimes.com
3. http://www.bbc.com/news/world-asia-india-56007448
4. http://rockandice.com/snowball/the-secret-of-nanda-devi/
5. http://www.bbc.com/news/magazine-29274491
6. wikileaks.org
7. www.indiatoday.in
8. wikileaks.org
9. www.washingtonpost.com
10. https://www.thehindu.com/books/books-reviews/ascent-and-exploration/article19433999.ece
11. Hugh Thompson, *Nanda Devi: A Journey to the Last Sanctuary*, Hachette Book Publishing, February 2005, previously published by Orion Publishing in April 2004.
12. http://savitrithepoem.com/authors-note.html
13. Sri Aurobindo, *Savitri: A Legend and a Symbol*, Sri Aurobindo Ashram Publication Department, Pondicherry, June 1940.

**Chapter Fifteen: The Balding of Our Mother**

1. https://sanctuarynaturefoundation.org/award/anne-wright

2.  https://www.outlookindia.com/outlooktraveller/travelnews/ story/61817/wildlife-conservationists-belinda-wright
3.  https://gulfnews.com/world/asia/india/lifetime-service-award-for-anne-wright-1.1263776
4.  https://www.kiplingcamp.com/anne-wright.html
5.  https://www.dailyo.in/politics/indira-gandhi-birth-anniversary-wildlife-protection-conservation-bengal-tiger-india/story/1/7466.html
6.  https://www.naturesafariindia.com/conservationists-in-india/ indira-gandhi/
7.  https://www.conservationindia.org/resources/betraying-indias-wildlife
8.  https://www.telegraphindia.com/opinion/no-lack-of-warning-something-horribly-wrong-in-the-himalaya/cid/283638
9.  https://www.thebetterindia.com/163009/women-freedom-fighter-himalayas-quit-india-news/
10. https://www.downtoearth.org.in/blog/mira-behn-a-friend-of-nature-31306
11. https://stb.univie.ac.at/news-events/ detail/news/mirabehn-after-gandhi/? tx_news_pi1%5Bcontroller%5D=News&tx_ news_pi1%5Baction%5D=detail& cHash=720dda48cb3041ebdd142dc485c4e82e
12. https://www.hindustantimes.com/india/uttarakhand-floods-the-prophecy-that-was/story-uIADIIsf5zTAEK3tDXT5gM.html
13. https://bioone.org/journals/mountain-research-and-development/ volume-24/issue-4/0276-4741(2004)024%5B0312%3AFTADI T%5D2.0.CO%3B2/Fuelwood-Timber-and-Deforestation-in-the-Himalayas/10.1659/0276-4741(2004)024[0312:FTADIT] 2.0.CO;2.full#:~:text=The%20deforestation%20rate%20in%20 the,the%20world%20(IUCN%202002).&text=Deforestation%20 in%20the%20Himalayan%20region,Moddie%201981%3B%20 Myers%201986).
14. https://www.iatp.org/news/himalayas-deforestation-could-lead-to-plant-animal-loss
15. https://iasgoogle.com/how-is-deforestation-of-himalayas-disturbing-the-ecological-balance-of-north-india-250-words/
16. https://www.worldwildlife.org/stories/saving-himalayan-forests
17. https://www.jstor.org/stable/3673213

18. https://www.researchgate.net/publication/232669667_Fuelwood_ Timber_and_Deforestation_in_the_Himalayas
19. https://economictimes.indiatimes.com/news/politics-and- nation/indias-natural-forests-half-of-what-ministry-claims/ articleshow/38504925.cms
20. https://www.downtoearth.org.in/news/maximum-devastation- occurred-in-areas-of-maximum-forestland-diversion-41483
21. https://www.thehindu.com/opinion/op-ed/nature-avenges-its- exploitation/article4834480.ece
22. https://www.thethirdpole.net/en/culture/displacement-and- deforestation-on-kedarnath-route/
23. https://nvdatabase.swarthmore.edu/content/indian-villagers- protest-tehri-dam-construction-2001-2002
24. https://india.mongabay.com/2021/05/obituary-sunderlal- bahuguna-end-of-an-era-for-indian-environmentalism/
25. https://frontline.thehindu.com/books/the-dam-debate/ article8123541.ece
26. https://www.downtoearth.org.in/coverage/protest-damned-28303
27. https://www.dw.com/en/five-ways-mega-dams-harm-the- environment/a-53916579
28. https://www.theigc.org/blog/water-power-mega-dams-mega-damage/
29. https://news.mongabay.com/2018/11/mega-dam-costs-outweigh- benefits-global-building-spree-should-end-experts/
30. https://www.scidev.net/asia-pacific/news/ancient-trees-reveal- brahmaputra-mega-dam-risks/
31. https://gebe.foei.org/good-energy-bad-energy/destructive-energy- sources/megadams-a-destructive-energy-source/
32. https://en.wikipedia.org/wiki/Dam_failure
33. https://economictimes.indiatimes.com/news/international/world- news/why-is-china-facing-record-floods/articleshow/84612391. cms?from=mdr
34. https://www.reuters.com/article/us-china-weather-floods-dams- idUSKCN24N047
35. https://www.japantimes.co.jp/opinion/2021/06/22/commentary/ world-commentary/cpc-one-hundred-years-environmental- devastation/
36. https://www.hindustantimes.com/world-news/melting-glaciers- may-disrupt-china-s-plan-to-build-dam-over-brahmaputra-in- tibet-101619621981025.html

37. https://en.wikipedia.org/wiki/Earthquake_zones_of_India#:~:text=Jammu%20and%20Kashmir%2C%20Ladakh%2C%20Himachal,is%20also%20in%20Zone%204.
38. https://www.jagranjosh.com/general-knowledge/list-of-earthquake-seismic-zones-in-india-1591274253-1
39. http://www.iitk.ac.in/nicee/EQTips/EQTip04.pdf
40. https://indianexpress.com/article/india/high-risk-seismic-zones-in-india-how-prone-is-your-city-to-earthquakes/
41. http://usdma.uk.gov.in/earthquake-13.aspx
42. https://www.hindustantimes.com/india-news/over-85-uttarakhand-districts-hot-spots-of-extreme-floods-analysis-101613031554384.html
43. https://timesofindia.indiatimes.com/city/dehradun/chamoli-uttarkashi-to-get-earthquake-warning-systems/articleshow/48178423.cms
44. https://en.wikipedia.org/wiki/1991_Uttarkashi_earthquake
45. https://www.hindustantimes.com/india/uttarkashi-earthquake/story-I9KQPRPWfbnLvT75LBcNXM.html
46. https://onlinelibrary.wiley.com/doi/abs/10.1111/j.1365-3121.1994.tb00637.x
47. https://frontline.thehindu.com/science-and-technology/article30193609.ece
48. https://nicee.org/eqe-iitk/uploads/EQR_Uttarkashi.pdf
49. https://www.softschools.com/difference/mercalli_scale_vs_richter_scale/461/
50. http://www.differencebetween.net/science/difference-between-richter-scale-and-mercalli-scale/
51. Kristina Gale-Kumar, *The Scriptures Are Fulfilled,* Cardinal Enterprises, 1991.
52. https://timesofindia.indiatimes.com/city/dehradun/noted-photographer-swami-sundaranand-passes-away/articleshow/79945425.cms
53. https://www.meaus.com/himalaya-sundaranand.htm
54. Swami Sunderanand, *Himalaya: Through the Lens of a Sadhu,* Tapovan Kuti Prakashan Publisher, January 2001.
55. https://blog.yoga.in/2020/03/25/swami-sundaranand-on-the-eightfold-path/
56. https://www.chinmayamission.com/our-homage-and-reverential-pranaams-to-swami-sundarananda/

57. https://www.outlookindia.com/newsscroll/ukhand-cm-pays-homage-to-swami-sundaranand/1998980
58. https://peoplepill.com/people/swami-sundaranand
59. The Holy Bible, the King James version, John 1:1, New Testament, 1611.
60. https://www.independent.co.uk/climate-change/news/why-the-haiti-earthquake-may-not-have-been-a-natural-disaster-6275044.html
61. https://paleoseismicity.org/things-that-cause-earthquakes/
62. https://www.downtoearth.org.in/news/earthshaking-intervention-15816
63. https://www.templepurohit.com/shiva-tandava-lord-shiva-cosmic-dance/
64. https://www.iucn.org/sites/dev/files/import/downloads/arborvitae27.pdf
65. http://ij-tejas.com/paper/vol2Issue2/6.pdf
66. https://news.mongabay.com/2011/01/did-haitis-deforestation-hurricane-trigger-deadly-earthquake/
67. http://www.reuters.com/article/us-malaria-amazon/cleared-forests-lead-to-rise-in-malaria-in-brazil-idUSTRE65F61720100617

## Chapter Sixteen: The Final Transplantation

1. https://sanskritdictionary.org/ai
2. https://sanskritdictionary.org/sa
3. http://saibaba.ws/articles/isaissai.htm
4. https://www.facebook.com/saiCallingShirdi/posts/one-day-a-man-asked-sai-baba-meaning-of-saiso-baba-said-this-name-sai-is-made-of/1029528730417159/
5. https://www.thelivingurn.com/blogs/news/hindu-funerals
6. https://www.theguardian.com/global-development/2020/oct/14/not-just-a-dog-bite-why-india-is-struggling-to-keep-rabies-at-bay#:~:text=India%20has%20around%2020%2C000%20rabies,cases%20of%20rabies%20in%20India.
7. https://www.nytimes.com/2012/08/07/world/asia/india-stray-dogs-are-a-menace.html
8. https://www.who.int/india/health-topics/rabies
9. https://www.thehindubusinessline.com/news/world-rabies-day-rabies-killed-more-people-in-india-in-the-last-5-years-than-covid-19/article32708436.ece
10. https://en.wikipedia.org/wiki/Prevalence_of_rabies

## Chapter Seventeen: Weaving Together the Tapestry of Life

1. https://www.science.org/news/2019/05/wood-wide-web-underground-network-microbes-connects-trees-mapped-first-time
2. https://www.newyorker.com/tech/annals-of-technology/the-secrets-of-the-wood-wide-web
3. https://www.youtube.com/watch?v=5MSq_NzpMKk
4. https://www.brightvibes.com/1368/en/discover-how-trees-secretly-talk-to-each-other-using-the-wood-wide-web
5. https://www.nytimes.com/interactive/2020/12/02/magazine/tree-communication-mycorrhiza.html
6. https://www.youtube.com/watch?v=oVK9TCXZz6I
7. https://www.asktherightquestion.org/trees-wood-wide-web-dan-durall-suzanne-simard-ted-ecology/
8. https://www.labroots.com/trending/plants-and-animals/14169/parrots-smarter-5-year-old-human-children
9. https://news.harvard.edu/gazette/story/2017/12/harvard-researchers-test-intelligence-of-african-grey-parrot/
10. https://www.clockguy.com/Olivers/JoplinPages/AlexandrineParakeetInfo.html
11. https://link.springer.com/article/10.1007/s41055-016-0003-z
12. http://www.fao.org/news/story/en/item/1194910/icode/
13. https://www.foodnavigator.com/Article/2019/11/13/Insect-apocalypse-poses-risk-to-food-production
14. 'Defaunation in the Anthropocene', Science.org.
15. https://www.sciencedirect.com/topics/agricultural-and-biological-sciences/pollinator-decline
16. https://theconversation.com/bees-how-important-are-they-and-what-would-happen-if-they-went-extinct-121272
17. https://www.nature.com/articles/s41467-019-08974-9
18. https://www.downtoearth.org.in/blog/forests/leaf-coalition-s-proposal-is-a-step-forward-in-saving-forests-indigenous-peoples-77745
19. https://www.nature.com/articles/ncomms11351; Anand Osuri, National Centre for Biological Sciences in Bangalore, Research Scientist, Earth Institute, Columbia University.
20. http://indiaclimatedialogue.net/2016/03/21/varying-rainfall-threatens-biodiversity-western-ghats/
21. https://thewire.in/65037/deforestation-reducing-monsoon-rainfall-in-india-new-study/

22. https://sandrp.wordpress.com/2013/07/26/climate-change-in-western-ghats-4x4-report-and-beyond/

23. 'Animal Biodiversity Key Part of Carbon Cycle', Stanford News.

24. 'Social Cost of Carbon Emissions in Spotlight', *Nature*.

25. 'What's Causing the Sharp Decline in Insects, and Why It Matters', Yale E360.

26. 'Insect Armageddon', *New York Times*.

27. https://www.theguardian.com/environment/2019/feb/04/a-third-of-himalayan-ice-cap-doomed-finds-shocking-report?CMP=Share_iOSApp_Other

28. https://www.theguardian.com/environment/2019/feb/10/plummeting-insect-numbers-threaten-collapse-of-nature

29. '"Pollination crisis" Hitting India's Vegetable Farmers', BBC News.

30. https://news.stanford.edu/2017/10/09/animal-biodiversity-important-part-carbon-cycle/

31. https://www.nature.com/articles/s41559-017-0334-0

32. https://blog.conservation.org/2016/04/wildlife-loss-in-tropical-forests-is-bad-news-and-not-just-for-animals/

33. https://www.nature.com/articles/ncomms11351

34. https://timesofindia.indiatimes.com/life-style/relationships/pets/banned-in-india/articleshow/64691806.cms

35. https://www.hindustantimes.com/india/birds-as-pets-illegal-did-you-know/story-cDqX0uJhu0lHDp3Ed0q4lJ.html

36. https://www.animallaw.info/article/overview-animal-laws-india

37. http://www.awbi.org/awbi-pdf/APL.pdf

38. https://www.downtoearth.org.in/coverage/free-as-a---bird-24828

39. https://www.wildlifecenter.org/human-imprinting-birds-and-importance-surrogacy

40. https://www.betterhelp.com/advice/general/understanding-imprinting-psychology/

## Chapter Eighteen: Living within the Heart of the Mother

1. https://www.healthbenefitstimes.com/coral-tree/

2. http://herbs-treatandtaste.blogspot.com/2012/02/indian-coral-tree-history-uses-and.html

3. https://www.worldlandtrust.org/species/mammals/nilgiri-langur/#:~:text=Threats%20and%20Conservation,5%2C000%20left%20in%20the%20wild.

4.  https://www.thehindu.com/thread/reflections/nilgiri-langur-endangered-by-myths/article29323104.ece
5.  https://endangeredinnilgiris.wordpress.com/2015/11/25/nilgiri-langur/
6.  https://www.thenewsminute.com/article/habitat-loss-and-poaching-threaten-survival-elusive-nilgiri-langur-104175
7.  The Holy Bible, the King James version, Mathew 4:4, New Testament, 1611.
8.  https://www.birminghamzoo.com/animal/north-american-river-otter/#:~:text=Otters%20are%20what%20we%20call,been%20polluted%20or%20is%20unhealthy.
9.  https://www.researchgate.net/publication/235330186_Is_the_otter_a_bioindicator
10. https://www.paws.org/resources/river-otters/
11. https://www.wti.org.in/news/delhi-police-seize-leopard-and-otter-skins/
12. https://www.newindianexpress.com/states/karnataka/2019/sep/02/india-gets-top-protection-for-river-otters-but-experts-say-this-is-not-enough-2027661.html
13. https://www.drishtiias.com/daily-updates/daily-news-analysis/proposals-to-change-in-cites-listing
14. https://onlinelibrary.wiley.com/doi/full/10.1111/j.1936-704X.2016.03212.x
15. https://www.secem.es/wp-content/uploads/2013/03/G-10-NE-21-Ruiz-Olmo-et-al-227-237.pdf
16. https://www.fs.usda.gov/Internet/FSE_DOCUMENTS/fseprd530668.pdf
17. https://en.wikipedia.org/wiki/Pamela_Malhotra
18. https://wcd.nic.in/nari-shakti-awardees-ms-pamela-gale-malhotra
19. https://en.wikipedia.org/wiki/SAI_Sanctuary
20. https://www.deccanherald.com/content/600106/nari-shakti-puraskar-three-state.html

## Chapter Nineteen: From Love-Posts and Bears to the Gentle Giants of SAI

1.  https://pubmed.ncbi.nlm.nih.gov/16452075/
2.  https://www.thehindu.com/sci-tech/science/leaf-colour/article4627493.ece
3.  https://www.smithsonianmag.com/smart-news/did-ancient-magnetic-field-reversal-cause-chaos-life-earth-180977072/

4.  https://climate.nasa.gov/news/3105/earths-magnetosphere-protecting-our-planet-from-harmful-space-energy/
5.  http://www.tree-care.info/uktc/archive/2005/msg04701
6.  https://www.lynchburgparksandrec.com/tree-hugging-hippies-right-part-iii/ AND https://www.lynchburgparksandrec.com/tree-hugging-hippies-right-part-iv/
7.  https://wildtreeadventures.com/2020/04/22/hugging-trees-is-good-for-us-and-the-trees/
8.  https://www.careelite.de/en/alexander-von-humboldt-quotes-sayings/
9.  https://www.poetryfoundation.org/poems/43687/the-tyger
10. https://interestingliterature.com/2017/03/a-short-analysis-of-william-blakes-the-tyger/
11. https://www.kqed.org/science/1926248/how-elephants-listen-with-their-feet
12. https://www.youtube.com/watch?v=iYM9oXftLIQ
13. https://elephantconservation.org/elephants/just-for-kids/
14. https://www.oysterworldwide.com/news/interesting-facts-about-elephants/
15. https://news.mongabay.com/2018/10/loss-of-forest-elephant-may-make-earth-less-inhabitable-for-humans/

## Epilogue: Reflections from the Past, Visions of the Future

1.  https://wwf.panda.org/discover/our_focus/biodiversity/biodiversity/
2.  https://www.theguardian.com/environment/2010/aug/16/nature-economic-security
3.  https://www.un.org/sustainabledevelopment/blog/2019/05/nature-decline-unprecedented-report/
4.  https://now.tufts.edu/articles/extinction-crisis
5.  https://www.worldwildlife.org/threats/deforestation-and-forest-degradation
6.  https://ypte.org.uk/factsheets/rainforests/what-are-the-threats-to-the-rainforests
7.  https://www.theguardian.com/global-development-professionals-network/2017/jan/23/destroying-rainforests-quickly-gone-100-years-deforestation
8.  https://www.theguardian.com/environment/2019/sep/12/deforestation-world-losing-area-forest-size-of-uk-each-year-report-finds

9.  https://www.bbc.com/news/science-environment-49679883 http://www.fao.org/state-of-forests/en/
10. https://www.conservation.org/blog/nature-now%E2%80%99-in-new-film-climate-heavyweights-make-plea-for-the-planet
11. https://www.conservation.org/video/nature-now-video-with-greta-thunberg
12. https://www.nationalgeographic.com/science/article/why-climate-change-is-still-the-greatest-threat-to-human-health
13. https://www.nationalgeographic.com/environment/article/heat-related-deaths-attributed-to-climate-change
14. https://www.nature.com/articles/s41558-021-01058-x
15. https://edition.cnn.com/2019/06/04/health/climate-change-existential-threat-report-intl/index.html